Y0-EFO-954

To Glori

The Administration
of Justice System

*Consulting Editors for the Holbrook Press
Criminal Justice Series*

Vern L. Folley

Richmond Regional Criminal Justice
Training Center

Donald T. Shanahan

Associate Director, Southern Police Institute
and University of Louisville

William J. Bopp

Director, Criminal Justice Program
Florida Atlantic University

The Administration of Justice System

AN INTRODUCTION

Donald T. Shanahan
University of Louisville

HV
8138
.A56

HOLBROOK PRESS, INC.   **BOSTON**

INDIANA PURDUE LIBRARY FEB 19 1979 FORT WAYNE

© Copyright 1977 by Holbrook Press, Inc., 470 Atlantic Avenue, Boston. All rights reserved. No part of the material protected by this copyright notice may be reproduced or utilized in any form or by any means, electronic or mechanical, including photocopying, recording, or by any informational storage and retrieval system, without written permission from the copyright owner.

Printed in the United States of America.

Library of Congress Cataloging in Publication Data

Main entry under title:

The Administration of justice system.

    Includes bibliographies and index.
    1. Criminal justice, Administration of—United
States. I. Shanahan, Donald T., 1932–
HV8138.A56   364   76–27298
ISBN 0–205–05597–4

Contents

Contributors

GARY B. ADAMS is an Assistant Professor of Criminal Justice at the California State University at Long Beach. Dr. Adams holds a D.P.A. from the University of Southern California.

MARY ANNA BADEN, Ph.D. is a Professor of Social Science at Florida Atlantic University.

WILLIAM J. BOPP, Ph.D. is a Professor and Director of Criminal Justice at the Institute of Behavioral Research, Florida Atlantic University. Professor Bopp is the author of numerous books, including *Police Personnel Administration* and *Police Rebellion*.

NEIL C. CHAMELIN is the Administrator, Police Science Division, Institute of Government, Athens, Georgia.

GEORGE F. COLE is Associate Professor, Department of Political Science, the University of Connecticut. Professor Cole is the author of numerous publications including *The American System of Criminal Justice* and *Public Policy Toward the Criminal Courts*.

PAUL F. CROMWELL, JR. is a Professor of Criminology, San Antonio College, San Antonio, Texas. Professor Cromwell has coauthored *Police Community Relations* and *Penology*.

EUGENE H. CZAJKOSKI is Dean, School of Criminology, Florida State University, Tallahassee, Florida.

WILLA J. DAWSON is a lecturer in the Administration of Justice, San Jose State University, San Jose, California. Miss Dawson received her masters degree in Criminology from the University of California, Berkeley.

WILLIAM E. EASTMAN is a Lieutenant and Team Manager, Culver City Police Department, Culver City, California.

GORDON F. N. FEARN, Ph.D. is a Professor of Social Science at Florida Atlantic University, Boca Raton, Florida.

PETER FEUILLE is Assistant Professor of Organization and Human Resources, State University of New York at Buffalo. Dr. Feuille received his Ph.D. in Organizational Behavior, Industrial Relations, University of California, Berkeley. Dr. Feuille is the author of many publications and monographs about police personnel, especially in the area of Labor Relations and Police Union activity.

VERNON FOX, Ph.D. is a Professor of Criminology, Florida State University, Tallahassee, Florida. Dr. Fox has written extensively in the field of Criminology and has been honored on many occasions including by *Who's Who in the World*.

ROBERT R. J. GALLATI, S.J.D. is one of the greats in the field of police administration. Together with A. C. Germann and Frank D. Day, he authored *Introduction to Law Enforcement and Criminal Justice*.

ALBERT C. GERMANN, D.P.A. is Professor of Criminology, Department of Criminal Justice, California State University, Long Beach, California. Dr. Germann has authored *Police Personnel Management, Police Executive Development,* and together with Robert Gallati and Frank Day, *Introduction to Law Enforcement and Criminal Justice*. His other writings have appeared in *Police, The Police Chief,* and *The Journal of Criminal Law, Criminology, and Police Science*.

R. PAUL McCAULEY, Ph.D. is Assistant Professor, School of Police Administration, University of Louisville, Kentucky. Dr. McCauley is also Director of Graduate Studies in the Administration of Justice. He is coauthor of a text, *Introduction to Criminal Justice*.

JAN C. MENNIG is the Chief of Police, Culver City, California.

GORDON E. MISNER is Professor, Administration of Justice, University of Missouri at St. Louis.

CHARLES E. MOYLAN, JR. is Associate Judge, Court of Special Appeals, State of Maryland.

THOMAS A. REPPETTO is a Professor, John Jay College of Criminal Justice, the City University of New York.

MICHAEL SCHWARTZ, Ph.D. is Professor, College of Social Science, Florida Atlantic University, Boca Raton, Florida.

DONALD T. SHANAHAN

PAUL M. WHISENAND, Ph.D. is a Professor and Chairman of the Department of Criminal Justice, California State University, Long Beach. Dr. Whisenand has written extensively in the area of Criminal Justice, including nine text books and over twenty-four articles.

About the Author

The author is currently Associate Professor at the School of Police Administration, University of Louisville, Louisville, Kentucky and is Associate Director of the Southern Police Institute. He holds an associate of arts degree from Eastern College, a bachelor of science in Police Administration from the University of Baltimore, Maryland, and a master of education degree from Coppin State College, Baltimore, Maryland. He has also attended American University and Mt. Vernon School of Law and is doing postgraduate work at the University of Louisville's Institute of Community Development.

He was a member of the Baltimore City Police Department where he served in most line and staff positions, including officer in charge of the Planning and Research Division, Director of Records and Lieutenant Colonel, and Chief of the Patrol Division.

He has taught numerous police-related courses in undergraduate and graduate programs besides those of the Southern Police Institute. He has been a consultant for the International Association of Chiefs of Police on police management and implementation of innovative departmental programs. He has lectured extensively on police administration subjects for the International Association of Chiefs of Police, Southern Methodist University, University of Texas, Sam Houston State, and the Southwest Legal Foundation, to name a few.

He has published articles in the magazine *Police Chief* and recently published a textbook (with instructor's manual) entitled *Patrol Administration: Management by Objectives* (Holbrook Press, 1975).

Preface

This book is designed to meet the needs of the students of justice administration. Communication and understanding between Criminal Justice System I participants and the larger Criminal Justice System II* must precede any effective program to improve the administration of justice. An integral part of their communication and understanding is to be able to address common problems and issues in an enlightened manner. The author has presented original writings in this text to provide a contemporary setting within which the philosophy, goals, and potential results of the administration of criminal justice can be explored. There is no denying the importance of the issues contained in the text and no denying the need for objective analysis of each.

There are some scholars who believe that by the year 2000, criminal justice practitioners will exist as a single unit, rather than in today's component parts. The validity and relevancy of this view may be an issue itself. However, the author believes that only through the study of each component, and then through an analysis of a systems approach, can the question of component practitioners versus criminal justice practitioner be answered intelligently and effectively. Exchange programs on criminal justice career development may satisfy the needs of the administrator of criminal justice.

This book should enable students to view the issues and problems of the administration of criminal justice in the contexts of today and the future. This text was produced with the author's view that criminal justice administration participants are professionals or potential professionals.

Where can this book be used? It can be used in the following courses: introduction to the administration of justice; police administration; correctional administration; court administration; probation and parole administration; the criminal justice system; seminars or work-

*Defined in the National Advisory Commission on Criminal Justice Standards and Goals report *Criminal Justice System* (Washington, D.C., 1973).

shops in any of the preceding; selected topics, problems, or issues in criminal justice; second courses on advanced police administration; corrections administration; court administration; parole and probation administration; and executive development or middle management/ supervisory training within any of the agencies. It may also be used in any two-year, four-year, or graduate program of criminal justice, or as a supplement in the political sciences and social sciences. It has merit for our law schools, schools of criminology and urban affairs, or community development programs. The author hopes that this text will find its way into the schools of public administration, law, and institutes of government throughout this country.

I wish to acknowledge and express my appreciation to the highly respected authors who took their valuable time to write their respective chapters for this book. When presented with the idea behind the text, the contributing authors were highly enthused—over their individual contributions to the project, but especially over the text as a totality. Each author felt there was a need for the text, that it would make a valuable contribution to the field of justice administration, and that the other contributing authors were of the highest caliber. I hope the final result meets with their approval, since my intention has been to meet the standard of excellence for education—*quality of intellectual content.*

Introduction

It is most important to point out that the contributors to this book were selected very carefully because of the objectives the author hopes to achieve. Each contributor was asked, and has graciously complied with the request, that the chapter be written expressly for this book and be issue-problem oriented. The objective is to stimulate reactions—either agreement or disagreement—and to show applications (the reactions can be synthesized and applied realistically to situations). The atmosphere thus created is conducive to diverse views about the administration of justice in general, and about the selected issues and problems contained in this book specifically.

Administration of justice practitioners will have to deal with Criminal Justice Systems I and II; systems vs. nonsystems; acceptance, rejection, or modification of standards and goals; professionalism; personnel problems; discretion; education; processes of justice; juvenile offenders; punishment; rehabilitation; and parole and probation. To deal with these issues will require objectively drawn conclusions if we are to optimize our country's effectiveness in maintaining a lawful and just society. Such conclusions must be made in a changing society and within our legal and political framework.

This text identifies the special issues and problems facing the participants who traditionally are held accountable for the administration of justice. Even though the community (society) plays an important role in the responsibility for criminal justice, this book cannot attempt to address the voluminous issues relating to the community.

What are the objectives of the administration of justice? Can they be achieved through the cooperation of the system's components? Exactly how much impact does each component have on crime? What are the assets and liabilities of the components as they exist today? Can the administration of justice handle the impact of technology? What data are necessary to improve the effectiveness and quality of justice in America? What constitutional limitations have an effect on the administration of justice as viewed by each of the components? The challenges facing our future justice administration leaders are worthy of much discussion, serious questioning, visionary contemplation, and diverse input from all concerned with the American way of life. This is especially true for both students in the administration of justice programs in our colleges and universities and practitioners throughout our country. Hopefully, this book will provide the stimulus to use a diversity of knowledge and ideology to meet the challenges and succeed in resolving them effectively. Communication of the real issues across the spectrum of the justice administration components is vital in order to achieve the cooperative effort necessary to solve specific issues. First, the issues must be identified; this text can be a start in that direction by identifying controversial issues that can be debated and elaborated upon by instructors and students.

The Administration of Justice System: An Introduction is in four parts containing twenty-one chapters. Several Topics for Discussion designed to assist in stimulating discussion are included after each chapter. Part 1, The Administration of Criminal Justice, consists of four chapters designed to give an overview of three important aspects impacting the other three parts. Chapter 1 analyzes the systems approach and its relevancy and potential problems for the administration of justice; Chapters 2 and 3 address the issue of higher education and the impact it has had, may have, or should have on justice administration; and Chapter 4 overcomes a difficult challenge in synthesizing the findings and recommendations of the National Advisory Commission on Criminal Justice Standards and Goals reports. A provocative view and spirited approach is revealed.

Part 2, The Police, consists of eight chapters, each addressing an important issue or problem especially for the police administrator or potential police administrator. Chapter 5 describes the need for reviewing the police organization as it exists and what it should look like in the future; the need to communicate to the public their responsibility in reducing crime; and the need to identify the contents of true professionalism. Chapter 6 takes over where Chapter 5 left off, questioning some myths about professions and analyzing the status of police to attempt to determine whether police work is a profession as opposed to a craft. Chapter 7 focuses on the police labor movement and the impact this movement has on such issues as policy, manpower development and deployment, the process of labor relations (including collective bargaining), professionalization, politicians (internal and external), and discipline. Chapter 8 looks at the human side of the police organization and follows Chapter 7 in the discussion of discipline. The traditional approach to police organizational structure and the impact this approach has had on motivation, morale, and conflict is reviewed. Issues involving participatory management, achievement, recognition, and a sense of belonging emerge from this chapter. Chapter 9 presents a new approach to delivering police service to the community. Modern management practices, including organizational design based on achieving stated objectives, is the synthesis of this delivery system. Chapter 10 deals with the issue of technology in general, including specific areas of identification and intelligence system technology, optical technology, statistical technology, facsimile technology, criminalistic technology, and criminological theory and research. What impact, if any, has technology had on the control of crime? Are there any obstacles hindering the effective use of technology as applied to the administration of justice? These questions and many others are addressed in this chapter by Dr. Gallati. Chapter 11 takes a critical look at the performance of our police agencies regarding how well they walk that fine line between allowing personnel a desirable amount of freedom and assuring community security. Dr. Germann's "Police Power vs. Citizens Rights: The Delicate Balance" will stimulate the thinking and diverse views of all involved in the administration of justice. While Chapter 10 on technology analyzes privacy and liberty from the legal and technological viewpoints, Chapter 11 analyzes privacy and liberty from the legal and humanistic viewpoints. When Chapter 11 is read in conjunction with Chapter 10, the stage is set for an exciting intellectual discussion which will promote controversy and enthusiasm, thereby accomplishing the learning objectives of the text. Chapter 12 assesses the value of police-community relations as they exist in our country today and discusses how they could exist. Basic history or philosophy regarding the issue of the role of the police versus the role of the community is focused upon. This chapter also identifies the effects that traditional police-community relations have on the police as an organization and as individuals. A central problem brought out in the chapter is the role conflicts of police officers; practical examples are given by using actual projects from various parts of the United States.

Part 3, The Law and the Courts, is made up of four chapters. Chapter 13, "The American Criminal Lawyer: A Role Definition," deals with an issue not previously addressed as it is within the context of this text. The role is viewed as a concept for analysis using criminal practice, environment, and relations with clients as parts of the analytical spectrum. Chapter 14 takes a hard look at the traffic courts of our country. Several issues and problems are highlighted along with a critique of reforms. Questions such as what might take the place of traffic courts and the enormity of such a transition are discussed realistically. This chapter will promote intellectual discussion and creative and innovative thought. Chapter 15 analyzes the past, present, and future of the court administrator concept. The definition of the function, qualifications, and need for the court administrator is explained in the context of the potential contribution to the administration of justice. Chapter 16 does exactly what the title implies: it discusses the issues and controversies of plea bargaining, the grand jury concept, bail and release on recognizance, and capital punishment.

Part 4 has five chapters on corrections. Chapter 17 "Toward a Workable Theory of Rehabilitation," relates to the issues of roles, role changes, labeling, self-concept, and the social psychology of rehabilitation. Chapter 18 discusses the magnitude, cost, and causation of the problems related to the juvenile offender. This is done in a general way, pointing out several important factors associated with these issues. Also, there is an indepth analysis directed at the theories of strain-producing environments which spawn the use of drugs, alcohol, marijuana, hallucinogens, stimulants, depressants, and opiates. Chapter 19 entitled "Institutional Confinement: Countdown to Explosion" reviews the sentence, correctional client, correctional institutions, the atmosphere or setting in which the explosion takes place, and ways of defusing the bomb. All of these factors are involved in the issue of how correctional facilities should be operated. The issues presented tend to be about philosophy and methodology, which makes for an interesting debate between participants in the classroom. Chapter 20 focuses on community-based corrections, an emerging concept with differing viewpoints and expectations. The reduction of institutional isolation, intensification of social ties in the community, and national interest highlight the discussion of this controversial issue. Chapter 21 "Probation and Parole" begins with the fundamental issues of the philosophy and missions of probation and parole. Next, the chapter critically analyzes the intermediate issues of due process, plea bargaining by probation officers, conditions of probation and parole, and procedures for dealing with parole and probation violators. This chapter touches on the delicate issue of the use of punishment by the probation and parole officer.

1

The Criminal Justice System

Chapter I has presented some difficulties. Thought was given to deleting quotations and adding subheadings. However, since the authors of the quotations were selected deliberately for the purpose of providing widely representative viewpoints, to leave any of them out of the chapter would weaken its central point: there is no one way to define or to use the systems approach. The examples used in the last part of the chapter are intended to show the current application of the varied definitions of the systems approach to the administration of justice, as well as to point out the need for the continuing use of this approach. It would be improper to paraphrase and not give credit to the respective authors. Much of the material included in the first chapter has to do with nonsystem arguments, since my intent was to develop an issue-oriented book. I have attempted to bring out the issues surrounding the need for a systems approach to justice administration.

Why should the administration of justice address the systems issue? Many scholars believe the only way to effectively administer justice in America is for the output of one component of the criminal justice system to be understood by the accepting component as an input; each component must understand where he fits in the whole administration. For example, what kind of an input is a criminal to the correctional institution if the person has been, in his own mind, mistreated by police, prosecution and courts?

The issue of using a systems as opposed to a nonsystems approach is a very real one. This is exemplified in the chapter by contrasting the crime control model and the due process model of justice administration. One possibility would be to develop a synthesis from the opposing positions. I suggest that part of this synthesis could be to determine who the multiple offenders are and take them off the streets. This will assist realistically in reducing crime, and at the same time will increase the ability of the system to satisfy the end of justice. This suggestion is concurrent and compatible with a need statement such as "American cities need a 5 percent average reduction in crimes against property for the next five years." The suggestion is certainly commensurate with the designated responsibility of the public agencies assigned to the task of crime control.

Effective and realistic criminal justice education should be an agent for change by educating criminal justice practitioners to view the administration of justice not so much as a system, but as an effective criminal justice process. The second chapter in this part discusses criminal justice education as a unifying force. Dr. Gordon Misner is not at all certain that criminal justice education should have any special unifying force. He ably presents his view on this most important issue. In the area of education the Law Enforcement Assistance Administration has had an impact on the administration of justice. What has education done with the resources provided by the Law Enforcement Assistance program? Chapters 2 and 3 are intended to elicit views about the real value of criminal justice education, with regard to objectives, curriculum, programs, quality presentation, evaluation, and accreditation.

I have included chapter 3 for four reasons: first, so that readers may have another view of the impact criminal justice education (especially police higher education) may have on the administration of justice; secondly, because experience has shown that effective change can take place through transmitting ideas from educators to practitioners (this does not mean that practitioners do not think, but their day-to-day problems tend to obstruct the pursuit of free thinking); thirdly, the criminal justice education faculty has developed competence to the point where it is realistic to expect police administration to be accepted as a discipline; fourthly, the practitioners reaching the administrative level of many criminal justice agencies today appear willing to approach their work In a spirit of scientific inquiry, in order to establish objectives, priorities, and decisionmaking. Although this chapter was not written specifically for this book (I wrote and delivered it as a paper before the American Academy for Professional Law Enforcement), I felt it contributed to the discussion in an issue-oriented manner. Hopefully, this contribution will be accepted in the manner in which it is intended, to enhance the intellectual discussion of issues in justice administration.

In chapter 4, Dr. Paul Whisenand was requested to perform an extremely difficult task. I believe he has shown a unique ability in achieving the synthesis objective. I say this even if the chapter serves, at a minimum, as an incentive to discuss the National Advisory Commission's Reports.

At first glance it would seem that given the resources, the goals for crime reduction as stated by the NAC (National Advisory Commission on Criminal Justice Standards and Goals) are achievable. However, reviewing past performances and allocated resources and evaluating the length of time it takes to implement effective changes necessary to achieve the goals, they are totally unrealistic. This does not mean that any of the participants should stop trying. What it does mean is that unrealistic goals tend to result in frustration, and there is already enough frustration existing today due to incompetent management alone. Why add to the level of frustration by introducing unrealistic goals? Additionally, the word "leadership" rarely is seen throughout the reports, although leadership is crucial in producing any kind of goal achievement. I strongly believe that by emphasizing leadership and by setting as a first priority the concept of "crime prevention," criminal justice institutions and the citizens of our country can reduce crime.

There is much work to be done in the field of justice administration. Dr. Whisenand has pointed out most significantly the importance of having standards and goals as a historical data base. His critique and synthesis of these reports offers students a foundation for thinking about and applying objective evaluations of the reports for the future.

1

The need for a systems approach
to justice administration

INTRODUCTION

It has become popular in the past few years to refer to the administration of justice as a "nonsystem" approach. Most authors or speakers, however, go on to point out that it is not a nonsystem, after all; rather it is a poorly working system that could be improved by the applications of modern systems theory principles.

Systems analysis theory jelled during World War II, gained momentum as a conceptual model in the 1950s, stimulated interest in its broader application in industrial and governmental management in the 1960s,[1] and has continued to gain proponents in the 1970s. As with any popular or rapidly developing theory, it is not without its critics. Even among its advocates are those who caution that the systems approach is no panacea.

Two central themes seem to emerge from the discussions. The first has to do with whether or not those involved with the administration of justice are operating in a system or in an amalgamation of agencies. If it is the second, the questions have to do with whether or not these activities can be organized into a system and, if this is possible, is it advantageous? The second theme is based on the assumption that there is, in fact, an identifiable administration of justice system and that it can be advanced considerably by utilizing conceptual models emanating from systems analysis.

PROBLEM OF DEFINITION

A review of the literature reveals wide disparity in the way the term "systems" is used and the meaning behind the usage. Ida R. Hoos cites a dictionary yield of no less than fifteen different classes of meaning for the word "system"[2] and goes on to point out that almost all definitions are acceptable by proponents of the systems approach. This leads to serious difficulty:

> Lack of a firm definition leads persons engaged in systems analysis ... [to see] the system as what they say it is, what they conceive it to be. This they study; this they manipulate according to the rules they have set. In this way, other systems are ... [by force of circumstances] delimited. ...[3]

Some authors explain, by analogy, their conceptual framework in terms of a mechanistic model[4] while others contend that the systems approach "really consists of a continuing debate between various attitudes of mind with respect to society."[5] Walter Buckley provides an excellent discussion of the limitations of the early classical equilibrium theory and organic models and goes on to say that currently:

> This scientific worldview ... [has] led away from concern for inherent substance, qualities, and properties to a central focus on the principles of organization *per se,* regardless of what it is that is organized.[6] ... The kind of system we are interested in may be described generally as a complex of elements or components directly or indirectly related in a causal network, such that each component is related to at least some others in a more or less stable way within any particular period of time.[7]

The interest in the systems perspective cuts across several disciplines. Buckley's interest is in sociological research application. Psychology has its proponents, e. g., Gestalt therapy. The discipline embracing systems theory that has the greatest appeal to justice administrators is the management field. This is attributable to a growing recognition that, due to the discretion granted personnel at all levels, the administration of justice field has managers, in the technical sense, at all levels: patrolmen oversee their beats; probation officers manage caseloads, etc. Also, with an increasing interest in interdisciplinary approaches, more patrolmen, correctional workers, law enforcement, corrections and court administrators are gaining new working tools from the public administration curriculum. The vernacular of administration of justice personnel is sprinkled liberally with systems terminology—input, output, interface—particularly for those above the entry level. This is so even for those who do not strictly agree with or adhere to the systems approach. The terminology has influenced the field in subtle ways.

One feature that appears to be relevant in defining or analyzing administration of justice systems is that of interdependence. For example, it became immediately evident at the outset of the California Correctional System Study that a clear definition would have to be adopted in order to provide a benchmark for the continuing analysis. It was articulated as follows:

> It is crucial that corrections in California be viewed as a system, however vast and complex, with its parts so interrelated that the malfunctioning of any component part has disruptive reverbera- tions throughout the whole system. In short, if one thread breaks, the whole cord is weakened.[8]

(Obviously, this definition has been applied solely to corrections, thus, it could be argued that corrections would be considered either a component or a subsystem in the broader view. This matter will be taken up later.) The critical point is that whatever happens in one component has its effect on the rest of the organizational arrange- ments. There are no self-sufficient islands.

The other relevant feature is that of pragmatism—the notion that there is purpose in the design. This is best exemplified in the following:

> ... it will be helpful to define systems more precisely as *an array of components designed to accomplish a particular objective ac- cording to plan.* There are three significant points in this definition. First, there must be a *purpose,* or *objective,* which the system is de- signed to perform. Second, there must be design, or an *established arrangement* of the components. Finally, inputs of information, en- ergy and materials must be allocated according to *plan.*[9]

The components or subsystems are readily identified: law enforce- ment, courts, corrections and, more recently, the community. The goal is the reduction of crime, and the order of achieving the goal is well established in procedural law, that is, a defendant must be processed in a certain manner through each component of the justice system. The interrelatedness is most obvious in crises. When one component becomes ineffectual, the others experience an inordinate strain on their resources.

NONSYSTEM VIEWPOINTS

One major impediment to the full implementation of the systems approach in the administration of justice lies in the heart of Anglo- American legal provisions. That is, the commitment to the adversary proceeding. The principle actors—the prosecuting and defense attorneys—must, by definition, be lined up as opposing forces. The other participants who represent the other components tend to align themselves on one side or the other. It is rare to see a neutral participant, in the strictest sense, except for the judge, and even his detachment and objectivity comes into question from time to time depending upon the observer's frame of reference.

The systems view calls for a broader perspective for cooperation and coordination, for shared decision making, compromise on priorities and, above all, a commitment to change to meet the agreed-upon goals and objectives. All of this runs counter to the nature of the adversary approach. The closest semblance to the systems approach is embedded in the present practice of plea negotiations, and this practice has been open to serious question recently.

The question then is whether efficiency should override the concerns for effectiveness.[10] This is best portrayed in the two models intended to amplify the competing values developed by Herbert Packer, the crime control model and the due process model.[11] The crime control model is compared to assembly-line justice, or maximization of efficiency, while the due process model is seen as an obstacle course but more effective in terms of satisfying the ends of justice in the ideal. The systems analysis approach forces the competing values to the surface for examination. The ensuing discussion occasionally bogs down in even deeper divisiveness.

For example, one defense attorney might argue that justice is served when he can get the best "deal" for his client, providing the devices used are legal and ethical. These might include a form of artistry before the bench, astute plea bargaining, power plays, or whatever he deems to be necessary. Another attorney might feel this is a poor substitute for affording the accused the "real" due process provisions: his day in court, a chance to be heard, a trial in which he is judged by a jury of his peers, and so forth. A systems approach necessitates agreement on not only objectives but also on means. To reach such an agreement, one of the two above-described positions would have to be discarded, if the consensus resulted in one of those two extremes. On the other hand, both attorneys might experience some dissatisfaction if a middle-of-the-road compromise became acceptable.

This disparity in values and viewpoints is critically apparent in workers from differing components of the justice system. Furthermore, this might be expected when considering the nature of their respective responsibilities and working arenas. Daniel Freed in his article, "The Nonsystem of Justice," elucidates the problem:

> The police see crime in the raw. They are exposed firsthand to the agony of victims, the danger of the streets, the violence of lawbreakers. A major task of the police officer is to track down and arrest persons who have committed serious crimes. It is often discouraging for such an officer to see courts promptly release defendants on bail, or prosecutors reduce charges in order to induce pleas

of guilty to lesser offenses, or judges exclude incriminating evidence, or parole officers accept supervision of released persons but check on them only a few minutes each month.

Yet the police themselves are often seen by others as contributing to the failure of the system. They are the target of charges of ineptness, discourtesy, brutality, sleeping on duty, illegal searches. They are increasingly attacked by large segments of the community as being insensitive to the feelings and needs of the citizens they are employed to serve.[12]

Freed goes on to point out that judges "may sit long hours on the bench in an effort to adjudicate cases with dignity and dispatch, only to find counsel unprepared, weak cases presented," and so forth. Correctional officers are "dismayed at police officers who harass parolees, or at a community which fails to provide jobs or refuses to build halfway houses for ex-offenders."

It is extremely difficult to appreciate fully the difficulties others encounter in the normal course of carrying out their duties or to feel the weight of their responsibility. However, until recently, there was very little communication between the personnel in justice administration; what communication did exist generally was limited to discussion of procedures of a particular case. Some of the increase in understanding of the others' positions came about with the advent of such devices as sensitivity training for police officers and correctional officers. Another was one of the spinoff benefits of juvenile diversion projects in which police officers gained the experience of performing tasks traditionally handled by probation officers. And, at the administrative level, the local criminal justice planning boards have provided the opportunity for administrators in criminal and juvenile justice to gain knowledge and understanding of the problems of their counterparts in other components of the system. However, these effects are minor when considering the needs for increased communications to bring about the understanding and appreciation necessary to effectuate a systems approach.

Many other factors traditionally have contributed to disparity in the field of justice administration. Harry More cites several:

- The magnitude and complexity of the system serves to create tensions resulting in a negative congruence pattern.
- Interagency controls are minimal.
- The controls exerted by one element of the system over the other are clearly criminal process-oriented and have limited impact in terms of affecting the overall administration of other justice agencies.
- Intensified criticism engenders a hostile response and as the justice actors close ranks within an agency the psychological and physical barriers become increasingly insurmountable.

- Conflict is not only a matter of component isolation, but has been evident in jurisdictional disputes of law enforcement agencies.
- Each justice agency develops a social structure, traditions, customs, and a culture which serve as organizational stabilizers and reinforcers of a closed system with impermeable boundaries.[13]

It is evident that there are other more subtle influences. Historically, we have preserved the prerogatives of "home rule" which contributes notably to the autonomy of agencies. The high level of discretion granted those working in criminal and juvenile justice agencies has been assiduously protected, and this has contributed to individual autonomy. Finally, there has been a trend toward specialization; consequently, a type of professional respect is granted others. This respect precludes a closer investigation of the activities of others; it is assumed that the others' expertise facilitates appropriate decision making.

Those in the field fully appreciate their individual and agency autonomy and, quite naturally, resist attempts to bring about a more systematic approach, since they interpret this as a sacrifice to their working flexibility. They object to becoming cogs in a machine and believe that will be their fate.[14] There is some reality to this conception in that some proponents adhere to the mechanistic model. Also, the systems view is a broad view and, due to the critical and immediate nature of the majority of the assignments, it is exceedingly difficult to place oneself far enough away to see the forest as well as the trees. This is a luxury afforded administrators and researchers. It is not conducive to creating a change-making milieu when chiefs are dedicated to upgrading and improving the operations while the troops are resisting, either overtly or covertly.

Hoos[15] very succinctly points out the myriad pitfalls in accepting the systems approach as a panacea. One of the most significant dangers is that systems analysis can limit conceptualizations; hence, results of the findings may be grotesquely skewed or out of optimum focus. She cautions that:

> ... it should be remembered that most analysts are technically oriented. This means they view the situation in terms of their tools and trade. Operating on the assumption that theirs is the *systematic* way, they have focused on the tangible and the measurable and have pursued an arbitrary and eclectic course, all in the name of systematic analysis. The analyst's delineation of the objectives has been seen to influence profoundly his model and to affect his choices, assignment of weights, and even so seemingly quantitative a procedure as his allocation of costs and benefits.
>
> The point cannot be stressed enough that *discriminatory value judgments prevail throughout systems analytic procedures.* ... The hidden imprint starts with the selection of goals, itself a normative

matter, and goes on to bias the direction of the study through designation or neglect of alternatives, ascription of relevance to the various possible factors, and the development of criteria for the reliability of the data base.[16]

An example how this develops is seen in Appendix C of the *National Advisory Commission on Criminal Justice Standards and Goals*, "Program Evaluation and Measurement," prepared by the Los Angeles County Sheriff's Department.

Ironically, the need statement is difficult to evaluate. Perhaps there are too many needs or perhaps the needs arise from problems that are too large. The world "needs peace" and the nation "needs a crimeless society" but these two needs are too vast, too amorphous, to permit the problems to be defined. Better to say "the world needs a nuclear arms treaty with the Soviet Union" or that "American cities need a 20 percent reduction in theft." These needs are less extravagant, far more achievable, and well within the framework of the "divide and conquer" strategy of the systems analyst.[17]

The limitations arise from the subtle shading of values and from the adherence to the scientific method as *the* method, implying that it is the best method, or perhaps the only approach, for getting a conceptual handle on the problems. Only those factors which are readily available for empirical measurement *should* be considered; otherwise, the data get "soft" or "mushy." In view of the complexity of human problems, how many other factors, beyond the measureables, impact upon the system?

In the above quote the author suggests reducing the goal to measure the reduction in the percent of a particular type of crime. Assuming that this could be documented over a period of time using the traditional measure, arrest records or theft reported to the police, it would turn out to be a worthless endeavor. New victimization studies[18] have shown that the level of criminality, as measured by the reported or recorded, has been grossly underestimated. Obviously, it could be argued that it is a poor stance to stop conducting research until better methods of measurement are in, but it has been recognized for many years that the only available crime statistics *were* inadequate. And yet, much of the federal money that has been funnelled through the states has been awarded on the basis of grant applications claiming to be able to reduce criminality by a stated percent.

Hoos' text is replete with examples of cautionary measures to be employed. Included in her concluding remarks is this:

Refinement of methodology has led only to greater preoccupation with abstraction while the mythology that social problems can be solved remains unchallenged. In fact, this false assumption plays an important part in the perpetuation of the magic spell which promises a technology to solve social problems.

This is not to say that systematic approaches do not have a contribution to make to the understanding of social process and improvement of the social condition. The problems besetting mankind are plentiful, complex, and multifaceted enough to provide challenge to and invite commitment of professionals from a variety of disciplines. The clearly nonlinear, normative, and value-laden dimensions of these problems need deter the efforts of only those experts who approach with predetermined solutions. The systems approach, if it is ever to become conceptually sound, must be a genuine multidisciplined endeavor, in which contributions from the pertinent fields of knowledge are meaningfully synthesized, and not merely homogenized into a synthetic and symbolic language.[19]

IMPACT ON ADMINISTRATION OF JUSTICE

It is more common than not to hear and read references to "the system" of administration of justice. In fact, allusion to the "non-system of justice" sounds contrived and, as mentioned above, prepares the listener for an explanation. Common usage of the systems terminology signifies at least some level of acceptance that administration of justice meets the criteria of a system.

One view of the systems approach is that it is a manmade, artificial contrivance designed as a methodological tool. At the other extreme are those who see the world as a system,[20] a world order composed of both physical and social systematized associations which are natural. This reasoning follows along the lines that we traditionally have banded together to work toward common goals. The first view emanates from a notion of what ought to be while the second depicts what is—it is descriptive.

Part of the difficulty in reaching an adequate systems perspective is that a system may be described as closed or open. The closed system definition is, of course, extremely limited, which makes its application virtually worthless for analyzing the administration of justice functions. We refer to an information system, a communication system, a transportation system, or a criminal justice system, and when inferences are drawn that these are closed systems, the description becomes inadequate as a conceptual model. As Churchman so well portrays, ". . . every system is part of a larger system."[21] Or, to borrow again from the business management field:

A business firm can be considered as an integrated whole where each system, subsystem, and supporting subsystem is associated with the total operation. Its structure, therefore, is created by hundreds of systems arranged in hierarchical order. The output of the smallest system becomes input for the next larger system, which in turn furnishes input for a higher level.[22]

The administration of justice system is a part of the social order system in a city, in a county, and so on to the international order systems. The recognition and appreciation of this stands to improve administration of justice significantly. Unfortunately, the police have been handed the responsibility for *controlling* the "crime problem," when they have limited resources for responding to anything more than the manifestations of the problems. Correctional officers are expected to "correct" those legally defined as criminally deviant in a relatively short time when it is known that, for the most part, the psychological and social environments from which they came are grossly inadequate. In essence, the police and correctional officers are expected to do what others in the community could not do and are then blamed for the increased crime and recidivism rates. Law enforcement and corrections are but a part of a larger social order system, not closed systems sufficient unto themselves.

Fanning the fire are those with simplistic notions regarding "handling the crime problem" and who have little interest in contributing anything more than expressions of righteous indignation. And there are those politicians who capitalize on this for campaign platforms. Many authorities in the administration of justice field have commented on this, among them Norval Morris and Gordon Hawkins, "Politicians Who Would Be Reluctant to Pose As Experts in Biochemistry or Astrophysics Do Not Hesitate to Peddle Fashionable Nostrums and Panaceas for the Crime Problem."[23] Fortunately, the instant experts are few; unfortunately, however, they are vociferous and, consequently, stimulate negative influence.

A significant breakthrough in the awareness of the hierarchal order of systems as it applies to administration of justice is the recognition that one of the valuable components, heretofore minimized, is the community or as the National Advisory Commission Reports describes it, Criminal Justice System 2. It is explained thus:

> Criminal Justice System 1 is well known. It is the traditional series of agencies that have been given the formal responsibility to control crime: police and sheriff's departments, judges, prosecutors and their staffs, defense offices, jails and prisons, and probation and parole agencies.
> There is a broader implication of the term. For a system is merely a group of parts operating in some coordination to accomplish a set of goals. Many public and private agencies and citizens outside of police, courts and corrections are—or ought to be—involved in reducing and preventing crime, the primary goal of criminal justice.[24]

The Commission report, *Community Crime Prevention,* is well stocked with far-reaching examples of how Criminal Justice System 2 can interact effectively with Criminal Justice System 1. Most important among the recommendations and suggestions are those that deal with factors that have been well documented as precipitators to criminality. It is a means for addressing the other side of the coin, dealing with causes as well as effects.

Some of the types of formalized programs along these lines that have proven to be highly effective are the youth service bureaus, community school projects and juvenile diversion projects. There are numerous distinct advantages. The most salient are that: 1) they utilize community resources that are already established and available, thereby preventing a money and time drain on criminal or juvenile justice agencies; 2) they deal with the problems in a natural environment where varied means of social control are available beyond those available through legal sanctions; 3) they go a step beyond traditional measures in which available resources are used. They analyze the problems, document unmet needs, and work cooperatively to create needed resources; 4) finally, as a result of representatives from different agencies and disciplines working together as teams, there is optimal input into decision making. There is the opportunity to share expertise in a highly valuable way.

There are innumerable ways in which citizens may become involved.[25] Rather than being a meddlesome drain on the system, their contributions could very well provide those much needed bridges to increased effectiveness. This approach meshes with the democratic ideals that have been propagated throughout this country's history.

It has become increasingly tiresome to hear, "If we can put a man on the moon, why can't we handle our human problems?" For those who failed to see the complexity of human nature in the past, it should be imminently clearer through systems analysis. The President's Commission on Law Enforcement and the Administration of Justice was the first major study to approach the subject from a systems viewpoint. There are now more academicians pointing up the complexities of the interactions central to administering justice. Blumberg portrayed this very well in regard to the judicial processes.[26] And Neubauer continues with this theme:

> While the police, prosecutor, judge, and defense attorney represent separate institutions, they must work together. In carrying out their assigned tasks, these law appliers interact on an almost daily basis. Such interactions are crucial because no one law applier can make decisions independently. Each must consider the reactions of others.[27]

He goes on to point out that the court is a social system in which consideration of political and social pressures is of utmost importance in achieving an adequate level of analysis. Ultimately, there is a much more accurate assessment of the decision making process; what kind of information is relevant, where and how the power or influence emerges, and who contributes input. The former linear model used to describe critical decision making masked the wide variety of options that are actually available at each point.

The advent of federal funding has stimulated a necessity for more precise evaluation. Evaluation efforts are still short of an effective level; however, the efforts have focused discussion on areas that were long overdue for clarification. Among these are goals and objectives, resources, and a more accurate estimate of what kind of and how much of services an apportioned amount of money will buy. As a result, there is a clearer picture of which agency, or combination of agencies, can best deal with justice administration problems. And this, combined with the awareness of finite public financial resources, has synthesized a systems view. Evaluation efforts also help to surface the realization that the assumed causal linkages of the past are totally inadequate—i.e., attempts to design a delinquency prevention program located in the community where there are multitudinous variables that could affect outcome.

Except for the larger metropolitan agencies, the implementation of a systems analysis probably surpasses the capability of most administration of justice systems at the present time. However, the smaller agencies should be able to capitalize on the experience of the larger ones in the next few years. Some may be able to hire federally funded consultants in order to explore new conceptual areas or to implement programs based on proven results, for example, program budgeting, comprehensive planning, operation analysis, and so forth. Furthermore, the National Advisory Commission reports, *Criminal Justice System* and *Community Crime Prevention*, both provide well-developed and documented guidelines.

The systems perspective facilitates some of the changes occurring in a more positive, fruitful direction. One of these directions is toward interdisciplinary approaches. A wry comment on recent trends is that if we continue the trend in specialization, those from different disciplines will have little about which to communicate to one another. One need to keep the communications bridges functional was discussed above. Beyond that, there is a need to be able to become more eclectic; administration of justice systems will continue to profit by drawing from the fields of economics, public administration, management, sociology, psychology, finance, and many others. The systems approach necessitates drawing on varied disciplines, hence, it furnishes a common ground for bringing in the best from the various areas of expertise.

The administration of justice system was able to come up with new methodologies after the smoke cleared from the social disruptions of the 1960s and after it recovered from its shock. However, it is not necessary to experience trauma to shake loose some of the old ineffectual methods. Churchman suggests that the unfamiliar questions of the systems analysts are sufficient to trigger the postulation of alternatives. It is not particularly productive to ask those who have been performing tasks over a period of years with minimum efficiency to devise creative alternatives. The outside consultant or the new methodology frequently is the needed catalyst.

Some of the newer approaches are born of the philosophical models that assume conflict as a basic premise. This premise should be more obvious to those working in the administration of justice system than to those in most other disciplines but, until recently, there was a strong adherence to the order model. More states, "System legitimacy can only be attained if there is concerted effort to maintain a reasonable balance between the collective need and individual rights."[28] Maintaining this balance calls for dynamic solutions.

We have been witness to a marked change in the ways the "disenchanted" deal with the established order in the last decade. A basis for this approach is described by Martin and Shattuck:

> From the viewpoint of the conflict theorist interested in social change, communities are perceived as involving more than one system; there is a recognition of the legitimacy of cultural pluralism; the existence and rights of political minority subcommunities are acknowledged; structural inequalities between different collectivities are of concern in public policy terms; and most significantly, minority subcommittees are encouraged to challenge and bargain with the *status quo*.[29]

The authors proceed to point out that those who operate programs under the tenets of this model work within the framework of the law, bargaining for what they perceive to be legitimate and needed changes rather than engaging in destructive activity that creates a negative reaction.

CONCLUSION

Administration of justice can be regarded as a system by most standards. It may be a poorly functioning system but it does meet the criteria nonetheless. The systems approach is still in its infancy; as an approach it has affected administration of justice in many more ways than are listed here and holds greater promise for the future.

It is, by no means, a cure-all, or final answer. There are many other factors to be taken into consideration. For example, Freed reminds us:

> There are, of course, no shortcuts to the reduction of crime. More money and personnel, new equipment and revised procedures will all be essential to the goal. Yet without new organizations and relationships to help spend money wisely and use personnel well, history suggests that significant changes are unlikely.[30]

Refinement and agreement in regard to definition and explanation are essential. Efforts to advance administration of justice could be seriously curtailed unless this problem receives some serious attention in the near future. Additionally, there are many other cautionary measures to be exercised, as so aptly documented by Hoos. Most important, a view of the system as static, closed, mechanically analogous, and exclusively technical should be avoided absolutely.

A systems approach has already facilitated positive movement. It is providing the stimulus and foundation for new programs which are not only effective but are also compatible with democratic ideals and individual freedoms. We cannot afford—at the cost of lives, money, and freedoms—to cling to the old conceptual models.

NOTES

1. C. West Churchman, *The Systems Approach* (New York: Dell Publishing Co. Inc., 1968), p. x.
2. Ida R. Hoos, *Systems Analysis in Public Policy, A Critique* (Berkeley: University of California Press, 1972), p. 16.
3. Ibid., p. 17.
4. See: Alan Coffey, Edward Eldefonso, and Walter Hartinger, *An Introduction to The Criminal Justice System and Process* (Englewood Cliffs: Prentice-Hall, 1974), pp. 6–7.
5. Churchman, *The Systems Approach*, p. xi.
6. Walter Buckley, *Sociology and Modern Systems Theory* (Englewood Cliffs: Prentice-Hall, 1967), p. 36.
7. Ibid., p. 41.
8. California Board of Corrections, *California Correctional System Study, The System* (Sacramento: California State Printing Office, 1971), p. 5.
9. Richard A. Johnson, Fremont E. Kast, and James E. Rosenzweig, *The Theory and Management of Systems*, 2nd edition (New York: McGraw-Hill Book Co., 1963), p. 113.
10. Efficiency is used here as a method by which a process is completed with a minimal investment of time, energy, and money while effectiveness connotes the attainment, or close approximation, of stated goals or postulated ideals. Efficiency equates with costs, effectiveness with benefits.
11. See: Herbert L. Packer, *The Limits of The Criminal Sanction* (Stanford: Stanford University Press, 1968), Chap. 8.
12. *National Commission on the Causes and Prevention of Violence, Law and Order Reconsidered* (Washington, D.C.: U.S. Government Printing Office, n.d.), pp. 267–268.

13. Harry W. More, Jr., and Richard Chang, *Contemporary Criminal Justice* (San Jose: Justice Systems Development, 1974), pp. 32–35.
14. See: Williams Exton, Jr., *The Age of Systems, The Human Dilemma* (n.p.: American Management Association, 1972), pp. 138–180.
15. Hoos, *Systems Analysis in Public Policy, A Critique.*
16. Ibid., pp. 130–131.
17. *National Advisory Commission on Criminal Justice Standards and Goals, Criminal Justice System* (Washington, D.C.: U.S. Government Printing Office, 1973), pp. 225–226.
18. See: Carol B. Kalish, *Crimes and Victims, A Report on the Dayton-San Jose Pilot Survey of Victimization* (Washington, D.C.: National Criminal Justice Information and Statistics Service, 1974).
19. Hoos, *Systems Analysis in Public Policy, A Critique,* p. 247.
20. See: Ervin Laszlo, *The Systems View of The World* (New York: George Braziller, 1972).
21. Churchman, *The Systems Approach,* Chap. 3.
22. Johnson et al., *The Theory and Management of Systems,* p. 113.
23. Norval Morris and Gordon Hawkins, *The Honest Politician's Guide to Crime Control* (Chicago: The University of Chicago Press, 1969), p. 237.
24. *National Advisory Commission on Criminal Justice Standards and Goals, Criminal Justice System,* p. 1.
25. *Law and Order Reconsidered.* See Freed, pp. 281–284 for an extensive list. Also, see: "Modernizing Criminal Justice through Citizen Power," a pamphlet put out by the U.S. Chamber of Commerce (Library of Congress Card Catalog Number 73–85301) which suggests methods for citizens to help implement recommendations put forth in federally supported studies and the American Bar Association reports.
26. Abraham S. Blumberg, *Criminal Justice* (Chicago: Quadrangle Books, 1967).
27. David W. Neubauer, *Criminal Justice in Middle America* (Morristown: General Learning Press, 1974), p. 12.
28. More et al., *Contemporary Criminal Justice,* p. 30.
29. John M. Martin and Gerald M. Shattuck, *Community Intervention and the Correctional Mandate,* working paper submitted to the President's Commission on Law Enforcement and the Administration of Justice, 1967, p. 13.
30. Freed, *Law and Order Reconsidered,* p. 274.

TOPICS FOR DISCUSSION

1. Discuss the administration of justice as a system/nonsystem.

2. Discuss the reasons why there is a lack of consensus on defining the term "systems."

3. Discuss how the administration of justice in the United States could be more effective.

4. Discuss wheher it is feasible to design, develop, implement, and evaluate a master plan for the administration of justice at the federal, state, and local levels.

5. Discuss the development of a synthesis based on the crime control model and due process model of justice administration.

6. Prepare a need statement, present the statement, and then discuss each statement.

2

GORDON E. MISNER

Criminal justice education: the unifying force?

INTRODUCTION

When attempting to deal with a subject such as this, there is a tendency to rush to the bookshelf and wrestle with *Bartlett* or some similar reference source on quotations. I will resist doing this, being uncertain really how productive that exercise would be. The fact that we are where we are today in criminal justice education may actually be *because of* the fact that some earlier writers on the subject *did* rely on Socrates, or Augustus, or Hobbes, etc. This is certainly not to discount the importance of what these great writers had to say; the point is they probably had precious little to say about criminal justice education. If a reader finds them quoted in a piece on criminal justice education, on LEEP, or on modern criminal justice, the reader would be well advised to read especially critically. The author using their quotations may have quoted them completely out of context. More to the point, they may have been quoted only to bolster arguments that lacked any intrinsic merit of their own!

I do not generally accept the notion that education is, or should be, the unifying force in criminal justice. In fact, it is not at all certain that criminal justice education should have any special unifying force! But, first things first. We have, as a nation, tended to place entirely too heavy and uncritical a reliance upon education and simple credentialling. We are a credentials-conscious society, placing an unbelievable amount of faith in education as being the solution to all of our social and technological problems. Seventeen- and eighteen-year-olds who have demonstrated little interest or aptitude in college-level work have often been pressured, in droves, to enroll at the nation's colleges and universities. Those who resisted the pressure or

aptly demonstrated their lack of interest and aptitude have often been automatically stigmatized as "lesser beings." Vocational education has become "second best." There is ample evidence, in all of our great urban centers, that vocational and technical education has been placed very low on the policy-maker's priority system.

The point is that criminal justice may have fallen—or have been gently pushed—into the same trap, into the trap of placing an over-reliance upon higher education. There are objectives that institutions of higher education can accomplish very effectively; at the same time, we must admit that there are also objectives that higher education cannot achieve effectively. Serving as the unifying force in criminal justice may be one notable example.

Criminal justice education and the Law Enforcement Education Program (LEEP) are not precisely synonymous, but LEEP figures for financial investment will give a close approximation of the number of students currently involved in some form of criminal justice education. In fiscal 1975, for example, the federal government's budget for the LEEP program was approximately $40 million. This involved some form of financial assistance to nearly 100,000 students enrolled in academic programs at approximately 1,000 institutions throughout the nation. In addition to LEEP, of course, each of the State Planning Agencies in the nation were investing some funds in criminal justice education endeavors. There were also federal monies in the form of support for vocational education, vocational rehabilitation, and through the Veterans Administration. In 1975, therefore, a reasonable estimate of the financial investment in criminal justice education would be approximately $100 million. *For one year*, that represents $1,000 for each of the 100,000 enrolled students. That amount also represents approximately $166 for each of the total 600,000 criminal justice practitioners in the nation! That is a hefty amount of money to invest in any endeavor, especially since the figure represents an *annual* investment. The impact of all of this may be hard for many of us to explain or defend

THE CRIMINAL JUSTICE "SYSTEM"

For the past ten years, our ears and our minds have been assaulted with the phrase, "criminal justice system," and we have been reminded reprovingly of the fact that criminal justice is actually a "nonsystem." Obviously, the fact that criminal justice was a nonsystem was something bad. After all, the experts made their frequent comments about the matter in reproving and scolding tones. The statement of the "fact" was impressive enough, but it was followed by various endeavors imploring us to take action. We have heard, read, or been told that it is our national and individual duty to improve the criminal justice system, working conscientiously and diligently to turn the nonsystem into a system!

At this point, it would be useful to review a statement made in *The Challenge of Crime in a Free Society* in 1967:

> The system of criminal justice America uses . . . is not a monolithic, or even a consistent, system. It was not designed or built in one piece at one time. Its philosophic core is that a person may be punished by the government if, and only if, it has been proved by an impartial and deliberate process that he has violated a specific law. Around that core, layer upon layer of institutions and procedures, some carefully constructed and some improvised, some inspired by principle and some by expediency have accumulated. . . . The entire system represents an adaptation of the English common law to America's peculiar structure of government which allows each local community to construct institutions that fill its special needs. Every village, town, county, city, and state has its own criminal justice system, and there is a federal one as well. All of them operate somewhat alike. No two of them operate precisely alike.[1]

It is obvious, to any informed observer of the criminal justice processes, that the above statement is an accurate reflection of the "criminal justice system." Criminal justice is obviously not a system; some of us would argue the point that it should not be restructured to become a system.

One of the problems involved in this whole matter is confusion about the term "system." Unfortunately, the term has both a popular, common-sense *set* of meanings, and it also has a more precise, objective meaning compounded by a group loosely called "system scientists." If the proponents of a "criminal justice system" are using that term in its scientific sense, one would wonder how really popular the concept would be! Fresh out of Watergate and all of its ramifications, many of us would question whether it is really desirable to have a fully integrated criminal justice system, with a centralized decision-making authority, and sharing a common information base. There is at least a remote possibility that our founding fathers were wiser than many of the current advocates of a criminal justice system. It was they—the founding fathers—after all, who set up the basic outlines of our governmental system. This includes its federal features, its concept of judicial supremacy in the law area, the whole notion of limiting centralized authority by delegating the responsibility of criminal law to the several states, and the idea of creating an explicit separation of powers.

The criminal law, our particular social and political heritage, and the needs of the general public for an effective and systematic governmental apparatus are the principle unifying forces in the field of criminal justice. Criminal justice education can be supportive and complementary of these. However, it would be inappropriate, presumptuous, and hopelessly frustrating to conceive a criminal justice education as having a principle role to play as a unifying force.

CRIMINAL JUSTICE EDUCATION

Criminal justice education had its essential beginnings in the World War I period when August Vollmer began to teach occasional courses at the University of California, Berkeley. The first degree-granting program began in 1931 at San Jose State College in California, greatly influenced by the ideas and concepts of Chief Vollmer. By the time this author began a college teaching career in 1956, there were fewer than 30 degree-granting programs in the nation. Most of these were on the junior or community college level in California. The only four-year institutions or universities that had established programs at that time were: San Jose State College, Michigan State University, University of California, Washington State College, Indiana University, and four other State Colleges in California (Sacramento, Los Angeles, Long Beach, and Fresno).[2]

In 1956, therefore, there were approximately twenty-seven institutions with fewer than 5,000 majors in police science, criminology, or similarly named programs. Twenty years later, we had approximately 100,000 majors. Few, if any, fields of study have ever experienced the rapid growth that criminal justice education has enjoyed or endured.

Any endeavor growing as rapidly as criminal justice education has grown will experience quality control problems. Criminal justice education has been no exception, and the field has been bedeviled with a series of problems. Principally, these have centered around three different, but related, matters. First, there has been no general agreement on the matter of educational objectives in criminal justice; second, there has been a scarcity of qualified faculty. Finally, there has been a scarcity of appropriate learning materials. Much of the discussion that follows will focus upon one of these matters, namely the educational objectives of criminal justice programs. At the same time, the discussion that follows will tangentially address the other two matters: faculty and learning resources.

What are appropriate educational objectives for criminal justice programs? Certainly there can be and should be variations in these. These variations may reflect the locale of the institution, its overall educational mission, the qualifications of faculty members, etc. For example, a community college located in an agrarian, midwest state, having a faculty principally educated and experienced in the corrections field might have one set of educational objectives. A large west coast university, located in one of the nation's largest metropolitan areas, and boasting a diversified and distinguished faculty of more than twenty members will probably have another set of objectives. In the case of the first institution, it would be unrealistic—actually ludicrous—for the faculty to concentrate their attention on urban policing. In the case of the west coast institution, it would be equally unrealistic for the faculty to focus their attention only upon urban policing.

The point is that educational objectives are arrived at in a number of different ways. There are a series of justifiable, different inputs into the process. One of these is the locale, another can be called the "institution's setting" or bias, and yet another input could be the perceived needs of the community served by the institution. *Underpinning each of these inputs, however, should be the philosophical, historical, and governmental core of our criminal justice processes.*

If we can assume higher education institutions and their faculties wish to impart correct information, then the starting point for any criminal justice program should be an understanding of that short statement from *The Challenge of Crime in a Free Society* quoted on page 22.

If we review and analyze that statement, we will see that it delineates several different crucial and fundamental statements about criminal justice in the United States. These can be listed as follows:

1. Criminal justice in the United States is not a monolithic system.
2. It was not consciously designed.
3. Therefore, it cannot be a consistent system, or perhaps a system at all.
4. Criminal justice processes in the United States were not built at one time.
5. Rather, criminal justice consists of layers upon layers of institutions.
6. Some were developed only for governmental expediency.
7. Criminal justice in the United States represents an adaptation of English common law features.
8. To our own peculiar governmental system.
9. As a consequence of this, federalism and local determination of governmental form have been key considerations in the development of criminal justice.

10. Every town, village, county, city, and state has its own particular criminal justice process.
11. The national government also has a criminal justice process to handle violations of federal criminal law.
12. There is a large amount of commonality in criminal justice throughout the United States.
13. But criminal justice processes in no two locales or jurisdictions are identical.
14. Throughout its historical development, criminal justice in the United States has been continually influenced by its emphasis upon an enlarged concept of due process of law.

The above listing is a formidable statement. Educating students so that they would have a genuine understanding of what is encompassed in that statement would represent a noteworthy educational objective. Unfortunately, too little of that simple statement undergirds criminal justice education at the present time. Certainly none of the earliest programs—1931 to 1961—manifested any ostensible appreciation of the "message" of that statement. The vast majority of those early programs focused their "system" attention upon the police, almost exclusively. (Only one or two of the programs in existence prior to 1960 emphasized any interest in other component sectors of criminal justice, i.e., courts, corrections, juvenile justice, etc.) Because of the preoccupation with the police, the bias of most of those early programs was toward viewing due process as simply an unwanted and resented encumbrance to police efficiency.

Therefore, rather than adapting a "systems" view or stance, the earliest programs in criminal justice took actually an opposite stance. Essentially, they informally or formally adopted the view that focusing upon a single segment of criminal justice would result in some tangible social benefit. Retrospectively, that view could be vigorously criticized.

This resurrects the main subject of this chapter, namely whether criminal justice education should attempt to become a unifying force in criminal justice. Given our historical development, the philosophic thrust of our various justice institutions, and the generally low credibility of higher education in "the real world," that objective would be impossible to achieve. Hopefully we are not foolish enough to desire it!

The criminal justice "system" in the United States is nonunitary, and given its historical development, it was apparently meant to be that way! Criminal justice in this nation is fragmented—by component, by jurisdiction, and by goals. Criminal justice is uncoordinated; that is, there is no single executive nor committee which has authority over the diverse components of the operation. This is true in each of the states, and in the national system. This means that not even the fifty governors, nor indeed the President of the United States, have been given such authority. Apparently a few have tried—unsuccessfully!

These unsystematic features of criminal justice are sources of irritation and frustration to many criminal justice practitioners and others. Certainly, many students and professional observers of criminal justice operations are appalled by the many delays, the many inefficiencies, the many miscarriages of justice. However, many who uncritically adopt the "systems point of view" may be unconsciously endorsing a cure which is worse than the illness.

If we were truly to be interested in creating a system of criminal justice, we would have to restructure our whole approach to the matter. First, we would have to do away with the principle of separation of powers which deliberately separates the three principal departments of government: legislative, executive, and judicial. Certainly, we would have to combine the executive and the judicial branches, giving the executive both the appointing authority and the actual control over management of our courts systems. We would also have to change the most common means of selecting prosecutors, from elective to appointive by the executive branch.

At the present time, one principal reason for the lack of coordination in criminal justice matters is due to the fact that various component parts have established different sorts of goals. Often, these goal statements actually conflict with the goal statements of other components. For example, courts may be very much attached to the concepts of fairness and to due process; they may see "discovery" procedures and pretrial conference as means of speeding up their own functioning. Prosecutors and police may not share these goals of the courts. In fact, these goals of the judiciary may be in direct conflict with the goals of the police and prosecutors.

Courts may also take very seriously their sworn duties to uphold the Constitution. In such a circumstance, if they are asked to avoid housing prisoners in a particular jail because its conditions represent cruel and unusual punishment, the courts may very well intrude into areas that corrections administrators view as their exclusive territories.

The point is the potential sources of conflict between component agencies in criminal justice are limitless. Conceiving of criminal justice as a system may not be the ideal solution to our current problems. In fact, the day is long past when we could realistically do this, even if we were serious about using the term "system" in its precise meaning. Criminal justice education should deal with actualities, rather than perpetuate the myth that criminal justice should somehow be a system.

Most of the criminal justice programs in the nation initially were strongly biased toward dealing in some fashion with improved police efficiency. Despite their official names, many of the criminal justice programs throughout the nation are still actually police administration programs in disguise. Let me emphasize that I do not object to the fact that these programs devote primary attention to the police. This can be perfectly appropriate, in and of itself. It is inappropriate only when these "police" programs attempt to *reform* criminal justice operations taking only the police into consideration. Actually, the author would argue that this is a crucial disservice to the students in such programs; for by doing this the programs are doing little to prepare the students for the hard realities of the operating world.

Surely, some would argue in favor of doing away with federalism, and replacing it with a unitary system of government. Surely, some may even argue for doing away with the doctrine of separation of powers. (After all, the logic goes, what do legislators and other politicians know about criminal justice problems. Really how interested can they be in improving system performance?) The best that can be said at this point is that there are a tremendous number of typical voters around the land who would probably resist this move, even if it promised to "make the streets safe" again!

All of this may sound very remote from the discussion of educational objectives. It isn't; it is directly in point. Recently, Bruce Olson—formerly a policeman and now a university professor—made the following statement, directly in line with the discussion:

> ... nothing could be more stultifying than if one academic segment or criminal justice subsystem (i.e. police, corrections, defense, courts, prosecutions, prisons, etc.) captured the curriculum and fashioned it to its own narrow purposes.... [The] writer is convinced that the possibility of developing a socially responsive criminal justice professional is very remote if only one group or another dominates the education field and successfully defines the means and ends of criminal justice training and education.[3]

The point made by Olson is crucial, namely that the domination by one particular segment—of either academe or of criminal justice—can be self-defeating.

An appropriate example may be taken from systems science. One situation that systems people attempt to avoid is "suboptimization." When some function is suboptimized, it simply means that the whole mechanism is running out of balance, and that the performance of some emphasized subfunction is threatening to become detrimental to the entire operation. In an example from aircraft production, suboptimization would occur when the performance of one "subsystem" was out of synchronization with the production of the rest of the operation. The objective is to build whole airplanes. There might be two and one-half starboard wings for every one fusilage! Obviously, the aircraft production system—as a whole—is not operating very effectively.

The term suboptimization can be used in other settings. It is appropriate to use it in this present discussion of criminal justice education. What has transpired as criminal justice education has actually been an unfortunate mixture called police science or law enforcement administration; it has been a witches brew of wishful thinking and suboptimization. More importantly, it has been a sub-suboptimization. By focusing primarily on the police, we have committed our first sin of suboptimization. By primarily featuring the criminal investigation and traffic subfunctions of the police, we have committed a double sin of suboptimization! In other words, what has taken place—and is still taking place—in many programs is a concentration upon only approximately 25 percent of the police function. The function of the police in most jurisdictions is much broader than a combination of criminal investigation and traffic enforcement. Three-fourths of the police task involves other totally different types of activities. Detective commanders and traffic division heads may not see it this way, but the evidence is weighing heavily against them!

In summarizing this point of view, it is imperative that criminal justice education have as its central objective, the accurate reproduction of criminal justice as it functions in the American governmental setting. The study of comparative criminal justice—in other governmental settings—would certainly be a useful teaching approach, but the primary objective should be a thorough familiarization with the functioning in an American setting. Other educational objectives should somehow be functionally related to this overall objective.

Unfortunately, only a small number of our criminal justice faculty and very few of our textual materials are ideally suited for the task proposed. Many of our faculty—perhaps the majority throughout the nation—are products of careers in the police field, or other operating components. They may be ideally prepared to teach certain subject matter, but not very well prepared at all to deal with this particular approach to criminal justice education. (Many textual materials will be of little help in this regard.) Therefore, it is imperative—for this if for no other reason—that criminal justice programs be effectively linked to other subject matter fields, particularly to the social sciences.

To achieve the educational objective outlined in this chapter, the faculty involved ideally must represent an amalgam of criminal justice, law, history, sociology, and political science. Few persons individually possess the skills, insights, and experiences necessary to relate criminal justice and its subfunctions to its actual working setting, to its historical, social, and governmental framework. This is not to say that criminal justice programs around the nation are staffed with unqualified persons. What the statement says is that few, if any, individuals have the qualifications to do "the whole job" by themselves.

Many students will resist this approach to the subject matter, derisively referring to it as an "American civics" approach. Many students are pragmatists, who want to get an "education," get a job, and get to work. Because of their experience with civics in junior and senior high schools, they may be "turned off" to traditional and hackneyed approaches to the subject matter. This is where excellence of teaching enters. The superior teaching faculty, representing a variety of perspectives and subject matter fields, should be able to relate the substance of criminal justice to its operating, real world environment. Many students may complain that they enrolled in college for something other than a traditional "civics" program, and indeed they did. Hopefully, they will get a criminal justice program soundly based in American heritage, a broadly conceived program that seeks to show the relevance of American institutions to the whole matter of criminal justice. For the "nuts and bolts" student who wants only practical material, things that will make him a better policeman or correctional worker, we can only say the following: "Being highly practical can, in the end, be very impractical."

Too many criminal justice programs are so "practical" as to be, in the long run, a real disservice to students. How can a student be effective in the police world without knowing something of the essence of due process? How can we possibly serve our community without knowing its institutions and their heritage, without knowing something about the vested interests in the community, without knowing about the fact that vested interest is not the same as community-shared interest? Personally, we may reject some of the latest notions about due process of law. We also may reject the notion that the political heritage of a community has any relevance to governmental service. In fact, we can even adopt the notion that the term "local government" refers to all those other "civic" functions, but it doesn't include policing, or corrections, or any other criminal justice matter.

We are certainly free to do this, if we can reconcile it with our own conscience, and with the social conscience of our immediate family and work associates. We should be advised, however, that our view is contrary to more than two hundred years of painful history. More than that, we cannot in good conscience accept our oath of office, for that involves our swearing to uphold and protect the Constitution. In fact, we should be aware of the fact that we may be running some chance of being formally charged in the future with a serious offense, namely the abuse of office.

CONCLUSION

Criminal justice education deals, in a central fashion, with one of the most important aspects of democratic self-government. All organized societies have developed systems of self-defense, systems designed to manage the incidence of criminal and delinquent behavior. Ours is a highly organized society, founded upon principles that sounded revolutionary at the time of their inception, namely the principle of self-government and all that idea encompasses. Involved in this concept was the notion that free people could govern themselves, and that government would possess only delegated powers. Theoretically, the people could withdraw these powers whenever governmental agents exceeded their authority. In actuality, this has seldom been done, and is difficult to do. However, our system of government also involves the genius of a separation of powers and a system of checks and balances.

Criminal justice works within this framework in the United States. In addition, it works within a legal framework, undergirded throughout by the concept of due process of law. These phrases *democratic self-government, delegated powers, separation of powers, checks and balances, due process of law,* etc., are more than clichés or idle phrases taken from some elementary civics text. Rather, they represent the fabric of criminal justice in a democratic society. As such, they become the foundation of any relevant criminal justice education program. Neither criminal justice nor any of its subfunctions can operate in a cultural vacuum. One can reject one's history, but only at his own peril.

> *If men could learn from history,*
> *what lessons it might teach us!*
> *But passion and party blind our eyes,*
> *and the light which experience gives*
> *is a lantern on the stern, which shines*
> *only on the waves behind us!*
> Samuel Taylor Coleridge . . . 1831

NOTES

1. President's Commission on Law Enforcement and Administration of Justice, *The Challenge of Crime in a Free Society* (Washington, D.C.: U.S. Government Printing Office, 1967), p. 7.
2. For an excellent historical outline and discussion of issues involved in criminal justice education, see Charles B. Saunders, Jr., *Upgrading the American Police: Education and Training for Better Law Enforcement* (Washington, D.C.: Brookings Institution, 1970), 182 pp. Although Saunders' book focuses

upon the police, much of his discussion is generally relevant to criminal justice as a whole.

3. Bruce T. Olson, "Notes on a Philosophy of Criminal Justice Education," (Los Angeles: Center for the Administration of Justice, University of Southern California, October 1974), 14 pp. (mimeo) p. 2.

TOPICS FOR DISCUSSION

1. Discuss whether criminal justice education should attempt to act as a unifying force in criminal justice.

2. Discuss the objectives that institutions of higher education can accomplish in the field of criminal justice.

3. Discuss the possibility of measuring the effectiveness of the Law Enforcement Assistance Administration.

4. Discuss the possibility of measuring the effectiveness of the Law Enforcement Education Program.

5. Discuss ways educational institutions can better use the funds provided by the Law Enforcement Assistance Administration.

6. Discuss each of the statements in the list (page 24) concerning the fundamental, crucial statements about criminal justice in the United States.

3

DONALD T. SHANAHAN

Education for police service
(professional or liberal arts)

INTRODUCTION

Traditionally, the study of liberal arts was reserved for the upper classes or the socially elite of our society. In ancient Greek and Roman societies, and to some extent in modern Europe today, the study of liberal arts was designed to improve a person's mind and develop his understanding of the world about him; liberal arts had no vocational end; i.e., they were not designed to teach a man how to make a living, but how to live.

With the widening of the base of education or the democratization of mass education, liberal arts carried over to the new system of education. However, because the participants in this educational process were from all elements of society, most of whom had to learn how to make a living, the original purpose of liberal arts—teaching a man how to live—was changed partly to teaching a man how to earn a living. The question that arises at this point is, "How can we accommodate teaching a man how to live to teaching a man how to earn a living?"

The professional police practitioner must understand people, their interaction, and the environment as well as being competent in the professional aspects of his profession.

PROPER MIX

There is no trichotomy among academic, professional, and liberal arts: i.e., professional and liberal arts education are academic. It is not an either/or situation, but a situation that supports and complements. Professional education is as sterile without liberal arts as liberal arts is without utility in today's society. Neither liberal arts alone nor professional education alone is the panacea to higher education for police. The issue is in determining the proper proportion of each, the right mix, if you will.

Higher education for police must serve as a unifying force to bring together police and the other components of the administration of justice. The objective of this action should not be to develop a criminal justice system as such, but to develop practitioners who are capable of providing our country with an effective criminal justice process. Police administration can and should be a discipline just as policing can and should be a profession.

Effective and realistic police educators should be, and in many cases are, change agents. Police educators can assist in achieving the objectives of acting as a unifying force by educating police administrators and potential police administrators in meaningful traditional areas, such as the liberal arts; education in the professional school, as well, should be geared to a changing society. An example is the recent concept of team policing as introduced to a group of patrol administrators by Mr. Quinn Tamm, past executive director of the International Association of Chiefs of Police. Mr. Tamm's remarks are as follows:

> It is unrealistic to expect that innovative programs will not create problems. But most of these problems are solvable and they should certainly not deter departments from giving innovative programs an adequate opportunity to prove themselves. I think the best approach is—and has always been—a willingness to experiment with new ideas and new concepts without abandoning the old methods and procedures until the new ones have been proved superior.[1]

There should not be change for the sake of change, but there should always be a willingness to change when improvement would be the result. However, we also should take heed from the Ford Foundation's William C. Pendleton, who has conducted a study of the problem concerning large-scale intervention of universities in national and local affairs, when he states: "When academicians get beyond analysis of options into the area of advocacy and decision-making, there is a clear risk of misjudgment."

My colleague, Professor B. Edward Campbell, in an unpublished paper entitled "Developing a Philosophy for Higher Education in Police Administration" makes two significant points. First, in a section subheading *A Typical Police Administration Curriculum*, Professor Campbell identifies four major parts: Administration and

Management, Technical Courses, Law, and Basic Liberal Arts or General Education Courses. Secondly, in the section *Some Future Goals*, Professor Campbell describes several objectives for professional practitioners. When Professor Campbell addresses the fourth part of a typical curriculum, he states:

> The fourth part consists of basic liberal arts or general education courses. Communication skills, natural sciences, social sciences, political science, history, humanities, and behavioral sciences make up this part. Often this phase of the curriculum is relegated to a minor position, if not in terms of time, in terms of esteem. Quantitative literacy seldom is developed in students during the study of these courses. Students sometime look upon these courses as an unnecessary nuisance rather than as a fundamental foundation. Police educators frequently nurture this attitude among students.[2]

Under the section, *Some Future Goals*, Professor Campbell states:

> Police administration education needs very much to escape the shackles of perennialism. This is not to say that such topics as history, for example, as a part of the basic arts and sciences, or jurisprudence, for example, as part of the professional arts and sciences have no place in the curriculum. Nor do I intend to suggest that police administration should be spared the study of subjects intended primarily to transmit the traditions of culture. On the contrary, too many of the police administration curriculums appear to slight this crucial aspect of education. Too many students opt to slough off the cultural courses. What I do suggest is that police education be moved from the trailing edge of society.
>
> Our society continually exhibits change. The administration of justice needs to be geared to a changing society—not a static society. Education for positions in this justice system needs to be pushed out to the growing edge of this society. Again, I do not call for the discarding of useful and worthwhile traditions nor change for the sake of change. And neither do I contemplate wasting college class time allowing each new group of freshmen the expensive luxury of rediscovering the wheel or the alphabet or the microscope or the autoanalyzer. Professional practitioners need to be able to sense changes in the goals of the people they swear to serve. They need to learn how to adjust to new techniques, methods, tools, and procedures. They need to know when to discard worn out and thus ineffective approaches to problems. They need to learn how to acquire new knowledge. They need to learn how to investigate problems objectively, to evaluate their findings, and to establish priorities in applying their resources, not so much in terms of things as in terms of people.[3]

There is an overwhelming need to understand the importance of the liberal arts contribution in achieving the objectives of the police profession. How can professional police practitioners sense changes in the goals of the people they swear to serve if they are not aware of

James Q. Wilson's *Varieties of Police Behavior* or *Dilemmas of Police Administration?* To sense the changes, they must be aware of the economic and social forces working on the environment, nationally and locally. They need to know the effects, for example, that population changes and unemployment may have on crime identification, crime reduction, service quality, and service volume. The specific demands or objectives of a community may be different from neighborhood to neighborhood.

How can the professional police **pract**itioner learn how to adjust to new techniques, methods, tools, and procedures? What will he think when he reads a research report from the National Institute of Law Enforcement and Criminal Justice (Research center for LEAA) in the areas of planning or personnel? Will he be able to transform the findings and apply them to his own agency? Will he be able to recognize the appropriate time for calling in experts to assist? Will he anticipate the need for research assistance? Mr. David J. Farmer, of the National Institute of Law Enforcement and Criminal Justice, points out four problems in police research: 1) practice and methodology gap; 2) the "experiment interruption" tendency; 3) the data base problem; 4) the significance issue.[4] How will the professional police practitioner resolve these problems without the proper mix of liberal arts and professional school education?

How will he know when to discard worn out and thus ineffective approaches to problems? How will he know the techniques of completed staff work, problem solving conferences, and brainstorming without the proper mix? The professional police practitioner must be able to select alternative approaches to prison riots; therefore, he should know some of the reasons why prisoners riot. He must direct his agency in response to demonstrations about busing; therefore, he must understand the body politic and its parts to be able to be flexible in his police approach within the federal process. Should he not have a philosophical background so he can set frames of reference?

The professional police practitioner needs to know how to acquire new knowledge. He must know where to go to find information about defining tasks, sensitivity, tolerance of personality differences, communication skills, and diagnostic skills. He must know how to use the library, to know what to read, to know what lectures to attend, to know what issues should be addressed with other leaders in the field. He must know when and how to distinguish between gut decisions and scientifically validated decisions and when to use each.

How does the professional police practitioner learn how to investigate problems objectively? This can happen only when the exercise is performed in an atmosphere where a hypothesis can be stated, an antithesis can be espoused, and a realistic synthesis can result. A

climate of agreement, disagreement, and a tolerance of diverse viewpoints is necessary to bring about objectivity. An analysis of the
potential consequence and ramification of selected decisions in an
objective manner is necessary to produce a proper evaluation of
decisions.

In this day of measurement, accountability, and productivity in the
public sector, there is a dire need for professional police practioners
to be able to establish priorities in applying their resources, especially
in terms of people. In a recent interview with Chief of Police Thomas
J. Cullinane of Washington, D.C., he was asked the question "What
will you do after you lose these several hundred men?" (The department was about to lose personnel.) Chief Cullinane said "We will
have to reestablish our priorities, and you know how difficult that is."

I submit that the professional police practitioner of today and
tomorrow who must face the complex problems of our society generally
and the administration of justice specifically cannot effectively fulfill
his responsibility unless he has the proper mix of liberal arts and professional education.

EDUCATIONAL OBJECTIVES

More and more, colleges and universities are setting their sights on
career education—the training of Americans for better working lives.
This has been described as *Career Training*, The New Realism. A
major priority of President Ford and the U.S. Office of Education, it
is also attracting support from Congress, which appropriated $10
million for career education this year, and from business, industry,
organized labor and such groups as the National Urban Coalition.

What they are pushing is the view that career education is lifelong, from prekindergarten years well into retirement. In college,
students are encouraged to make early career choices and acquire
professionalism.[5]

U.S. Education Commissioner Terrel Bell said: "The college that
devotes itself totally and unequivocally to the liberal arts today is
just kidding itself. Today, we in education must recognize that it is
our duty to provide our students with salable skills."[6] Career education is seen as aiming to make work purposeful and satisfying for the
individual, without neglecting Shakespeare.

A federally aided study carried out by Harvard University and
Massachusetts Institute of Technology reports that the value of a
college degree in terms of jobs and upward mobility is fading—
with the result that "large numbers of young people, for the first

time, are likely to obtain less schooling and potentially lower occupational status than their parents."

... educational theorists see a historical landmark and the central problem confronting U.S. schools, colleges, parents, taxpayers, teachers, and students in the 1970s. Professor Arthur G. Powell, associate dean for academic affairs at Harvard's Graduate School of Education, puts it this way: "Schools are a litmus paper which tells us what the community thinks education should be. The basic concepts of schooling really didn't change much from the 1890s through the 1960s because, for most of that time, there was a consensus on what the public wanted from education.

"Now educators are not sure what direction to take, and colleges and high schools let students do their own thing from a large array of electives. In other words, the public consensus has broken down."

Where does this leave police education? What should we do about the change in theory and the identification of directions with regard to police education?

DIRECTION FOR CHANGE

Some of this direction may come from the practitioner Clarence M. Kelley. In his address to the 80th annual conference of the International Association of Chiefs of Police, September 1973, entitled "Receptiveness to Change," Mr. Kelley addressed the future for police administrators:

Planning and Evaluation
Obviously we do not want arbitrarily to discard what is good, what is working, what is performing well. But, we must be willing to analyze, to test, to evaluate, to see what can be.

Substantive Changes
Let's be honest with ourselves. Most of the substantive changes we have made as a profession in recent decades have been dictated by external pressures. Too often we have instituted changes under compulsion and coercion. Rather, we need to inculcate into our personnel, at all levels, an attitude which encourages creative and innovative thinking. We need to encourage a perception of change as part of the thinking process of the officer as he carries out his daily assignments. We want him to seek more efficient and effective ways of accomplishing his goals. Actually, in the long run—and this is a basic point—the specific changes effected are often not nearly as important as *efforts to build an organization capable of containing change.* (emphasis his)

Meeting the critical challenge of change
The anticipation of change means one thing above everything else in law enforcement: professional training.

One way to constructively master change is through professional competence and training.[7]

Higher education can only meet the needs of the police practitioner
in fulfilling the challenges stated by Mr. Kelley through carefully
designed courses of education which contain liberal arts and professional programs. I strongly believe that this approach will enable
higher education to assist in producing police leaders capable of:
being sensitive to the peculiar needs of policing in a free society,
analyzing ambiguous situations, and achieving order within the re-
straints of the democratic process.

As time passes, more and more police practitioners recognize the
need for and the value of college and higher education. It is my belief
that these practitioners also believe higher education is the most effective stimulus for police practitioners to reexamine the many assumptions about police procedures.

Higher education must address the problem of developing the
necessary body of knowledge, curriculum, and accreditation. This can
be done only after objectives of higher education for police are stated.
With this in mind, I submit the implementation of recommendation
15.1 of the National Advisory Commission on Criminal Justice Standards and Goals, *Police*, as our strategy point. Recommendation 15.1
reads as follows:

RECOMMENDATION 15.1

IDENTIFICATION OF
POLICE EDUCATIONAL NEEDS

It is recommended that a national body comprised of *educators,
police,* and *other criminal justice administrators be formed immediately to establish curriculum guidelines for police educational
programs.*
    This national body should identify the educational needs of the
police service, including the needs of the *police generalist, the
police specialist, and the police manager.*
    1. Having *identified these educational needs,* this *national
body should prepare a model curriculum* that will *satisfy* the Nation's law enforcement needs.
    2. This national body should urge the modification of exist-
ing police educational programs and, where none exist, the institution of new programs designed upon the model curriculum.[8]

In conclusion, I would like to relate two quotes that I found when
reading the book *Upgrading the American Police* by Charles B. Saunders, Jr. The first is by Alfred North Whitehead:

There can be no adequate technical training which is not liberal and no liberal education which is not technical: that is no education which does not impart both technique and intellectual vision.[9]

The second quote is by Leonard E. Reisman and reads as follows:

How do you educate policemen? First, teach them "like anyone else" and second, "teach them the practice, techniques, needs, and milieu of police work.[10]

NOTES

1. Quinn Tamm, *A Conference on Managing the Patrol Function* (Washington, D.C.: Police Foundation, 1974).
2. B. Edward Campbell, *Developing a Philosophy for Higher Education in Police Administration,* Unpublished Paper (Louisville, Ky.: University of Louisville, School of Police Administration, 1974), pp. 4–5.
3. Ibid, pp. 11–12.
4. David J. Farmer, "Police Research Program," *The Police Chief,* (Gaithersburg, Md.: International Association of Chiefs of Police, March 1975) p. 68.
5. Crisis in the Schools," *U.S. News & World Report,* Sept. 1975, pp. 48–51.
6. Ibid, p. 51.
7. Clarence M. Kelley, "Receptiveness to Change," *Police Chief,* Gaithersburg, Md.: International Association of Chiefs of Police, 1973.
8. National Advisory Commission on Criminal Justice Standards and Goals, *Police* (Washington, D.C.: 1973), p. 378.
9. Alfred North Whitehead, *The Aims of Education* (New York: Mentor Books, 1953), p. 58.
10. Leonard E. Reisman, "How Do You Educate a Policeman?" *AAVW Journal* (May 1967), p. 688.

TOPICS FOR DISCUSSION

1. Discuss the need for liberal arts and professional education in the field of justice administration.

2. Discuss the criminal justice system vs. criminal justice process.

3. Discuss whether the measurement of productivity in criminal justice is possible.

4. Discuss the potential members (organizations) of the National Body outlined in Recommendation 15.1 of the National Advisory Commission on Criminal Justice Standards and Goals report—*Police.*

5. Discuss a list of police myths (assumptions) that have evolved over the years; for example, organization structure, degree of preventive patrol effectiveness.

6. Discuss the local community's view of what education should be.

4

PAUL M. WHISENAND

Synthesis and critique of the findings
and recommendations
of the national advisory commission
on criminal justice standards and goals

A NATIONAL STRATEGY TO
REDUCE CRIME

Goals for Crime Reduction

The Commission proposes as a goal for the American people a 50 percent reduction in high-fear crimes by 1983. It further proposes that
crime reduction efforts be concentrated on five crimes by 1983. The
goals for the reduction of these crimes should be:

- Homicide: Reduced by at least 25 percent by 1983
- Forcible Rape: Reduced by at least 25 percent by 1983
- Aggravated Assault: Reduced by at least 25 percent by 1983
- Robbery: Reduced by at least 50 percent by 1983
- Burglary: Reduced by at least 50 percent by 1983

Priorities for Action

The Commission proposes four areas for priority action in reducing
the five target crimes:

- Juvenile Delinquency: The highest attention must be given to
  preventing juvenile delinquency and to minimizing the involve-

40

ment of young offenders in the juvenile and criminal justice system, and to reintegrating juvenile offenders into the community.
- Delivery of Social Services: Public and private service agencies should direct their actions to improve the delivery of all social services to citizens, particularly to groups that contribute higher than average proportions of their numbers to crime statistics.
- Prompt Determination of Guilt or Innocence: Delays in the adjudication and disposition of criminal cases must be greatly reduced.
- Citizen Action: Increased citizen participation in activities to control crime in their community must be generated, with active encouragement and support by criminal justice agencies.[1]

This chapter presents a summary review and evaluation of the standards and recommendations of a most significant study conducted by the National Advisory Commission on Criminal Justice Standards and Goals (NAC). The work of NAC began in October 1971 and lasted almost two years. The overview report *A National Strategy to Reduce Crime* was released on January 23, 1973, while the more comprehensive documents did not appear in print until mid-1973. By title the reports are: *Criminal Justice System, Police, Courts, Corrections*, and *Community Crime Prevention*. The Law Enforcement Assistance Administration (LEAA) provided $1.75 million in discretionary grants for the work of NAC. The immediate future will reveal whether or not the monies produced the intended results—to improve the capability of the Criminal Justice System (CJS) in conjunction with the community (CJS/C).

At this point, I would want the reader to share with me the challenge and frustration of capsulizing over 1,000 pages of material that in turn contain nearly 400 standards and recommendations pertaining to the CJS/C. Additionally, NAC has antecedent underpinnings that should be discussed in order to better comprehend the reasoning and importance of the various standards. Further, there is, in particular, a complementary (perhaps even competitive) set of standards to NAC's that should be addressed at this time. At best, this chapter should serve as an impetus to the reader for personally perusing the NAC reports. At worst, I am fearful of misinterpreting the subject at hand to the extent that you may build false expectations concerning their relevance or lack of same. In either event, I must presage, most affirmatively, that the NAC reports will be a predominant spark of reflection and action during the latter half of this decade.

The remainder of this chapter is partitioned into five sections as follows. First, one of the major cornerstones and incipients for NAC— The President's Commission on Law Enforcement and Administration of Justice (1967)[2]—is brought into perspective. Second, the goals and processes utilized for their attainment by NAC are described. Third, and very succinctly, the content of the NAC reports are highlighted. Fourth, NAC and a recent similar endeavor by the American Bar Association Project on Standards for Criminal Justice are compared to one another. Fifth, and finally, the chapter offers an evaluation of the NAC recommendations.

PRE-NAC: THE EARLIER CHALLENGE

The report makes more than 200 specific recommendations—concrete steps the Commission believes can lead to a safe and more just society. These recommendations call for a greatly increased effort on the part of the federal government, the states, the counties, the cities, civic organizations, religious institutions, business groups, and individual citizens. They call for basic changes in the operations of police, schools, prosecutors, employment agencies, defenders, social workers, prisons, housing authorities, and probation and parole officers.

But the recommendations are more than just a list of new procedures, new tactics, and new techniques. They are a call for a revolution in the way America thinks about crime.

Admittedly, there are many cornerstones in the NAC "foundations." Typically, a writer/researcher/scholar begins his or her discussion of criminal justice "commissionitis" with the Wickersham Commission (1935).[3] Space does not permit a review of the numerous commissions that predate the NAC. One in particular, however, necessitates some commentary—the President's Commission on Law Enforcement and Administration of Criminal Justice (President's Commission).[4] The President's Commission provided a series of reports that contained, as previously mentioned, over 200 recommendations on how to improve the delivery of criminal justice services for reducing the severity of crime in this nation. As a result of its analytical research and conceptualization, the President's Commission proposed that:

> Despite the seriousness of the problem today and the increasing challenge in the years ahead, the central conclusion of the Commission is that a significant reduction in crime is possible if the following objectives are vigorously pursued:
> First, society must seek to prevent crime before it happens by assuring all Americans a stake in the benefits and responsibilities of American life, by strengthening law enforcement, and by reducing criminal opportunities.

Second, society's aim of reducing crime would be better served if the system of criminal justice developed a far broader range of techniques with which to deal with individual offenders.

Third, the system of criminal justice must eliminate existing injustices if it is to achieve its ideals and win the respect and co-operation of all citizens.

Fourth, the system of criminal justice must attract more people and better people—police, prosecutors, judges, defense attorneys, probation and parole officers, and corrections officials with more knowledge, expertise, initiative, and integrity.

Fifth, there must be much more operational and basic research into the problems of crime and criminal administration, by those both within and without the system of criminal justice.

Sixth, the police, courts, and correctional agencies must be given substantially greater amounts of money if they are to improve their ability to control crime.

Seventh, individual citizens, civic and business organizations, religious institutions, and all levels of government must take responsibility for planning and implementing the changes that must be made in the criminal justice system if crime is to be reduced.

In terms of specific recommendations, what do these seven objectives mean?[5]

Perhaps the most distinguishing features of the President's Commission are: (1) it was nationally well timed and socially critical, and (2) it resulted in a few changes at the federal level, and (3) relatively none at the community level. I am not saying that the President's Commission was irrelevant or useless. On the contrary, it fulfilled a paramount purpose—to focus public attention on the CJS. Moreover, it impressed upon the citizenry that the community must be intimately included in any concerted effort to measurably reduce crime. Hence, the concept of a CJS/C was sagaciously pronounced and emphasized.

The results were far from successful. Yet, a fairly firm basis for confronting the challenges of the seventies as compared to those of the sixties was laid. Quite simply, the following happened because of, or maybe even in spite of, the President's Commission:

1. The CJS was visualized as a CJS/C.
2. The CJS agents started to or were encouraged to cope with their problems in a systematic rather than a separatist manner (the cops became more communicative with the jurists and corrections personnel, and vice-versa).
3. The CJS was revealed as a social system very gravely in need of *help*.
4. The federal government began to promulgate administrative mechanisms to assist state and local CJS's.
5. The public had certain expectations of the CJS.

6. The public expectation of a crime rate that was abated in reality as well as perceptually.

For a few moments, please return to the quotation from the President's Commission. Take note of the wording. In essence, broad and highly significant goals were outlined. Specific recommendations, regretfully, were not. The so-called *challenge* was cogently presented; the means for meeting the challenge were not so clearly defined. Coincidentally, the final chapter in the overview report speaks to "a national strategy" on what should be done to meet the challenge of crime in our society. Explicitly . . .

> The responsibility of the individual citizen runs far deeper than cooperating with the police or accepting jury duty or insuring the safety of his family by installing adequate locks—important as they are. He must respect the law, refuse to cut corners, reject the cynical argument that "anything goes as long as you don't get caught."
>
> Most important of all, he must, on his own and through the organizations he belongs to, interest himself in the problems of crime and criminal justice, seek information, express his views, use his vote wisely, get involved.
>
> In sum, the Commission is sure that the Nation can control crime if it will.[6]

In retrospect, the President's Commission is a paradox. The President's Commission could be assessed as a failure by some, although others might feel inclined (as I do) to more favorably weight the commission as a cost/beneficial study that had a far-reaching, and not short-term, proclivity for solidifying and perfecting the concept, if not the activities, of our CJS. For those who carefully inspect both reports (President's Commission and NAC) will discern that the former is more circumspect, while the latter asserts an unequivocal routing to the reduction of crime. Maybe the single most important result of the President's Commission was to place the federal government in a position of frontally assaulting the problems of local policing. The 19 commissioners, 63 staff, 175 consultants, and hundreds of advisors decided to act as midwives to a concept of crime reduction via better CJS/C. NAC, it seems to me, is the next logical iteration above and beyond the findings and recommendations of the commission. The impact of NAC, similar to that of the President's Commission, is totally dependent on its ability to gain access to the means of change within our society. For those who desire a perspicacious understanding of NAC, I would strongly suggest that you spend some time reading the commission's reports. If one does not possess the requisite amount of time, I would only add that the majority of President's Commission's findings are contained in a different format within the NAC reports.

NAC: PURPOSES AND PROCESSES

The commission's report is one of the greatest accomplishments of the Law Enforcement Assistance Administration in its first five years of operation. It will be one of the guides in determining LEAA policies and in evaluating the efficacy and effectiveness of its programs.

However, we are not endorsing the commission's recommendations. LEAA does feel, however, that the process employed by the commission in its efforts to set standards and goals is a process that should be commended to every criminal justice agency in this country.

The commission has stated this clearly in its report, "A National Strategy to Reduce Crime." It said:

> Operating without standards and goals does not guarantee failure, but it does invite it.
>
> Specific standards and goals enable professionals and the public to know where the system is heading, what it is trying to achieve, and what in fact it is achieving. Standards can be used to focus essential institutional and public pressure on the reform of the entire criminal justice system.

LEAA is undertaking a detailed analysis to determine the means by which it can establish a process for utilizing the commission's proposals.

> Though our plans are not yet final, we are beginning work on a series of possible grants to help implement commission proposals in such areas as speeding trials and reducing police response time. These would be demonstration efforts, and the successful results would be disseminated throughout the nation.
>
> We have also established a management committee that is developing detailed objectives that LEAA can utilize in assisting the states to implement standards and goals, to measure their performance in reducing crime, and to develop plans for action.
>
> It is not our intention to impose these standards on states and units of local governments, but rather to assist and encourage them to get through the process of analyzing their criminal justice systems and to adopt such standards as each state and unit of local government finds appropriate and necessary.[7]

As related earlier, $1.75 million (yours and mine) were expended on NAC. Professionally and personally, I believe that the monies were appropriately spent. Correct or not, we now possess a set of highly concrete and "challenging" (there is that word again) criminal justice standards and recommendations. The intent of NAC is equally paramount and perplexing for our nation. On the one hand, we may have the answer(s) to our problems; on the other hand, we may be confronted with nothing more than solutions that do not respond to the issues.

The purpose of NAC seems somewhat self-evident—to clarify and set into motion many of those precepts expressed in 1967. Interesting parallels can be easily drawn between NAC and the President's Commission. For example:

> A National Criminal Justice Statistics Center should be established in the Department of Justice. The Center should be responsible for the collection, analysis, and dissemination of two basic kinds of data:
> Those characterizing criminal careers, derived from carefully drawn samples of anonymous offenders.
> Those on crime and the system's response to it, as reported by the criminal justice agencies at all levels.[8]

The above has been established within LEAA. Other similar linkages between the two commissions could be depicted; however, the main message should be patent—NAC is singularly bent upon "getting things done." Basically speaking, NAC is operationally oriented. To illustrate this proposition, the following is cited as but one case in point.

STANDARD 19.1

FOUNDATION FOR INTERNAL DISCIPLINE

> Every police agency immediately should formalize policies, procedures, and rules in written form for the administration of internal discipline. The internal discipline system should be based on essential fairness, but not bound by formal procedures or proceedings such as are used in criminal trials.
> 1. Every police agency immediately should establish formal written procedures for the administration of internal discipline and an appropriate summary of those procedures should be made public.
> 2. The chief executive of every police agency should have ultimate responsibility for the administration of internal discipline.
> 3. Every employee at the time of employment should be given written rules for conduct and appearance. They should be stated in brief, understandable language.
> In addition to other rules that may be drafted with assistance from employee participants, one prohibiting a general classification of misconduct, traditionally known as "conduct unbecoming an officer," should be included. This rule should prohibit conduct that may tend to reflect unfavorably upon the employee or the agency.
> 4. The policies, procedures, and rules governing employee conduct and the administration of discipline should be strengthened by incorporating them in training programs and promotional

examinations, and by encouraging employee participation in the disciplinary system.[9]

While seemingly somewhat mundane, the above "standard" if adopted by a statewide planning agency (SPA) or a local criminal justice agency could produce vastly beneficial effects. The implementation of other related standards could, in turn, generate deserved results within the CJS of considerable magnitude. Note once again . . .

STANDARD 14.1

MAINTAINING INTEGRITY
IN THE LOCAL PROSECUTOR'S OFFICE

1. States should redefine their law enforcement districts so as to combine smaller jurisdictions into districts having sufficient workload to support at least one full-time district attorney.
2. States should devise training standards for prosecution service, and should provide prosecutors' salaries that will attract the best-qualified personnel.
3. All local prosecutors and their staff attorneys should be prohibited from engaging in partisan political activity. Local prosecutors who are elected should be elected in nonpartisan elections.
4. All local prosecutors should be required to publish and make available annual reports detailing the deployment of personnel and resources during the preceding reporting period. Such reports should disclose the number of cases pending, hours spent in court and before the grand jury, and other details cataloging the number and kinds of cases handled by the prosecutor and their status at the time of reporting. Reports should be available for public inspection.[10]

NAC, then, is a sincere and intensified effort to transfer concepts and concerns from theoretical drawing boards into the milieu of functional society. Thus NAC proposes standards and recommendations for the CJS/C that are designed, in rather precise terms, to rectify existing deficiencies. Rather than "regurgitate the obvious," NAC exposes the significant in such manner that minor achievements can be, if implemented, aggregated into major accomplishments.

NAC: The Content

A commission of state and local officials today presented Attorney General Elliot L. Richardson and LEAA Administrator Donald E. Santarelli with a massive, detailed master plan to reduce crime and improve criminal justice throughout the nation during the next ten years—and to provide a catalyst for continuing improvement.[11]

Other recent Commissions have studied the causes and debilitating effects of crime in our society. We have sought to expand their work and build upon it by developing a clear statement of priorities, goals, and standards to help set a national strategy to reduce crime through the timely and equitable administration of justice; the protection of life, liberty and property; and the efficient mobilization of resources.[12]

Because the commission was developing standards, the emphasis of its efforts was placed not only on what was desirable but also on what was workable and practical. Many standards are based upon successful models that are operational in one or more places in the country. Many models were found that had never been documented before. Where no model existed, standards were based upon concepts that the task forces and the commission felt were necessary for crime reduction.

Finally, some of the standards, upon initial reading, may not appear to be directly related to crime reduction. Examples include standards dealing with expansion of the constitutional rights of convicted offenders, elimination of plea bargaining, expansion of the right to counsel, the use of summons in lieu of arrest, and integrity in government. In setting such standards, it was the opinion of the commission that to foster respect for the criminal laws and to win the respect and cooperation of all citizens, the agencies and officials of the criminal justice system and the governing authorities of this country must themselves respect the law and must act fairly and justly toward all citizens.[13]

A cursory examination of the above quotations indicates that the NAC reports are (or, were intended to be): (1) sufficiently comprehensive to encompass those institutions and functions that interfere with the CJS, (2) comprised of highly specific standards and recommendations that pertain to the CJS/C, (3) pragmatically oriented, (4) in a major way based on earlier studies, and (5) dedicated to the reduction of crime in our society. Preceding as well as subsequent pages contain examples of the various standards and recommendations. I do not (moreover cannot) either describe or synopsize them for you. In presenting such a list in the overview report, *A National Strategy to Reduce Crime*, NAC consumed nearly thirty pages to do so (pp. 249–278). I would, however, warn those of you who believe that a quick reading of this list will provide an understanding of the NAC reports that you err. Unfortunately, a greater commitment of your time is necessary to adequately comprehend them. For, all of the standards and recommendations are expressed as a series of paragraphs that are then followed by a commentary that explicates, usually by example, the intent and purpose of the proposed standard.

The first page of this chapter contained NAC's primary goals for crime reduction and paramount priorities for action. Before reading further, it may be worthwhile to briefly review them. Let us now look at what NAC termed "key" proposals.

To begin with, John R. Plants, Chairman, Advisory Task Force on Information Systems and Statistics, writes as a forward to NAC's *Criminal Justice System:*

> The accent in this volume is on management and budget planning, systems analysis, information systems, evaluation, training of personnel, and criminal code revision.
>
> Planning for resource allocation is one of the most important functions that a criminal justice agency performs. Proper planning, which makes maximum use of available information, can enable a police department to reduce crime in its jurisdiction without adding manpower, a court to unclog its calendars without employing additional judges, and a corrections agency to improve its rehabilitative efforts without expanding its facilities.
>
> The nature of available criminal justice data is another crucial factor. So much of it is incomplete or fragmented among unrelated, uncoordinated, and duplicative systems that many agencies that would like to use an information bank in planning, budgeting, and evaluation, for example, have no viable access to one.[14]

In regard to the CJS, NAC proffered expansive reforms and refinements in the CJS at the state and local levels of government. Among the many, those considered as highly important are:

- Development by states of integrated multiyear criminal justice planning.
- Establishment of criminal justice coordinating councils by all major cities and counties.
- Establishment by each state of a Security and Privacy Council to develop procedures and recommendations for legislation to assure security and privacy of information contained in criminal justice information systems.
- Creation by each state of an organizational structure for coordinating the development of criminal justice information systems.

Jack Michie, Chairman, Task Force on Community Crime Prevention, related in the foreword to NAC's report on *Community Crime Prevention:*

> "We, the People . . ." has always been a cornerstone of American democracy. But technology, urban stress, and the pace of change in America have produced a society in which it is difficult for "the People" to exercise their responsibility to participate. As society places more responsibility on its institutions, it places less on itself. Much of the alienation in America may result from the lack of power citizens feel in relation to the institutions they have set up to run their lives.
>
> One area where citizen participation is critical is law enforcement. Rather than relying solely on their institutions, citizens must

share the responsibility. This volume promotes a system of mutual responsibility between citizens and the criminal justice system.

This Commission is the first to focus on the community as a partner in the crime reduction effort. Other commissions have studied various elements of community participation, but never before has a blueprint been drawn up that sets out citizen responsibilities in all areas of social life that can contribute to crime reduction.[15]

Concerning the community, NAC proposed that you and I make a personal contribution to the reduction of crime, and further that we assist in establishing or bettering the crime prevention program of our state and local governments. Prime recommendations are:

- Increased citizen contribution to crime prevention by making homes and businesses more secure by participating in police-community programs, and by working with youth.
- Expanded public and private employment opportunities and elimination of unnecessary restrictions on hiring ex-offenders.
- Establishment of and citizen support for youth services bureaus to improve the delivery of social services to young people.
- Provision of individualized treatment for drug offenders and abusers.
- Provision of statewide capability for overseeing and investigating financing of political campaigns.
- Establishment of a statewide investigation and prosecution capability to deal with corruption in government.

E. M. Davis, Chairman, Task Force on Police, asserts in the foreword to NAC's report on the police:

> The *Report on Police* is intended as a practical document. It provides standards designed for the police administrators, other criminal justice practitioners, political figures, and interested readers seeking a clear insight into the "real" world of the American police service.
>
> A strong emphasis persists throughout the *Report on Police*, brought about at the request of the Task Force itself, to identify programs that have a proven record of effectiveness and to draw upon those programs in developing standards. It is strongly felt that this report represents the most up-to-date and proven experience in the police field available today.
>
> To some extent the report stresses procedural areas and goes into some detail covering the area of investigations and arrests. Time and limitations imposed to avoid duplication of other Commission reports dictated that some subjects be given less emphasis. The desire to prepare a comprehensive document for the working administrator dictated that emphasis. It is hoped that the police service administrator can find in these pages, presented in one

place, reasonable and practical answers to questions he must face every day.[16]

Relative to the police, NAC emphasized that the delivery system for outputting police services be significantly enhanced at the city and county levels of government. Principal recommendations are:

- Consolidation of all police departments with fewer than ten sworn officers.
- Enhancement of the role of the patrolman.
- Increased crime prevention efforts by police working in and with the community.
- Affirmative police action to divert public drunks and mental patients from the criminal justice system.
- Increased employment and utilization of women, minorities, and civilians in police work.
- Enactment of legislation authorizing police to obtain search warrants by telephone.

In NAC's report on courts, Daniel J. Meador, Chairman, Task Force on Courts, writes in the foreword that:

> To some extent, the scope with which various areas are covered represents a judgment as to their relative importance. The report, for example, does address in some detail the procedures for the formal litigation of a criminal prosecution. But, in recognition of the fact that only a small percentage of criminal cases are formally litigated, the report devotes substantially greater space to the informal processes that determine most criminal prosecutions: screening, diversion, and plea negotiation. Some limits in the coverage of this report were imposed to avoid duplication of other reports. The Commission's *Report on Corrections,* for example, deals extensively with sentencing, so this report's coverage of that subject is correspondingly limited. Other limits are simply a concession to time and the need to address only the most important aspects of a problem.
> In its evaluation of alternatives to current practice, The Commission has not considered itself bound by existing law. It has felt free to recommend changes in the law, even if the law be of constitutional dimension, if that seemed desirable to achieve a more just and effective judicial process. However, it has endeavored to understand the rationale of existing legal requirements and to recommend changing them only when it has been convinced that these rationales are inadequate. As a result, there is wide variation in the extent to which implementing the standards in this report will require modification of the formal law.[17]

Pertaining to the courts, NAC advocated profound reorganizing and expediting of legal and administrative processes in the adjudication of criminal cases at the state and local levels. The recommendations in this instance, therefore, center on accelerating the procedures and practices for the ultimate determination of innocence or guilt. Paramount proposals are:

- Trying all cases within 60 days of arrest.
- Requiring judges to hold full days in court.
- Unification within the state of all courts.
- Allowing only one review on appeal.
- Elimination of plea bargaining.
- Screening of all criminal cases coming to the attention of the prosecutor to determine if further processing is appropriate.
- Diverting out of the system all cases in which further processing by the prosecutor is not appropriate, based on such factors as the age of the individual, his psychological needs, the nature of the crime, and the availability of treatment programs.
- Elimination of grand juries and arraignments.

The chairman of the Task Force on Corrections, Joe Frazier Brown, stated in the foreword to NAC's report on corrections:

> Recently, however, increased attention has been given to the systems aspect of criminal justice, recognizing that what happens in one part of the system affects all the other parts.
> Police, for example, are coming to agree with correctional authorities that as many young people as possible, consistent with protection of the public, should be diverted to education, employment, counseling, or other services which will meet their needs and thus help them avoid the stigma of a criminal record. Police departments in several areas have set up their own diversion programs.
> Courts have made an indelible imprint on corrections through recent decisions on violations of the civil rights of offenders. Whole State prison systems have been declared unconstitutional as violating the eighth amendment's ban on cruel and unusual punishment.
> In the light of these developments, this report goes farther than any previous study in examining the interrelationships between corrections and the other elements of the criminal justice system. The report includes, for example, discussions of jails, which are traditionally a part of law enforcement rather than corrections; of the effects of sentencing on convicted offenders; of the need for judges to have continuing jurisdiction over offenders they have sentenced; and many other subjects that previously might not have been considered within the realm of corrections.[18]

On the subject of corrections, NAC expressed that fundamental modifications in the correctional system were required at the state, county, and city levels of government! Of major consequence are:

- Restricting construction of major state institutions for adult offenders.
- Phasing out of all major juvenile offender institutions.
- Elimination of disparate sentencing practices.
- Establishment of community-based correctional programs and facilities.
- Unification of all correctional functions within the state.
- Increased and expanded salary, education, and training levels for corrections personnel.[19]

NAC additionally proposed a reexamination of all state criminal codes in terms of their relevancy and an elimination of the dangers presented by a plethora of handguns in our society. Specifically, the recommended courses of action are:

- Establishment of permanent criminal code revision commissions at the state level.
- Decriminalization of vagrancy and drunkenness.
- Elimination of importation, manufacture, sale, and private possession of handguns by January 1, 1983.[20]

At this time I feel confident of three things. One—that most of the criminal justice executives have heard, however vaguely, about the scope and purpose of NAC. Regretfully, I do not possess the same sense of confidence in their understanding of the NAC findings. Two—I am reasonably certain that some of the executives have studied parts if not all of the NAC reports. Three—I believe that very few of the criminal justice executives can arbitrarily dismiss them as being mundane when one views recommendations that seek to impact the substantive issues of:

- Privacy and security of data contained in criminal justice information systems.
- Statewide investigation and prosecution designed to erase corruption in government.
- Consolidation of all police agencies with less than ten sworn officers.
- Abolishing plea bargaining.
- Phasing out all major juvenile offender institutions.
- Elimination of the importing, manufacturing, selling and private possession of handguns.

Let us for a few moments back away from NAC so that we might expand our focus to that of a comparative framework whereby the

ABA's standards are addressed as they either concur or differ with NAC's.

NAC—VS. OR VIS-À-VIS—ABA

It would seem, and reasonably so, ludicrous to commission two similar studies during an almost identical period of time. The intent and volume of the NAC and ABA products are certainly more congruent than not. While I have not weighed (nor do I intend to weigh) the sets of reports, it is my surmise that they would be very close in content. On the surface, one can easily detect two significant physical differences between the two standards. (1) NAC's was released in 1973 while ABA's predated it one to two years and (2) NAC's standards are compressed into six large volumes, while the ABA's are contained in separate compact reports.

To reiterate, I would adjudge the two sets of reports to be more alike than not. Hence, I am saying that there are more parallels than incongruities between NAC and ABA findings and standards. The remainder of this section presents NAC and ABA standards in a very limited yet comparative mode.

First, let us examine the police. A preceding page contained a NAC Standard entitled "Foundation for Internal Discipline." The ABA, in turn, generated a related standard, to wit:

5.4   NEED FOR ADMINISTRATIVE SANCTIONS AND PROCEDURES

In order to strengthen administrative review and control, responsibility should formally be delegated to the police for developing comprehensive administrative policies and rules governing the duties and responsibilities of police officers together with procedures and sanctions for ensuring that these duties and responsibilities are met. Police administrative rules and procedures should establish effective investigative, hearing, and internal review procedures for alleged violations. Such procedures should include provisions for handling, monitoring, and reviewing citizen complaints in such a way as to ensure diligence, fairness, and public confidence. In developing such rules and procedures, recognition must be given to the need to conform procedures to administrative due process requirements, to develop means for ensuring impartial investigations, and to keep the public informed of all administrative actions as they are taken.[21]

Additionally, both NAC and ABA focused on the *role* of the police which resulted in:

ABA

7.2 IMPORTANT FUNCTION
OF PATROLMEN

The nature of police operations makes the patrolman a more important figure than is implied by his rank in the organization. He exercises broad discretion in a wide array of situations, each of which is potentially of great importance, under conditions that allow for little supervision and review. Even with the controls recommended in these standards, in the interest of developing a police profession as well as in the interest of improving the quality of police operations generally, the patrolman himself should understand the important and complex needs of policing in a free society and have a commitment to meeting those needs.[22]

NAC

ENHANCING THE ROLE
OF THE PATROL OFFICER

Every local government and police chief executive, recognizing that the patrol function is the most important element of the police agency, immediately should adopt policies that attract and retain highly qualified personnel in the patrol force.

1. Every local government should expand its classification and pay system to provide greater advancement opportunities within the patrol ranks. The system should provide:
    a. Multiple pay grades within the basic rank.
    b. Opportunity for advancement within the basic rank to permit equality between patrol officers and investigators.
    c. Parity in top salary step between patrol officers and non- supervisory officers assigned to similar operational functions.

2. Proficiency pay for personnel who have demonstrated expertise in specific field activities that contribute to more efficient police service. Every police chief executive should seek continuously to enhance the role of the patrol officer in providing status and recognition from the agency and in encouraging similar status and recognition from the community. The police chief should:
    a. Provide distinctive insignia indicating demonstrated expertise in specific field activities.
    b. Insure that all elements within the agency provide maximum assistance and cooperation to the patrol officer.
    c. Implement a community information program emphasizing the importance of the patrol officer in the life of the community and encouraging community cooperation in providing police service.
    d. Provide comprehensive initial and in-service training thoroughly to equip the patrol officer for his role.

e. Insure that field supervisory personnel possess the knowledge and skills necessary to guide the patrol officer.
f. Implement procedures to provide agencywide recognition of patrol officers who have consistently performed in an efficient and commendable manner.
g. Encourage suggestions on changes in policies, procedures, and other matters that affect the delivery of police services and reduction of crime.
h. Provide deployment flexibility to facilitate various approaches to individual community crime problems.
i. Adopt policies and procedures that allow the patrol officer to conduct the complete investigation of crimes which do not require extensive follow-up investigation, and allow them to close the investigation of those crimes.
j. Insure that promotional oral examination boards recognize that patrol work provides valuable experience for men seeking promotion to supervisory positions.[23]

Continuing, let us look at the courts. To illustrate, concerning plea bargaining:

ABA

4.1 AVAILABILITY FOR PLEA DISCUSSIONS

(a) The prosecutor should make known a general policy of willingness to consult with defense counsel concerning disposition of charges by plea.
(b) It is unprofessional conduct for a prosecutor to engage in plea discussions directly with an accused who is represented by counsel, except with counsel's approval. If the accused refuses to be represented by counsel, the prosecutor may properly discuss disposition of the charges directly with the accused; the prosecutor would be well advised, however, to request that a lawyer be designated by the court or some appropriate central agency, such as a legal aid or defender office or bar association, to be present at such discussions.
(c) It is unprofessional conduct for a prosecutor knowingly to make false statements or representations in the course of plea discussions with defense counsel or the accused.

4.2 PLEA DISPOSITION WHEN ACCUSED MAINTAINS INNOCENCE

A prosecutor may not properly participate in a disposition by plea of guilty if he is aware that the accused persists in denying guilt or the factual basis for the plea, without disclosure to the court.[24]

NAC

Standard 3.1

ABOLITION OF PLEA NEGOTIATION

As soon as possible, but in no event later than 1978, negotiations between prosecutors and defendants—either personally or through their attorneys—concerning concessions to be made in return for guilty pleas should be prohibited. In the event that the prosecution makes a recommendation as to sentence, it should not be affected by the willingness of the defendant to plead guilty to some or all of the offenses with which he is charged. A plea of guilty should not be considered by the court in determining the sentence to be imposed.

Until plea negotiations are eliminated as recommended in this standard, such negotiations and the entry of pleas pursuant to the resulting agreements should be permitted only under a procedure embodying the safeguards contained in the remaining standards in this chapter.[25]

Finally, in regard to corrections we find:

ABA

6.5 QUALIFICATIONS FOR PROBATION OFFICERS; OTHER PERSONNEL

(a) The educational and occupational requirements for probation officers should be possession of a bachelor's degree supplemented by:
>   (i) a year of graduate study in social work, corrections, counseling, law, criminology, psychology, sociology, or related fields; or
>   (ii) a year of full-time casework, counseling, community or group work experience in a recognized social, community, correctional or juvenile agency dealing with offenders or disadvantaged persons, or its equivalent as determined by the hiring agency.

(b) A significant number of probation officers in a department should have graduate degrees in one of the subjects enumerated in this section.

(c) While the core of any probation department should be professionally educated and trained personnel, it is desirable that the staff include individuals who may lack such professional qualifications but have backgrounds similar to those of the probationers themselves. In addition, in appropriate cases citizen volunteers should be used to assist probation officers.[26]

NAC

Standard 10.4

PROBATION MANPOWER

Each State immediately should develop a comprehensive manpower development and training program to recruit, screen, utilize, train, educate, and evaluate a full range of probation personnel, including volunteers, women, and ex-offenders. The program should range from entry level to top level positions and include the following:

1. Provision should be made for effective utilization of a range of manpower on a full- or part-time basis by using a systems approach to identify service objectives and by specifying job tasks and range of personnel necessary to meet the objectives. Jobs should be reexamined periodically to insure that organizational objectives are being met.

2. In addition to probation officers, there should be new career lines in probation, all built into career ladders.

3. Advancement (salary and status) should be along two tracks: service delivery and administration.

4. Educational qualification for probation officers should be graduation from an accredited 4-year college.[27]

From a brief reading of the above standards, one may draw a variety of conclusions. NAC and ABA are more similar than not. On the other hand, however, they are not identical. In terms of their congruencies both sets of reports: (1) carry the weight of prestigious committee/commission members and funding agencies (ABA/USA), (2) are comprehensive in scope, and (3) are replete with standards dedicated to improving the CJS. The differences between the two reports are (1) ABA stresses court activities while NAC is somewhat more balanced among the CJS subsystems, (2) ABA is more generalized in its recommended standards, in turn NAC is highly specific, and (3) ABA does not attempt to interrelate their findings as compared to NAC which created a systematic report that sought to integrate and describe a generic formula for changing our CJS. If looked upon as a team rather than as competitors, the ABA and NAC make a strong case for operationalizing standards that would measurably affect the capability of the criminal justice *delivery system*. Rather than debate the merits or lack of same of ABA and NAC, I hope that the strength of each would be identified and soon implemented by the cognizant agencies.

NAC: An Evaluative Commentary

It is assumed by now you have accurately predicted that my assessment of the NAC reports is quite positive. In essence, to a major
degree the NAC fulfilled its mission. More specifically, if polar and
opposing concepts were placed at the opposite ends of a five point
continuum (see Figure 4–1), I would ask this question: "Are the
NAC reports . . .?"

Hence, out of a hypothetical total of fifty possible points, I have
rated NAC as having compiled forty-two points or a percentile of
eighty-four. Setting aside fictitious points and percentages, I have
evaluated the NAC products as they would most likely impact the
CJS/C and found that they were organizationally functional, specific
in content, challenging to the CJS agencies and citizenry alike, in the
public interest, comprehensive in scope, and highly pragmatic in
terms of eventual application.

There are two other favorable comments to be made before

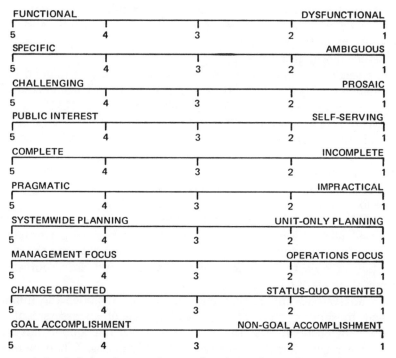

FIGURE 4–1 A five-point continuum showing polar and opposing concepts
of the NAC Reports.

potential problems and pitfalls are discussed. The first relates to the "public interest" question. Chapters and numerous standards in the NAC reports are devoted to citizen involvement in the delivery of CJS services.[28] Such concepts and terms are patent: citizen action, public right-to-know, neighborhood governments, government responsiveness, citizen representatives, community-based treatment, court-community relations, and developing community resources.

Enlisting the American conscience and active support on behalf of community crime prevention is at once an ironic and necessary procedure. It is ironic because of the hue and cry about the current volume of crime. It is widely assumed that the government and its agencies alone must respond to this demand and marshal all available resources to choke off crime at its roots.

This viewpoint neglects the certainty that unless a worried citizenry can translate its indignation into active participation in the search for and implementation of a solution, governments and their criminal justice systems inevitably must fall even further behind in their crime-control and rehabilitation efforts. Awakening the conscience of America is a necessity; if the multiplicity of factors that produce crime and delinquency are not recognized and remedied, more crime will occur, more of it will go undetected, and the inadequacies of the system thus will become even stronger incentive for further illegal activity.[29]

The second comment pertains to a construct that exploded into prominence during the late fifties and is currently of prime concern to the CJS/C—*evaluation*. Fortunately for us, the NAC reports underscored its essentiality.[30]

Evaluation is, or should be, an integral part of the planning and resource allocation process. Evaluation provides feedback on the results of previous planning efforts, prevents planning from occurring in a vacuum, and provides a corrective device to enable modification of previous planning efforts that were unsuccessful.

In the future, planners at all levels will have to become more concerned with the construction and interpretation of performance measures in evaluation efforts. Effective evaluation requires the clear definition of objectives, performance measures, and data sources in the initial stages of new programs.[31]

An analysis of any phenomenon invariably includes the human element to some degree. This particular type of an assessment or critique obviously affords the evaluator a sizeable opportunity to insert either consciously or inadvertently his biases. While in most instances NAC and I are sympatico, I am compelled at this time to point to a glaring deficiency that may not sink but that certainly impedes the NAC ship in its attempt to sail on a nationwide basis. In a single word, missing from NAC is a *management* emphasis. Naturally, there are other pertinent theories or techniques that you and I may cite as being absent. Albeit, none is more conspicuous in its absence than that of the "central mover"—management and the manager.

Any study as encompassing and exhaustive as NAC's would naturally cover, to some extent, the subject of management. Indeed, reference is made to management in two of the reports (Corrections and Courts). NAC's report on corrections devotes Chapter 13 to this subject, and I would add, does a commendable job of doing so. The other reports provide only limited and diffuse discussions of CJS management. Most appropriately, NAC's report *Criminal Justice System* would have been the logical location for its inclusion. Two parts of this report constituting eleven of its thirteen chapters are dedicated to planning and information of which both subjects are integral to the management of any socio-technical system. The criticality of competent management today as never before in large-scale organizations is emphatically voiced by Peter F. Drucker "... the essence of the manager is neither wealth nor rank, but *responsibility*"[32] (emphasis added). Further ...

The management of the non-business institution will indeed be a growing concern from now on. Their management may well become the central management problem, simply because the lack of management of the public-service institution is such a glaring weakness, whether municipal water department or graduate university.[33] And, I believe we should insert after the word university "or criminal justice agency."

The neglect of a management theme in the NAC reports both harbingers and sets a platform from which other barriers may be raised to block the implementation of NAC's recommended standards and goals. The problem can be visualized as management being the axle (crux) of rapidly moving wheels (activities). The spokes in turn serve as supportive braces (interaction with program and support activities). Thus graphically we see a wheel such as that shown in Figure 4-2.

Consequently, we find the circumference of the hypothesized NAC-Management wheel being comprised of two-plies of activities and sub-systems around a management hub. Thus one should be aware to the point of being alarmed that the eventual success of the NAC reports is inextricably linked to criminal justice management, and the reports failed to adequately pay testimony to its importance.

Well, it should seem that I have completed this coverage of NAC by relating that: (1) NAC is a meaningful set of reports, and (2) their contents stand little chance of being operationalized. In regard to the

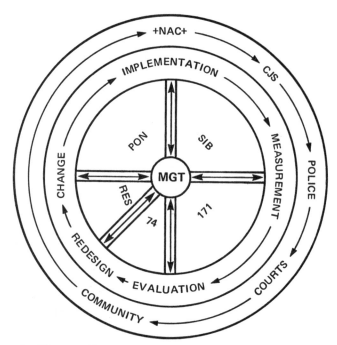

FIGURE 4–2   The NAC-management wheel

latter point, I think not. That is, I believe that NAC has a fighting chance, and a good one, to win its way into the operational bloodstream of the CJS/C.

Candidly, I daily grow more impressed and therefore more optimistic over the capability of criminal justice managers to manage the CJS. At the same time I cannot help, irrespective of all the gloomy reasons for not doing so, but see a spark of interest in our citizenry in backing the CJS in its efforts to reduce crime. As far as I am concerned, NAC fulfilled its goals, now it is up to you and me to support the CJS in achieving theirs. For, NAC could, all or in part, well become the battering ram to level the ramparts of resistance to organizational change and thus change obstacles into opportunities for making the CJS an effective and just system for delivering public services. In conclusion, NAC refined, added, modified—but moved forward little. It has made accessible to criminal justice executives everywhere what, up to now, had been the arcane knowledge of a few. NAC endeavors to place into general practice what, till this decade, had been the rare exception.

NOTES

1. National Advisory Commission on Criminal Justice Standards and Goals, *A National Strategy to Reduce Crime* (Washington, D.C.: U.S. Government Printing Office, 1973), p. ix.
2. *The Challenge of Crime in a Free Society,* A report by the President's Commission on Law Enforcement and Administration of Justice (Washington, D.C.: U.S. Government Printing Office, 1967), p. v.
3. An excellent bibliographical record of the various commissions devoted to an examination of the criminal justice system can be found in the article by Richard Myren, "Decentralization and Citizen Participation in Criminal Justice Systems," *Public Administration Review,* 32 (October 1972), 718–32.
4. The President's Commission (1967) generated, much like NAC, the following reports:

    • *The Challenge of Crime in a Free Society*
    • *Task Force Report: Drunkenness*
    • *Task Force Report: Assessment of Crime*
    • *Task Force Report: Juvenile Delinquency*
    • *Task Force Report: The Police*
    • *Task Force Report: Science and Technology*
    • *Task Force Report: Narcotics and Drug Abuse*
    • *Task Force Report: The Courts*
    • *Task Force Report: Corrections*
    • *Task Force Report: Organized Crime*

5. *The Challenge of Crime in a Free Society,* A Report by the President's Commission on Law Enforcement and Administration of Criminal Justice (Washington, D.C.: U.S. Government Printing Office, 1967), p. vi.
6. Ibid., p. xi.
7. Remarks by Donald E. Santarelli, Administrator, Law Enforcement Assistance Administration, U.S. Department of Justice, August 9, 1973.
8. Ibid., p. 269.
9. National Advisory Commission on Criminal Justice Standards and Goals (NAC), *Police* (Washington, D.C.: U.S. Government Printing Office, 1973), p. 474.
10. NAC, *Community Crime Prevention* (Washington, D.C.: U.S. Government Printing Office, 1973), p. 270.
11. Law Enforcement Assistance Administration, *News Release* (Washington, D.C.: U.S. Department of Justice, August 9, 1973), p. 1.
12. Russell W. Peterson in a Foreword to NAC's *A National Strategy to Reduce Crime* (Washington, D.C.: U.S. Government Printing Office, 1973), p. iii.
13. National Advisory Commission on Criminal Justice Standards and Goals, *A National Strategy To Reduce Crime* (Washington, D.C.: U.S. Government Printing Office, 1973), pp. 4, 5.
14. NAC, *Criminal Justice System* (Washington, D.C.: U.S. Government Printing Office, 1973), p. ii.
15. NAC, *Community Crime Prevention,* p. ii.
16. NAC, *Police,* p. ii.
17. NAC, *Courts* (Washington, D.C.: U.S. Government Printing Office, 1973), p. ii.
18. NAC, *Courts* (Washington, D.C.: U.S. Government Printing Office, 1973), p. ii.
19. NAC, *A National Strategy To Reduce Crime* (Washington, D.C.: U.S. Government Printing Office, 1973), p. xv.
20. Ibid.
21. Special Committee on Standards for Administration of Criminal Justice (ABA), *The Urban Police Function* (New York: American Bar Association, 1973), pp. 10, 11.

22. Ibid., p. 13.
23. NAC, *Police,* pp. 195, 196.
24. ABA, *The Urban Police Function,* pp. 104, 105, 107.
25. NAC, *Courts,* p. 46.
26. ABA, *Probation* (New York: American Bar Association, 1970), pp. 19, 20.
27. NAC, *Corrections* (Washington, D.C.: U.S. Government Printing Office, 1973), p. 337.
28. For examples, see NAC Reports: *Community Crime Prevention,* Chapter 1; *Corrections,* Chapter 7; *Courts,* Chapter 10; and *Police,* Chapter 3.
29. NAC, *Community Crime Prevention,* p. 2.
30. See NAC Reports: *Community Crime Prevention,* Appendix A; *Corrections,* Standards 9.10 and 15.5; *Police,* Recommendation 5.3 and Standard 4.2; and *Criminal Justice System,* Chapter 11 and 12, and Appendix.
31. NAC, *Criminal Justice System,* p. 14.
32. Peter F. Drucker, *Management: Tasks, Responsibilities, Practices,* (New York: Harper and Row, 1973), p. 6.
33. Ibid., p. 8.

TOPICS FOR DISCUSSION

1. Discuss why the word *leadership* is rarely found in the National Advisory Commission Reports.

2. Discuss the evaluation of selected parts of the NAC reports. (Have a student present the evaluation.)

3. Discuss the chances each NAC report has of being implemented.

4. Discuss the similarities between:

Wickersham Commission, 1935

The President's Commission, 1967

National Advisory Commission

5. Discuss the seven objectives suggested to be vigorously pursued if a significant reduction in crime is to be achieved.

6. Discuss the impact that those persons on the staff who wrote the standards and goals had on the results.

7. Discuss the possibility of having students complete a survey of local criminal justice agencies to determine how many have considered implementing selected standards and goals.

2

The Police

Until recently, the police have been the focus of our country's attempt to deal with the crime problem. More funds have been expended for upgrading police than any other component of justice administration. This trend is changing—rightly so—since police alone cannot be held accountable for crime increases. The problem of crime belongs proportionately to everyone in our country. Where have the police been, where are they now, and where are they going? Dr. Reppetto briefly discusses events leading up to police organizations as they exist today, and generates questions such as: Is there a need for specialized family crisis intervention units? How much change would have taken place in police ideology without the social impetus for change? What impact has behavioral science research had on such concepts as team policing? Does the police service need all college-educated personnel? What effect would requiring college educations for entrance have on the police agency's ability to hire minorities?

The police deal with crime control, peacekeeping, and service as their basic missions. The optimum formula for the amount of time spent to perform these missions have not yet been developed. What is known is that police spend more time dealing with noncriminal activity than they do with criminal activity, by a ratio of approximately 80 percent to 20 percent. It is doubtful that the percentages will change drastically in the next twenty years. Americans for the most part will demand the same kinds of police response in the future, and it appears that no other governmental agency is going to volunteer to relieve the police from performing the required tasks to meet citizen demands.

The government officials held most responsible for crime and violence are chief executives of our cities and metropolitan areas; however, these officials have too limited resources available to have a great deal of impact on resolving the problem.

In chapter 6, William J. Bopp sees professionalization of police as attainable, but not existing today. He defines police work as a craft because it lacks standards and legitimate accountability. Yet if we observe the other so-called professions, it is difficult to see any significant observance of professional standards and accountability. What criteria should be used to compare the status of police professionalization? Should the criteria be based upon that which is used by other recognized professions? Should the police develop their own set of criteria? If the police do develop their own set of criteria, what impact will this procedure have on the ability of the public to view police as professionals? One thing is certain, if police want to be identified as professional, they must afford professional status to their own sworn officers. Unnecessary regimentation, severe military organizational structure, restricted independent judgment, defensiveness to constructive criticism, and arbitrary resistance to change are some of the more obvious factors that must be confronted before professionalism can be attained. The atmosphere for a professional police organization must be set by the leaders so that the professional approach will permeate the entire organization. A logical result of this permeation will be that the police officer who works closest to the citizen (who place the mantle of professional on the police) will have the information, guidance, and proper direction to act with excellent independent judgment and adapt to ambiguous situations. This chapter should assist each student to determine his/her own feeling on professionalization.

Today it is rather obvious that police unions are here to stay. This fact has compounded the already difficult task of managing a police organization effectively, especially in the area of manpower deployment, discipline, and policymaking. However, the question does arise, "Have managers of police organizations improved in their ability to manage because of police unions?" The answer in most cases has been that, like it or not, unions have made police managers do their homework and realize that there is more than one type or style of management technique. Sharing power does not mean the loss of power. Where practical, allowing employees to participate in decisions that affect them does not necessarily mean that the manager's authority is being ignored. In some cases police unions have forced management to realize that it is accountable for the efficient and effective operation of the police agency. One department employee organization has gone so far as to publish an evaluation of the chief and draft a resolution of support. Police management must not only force decision-making but accountability to the level of execution. Increased compensation, authority, and responsibility should be accompanied by increased productivity and accountability. To increase productivity means to get a greater return for a given investment. For police work, productivity must be considered in relation to effectiveness. Effectiveness means making the most of the talents of police personnel. Clearly, unions, management, productivity, accountability, efficiency, and effectiveness point out the need for enlightened leadership on the part of both police unions and police management. Is it not true that police unions are here to stay? Since police unions can organize and bargain effectively, they must come to the conclusion, as have police administrators, that to survive they must play ball with each other. Professor Feuille has ably addressed the issues surrounding the police labor movement in this chapter.

What is the optimum design of a police organization? Can this question be answered or is the design of a police organization based on the goals, objectives, sophistication of employees, and all the other environmental influences that work in the individual police departments? I do not view the rigid semi-military structure as the answer; nor do I see as appropriate the move to the extreme of a pure democratic design. Formal structure, division of labor, status equivalent to ranks are characteristic of the traditional police organization and are not conducive to success in the rapidly changing society of the United States. However, the change that should take place, i.e., the move toward a democratic situation should be one of evolution where self-renewal and appropriate evaluation can act as guides indicating where on the continuum the structural design should stop. In chapter 7 Dr. Bopp points out that as a result of an acceptance of collective bargaining and organizational democracy by both labor and management class conflict in the private section has been largely removed. I believe it can work for the police profession, especially if there is a simultaneous use of management by objectives (MBO/R) for results. Class conflict should never be totally removed because it is healthy to have a small amount of conflict to induce honest input to decisionmaking. Couple the small amount of conflict with clearly thought out goals, objectives, and policy, and the result should be a healthy police agency capable of adapting to the demands of America's changing, complex society. The synthesis of the mechanistic and humanistic focus of management can only be one of amalgamation. A good place to start is with written philosophy, goals, objectives and policy.

As pointed out above, the amalgamation of the mechanistic and humanistic focus of management would result in a synthesis emphasized by a management style based on the principle of supportive relationships. Chapter 9 presents an example of a police agency that has reorganized and laid a foundation of goal achievement and support for officers actually performing the tasks necessary for achieving objectives. The development of a new program of this magnitude should always begin with an analysis of the capability of the organization to adapt to change, followed by participation in the planning process of the recipients of change, e.g., the persons who will be affected by the change. The consultant client model of change was used by the Culver City police department and found to be an effective method.

Scholars and practitioners have identified the police function to include law enforcement, order maintenance, and service. The Culver City police department identified the primary role or goal of police in modern society as the maintenance of ordered liberty. To achieve these objectives, the department adopted a fully integrated team policing concept using a colleague model. My view of the Culver City police department's approach to deliver services to the community is one of commendation and optimism. Students should find this chapter interesting because theory is applied. Organizational democracy and the delivery of service to the community are compatible.

This text would not have been complete without "Police Technology and the Challenge of Crime." I emphasize this for two reasons: first, because technology has and will continue to be a tremendous aid for police in their efforts to control crime; and second, because it points out the need for police administrators to be fundamentally sound in the field of scientific inquiry. The police administrator has available a wealth of information and the tools to gather that information; therefore, he must be able to examine, analyze and make judgments about the validity of the information. What will the police administrator do when he finds he cannot read a scientific research report presented to him? Is he competent if he is unable to comprehend and evaluate such reports? For example, what does the Kansas City, Missouri police department report on preventive patrol mean to my agency? He may answer, "I will hire a planning and research person capable of performing the task." Whatever he does, the fact remains "technology, scientific inquiry and the police administrator go together." Hopefully, this chapter will stimulate an awareness of the validity of the previous sentence.

In chapter 11, Dr. Germann identifies two scenarios depicting the relationship between police and citizens. One scenario includes the use or misuse of technology and police-public alienation. The second scenario involves the development of humane policy. It has been my experience that the second scenario has been developing for several years. I can remember very vividly explaining the difference between offensive and defensive weapons to hundreds of police officers preparing to enter sensitive situations such as prison riots, demonstrations, school disorders and welfare strikes. Offensive weapons were identified as chemical agents and people while all other weapons were described as defensive. There are many other examples of individual acts that were very humane and people-oriented that space does not allow me to list. Dr. Germann seems to be stereotyping police leadership. Is this stereotype deserved? Has police leadership broadened their view about organization, career development, and management techniques? Do bright, energetic, young officers become frustrated with today's police leadership and leave the organization prematurely? Have police attitudes and behavior changed since 1967? What has been the reader's experience regarding the college or university programs and open arenas for debate vs. disguised police academies? Does policing have to meet the criteria set forth by Dr. Germann before it can be said that there is a delicate balance between police power and citizens' rights? It is hoped that the student of justice administration will address the issues of the chapter and the questions mentioned above to determine where the police are in our society. The chapter is provocative, therefore, each student is encouraged to think objectively about the issues and draw his individual conclusions. Are we beginning the era of the safety welfare generalist/social scientist in the administration of justice?

The preceding chapter hopefully has generated in-depth thought and discussion about the status of police leadership and the performance of police officers with regard to the fine line between liberty and security. In chapter 12, Professor Cromwell presents the issue of police community relations, some of the problems facing laymen and business in improving the relationship, and a conclusion that I support wholeheartedly.

To effectively deal with the police community relations issue, we must deal with many other facets of the police and the conditions that exist when they relate to the community. Not the least of these facets is the role or the expected role an officer is to play. At one moment he must have the cunning and strength of the lion and the next moment he must have the gentleness of the proverbial lamb. Some people look upon the officer as a fascist oppressor while others see him as a Messiah. The officer has to play the role of priest, sociologist, lawyer, arbitrator, philosopher, and politician, all within a society that wants a policeman who cannot be bribed but a society that, at the same time, wants to bribe policemen. Does John Q. Public really want police? The rebellion against authority says no, but surveys have shown that most citizens feel they need and support the efforts of police.

There are those who suggest that police should make the improvement of police service their number one priority and automatically relations with the public will improve. But, what is meant by improvement of police service, increased arrests? reduced response time? courtesy? clearance rates? Is this what the community wants and needs? How do you identify the needs of the community? What are the objectives of police? Will the achievement of these objectives assist in a more effective administration of criminal justice? Within the objective of the police agency, has the problem of cultural shock been addressed when assignment of personnel is considered? What effect does assignment of personnel have on police community relations? What does a police officer say to a citizen when he is asked questions about the action taken or not taken with regard to a given situation? Most often an officer does not have time to answer the questions of bystanders. I submit that the officer must understand his role and the community must be informed about the police role.

5

THOMAS A. REPPETTO

New horizons
in police administration

INTRODUCTION

For the past decade American police administration has been in a state of dynamic change. While the origins of the change can be traced, the outcome remains uncertain—although available evidence does suggest some new horizons.

This chapter traces the roots of modern police administration; examines current trends and their relation to past, as well as present, social conditions; and attempts to forecast, from these trends, the forces that will shape future police departments. Throughout, the analysis will largely focus on the dominant element of American police service—the municipal level, particularly in the cities.[1]

HISTORICAL BACKGROUND

At least twice before in American history police administration has undergone upheaval similar in extent to that experienced today. In the early 19th century, public safety was provided by haphazard systems of private initiative, day police, night watchmen, sheriffs and constables; but with the growth of modern, industrial cities, such fragmented protection proved inadequate. Starting in the 1840s, the major Eastern cities began adopting a model of policing that had been established in London in 1829 under the auspices of Sir Robert Peel. The London model essentially replaced the public/private patchwork force with a uniformed semi-military body of regular municipal employees who assumed responsibility for both patrol and investigative functions, acquired the right to bear arms, and exercised fairly broad powers of arrest, search, and seizure.[2]

By the 1870s, the municipal police had assumed modern form, and patterns of policing differed little from the present. The bulk of the force was assigned to uniformed patrol. Officers then as now reported to duty at their precinct stations, stood roll call and went on patrol in specific geographical subdivisions of the precinct, under the supervision of an infrequently encountered sergeant. The familiar divisions between headquarters and precinct, patrol and detective, and supervisor and subordinate (the latter characterized by military ranks) are still apparent. In many cities, the only real changes have been technological: cars, radios, and computers have replaced the horse and buggy, telegraphs, and bound ledgers. However, the same changes have occurred in other aspects of life and work and are not peculiar to the police.

Because, however, the American police departments, unlike the London one, remained under the control of local government, they reflected the conditions prevalent around the turn of the century, the height of the machine politics era: i.e., intense political involvement, massive corruption, and very low levels of efficiency. Thus, a second era of major change in the police—occurring from the close of the 19th century to the early 1930s—can be linked with the reform movement of the Progressive Era. The appointment of Theodore Roosevelt to the presidency of the New York City Board of Police Commissioners in 1895 inaugurated this period, which was characterized by the widespread adoption of civil service, the introduction of scientific detective methods, the rise of the state police, and an unprecedented interest in the police by the professional and intellectual elite.[3]

With the creation of the FBI in 1933, and the passing of prohibition and the gangster era, reform was for the most part ended and police work settled into routine. Most of the lasting gains of the Progressive Movement occurred at federal and state levels, while municipal police departments remained largely in the traditional 19th century mold (although de jure reforms such as civil service did become institutionalized). Perhaps the most important development in municipal policing was the rise to primacy of the detectives, who, in the 19th century, had been a small and somewhat unwanted appendage to the patrol force.[4] By the 1920s the detective "bureau" dominated most police departments.

In the 1960s, police administration became a focus of interest once again, largely through police involvement with such social problems as the civil rights movement, urban crime and disorder, and youth protests. As the decade of the sixties began, American police service could be dichotomized into the traditional force, still plagued by politics, scandal, and poor performance, and the so-called professional or legalistic one where nonpartisanship, integrity, and technical efficiency were manifest.[5] The former and by far the most numerous group represented policing as it had developed in the 19th century. The professional style, advocated by Vollmer, O. W. Wilson, and W. H. Parker, derived from the reform era and exemplified classic bureaucracy of the managerial efficiency type.[6] The professional department was usually highly centralized, with all decisions (including relatively minor ones) made by the chief of police, who exercised his authority through a steep hierarchical chain of command. Both its dealings with the outside world and with its own employees were characterized by a military formality.[7]

Both the traditional and bureaucratic models were challenged by the events of the sixties. At present, new or seemingly new ideas abound; we are again in the midst of an era of change in the police service, and again it seems that the future changes will be shaped by the trends now under way.

CURRENT TRENDS

External

The social unrest of the 1960s particularly challenged the "professional" police view of the city as a single entity, without significant diversity of constituent neighborhoods and groups. Among professional departments, district stations were frequently closed or station boundaries and personnel periodically shifted in accordance with abstract managerial formulas, which diminished police/community ties. Reliance on motor patrol (as opposed to foot) also contributed to a loss of contact between police and local citizens. Finally, the emphasis of these departments on suppression of crime via aggressive patrol, stop and frisk, etc., at the expense of attention to less sensational but more voluminous order maintenance activities, tended to downplay the police role as a community service and highlight their role as an enforcement arm.

However, the social problems of the sixties—particularly those of minority populations—compelled the police once again to recognize diversity—both geographic and ethnic. Consequently, "community relations" and "social sensitivity" have become watchwords in policing. This has led to important organizational and functional reallocations with police departments. Since the bulk of routine contacts between officer and citizen are carried on at the uniformed patrol level, a new emphasis on patrol has emerged. Concurrently, it was the patrol division which was in the forefront of civil disorder. Thus, organizational primacy within police departments has clearly shifted away from detectives to patrol. This has been accelerated by the findings by some analytic studies which suggest that the bulk of criminal apprehensions are a result of patrol efforts, thus leading to a downgrading of the detective force.[8] While detectives decline in importance, new tasks such as the resolution of domestic quarrels receive increased attention and resources, as exemplified by the emergence of family crisis intervention units (FCIUs) in police departments.[9]

It is interesting that, while the impetus for change arose from current social conditions, the changes themselves constitute a return to traditional arrangements. An outstanding example is the neighborhood police team.[10] In essence, this involves the permanent assignment of a group of officers to a small geographic area where they are given considerable autonomy to deal with local problems. Thus, geographic stability and administrative flexibility facilitate territorial knowledge and integration. While the title is new, the concept describes the norm of traditional policing characterized by small precinct stations in which men spent long periods. Such commands were usually coterminous geographically with a political ward or district, which itself often encompassed an ethnic community and where—much to the despair of reformers—there was considerable interaction between police and community, ranging from the beat cop and the local pushcart peddler to the captain and the ward boss, both of whom ruled as feudal barons.

Internal

Within the police organization, the unrest of the sixties has reflected itself in a variety of—often quite contradictory—ways. In traditional police departments the rank and file could normally check the power of management through slackness and informality, without recourse to organized appeal. Also, a patrolman apprehended in a minor dereliction could expect leniency from his sergeant, since the sergeant was simply a patrolman with stripes.

However, with the growth of bureaucratic efficiency and the decay of machine politics, the necessity of more substantial protection was felt by the rank and file, and police unions developed. Since unionism coincided with the ideological quarrels of the sixties, management-labor struggles were fought out for public support in terms of "law and order" policy issues. Policy discussions coincided with contract negotiations in a most confusing way, so that, for example, the fourth

platoon issue in New York City[11] could—depending on one's perspective—be seen in terms of the equity of additional compulsory
night duty, managerial prerogative in work scheduling, or in the
protection of the public. So too the important issue of corruption was
caught up in labor-management disputes. The public demand for
governmental integrity, backed up by federal laws and investigative
manpower, led to the uncovering of major scandals in a number of
police departments, which then occasioned the institution of strong
"integrity controls," which in turn caused employee organizations to
object to the stringent practices of internal affairs units.

The past decade has also witnessed a demand for the entrance
into police service of college-educated, socially sensitive professionals.[12]
The certified expertise of the professional encourages a kind of functional autonomy, which, if carried to the beat level, would negate
the bureaucratic emphasis on hierarchy and centralization. Professionalism fits well with the self-actualizing service career sought by
many college graduates, but most police unions have resisted the
administrative arrangements that could attract large number of
college persons. For example, most employee groups oppose educational requirements for promotion, or extra pay based on college
attainment. Superior officer associations do not favor lateral entrance
at command level or the abolition of rank structures and military
titles. Thus, professionalism threatens both managerial and employee-centered bureaucracy.

Further, as the city populations change, the police, entrenched as
they are behind civil service regulations, become less representative
of the population. Attempts to alter civil service procedures, for
example, to permit the entrance of more minority persons, have met
with opposition from unions and others. But raising standards to the
college level, also resisted by unions and others, would make it even
more difficult to recruit minorities.

Thus, one school of thought argues for the traditional practice of
the admission to police service of local residents of minimum qualifications; another favors continuation of the status quo (managerial or
employee-centered bureaucracy) via retention of civil service practices; and a third suggests raising standards to the college level and
reshaping working procedures to fit professionalism.

Crime Control

Other trends in police service are a direct continuation of manage-
ment-centered bureaucracy and the emphasis on crime control. These
include improved command and control, computer-based resource
allocation, and development of staff specialities, especially in planning.

Also included among these are anti-crime techniques, such as crime specific operations,[13] anti-crime units,[14] security inspections,[15] and helicopter patrols. By and large these efforts present no conceptual problems for management, rank and file, or the community.[16] Thus, it is not surprising that most federal dollars are spent for such endeavors, not because the police choose solely to emphasize "hardware," but because it is the least controversial course to follow.

While major efforts have gone into improving police effectiveness against crime, recent studies have questioned police capabilities in this area. A Police Foundation study in Kansas City, Missouri, for example, reportedly found that the level of police patrol had no impact on the crime rate in the experimental areas.[17] Reiss, in a four-city survey, came to similar conclusions about the ineffectiveness of police patrol in preventing crime or apprehending offenders.[18] Indeed, a presidential task force calculated the probabilities of a patrolling police officer interdicting a robbery in progress at once in 14 years.[19] Regarding arrest and clearance rates, a Rand study of index crime arrests in New York City concluded that arrests for property crimes were largely random events, uninfluenced by the quality or quantity of police efforts, and that arrests for crimes against the person (murder, rape, and assault) were primarily attributable to information supplied to the police by victims, rather than to any special police techniques.[20]

Crime control is to the public the chief rationale for the existence and support of a police department. Should scholarly studies translate into common opinion, the entire perception of the nature of policing could be altered.

THE FUTURE

The foregoing discussion has identified few developments that could be termed new. The current environment of social unrest in American life is certainly not new. Crime and disorder have been high in other generations.[21] The administrative responses to contemporary demands appear largely characterized by a return to older forms. The internal bureaucratic struggles between management and labor are also traditional, although fought out in the new mode of police unionism and against the background of contemporary social issues. The application of modern management techniques to policing parellels developments in other occupations, while its anti-crime utility is as yet unproven. Even the intense governmental and scholarly interest in the police service have been known before.

However, three present day phenomena do appear unique and

may offer guides to the future. The first is the changing nature of urban life. American police administration has been dominated by central city police departments, yet the central cities are in decline. In many metropolitan areas, more people live in the suburbs than in the city, and crime and other problems are tending to follow the movement of population.[22] As yet, no organization has arisen to police the new centers of population comparable to the police departments that developed in the growing cities of the 19th century. Instead, there is an amalgam of small local departments, state, county, or metropolitan jurisdictions.

Within the cities, the increase in low income minority populations and the spiraling crime rates do not bode well for urban safety. One presidential commission provided a gloomy forecast for the future:[23]

> ... In a few more years, lacking effective public action, this is how these cities will likely look:
>
> • Central business districts in the heart of the city, surrounded by mixed areas of accelerating deterioration, will be partially protected by large numbers of people shopping or working in commercial buildings during daytime hours, plus a substantial police presence, and will be largely deserted except for police patrols during nighttime hours.
>
> • Highrise apartment buildings and residential compounds protected by private guards and security devices will be fortified cells for upper-middle and high-income populations living at prime locations in the city.
>
> • Lacking a sharp change in federal and state policies, ownership of guns will be almost universal in the suburbs, homes will be fortified by an array of devices from window grills to electronic surveillance equipment, armed citizen volunteers in cars will supplement inadequate police patrols in neighborhoods closer to the central city, and extreme left-wing and right-wing groups will have tremendous armories of weapons which could be brought into play with or without any provocation.
>
> • High-speed, patrolled expressways will be sanitized corridors connecting safe areas, and private automobiles, taxicabs, and commercial vehicles will be routinely equipped with unbreakable glass, light armor, and other security features. Inside garages or valet parking will be available at safe buildings in or near the central city. Armed guards will "ride shotgun" on all forms of public transportation.
>
> • Streets and residential neighborhoods in the central city will be unsafe in differing degrees, and the ghetto slum neighborhoods will be places of terror with widespread crime, perhaps entirely out of police control during nighttime hours. Armed guards will protect all public facilities such as schools, libraries and playgrounds in these areas.

The challenge to the police is to develop an organizational form which fits the current urban environment and to become more effective against crime while maintaining good community relations and adhering to constitutional limitations. Possible means for achieving this will be discussed below.

A second major development is the accent on true professionalism which appears to be struggling to the surface in many police departments. Young workers, particularly from college backgrounds, are not amenable to the older patterns of authority, whether on the assembly line, in the military, or on the campus. One suspects that if police service attracts large numbers of college-educated youths, they will not accommodate themselves to managerial bureaucracy, municipal politics, or unionism in any of their classic molds. Rather, they will demand forms of participatory management and tasks that permit self-actualization.

How realistic is it to expect the police service to be composed of college persons when traditionally it has not attracted this group? From the supply side, it seems very likely. The colleges are already producing more graduates than can be accommodated in the occupations traditionally open to them and consequently, other occupations are being "upgraded" to absorb the excess. Policing seems an ideal candidate for such "upgrading," since the work is challenging, both technically and behaviorally, and extremely important to the society as a whole. Also, numerous academic criminal justice programs not only prepare individuals for criminal justice careers but, more importantly, provide easy access to college education for current practitioners. Whether the supply of the college educated will be matched by demand is another question, but some such demand appears a likely byproduct of the third phenomenon: the increase of federal participation in local police affairs.

In the 19th century, Americans missed the essence of the Peelian reform. While they adopted the organizational forms of the London police, they did not place ultimate responsibility for policing on the national government, as Peel had done. Despite various experiments with state control, American police service remained highly localized and thus controlled by the level of government weakest in terms of resources and strongest in terms of overt partisan politics. With the passage of the Omnibus Crime Control Act of 1968 and its subsequent revisions, has come an infusion of federal money into local police departments, and with the money, in familiar sequence, the creation of federal standards. While this may not prove an unmixed blessing, it will ultimately establish a federal minimum standard below which no local police department can operate. For the first time then, there is a potential—unrealized by past efforts—for national impact on police operations at the beat level. Even now, the main federal dispenser of police funds—the Law Enforcement Assistance

Administration (LEAA)—has placed pressure on the standards of local departments.[24]

Other federal agencies, enforcing legislation less directly related to police administration, will also increasingly influence police operations through their involvement in civil rights, administrative procedures, and other federally supervised activities. This federal presence suggests that no matter what the political situation in certain cities, gross inefficiency and corruption will not be tolerated.

Based on the foregoing, it seems likely that future police service will be rooted in the availability of quality personnel and the creation of nationally mandated standards. The precise organizational form in metropolitan areas is still conjectural. If the present city-suburban divisions are maintained, policing may continue to follow these boundaries—although federal and state funding may seek to force economies of scale. For those areas in which the strength of local government proves resistant to mergers, the most likely arrangement is some form of task division by level so that beat patrol would be carried on by local communities and support tasks such as records, communication, investigation, etc., would be vested in a metropolitan police department.

Also, future police operations may be shaped by the growing realization that the police alone can do little about crime and that their effectiveness varies considerably against specific offenses. This realization may entail greater involvement with the total community. The most common form of involvement heretofore has been in the area of mobilizing citizens to take responsibility for the surveillance of their surroundings and to call police when suspicious activities are observed. Going beyond this, police are seeking, with other social agencies, to divert delinquents, drug addicts, and other offenders from the criminal justice system. They are also beginning to interact with the urban planning community to influence the built environment and land use patterns.

Thus, crime control is coming to involve more than simple patrol and detective work on a case by case basis. Instead, it is seen as an effort to view crime in systemic terms and to mobilize the total physical, social, and economic resources of the community against it. There is also more emphasis on white collar crime and organized racketeering and less on public morals or minor property offenses. While classic police work of the arrest, search, and seizure variety is not likely to disappear, it will probably be of less importance in the future than other strategies.

As regards internal organization, it seems likely that communities will seek and that standard setters will require more rigorously qualified personnel, which will mean an influx of young college persons. Within police organizations, a work ethos more in harmony with societal trends, more congenial to educated recruits, and more oriented toward efficiency will probably emerge. Thus, it can be expected that police organizations of the future will be much less hierarchical and functionally specialized, i.e., there will be less division between patrolman-detective, juvenile, or traffic officer. There will also be less emphasis on formal authority and titles of rank and more emphasis on team work and fraternal discipline, based on loyalty to one's comrades. This is in contrast to hierarchical discipline derived from formal positions, whereby a subordinate is legally bound to obey his superior. Fraternal discipline is personal; hierarchical, impersonal.

No longer will the organization resemble a steep pyramid with all power at the top. More likely, it will be bell-shaped and career satisfaction will not lie solely in promotion but in professional fulfillment. Thus, an effective beat officer will not have to leave his post and become a supervisor any more than a successful doctor gives up operating on patients. At the beat level, neighborhood police teams will probably be the standard arrangement with mutual support among the members and collective participation in decision making. At higher levels, highly skilled individuals will carry out the complex control and support tasks in a collegial spirit with the chief as a first among equals. Concurrently, the distinction between sworn and civilian personnel will become blurred.

SUMMARY

In the future the police role will be that of coordinator or catalyst in a total community effort against crime, although the types of crime dealt with will differ to some extent from the present. They will also play a significant part in social service activities. Within police organizations there will be a professionalism characterized by high caliber personnel, participatory management, technical efficiency and integrity, based on national standards. Thus, policing may offer one of the most challenging, progressive, and socially useful careers of the late 20th century.

NOTES

1. In 1972, 75 percent of all police personnel were employed by local governments. See U.S. Department of Justice, *Expenditures and Employment Data for the Criminal Justice System* (Washington, D.C.: Government Printing Office, 1974), Table 4.
2. Works on the creation of the London Police include: Charles Reith, *The*

Blind Eye of History (London: Faber & Faber, Ltd., 1952), and Belton Cobb, *The First Detectives* (London: L. Faber, 1957). Accounts of the American adaptation are Roger Lane, *Policing the City, Boston 1822–1885* (Cambridge: Harvard University Press, 1967) and James F. Richardson, *The New York Police—Colonial Times to 1901* (New York: Oxford University Press, 1970).

3. For example, two important early works on police administration (*European Police Systems,* 1914 and *American Police Systems,* 1920) were authored by Raymond B. Fosdick, later President of the Rockefeller Foundation. Beginning in the 1920's, studies of police were undertaken by the Center for Criminal Justice at the Harvard Law School, founded by Dean Roscoe Pound and future Supreme Court Justice, Felix Frankfurter. H. Norman Schwartzkopf, a West Point educated regular army officer and World War II general, headed the New Jersey State Police from 1921–1936.

4. Detectives were often recruited directly from civilian life and many were ex-convicts. An account of the ambivalence of detectives in 19th century police departments is contained in Lane, *Policing the City,* Chapter 8.

5. An account of the characteristics of the two styles is found in James Q. Wilson, *Varieties of Police Behavior* (Cambridge: Harvard University Press, 1968), Chapters V and VI. See also Jerome H. Skolnick, *Justice Without Trial* (New York: John Wiley & Sons, Inc., 1966); Joseph D. Lohman and Gordon E. Misner, *The Police and the Community,* Vols. I & II (Washington, D.C.: Government Printing Office, 1967). Skolnick and Wilson (in earlier writings) both used the term professional. Later Wilson substituted "legalistic." The traditional style has also been referred to as "watchman" (Wilson) or "old line" (Skolnick).

6. A description of classic bureaucratic organization is found in Peter Blau, *Bureaucracy in Modern Society* (New York: Random House, 1962).

7. An illustration of the logical positivism which underlay the bureaucratic style of policing was provided by the popular TV series, "Dragnet," based on Chief Parker's Los Angeles Police Department. Week after week Sergeant Friday would caution citizens that all he wanted was the "facts," rather than values or opinions.

8. A typical analytic study is, President's Commission of Law Enforcement and Administration of Justice, *Task Force Report: Science and Technology* (Washington, D.C.: Government Printing Office, 1967), pp. 7–10 and Appendix B. For an extended discussion of the role of detectives, see F. Feeney and A. Weir, *The Prevention and Control of Robbery,* Vol. I, "Robbery Investigation," pp. 337–381. See also, Syracuse Police Department and General Electric Company, *Crime Control Team, Final Report* (National Institute of Law Enforcement and Criminal Justice, 1970).

9. The Family Crisis Intervention Unit is a body of officers specially trained to handle family disturbances. For a description see LEAA *Newsletter,* April 1974, Research Briefs.

10. For a description of team policing see Larry Sherman, et al., *Team Policing: 7 Case Studies* (Washington, D.C.: The Police Foundation, 1973); *Street Crime: Reduction through Positive Responses,* a Report by the Select Committee on Crime, U.S. House Report No. 93–358 (Washington, D.C.: Government Printing Office, 1973), Part II, 8; and National Advisory Commission on Criminal Justice Standards and Goals, *Police* (Washington, D.C.: Government Printing Office, 1973), Chapter 8.

11. This involved the issue of whether a fourth platoon from 6 *p.m.* to 2 *a.m.* was to be instituted in addition to the three tours of duty established by state law.

12. See President's Commission on Law Enforcement and Administration of Justice, *Task Force Report: The Police* (Washington, D.C.: Government Printing Office, 1967), pp. 126–127 and Commission on Standards and Goals, *Police,* Chapter 15.

13. This approach concentrates on attacking particular crimes such as burglary. See Joanne W. Rockwell, "Crime Specific—An Answer," *The Police Chief,* Sept. 1972, pp. 38–43.

14. For a description of special anti-crime units in various cities, see U.S. House, *Street Crime,* Part II, 2.
15. Many police departments now provide routine security inspections for residences and businesses. See Orin Church, "Crime Prevention—A Stitch in Time," *The Police Chief,* March 1970, pp. 52–54, and *Police,* pp. 68–69.
16. While anti-crime *concepts* are generally accepted, they often involve disputes over specific *tactics* such as the use of decoys or stop and frisk.
17. D. Burnham, "A Police Study Challenges Value of Anti-crime Patrol," *The New York Times,* November 11, 1973, p. 1.
18. Albert J. Reiss, Jr., *The Police and the Public* (New Haven: Yale University Press, 1971), pp. 94–96.
19. President's Commission, *Science and Technology,* p. 12.
20. Peter Greenwood, *An Analysis of the Apprehension Activity of the NYCPD* (New York: Rand Institute, 1970), pp. 28–37.
21. See President's Commission on Law Enforcement and Administration of Justice, *Task Force Report: Crime and Its Impact—An Assessment* (Washington, D.C.: Government Printing Office, 1967), pp. 19–21. Also, more policemen were killed in the Haymarket Riot in Chicago in 1886 than in any modern disorder.
22. See *FBI Uniform Crime Reports,* 1st quarter 1974 (Washington, D.C.: Department of Justice, 7/15/74); *New York Times,* July 16, 1974, p. 24; and John Conklin and Egon Bittner, "Burglary in a Suburb," *Criminology,* August 1973, pp. 210–211.
23. See Final Report of the National Commission on the Causes and Prevention of Violence, *To Establish Justice, To Insure Domestic Tranquility* (Washington, D.C.: Government Printing Office, 1969), pp. 46–47.
24. For example, LEAA has pressured police agencies to abolish height requirements, admit more minorities, and obtain more citizen input to policy formulation. LEAA-sponsored victimization studies have cast doubt on some police crime reporting procedures.

TOPICS FOR DISCUSSION

1. Discuss the major eras of change for police.

2. Discuss the need for team policing.

3. Discuss the possibility of increased internal change as a result of a more enlightened leader in the field of police administration.

4. Discuss the amount of potential change that may take place regarding citizens' expectations of police response and performance.

5. Discuss the chances of a national **police** force becoming a reality.

6. Discuss the advantages and disadvantages of limiting police organizations in America to states and metropolitan areas.

7. Discuss the qualifications of a police administrator as stated by the American Bar Association in "Standards Relating to the Urban Police Function."

8. Discuss the role of the police chief within the parameter of what he must do in order to successfully cope with the managing of a police organization; for example, formulating, writing, disseminating policy and goals; legitimate recruitment, selection, evaluation, promotion, procedures.

6

WILLIAM J. BOPP

On professionalization

As the title of this chapter clearly indicates, the concern herein is with police professionalization. However, in no way does the author wish to convey the impression that he is even remotely representing this work to be the definitive word on the subject, the treatise to end all treatises. On the contrary, the article intends to present a representative sample of some of the best and most influential ideas, written by persons of some note in the law enforcement community. But, in addition to a rehash of previously stated notions, there will be a discussion of prestige, the characteristics of existing professions, and myths that are perpetrated about professions.

The concept of police professionalization has been in the forefront of law enforcement's attention for the better part of a decade. It has so permeated the police imagination that one is hardpressed to skim the table of contents of any issue of a leading journal without finding a major article which, in one or another ways, is addressed to that most cherished subject. There is a certain sameness about these essays, but they are also characterized by their differences, for the students, professors, administrators, and practitioners who make up the criminal justice system view this terribly complex phenomenon in a variety of ways. Furthermore, the recommended methods by which the police hope to ascend to professional status are by no means the subject of widespread agreement between those who articulate their positions in the police print media.

Writers often look to Webster for a stock definition of a *profession*. However, the dictionary description of this grammatical construct has no meaning in our case because what is important is not the way in which Webster perceives the term, but the way in which the police themselves see it. When viewed in this context it appears that *profession* is seen by the police as the highest occupational status that a salaried government worker can attain, while the term *professional-*

ization is the movement to achieve that status. Bound up in this theme is an implicit assumption that there are a multiplicity of occupational roles that are characterized by status differentation, meaning that a pecking order exists in which jobs will be classified according to the amount of esteem they generate, with those exacting the highest esteem—the professions—being the most desirable. It will do well to initially discuss a primary reason why police officers— or anyone else for that matter—are so preoccupied with ascending upward, even if it is in name or title only.

THE IDEA OF PRESTIGE

It may be helpful to begin with a conclusion, one to which the author subscribes but which the reader is free to accept or reject. That conclusion is this: police work is not now a profession, although it may be classified as such in the future. In short, professional status has not been attained, but it is attainable. Proceeding from this first premise, a discussion of the idea of prestige is in order.

It is inarguable that Americans are conscious of class, that they are aware of the differences between groups. Since this article is about professionalization, class consciousness will be explored only as it relates to that concept. In any given community, there is a system of social ranking that is said to be a stratified one; that is, a number of roles usually carry the same general social rank and thereby constitute a relatively homogeneous stratum. For example, the work force in a particular poor blue collar neighborhood may be involved in over fifty different occupations, but it makes up a single stratum of relatively low rank because all its members work at unskilled jobs. If a man wished to upgrade his social rank, it would be necessary for him to make certain profound changes in his work situation.[1]

A man's occupation is his chief direct source of income and prestige, and indirectly for his wife and children.[2] And income and prestige continue to be unequally distributed between occupations. By way of definition, *prestige* may be said to be the amount of deference an individual receives and from whom according to a consensus prevailing in society.[3] It is precisely these two forces—to a major extent prestige and to a considerably lesser extent income—which will go a long way toward determining the satisfaction that a working person derives from work, and whether or not that person will be content with his or her social status in the community. Accordingly, there are ways in which workers will perceive their occupational role. Some workers will be satisfied with their work and the prestige it generates. Others will be dissatisfied with their work and its prestige.

Still others will be relatively pleased with their work, but disenchanted with the relatively low prestige attached to it.

In the first case, the worker may be said to have optimized his work situation. In the second, the worker is so dissatisfied with his occupational role that he must either change occupations or labor and live unhappily throughout his productive years. In the last case, the worker probably wishes to remain in his career field, but to take measures to enhance its prestige in the community. It may be logically stated that law enforcement is in this last category and that the primary thrust in police work is to do what is necessary to propel the police service upward, from craft status to professional status. Practitioners are finding, however, that mere press agentry designed to sell law enforcement as a profession is not enough, and that substantive modifications in personnel, standards, operations, and accountability must be initiated in order to achieve the upward mobility for which policemen lust. One can't push for a profession without conspicuously tinkering with the work environment, and unfortunately, internal modifications often cause organizational anxiety among workers, which in turn leads to discontent and labor militancy. The result is ironic: policemen who like their work but are dissatisfied with its prestige find that the work routine must be substantially changed, thereby creating restiveness in the ranks. But that is another story.

PERSPECTIVES ON THE NATURE OF PROFESSIONALIZATION

As has been previously stated, *profession*—the highest status a salaried public employee can attain—is the objective, while *professionalization* is the means by which a group, in this case the police, may employ to fulfill it. Practitioners and scholars in a position to do so often disagree on what is needed by law enforcement to become a profession, and when they do concur on the essential elements it is not unusual to find widespread disagreement over which aspects should be emphasized over others. The ultimate success of the trek toward a profession may, in fact, depend not only on the field's ability to find the right means to professionalize but on its wisdom in assigning the appropriate weights to the elements it has identified as necessary to reach its end.

When presenting varied perspectives on the same issue, it is helpful to keep in mind that those who write are often affected by the professional environment in which they operate, and by the dual shortcomings of interest and bias. Some examples: a police chief who is in the forefront of a state movement to enact police minimum standards legislation may, in his writings, overemphasize its importance in the total professionalization movement; a law enforcement administrator whose agency has just suffered a costly police strike may transmit his temporarily jaundiced view of unions into a polemic against employee organizations as they relate to professionalization; a criminal justice educator, with no practical experience, may demean the importance of training while overemphasizing his specialty, based on little more than his limited interests.

Still, with all the problems associated with surveying various points of view on the same idea, there is value in doing so, as long as the reader is careful to evaluate and logically assign reasonable weights to each perspective. Following are what the author believes are typical perspectives. The author will reprint only brief excerpts, but the ideas contained therein are faithfully representative of the writers' philosophy, and caution was taken to insure that they were not taken out of context. That is not to say that the following quotes express the partisan's entire philosophy so much as they denote his dominant one. They will be presented without analysis.

In 1912, Supreme Court Justice Louis D. Brandeis delivered a Commencement Day Address at Brown University. Brandeis had long been concerned that the American businessman had become overly concerned with the pursuit of profit, while overlooking ethical considerations. He decided to use the occasion to impress upon Brown's graduating class that they cultivate a mentality commensurate with the social responsibilities displayed by other professions. In his address, he pointed out that businessmen must begin to be judged by new and more humane standards. Although Brandeis' speech was aimed at fledgling businessmen, there is evidence to indicate that he felt it had more widespread application to a multitude of professions. Said Brandeis:

> The particular characteristics of a profession as distinguished from other occupations, I take to be these: *first,* a profession is an occupation for which the necessary preliminary training is intellectual in character, involving knowledge and to some extent learning, as distinguished from mere skill; *second,* it is an occupation which is pursued largely for others and not merely for one's self; *third,* it is an occupation in which the amount of financial return is not the accepted measure of success.[4]

Bringing the discussion back to law enforcement, many observers agree with Brandeis that mandated higher education is necessary to a profession and that education should be academic rather than vocational. According to Lyndon A. S. Wilson, Jr.:

> Departments must be encouraged to recruit the best young men

this country has to offer for perhaps the most difficult job around. The goal should be at least two years of liberal arts curriculum at an accredited institution as a condition of appointment, with incentives, including pay, to continue college-level work once on the department. This broader educational background would enable officers to learn new material more readily and cause them to be more articulate in dealing with the public, reducing the need for the use of force. Broader educational experience also develops tolerance for the attitudes of others, particularly the young.[5]

William Mathias subscribes to the foregoing approach, yet adds a synthesizing factor by contending that law enforcement is a component in a system called criminal justice, so it, along with other subsystems (i.e., courts and corrections), should be made aware of the role of the total system and of the subcomponents. Mathias contends that:

> It is not necessary that the various parts of the criminal justice system know the operational techniques of the others, but it is imperative that they have some understanding, and hopefully resultant appreciation of the philosophy and contribution of the criminal justice system.[6]

William Bopp accepts the criminal justice approach to education, but cautions that it may be too narrow. He propounds that criminal justice is a system in itself, yet it also is part of a larger system: public administration. Consequently, education must, in order to be effective, bring the various service professions—health, welfare, justice—together in order to ameliorate intergovernmental isolation.[7]

In a final comment on education, G. Douglas Gourley says that, though the issue of police education is on everyone's lips, its value has been overrated and its dangers have been softpedaled:

> Despite the many values of college education for policemen, there are dangers which cannot be ignored—dangers which lead me to believe that all policemen should not be college graduates.
>
> Because of the limited number of promotional opportunities within police agencies, there is a real danger that officers with college educations who cannot be promoted will become frustrated and bitter. This may result in them leaving the police service prematurely to accept other work more personally satisfying or financially rewarding, or because of pension or other involvements they may remain on the job doing as little as necessary and spending their available time and most of their energies on avocations or second jobs.
>
> The dangers of a college education arise not only after it has been achieved, but also during the process of acquiring it. Unfortunately, to some officers a college program is not a means of improving themselves as officers or even as potential supervisors and administrators but rather as an escape mechanism by which

they get away from the seamy police work which they actually dislike. Such officers may not do their fair share of police work in the field, but rather leave it to their noncollege fellow officers.

Another real danger is that a college degree, or for that matter even college attendance, gives some policemen a feeling of superiority which is detectable by their fellow officers and supervisors. This situation may result in a lack of esprit-de-corps and cooperation—a lack of team work so essential to good policing.[8]

Charles B. Saunders asserts that a system of on-going training—recruit and in-service—is a critical element in upgrading personnel. Considering that the human resource—people—is an agency's most precious commodity, Saunders says that:

At present, the only certainty of the law is that it does not begin to deal with the deficiencies of police manpower. It does not require any department to create a training system which meets the needs of all its personnel.[9]

Saunders' answer: 1) the establishment of a National Training Commission to obtain reasonable uniformity of state police training laws and create minimum standards for training at all governmental levels; and 2) increased federal support for training standards, instructional personnel, regional training institutes and the construction of new facilities.[10]

William W. Blanks has grasped upon the integrity issue as a foundation of the professionalization movement. Further, he asserts that it is first and foremost a departmental responsibility to maintain individual and institutional integrity, through a well-staffed, dedicated, internal investigating unit. Blanks, speaking of the Los Angeles Police Department, holds that:

The ability to recognize and correct one's own faults has long been the mark of integrity found in all successful organizations. As the patriot, Edmund Burke once said, "Public life is a situation of power and energy; he trespasses against his duty who sleeps upon his watch, as well as he that goes over to the enemy."

Today, when criticism of police seems to be the fashion, and when much of the public regards nearly every police act as suspect, this proclivity for self-correction becomes vital, indeed indispensable, to the very preservation of law enforcement itself.

The men and women of the Internal Affairs Division fully recognize the urgency of safeguarding the integrity of the Department to insure its continuance as an effective, viable counterforce in the battle against crime. They willingly accept the responsibility, for these are dedicated professionals of whom the Department can be justly proud. The diligence of their efforts helps to keep the LAPD shield bright with promise and shining with integrity, making it possible for each of its wearers to hold his or her head high and say proudly, in the words of the inimitable Sgt. Friday, of "Dragnet" fame, "This is the city, I work here, I carry a badge."[11]

O. W. Wilson and Roy C. McLaren have equated police professionalization with career development. That is, they believe that a true police professional is one who is the object of and subject to enlightened personnel administration initiated by progressive police administrators who encourage professional development and growth in the ranks. According to Wilson and McLaren:

> Progressive chiefs of police have been concerned about professionalism for many years, and in the past decade there has been increasing interest in professional career development through reorganization of the traditional police position classifications and promotion structures; encouragement of education; adoption of minimum standards, certification, and lateral entry; and encouragement of phased, departmental career-development plans.[12]

There is a growing labor movement in law enforcement that challenges the above notion that police administrators have a unilateral responsibility to professionalize their field. Police trade unionists are demanding a share in decisionmaking (through collective bargaining) based on their belief that the people most affected by administrative decisions should be included in the process whereby policy is articulated, a point underscored by Montreal policemen Jean-Guy Menard:

> I have been a militant in the policemen's brotherhood for 20 years and I don't hesitate to say that the arrival of unionism in the life of policemen has done more than anything else to professionalize the policeman and to render his service to the community more efficient.[13]

John Dussich feels that law enforcement should be concerned with those organizational, technological, and to a lesser extent hardware approaches that will assist in lowering the crime rate through a program of prevention. Says Dussich:

> It would appear that a more important concern than hardware is the demanding but not as visible need to develop effective operational systems to cope with police problems unique to each community. Systems that will provide each police agency with a smoothly working organization in spite of its physical resources. A system that would be capable of delivering the needed services. It should also be able to correct itself, thereby continuously improve its policies. Developing operationally effective policies requires a tremendous amount of effort and understanding. It requires expertise in the areas of organization, management, per-

sonnel administration, human engineering, public relations, urban planning, law enforcement, government, law, criminal justice systems, sociology, psychology, systems analysis, cybernetics, research and development, and others. The macroscopic as well as microscopic perspectives are both necessary if a meaningful policy plan is to be developed. Once an effective set of operating procedures is implemented, an agency might start concerning itself with augmenting its physical resources and interfacing these to an already efficient structure.

This is not to say that one concern comes before the other. Both approaches need to be attended to simultaneously, but the efficacy of an agency's policies must be one of the main priorities if any effective work is to be done toward the ultimate goal of reducing the crime problem.

Today the emphasis is on speeding up the time between the commission of an offense and its subsequent punishment. This means greater emphasis must be given to organizational as well as technological improvements. A systems-oriented approach is an effective way to accomplish this task. Not only should the police organizational efforts be aimed at detection and apprehension, but it should also devote a sizeable effort to such programs as community services, manpower improvements and crime prevention progress.[14]

Robert Daley believes that police professionalism is inextricably bound up in the ability of the police to enlist the support of the public it serves. Daley was the public information officer for the New York Police Department, and he feels that at the core of the police-community relations problem is the inability or unwillingness of law enforcement to explain itself and its policies to citizens. Daley says that:

Policemen on the whole have always tended to embrace secrecy like some sort of a beautiful mistress. Entire departments have espoused secrecy for decades. And then we wonder why the people don't love us. Think about it for a minute. Most people don't like dark places. Dark places seem haunted and very dangerous. And so people have neither trusted nor admired their police departments; they have been afraid of their police departments, in part, because there has been far too much mystery surrounding them.

I have been on a number of rooftops and in a number of alleys at night where we were looking for evidence connected to a crime: guns, bullets, whatnot. These were foreboding places until our special Emergency Service Squad arrived with their portable floodlights and turned foreboding darkness into the brightness of a day at the beach.

In New York we have been trying, in effect, to turn those same floodlights, wherever possible, on our department and on ourselves and what we do—knowing that at times our own mistakes will show up, and even our own incompetencies but knowing also that the majority of times we will be shown as the brave and dedicated public servants which most policemen are. I don't see where this department has anything to fear from the floodlights. And I suggest that the image of the police in this country would rise enormously if other departments turned their floodlights on themselves too. The object, again, is simply to win the people back, thus making all our jobs a good deal easier than they are now.[15]

David C. Couper's preoccupations are also with the delivery of police service and with the recurring problem of police community relations. However, the quick delivery of services to citizens is not the primary issue with Couper, who strongly believes that:

The elusive goal of police professionalism will continue to be unattained unless some new concepts in the police service are considered. Some of these concepts deal with institutional changes to facilitate a humanitarian and service response to social problems. The development of this concept would be aided by police officers who see themselves as social workers, public servants, and community advocates with an allegiance to, and governed by, the Constitution in criminal justice matters. If experiments with police organizational structure, upgraded entrance requirements, dress, use of paraprofessionals, technicians and other nonsworn personnel, and post-professional training are not conducted, then police will continue to be hamstrung by gross incompetence and inefficiency in dealing with community needs and developing public support in matters of crime prevention and law observance.[16]

CHARACTERISTICS OF THE EXISTING PROFESSIONS

The author has surveyed a number of recognized professional occupational groupings to determine their major characteristics. In arriving at what does or does not constitute a profession, only one question was asked: does the public view the occupation as a profession? If the answer was in the affirmative, the group was included in the survey. Although this query was directed at separating the professions from all other types of undertakings, it has major implications for the subject at hand because, despite all the innovations law enforcement adopts in its quest to become a profession, the objective will not be achieved unless and until the public, in its wisdom, actually believes law enforcement is a profession.

The professional groups studied include attorneys, physicians,[17] nurses, elementary and secondary school teachers, professors, engineers, chemists, social workers, and airline pilots. Some selected characteristics of these professions will follow. First, a few words of explanation. The upcoming list contains items which may be more characteristic of one group than another, meaning that the discussion represents a synthesis of values rather than a grouping of universal attributes. So care must be taken by the reader in making sweeping generalizations based upon the articulation of one principle that may have strict application to seven of the nine professions, loose application to one, and no applicability to the other. Moreover, in no way are the following characteristics to be viewed as anything even remotely approximating a complete listing. It is admittedly selective, but the selection was made so that the fruits of the study would be relevant to this essay. One additional comment is in order: the generalizations made denote the optimum situation of the professions studied, even though less than the optimum often exists in the real world.

A Higher Loyalty

Professionals in the groups studied exhibit a loyalty above and beyond that given to the agency, institution, or corporation which employs them. This is not to say that they are disloyal to higher authority; nothing could be further from the truth. But, the highest loyalty of professionals surveyed is directed first at their professions and their clientele, and second at the employing authority. Physicians, for example, are strongly dedicated to medicine and their patients, while dedication to the hospital in which they practice is quite secondary. The same holds true for nurses, teachers, professors, social workers, and others.

Licensing

Most professionals are officially licensed or certified to practice or pursue their calling. In the case of airline pilots, the federal government is the certifying authority, while for physicians, attorneys, nurses, teachers, and professors it is usually the state. In the licensing/certification procedure, professional associations or unions usually play an active role in articulating criteria, in testing, in enforcement, and in applying sanctions, either officially or semi-officially.

Education

Most professions have a minimum requirement of a baccalaureate degree of a specialized nature. Many require advanced graduate work to qualify for basic entry-level training. In those few cases in which education is waived (e.g., airline pilots), it is done so only for demonstrated skill and documented ability.

Growing Emphasis on Teamwork

In most of the professions studied, there appears to be an increasing emphasis on teamwork, wherein an individual's skills and strengths can be better utilized. Team teaching, for instance, is in vogue, as is team nursing, the use of group dynamics in social work and interdisciplinary instruction in higher education.

Use of Paraprofessionals

Along with the growing emphasis on teamwork has come the realization that different levels of expertise are required of professionals, and that the most highly trained and competent persons should be assigned to the most important jobs. In public education, teacher aids are employed to free teachers from the busywork which detracts from their main role. In higher education, graduate assistants perform the same function. In nursing, registered nurses supervise aids, orderlies, and practical nurses, as well as volunteers. In medicine, nurses and skilled paraprofessionals perform tasks previously reserved for physicians (e.g. midwives, anesthetists, etc.). In social work, interns are assigned to field work on a college credit basis.

Specialization

Contrary to the trend toward producing generalists in some occupations, the professionals studied seem to embrace the idea of specialization. In fact, the movement to specialize in the professions appears to be growing. Attorneys may be in general practice, but they are usually more preoccupied with one phase of the law than others. Even assistant district attorneys in metropolitan areas, while generally concerned with the criminal law, tend to focus on one major aspect of it (i.e., traffic, fraud, organized crime, capital offenses, etc.). It is axiomatic that physicians and surgeons are highly specialized—the general practitioner may be becoming a rare species. Teachers in secondary schools and professors not only specialize by discipline, but often narrow their concern to an aspect of that discipline. Chemists' research interests are usually quite limited. Nurses, while chiefly generalists, also are beginning to specialize by clientele and by function (e.g. psychiatric, delivery room, obstetrics, surgical, etc.).

Codes of Conduct

Most professions are governed by a strict code of conduct, violations of which can lead to sanctions in the form of censure, suspension, an effect on one's license to work, or membership in the union or employee organization. The enforcement of these codes often assumes the force, if not the actual authority, of law, and their legitimacy is usually unquestioned because, when drafted, the codes had what was akin to universal acceptance. This is apparently so because practitioners at all working levels had input in their articulation, not just the aristocracy of the profession, the ruling oligarchy. Unions and professional organizations were not eliminated from participation.

A Disdain for Administrative Assignments

The author is about to make a sweeping generalization, but one which is heavily supported by data and the force of personal experience. Professional practitioners in the grouping surveyed exhibit a general disdain for administrative work. That is, few wish to move into administrative or management positions, for it would mean that they would no longer be able to pursue, on a fulltime basis, their chosen line of work. Thus, most prefer to operate on the level at which they entered their professions with occasional lateral transfers or advanced training which permits greater specialization. Surgeons wish to remain surgeons and not be directors of staff; few professors wish to be deans; airline pilots wish to fly airplanes not sit at desks; devoted teachers love their classrooms; nurses are usually content to minister to the infirm, not administer other nurses. And it is not unusual to find that professionals who have mastered their calling are remunerated more generously than those who supervise them, and command considerably more prestige in their specialties than administrators. In those professions that have an hierarchical structure, it is common to find that line operatives will accept one promotion to a first-line supervisory position that permits them to stay in the field, but will refuse higher rank which philosophically separates them from their colleagues and physically separates them from their clientele. In those cases in which administrative positions are highly prized, it is often because: 1) professionals feel a need to reform the agency involved; or 2) the remuneration and rewards at entry level are too low.

Intellectual Standards, Skills, and Physical Criteria

In the professions, the emphasis is on the cultivation of skill through an individual commitment to a rather rigorous set of relevant intellectual standards. All fledgling professionals, in order to make it into their field, must dedicate themselves to a challenging course of study designed to mold them into what it takes to successfully operate in their chosen area. In short, the emphasis is on *functional* means and objectives, not on *ceremonial* ones. Height, weight, sex, eyesight, hearing, personal habits, temperament, mannerisms, dress, hair style, and the like are only important as they relate, directly and unequivocally, to the ability to perform the job. Rules of conduct and deportment are based on the idea of maximizing the probability of success, and not on the whims of administrators concerned with standardizing behavior for the sake of mass conformity. True professionals are permitted—even encouraged—to retain their individuality, even in a team effort.

This partial list, containing as it does some brazen generalizations, nevertheless represents, in the author's view, accurate and relevant material, which the reader is free to accept, reject, modify, or challenge. In any case, it is food for thought, especially when one attempts to place it in a law enforcement context, for law enforcement, if it hopes to become a profession, cannot afford to isolate itself from the existing family of professions.

SOME MYTHS ABOUT PROFESSIONS

It is a sorry state of affairs that some police managers have used the idea of a "police profession" to resist real reform. This resistance has come in the form of accusing proponents of a given concept of furthering an idea which is "unprofessional." The idea of a law enforcement profession is so deeply entrenched in the police imagination that the label "unprofessional" carries with it a terrible connotation, for to be "unprofessional" affects not only the individual in question but all his colleagues as well by retarding the field from advancing. As a result of this tactic, it is desirable that a few commonly perpetrated myths about professions be discussed.

Professionals Do Not Unionize or Collectively Bargain

Because of the onslaught of a police labor movement, with its emphasis on militancy and activism, and with a desire to collectively bargain, litigate, insert itself in policy decisions and occasionally engage in job actions, some police managers have become vitally concerned with rank and file encroachment into areas previously thought to be safely in management's realm. Alarmed over this possible intrusion, managers have tended to view unions and collective bargaining as "unprofessional." Although unions may be all right for laborers—plumbers, bricklayers, factory workers, and the like— they are said to be inappropriate for professionals. True professionals, according to this perspective, belong to professional associations, not to unions. Few other myths have been so consistently perpetuated; few have been so utterly inconsistent with reality.

Professionals do unionize, and many have a long history of it. They also collectively bargain, often with great enthusiasm. Moreover, there is an increasingly blurred distinction between professional associations and unions. These formerly separate and distinct organizations now engage in the same general types of behavior. Probably two major exceptions are the bar and medical associations, but that is because physicians and attorneys in the private sector set their own hours, working conditions, operating policies, and fees. Obviously, if professionals in other walks of life, including the police, could have this kind of authority over their affairs, labor relations would have no fascination. This obviously is not the case, so unionization and its adjuncts are an organizational reality in the various professions: teaching, nursing, flying, social work, and the like. Even physicians and surgeons who work for wages employ it and its concomitants.

There is nothing inherently professional or unprofessional in unionization and collective bargaining. These phenomena may be used to advance or retard professional status, but are not indicative, in and of themselves, of whether or not an occupational group is or will be a profession.

True Professionals Are Not Technically Educated

It is almost dogma in academia that policemen should be broadly educated, in lieu of technical, vocational, "nuts and bolts" training. If one reads the journals consistently or attends professorial conventions the term most used to demeaningly describe this academic approach is "how to handcuff" training. There are even clearcut distinctions made between training—which is oriented toward learning skills—and education—which is intellectual in nature (as in the Brandeis argument).

It is not the purpose of this discussion to evaluate the types of education police officers should receive. But it is purposeful to address the discussion to education as it relates to a profession. There are a multiplicity of arguments an educator can effectively use to criticize technical education of the police while supporting broad-based liberal arts or social science education. But one argument which *must not* be used is that technical education (or professional education, or vocational education, or nuts and bolts education—whatever it is termed) is inconsistent with the ideals of a profession. The fact of the matter is, with the possible exception of social work, all the professions studied stress technical coursework in the major. Examinations that lead to licensing are almost exclusively concerned with technical matter. Few occupational groups are more consistently looked on as the epitome of professional status as law and medicine, which are almost entirely concerned with what, to the police, would equate to "how to handcuff." The same holds true for nurses, pilots, engineers, and chemists. Teachers must often take "methods" courses to qualify for certification. No generalizations may be made of professors, for their exposure to technical coursework depends on their individual disciplines. But the point is clear: mandated technical education training is not inherently unprofessional.

Professionals Are Autonomous

Professionals who work for wages, especially those in the public sector, do not enjoy anything that nearly equates to autonomy, despite an oft-perpetrated myth to the contrary. Police administrators often contribute to this misconception in order to resist civilian-dominated review boards, community control of police operations, or the intrusion of partisan politics into departmental affairs. As in the case of technical education, there may be quite extensive reasons to resist such interferences, but it is inaccurate to state that autonomy is a characteristic of the professions. Police administrators pressing for autonomy often point to physicians and attorneys to prove their case, as these two groups, at least in the private sector, are autonomous, free of community control, self-policing. Yet, this is somewhat akin to comparing apples and basketballs, for policemen and private sector doctors and lawyers are not nearly of the same genre, and may only be honestly compared when physicians and attorneys labor for wages.

When one does survey the wage earning professions, it soon becomes clear that, while some may be granted a good deal of operating independence, the institutional, community, or corporate authorities which granted that independence also demand that professionals be held accountable for their actions. Nurses in a county hospital, for example, must adhere to manuals full of policy and procedure. The paperwork, and its routing system, are infamously extensive in the social work bureaucracy. Teachers constantly bemoan the procedures whereby they are initially accountable for their output to administrators, and ultimately to the community, who are invited to participate in school activities. Accountability is a fact of life in the wage earning professions, and it is clear that the trend is toward making them even more accountable.

CONCLUSION

The conclusion of this chapter differs from others of its type by inviting the reader to reach his or her own conclusions, based upon the material presented, as incomplete as it is. It is hoped that, out of the often contradictory data on the subject, the informed person can meld the varying viewpoints into a cohesive philosophy.

In closing, there may be some worth in listing propositions that can be of assistance in placing the issue into clearer focus. Several of the following propositions relate directly to law enforcement, others are general in nature, but all have implications for the police movement to professionalize.

Proposition 1. Law enforcement is not now a profession, but professional status is attainable.

Proposition 2. No policeman will be a professional until all are.

Proposition 3. A great many true professionals wish and are encouraged to spend most or all of their careers working at the level of execution, directly with their clients, and not in administrative positions.

Proposition 4. Unions and employee organizations are generally encouraged to play an active role in those affairs which affect a professional's occupational destiny.

Proposition 5. Analogy has worth only when the occupational groups compared share a sufficient number of common properties to make the comparison valid.

Proposition 6. Despite all attempts by the police to professionalize, law enforcement will not be a profession until it is accepted as one by the general community.

NOTES

1. Melvin L. DeFleur, William V. D'Antonio, and Lois B. DeFleur, *Sociology: Man in Society* (Glenview, Ill.: Scott, Foresman and Co., 1971), pp. 82–83.
2. Ibid.
3. Jackson Toby, *Contemporary Society, 2nd ed.* (New York: John Wiley and Sons, 1971), p. 603.

4. Moses Rischin, *The American Gospel of Success* (Chicago: Quadrangle Books, 1968), pp. 119–120.
5. Lyndon A. S. Wilson, Jr., "Toward Police Professionalism: An Alternative to Repression," *Police* (July–August, 1971), p. 37.
6. William J. Mathias, "A Criminal Justice Curriculum for an Urban Society," *The Police Chief* (August 1969), p. 16.
7. William J. Bopp, *Police Personnel Administration* (Boston: Holbrook Press, 1974), pp. 395–396.
8. G. Douglas Gourley, "Higher Education for Police Personnel," *Law and Order* (February 1972), pp. 34–35.
9. Charles B. Saunders, Jr., *Upgrading the American Police* (Washington, D.C.: The Brookings Institution, 1970), p. 151.
10. Ibid., pp. 161–166.
11. William W. Blanks, "Guardians of Integrity," *Law and Order* (March 1972), p. 13.
12. O. W. Wilson and Roy C. McLaren, *Police Administration, 3rd ed.* (New York: McGraw-Hill Book Co., 1972), p. 291.
13. Jean-Guy Menard, "Professionalism or Servitude for Police?" *The Law Officer* (December 1971), p. 13.
14. John P. J. Dussich, "Where Are Our Priorities?" *Journal of Lambda Alpha Epsilon* (November 1971), p. 19.
15. Martin A. Greenberg, "The Police Officer of the Twenty-First Century: He Is Already on the Scene," *The Police Chief* (July 1972), p. 67.
16. David C. Couper, "The Delivery of Neighborhood Police Services," *The Police Chief* (March 1972), p. 15.
17. Only salaried attorneys and physicians are subjects of this study.

TOPICS FOR DISCUSSION

1. Discuss why professionalism is a valid goal for police.

2. Discuss the present status of police as a profession as opposed to a craft.

3. Discuss the possibility of developing realistic measures of productivity and accountability for police agencies.

4. Discuss the criteria that other accepted professions have met and determine if police are in the same category, or if police should be in the same category; e.g., there may be other criteria more relevant to the police field.

   J. A. Greening listed the following elements of a profession:

   1. An organized body of knowledge, constantly augmented and refined, with special techniques based thereon.

   2. Facilities for formal training in this body of knowledge and procedure.

   3. Recognized qualifications for membership in, and identification with, the profession.

   4. An organization which includes a substantial number of the members qualified to practice the profession and to exercise an influence on the maintenance of professional standards.

5. A code of ethics which, in general, defines the relations of the members of the profession to the public and to other practitioners within the group and normally recognizes an obligation to render services on other than exclusively economic considerations.

Professionalization is accomplished through:

1. Prescribed courses of study, standardized and geared to one another in high schools, colleges, and universities.

2. Application of prescribed methods in practice teaching, reading, briefing, etc.

3. Post-graduate courses, prescribed and administered if a specialized field is selected.

4. Internship for application of theory to practice for the purpose of developing skill.

5. Acknowledgement and acceptance of self-imposed ethical standards of professional practice and personal conduct.

6. Examination to determine fitness to practice and enter the profession.

7. Continuous study and research for improvement and advancement of professional techniques and their application within the profession.

5. Discuss the following:

The definition of a profession and the method of attaining that status provides a yardstick for measuring the present position of the police in terms of a standard of excellence. Outstandingly evident are a number of criteria that must be accomplished, including:

1. Mandatory educational standards
2. Lateral transfer
3. Transferability of retirement credits
4. Ethical standards
5. Career development program
6. Certification of eligible professionals
7. Specialized literature
8. Continuous research

7

PETER FEUILLE

Police officers as unionists:
the police labor movement

INTRODUCTION

A decade or so ago most police officers in most urban police departments belonged to low-key organizations that sponsored several social
events each year, fulfilled various fraternal functions, and perhaps
offered some insurance benefits at group rates. Today, most police
officers in these same cities are members of organizations that, in addition to the above functions, actively lobby in city halls and state
capitols, energetically seek voter approval on police-related ballot
measures, frequently file lawsuits against managerial officials, actively
speak out on police issues, and aggressively bargain with city and
police management for improved economic benefits and working conditions. In short, the average urban police officer of ten years ago belonged to a low-key social-fraternal organization; today he or she
belongs to a police union.[1]

What difference does the presence of a police union make in a
police department and in city hall? The answer, of course, depends
upon the issue involved, the union and management involved, and
whether the respondent is a patrolman or a chief, a taxpayer or the
mayor, the union president or the city's labor negotiator. Whatever
the practitioner's or observer's normative judgments about these
organizations, the fact is that in many cities they play an important
and sometimes decisive role in the resolution of most police personnel
matters and some law enforcement policy issues and thus merit serious
attention. Consequently, in this article I will consider several aspects
of police union-management relations, including an analysis of the
kinds of issues over which police unions have sought a voice, an examination of the various processes by which the unions have sought to

achieve their goals, some comments on the structure of police bargaining arrangements, and a brief discussion of the complex relationship among unionism, professionalization, and the quest for professional status.[2]

POLICE EMPLOYMENT ISSUES

Since the interested reader can find discussions of police employee organization development elsewhere they will not be repeated here.[3] Suffice it to say that existing police unions for the most part are not new organizations but trace their ancestry back—several decades in some cases—to police fraternal associations and civil service organizations. However, during the middle and late 1960s policemen in ever larger numbers began to express, sometimes in a very aggressive or militant manner, many employment-related grievances and demanded an organized voice in the resolution of their grievances. In this section we consider some of the issues over which police unions have been active and some of the methods they have used to attain their objectives.

Dollars

Policemen seem no less financially greedy than other occupational groups, and much of their unions' efforts have been devoted to securing increases in base salaries, premium pay, and economic fringe benefits. In most of the cities I have studied, collective bargaining with its attendant dispute resolution procedures has become the primary mechanism by which the unions seek more cash. It would be inaccurate to characterize union pressures as the sole or even primary cause of the recent large increases in police salaries,[4] but it also would be incorrect in an era of city budget stringency to say that police militancy on behalf of more money is unrelated to these pay increases. Police unions also are deserving of much of the credit for recent increases in pension and health and welfare benefits, and most notably for securing extra compensation for off-duty court time, standby time, call-back, and call-in, and time and a half pay for regular overtime. The most obvious effect of these union pressures has been to increase the costs of delivering a given bundle of police services to the community. It seems fair to conclude that police unions have played a major role in bringing police compensation practices into line with prevailing private sector pay levels (i. e., of craftsmen) and practices (i. e., premium pay for work beyond 40 hours per week, etc.). Whether one views this as good or bad depends largely upon whether one is a taxpayer shouldering the costs or a patrolman receiving the benefits.

Nondollar Issues

Manpower Deployment. Prior to the emergence of aggressive unionism, police managers apparently enjoyed almost unfettered discretion in the assignment, transfer, and general deployment of their human resources. Many unions have sharply reduced their deployment discretion. One set of constraints upon management's flexibility comes from the much higher price tags attached to overtime, court time, standby, etc. In addition to these higher dollar costs, many unions have pressed at the negotiating table for an increased use of seniority in determining job and shift assignments and transfers. A few unions have objected to the introduction of a fourth shift during high crime hours or have opposed changes in shift starting times. Many unions have objected to one-man cars (sometimes successfully, sometimes not), and the usual union posture in a large number of cities toward civilianization of certain police department jobs (e. g., parking and traffic enforcement, clerical, technical, etc.) is one of opposition (though the intensity of the opposition varies with the jobs being civilianized).

As in most organizations that have become unionized, police unions noticeably have reduced managerial discretion to deploy manpower, but most of these union efforts have stemmed from a desire to eliminate favoritism, to secure extra pay for extra duty, and to attain a greater degree of position security for senior employees. In several of the cities I have studied, police management interviewees complained of union-generated constraints that limited their ability to achieve the most effective matching of men and jobs, but when pressed for specific examples to support these claims they had none to offer.

Discipline. Police departments generally have relied upon a quasi-military form of organization and disciplinary administration to enforce compliance with desired forms of behavior, and thus the administration of the disciplinary process tends to be more important than in most work organizations. As with manpower deployment, police unions have had a significant impact upon the operation of the disciplinary process, also in the direction of reducing managerial discretion. Their primary impact has been to provide accused officers with some legal assistance and internal civil rights, to require management to be more equitable in the administration of justice, to secure disciplinary consistency and minimize ad hoc disciplinary actions, and to eliminate certain kinds of punishments (e. g., working with no pay on days off). As in the case of compensation practices, the net effect of union pressures has been to bring police disciplinary practices more in line with the rights enjoyed by organized employees in the private sector. Police unions have not taken away management's right to levy punishments, but they have required management to prepare better cases, to make the punishment fit the offense, and to administer the disciplinary process more equitably.

Grievance Procedures. When police collective bargaining becomes institutionalized in a particular city, one of the union's first demands typically is for the establishment of a grievance procedure culminating in binding arbitration. The grievance procedure is the vehicle or mechanism by which individual officers (usually with the union's support) may seek redress for any alleged infringement of their contractual rights, and more generally is the mechanism by which the union enforces the rights (and obligations) specified in the contract. These procedures have become the primary day-to-day mechanism by which the unions and managements test the limits of managerial prerogatives and the extent of the union's voice in determining employment conditions. As might be expected, some managerial actions or proposals have been stalled or even prevented by union use of grievance-arbitration procedures, and similarly, some union interpretations of various contractual clauses have been disapproved by arbitrators. While it may be premature to say that grievance-arbitration procedures are the norm in American police departments, in 1971 ten of twenty-two departments I studied had them, and almost every department I know of which has a collective bargaining agreement also has some kind of negotiated grievance procedure (though some of them provide for the chief's decision as the final step).

Law Enforcement Policy Issues

Police unions appear to me to have concentrated most of their resources upon the bread-and-butter benefits, day-to-day working conditions, and job and union security goals that American trade unions traditionally have sought. However, police unions also have devoted considerable efforts toward influencing various law enforcement policy issues: the types of weapons carried and the conditions regulating their use, the appropriate police response to civil disorders, institutionalized civilian review of police behavior, the functioning of other parts of the criminal justice system, the appropriate response to publicized police corruption, etc.

The Use of Force.   When the enforcement of the law or the use of force have emerged as conflict issues, the usual union response has been a "hard line" posture. For instance, police unions in Boston, New York, Baltimore, and Pittsburgh in the late 1960s publicly condemned managerial policies aimed at containing civil disturbances with minimum force rather than extinguishing them with maximum force—though these condemnations did not seem to have any visible operational impact. Regarding the use of force in nonriot, everyday policing, unions in several cities have pressed for heavier armaments for patrol officers and minimal restrictions on the use of weapons, frequently after attacks on policemen. While some of these efforts have been unsuccessful, in some cities police officers either carry heavier armament or have fewer restrictions on their use of weapons because of the efforts of their unions.

Civilian Review.   Police unions have been vehemently opposed to any organizational arrangement which even hints at allowing non-judicial civilians to normatively review police behavior. The most celebrated example is the New York City patrolmen's union 1966 electoral defeat of Mayor Lindsay's civilian review board. Police union lobbying and litigation in Philadelphia and Rochester resulted in the eventual demise of civilian review boards in those cities. Unions in Buffalo, Boston, Baltimore, Detroit, Pittsburgh, and Seattle have condemned and worked against established or proposed procedures and bodies which they perceived as permitting civilians to review police behavior. The general impact of these union political activities has been to defeat civilian review mechanisms where they existed and to defeat other civilian review proposals before they were implemented.

The Criminal Justice System.   Police unions have worked to affect the operation of other parts of the criminal justice system. In theory the pieces of the system work independently: the legislature defines criminal activities; the police make arrests; the prosecutor seeks indictments and decides which cases to prosecute; the judge passes sentence, etc. While in practice these are not always independent events, the interdependence that does exist may be affected by many different kinds of police union political activities. For example, unions in Baltimore, Dayton, Detroit, San Francisco, and Seattle made statements about engaging in court-watching (stationed observers in court to record the judicial disposition of criminal cases), and their statements invariably were couched in coercive language castigating judicial leniency (though only in Detroit was such a plan put into operation). Unions in few cities worked for or against the election or appointment of certain judges, and the Detroit patrolmen's union in 1969 went to considerable (but unsuccessful) effort to remove a local judge after he released a large group of blacks arrested at the scene of a shootout with the police.[5] A few unions were overtly or covertly involved in the election campaigns of local prosecutors or state attorneys general. A few unions reported lobbying to influence criminal statutes, and police unions frequently were involved in state and local efforts to reinstate the death penalty after the 1972 U.S. Supreme Court decision which outlawed existing death penalties. Finally, police union sympathies for and endorsements of "law and order" candidates for executive and legislative offices are well known.[6]

Corruption. As recent police scandals in New York, Philadelphia, Detroit, Indianapolis, Chicago, and Seattle have demonstrated, police corruption seems to be an enduring problem. Some police unions shy away from public involvement in corruption issues, but others may get involved by providing legal services to accused officers, mounting a public relations effort to proclaim the honesty of the vast majority of police officers, or trying to halt or limit a corruption investigation. Classic examples of the latter occurred in New York City where the patrolmen's union filed suit to block the Knapp Commission's 1970–71 investigation into widespread corruption in that city's department, and in Seattle where the union went to court and forced a new chief to stop using polygraph examinations during his internal investigations into the widespread corruption patterns that were disclosed in 1970. While there are too few data points to reach definitive conclusions, police union behavior over corruption issues seems similar to the behavior of the traditional professional associations: they are highly unlikely to be the first to call public attention to the problem; they are careful to insist that those who are charged are not representative of the class; and they are insistent upon due process for the accused.

Other Issues

In addition to the above issues, there is a myriad of other issues over which the unions have devoted considerable energies and resources. For instance, advanced education for police officers has been proposed or institutionalized in a large number of departments, and the unions usually have insisted upon playing a major role in the formulation and implementation of such plans. Some unions have been quite supportive of advanced education incentives and requirements, and others have been opposed (much of the variance seems to be accounted for by union leader personal preferences for or against college education). In general, police unions seem to be supportive of higher education

plans provided that the unions are integrally involved in the establishment of such plans (often via collective bargaining), that there are
longevity increases for officers who don't want to pursue higher education, and that the plan provides higher pay for increased increments
of education.

Some unions have been involved in recruitment and selection
issues, usually over the question of minority recruitment. Unions
usually oppose proposed changes in selection standards designed to
facilitate the recruitment of minority officers. Similarly, some unions
have sought to affect the promotion process by influencing the shape
of promotion criteria. While it is difficult to describe a consistent pattern, the basic thrust of union efforts has been to attempt to reduce
managerial discretion and opportunities for favoritism by pressing
for greater weight on seniority and written examination scores and
less weight on supervisory ratings and oral exams, and by insisting on
rigid adherence to civil service procedures.

Finally, a grabbag list: in Buffalo the union challenged management over the introduction of off-duty use of marked squad cars
by patrolmen; in several cities unions have pressed management for
improved maintenance of squad cars; in one city the union objected
to the design of a new police headquarters building; in Boston the
patrolmen's union clashed with the mayor over his proposed changes
in the colors of squad cars and uniform shirts; in Detroit the union
filed a grievance over the lack of downtown parking spaces; in several
cities unions have attempted to influence moonlighting regulations
and residency requirements; and in Pittsburgh the union fought a
lengthy but unsuccessful court battle to prevent the introduction of
metermaids for parking enforcement. The myriad of issues presented
in this section should emphasize that police labor relations are quite
pragmatic and situation-specific, and that the range of union interests
is very wide.

Union Impact

In the above discussion I noted several issue-specific union impacts;
in this section I discuss the unions' impact more generally. Basically,
the unions have provided the rank-and-file officers with an effective
voice in influencing employment issues and have required management to share with the union the decision-making authority on a wide
variety of personnel practices and policy issues. The unions have
sharply reduced managerial discretion to fix wages and benefits, to
deploy manpower, and to administer discipline. They have protected
employees against arbitrary and inconsistent managerial treatment,
and they have required management to view the department's human

resources as a much more expensive and valuable commodity. They have fostered the development of management by policy, and they have been a loud and sometimes decisive voice in many law enforcement policy debates. In sum, they have moved many police departments from a unilateral to a bilateral decision-making mode, and it is extremely unlikely that the "good old days" will ever return.

LABOR RELATIONS PROCESSES

The above examination of issues is only partially complete, for it did not include an examination of the various processes by which the unions have tried to wield influence. Not only does the shape of these processes affect the unions' impact on many issues, the unions have devoted considerable effort toward improving the process interaction structure to their perceived advantage. The most obvious examples are union efforts to secure favorable collective bargaining and dispute resolution legislation.

Collective Bargaining

The primary factor distinguishing the police unions of today from the police organizations of yesteryear is the presence of collective bargaining as a mechanism for organized union-management interaction over many of the employment issues discussed above. Police organizations in some cities long have lobbied and even dabbled in electoral politics; only since the late 1960s have most urban police unions been bargaining collectively with police and city management. Police unions also are more active politically than they used to be, but it is their status as exclusive bargaining agents that gives them a presence and visibility that they have not previously enjoyed.

The collective bargaining process, with its institutionalized visibility, negotiating teams and lists of demands, attendant dispute resolution procedures, and resultant written contract, is the cornerstone of the typical urban police union's representation policy. As a glance through the typical police contract will reveal, it is this process through which the union seeks most of its economic benefit and working condition objectives. The contract is also the source of a negotiated grievance procedure which the union may use during the life of the agreement to challenge managerial interpretations of various contractual provisions.

Because many bargaining subjects are perceived as distributive or win-lose issues, collective bargaining is an adversarial interaction process in which each side exerts leverage (or has the potential to do so) in order to secure as favorable terms as possible. The most obvious lever the union has is the ability to call a work stoppage of some kind (ranging from selected job actions to full-fledged strikes) which by disrupting some portion of the normal police services delivered to the community increases the cost to management of disagreeing with the union's proposed terms. Baltimore, Milwaukee, New York, Detroit, Pittsburgh, Rochester, and several smaller cities have experienced police strikes in recent years,[7] but as a proportion of all police bargaining relationships police strikes are relatively uncommon. More frequent are such job actions as traffic ticket slowdowns or speedups. In order to prevent police strikes, many state public sector bargaining laws provide for various forms of mediation, fact-finding, or arbitration to resolve negotiating impasses, and some unions have devoted considerable energies to obtaining and then manipulating these dispute resolution mechanisms for more favorable contract terms than might be obtained from management directly.

Politics

The key feature distinguishing public from private sector union activities are the roles played by political considerations and tactics. Private sector unions are no strangers to political action, but they rely on collective bargaining with private employers for direct membership benefits, and these bargaining interactions take place in the economic contexts of the employer's markets. In contrast, cities are political entities, ultimately controlled by elected officials, which exist to provide public services rather than make profits. These factors mean that municipal labor relations are conducted in the context of the relevant state and local political influence structures, and consequently the city unions must engage in political activities to strengthen their positions at the bargaining table. Many police unions, for example, have lobbied extensively with city officials to improve their bargaining position. If these contacts occur during ongoing contract negotiations they often are referred to as "end runs" (around the city's official negotiators). Similarly, many police unions have engaged in overt or covert electoral politics on behalf of candidates for mayor, city council, and state offices in the hopes of acquiring political IOUs which can be exchanged for valued considerations at a later date.

However, union political activities are not limited to strengthening the union's negotiating position. Many of the issues over which police unions have been active are not decided via collective bargaining but instead are resolved by traditional political tactics in various political arenas: electoral campaigns on behalf of various police-related ballot measures, lawsuits filed in various courts, lobbying the city council and state legislature, publicity campaigns to espouse a particular union position, etc. Many police working conditions are regulated by city charter provisions, city ordinances, or state statutes which are changed by the above kinds of political activities. In addition, the law enforcement policy issues discussed earlier are not very common subjects for the contract negotiation table (how could a police union contract provide for the judicial disposition of criminal cases?), and consequently are debated and resolved in political arenas.

Multilateral Labor Relations

The variety of processes that police unions use to seek their objectives, and the variety of managerial and other adversaries with whom they interact convince me that it is appropriate to describe police labor relations as being very multilateral in nature. This multilateralism includes several kinds of union-management activities in a variety of contexts: traditional collective bargaining activities such as contract negotiations, grievance negotiations, and work stoppages; traditional political interest group activities as described above in order to strengthen the union's position at the bargaining table; the same kinds of political activities over issues not decided at the bargaining table; and (as a special case of the preceding category) the same kinds of political activities where no police collective bargaining exists. While I believe that collective bargaining is the most important police union-management interaction mechanism, it also would be impossible to explain the range of adversarial interactions among the various parties and the scope and depth of the unions' impacts upon substantive employment conditions without frequent reference to union political activities connected and unconnected with collective bargaining.

CONCLUSIONS

The Development of Police Bargaining

The emergence of collective bargaining in policing has fomented considerable debate and speculation among practitioners and observers about the development of the most appropriate form of collective bargaining in the police industry. While my relatively limited research sample and the situational nature of labor relations make it hazardous to generalize, it is possible to note some patterns in police union-management relationships.

Private Sector Similarities. From one perspective, police bargaining relationships appear very similar to established bargaining relationships: after a sufficient showing of interest by the police officers in a particular bargaining unit (usually defined as some portion of the police department), a third party agency (usually a state public employee relations board) conducts a collective bargaining representation election; the organization chosen by a majority of the secret ballots cast enjoys exclusive representation rights; contracts usually are negotiated with professional labor relations officials reporting to top management; the posturing and rhetoric surrounding contract negotiations is often very similar to private sector experiences; the negotiated contracts are legally enforceable and cover a wide range of employment conditions; more and more of these contracts provide for grievance procedures culminating in arbitration; and the union typically becomes the effective voice of the rank-and-file worker. In addition, the unions' impacts noted earlier are very similar to those union impacts noted in the private sector[8] and among various occupational groups in the public sector.[9]

Bargaining Structure. An examination of police bargaining structure yields some similarities to and some differences from the private sector. As with many occupational groups in private employment (and elsewhere in the public sector) who have a strong sense of separate occupational identity (electricians, plumbers, airline pilots, and teachers are a few examples), police officers have insisted upon separate bargaining representation status limited to members of their own occupational group, or craft. This craft-type of representation means that each bargaining unit is limited to members of a particular police department, in contrast to the industrial-type bargaining units that may encompass several different occupational groups (as in the auto and steel industries, for instance).[10] Further, the police insistence upon separate representation frequently means that civilian employees of the police department are excluded from the sworn officers' bargaining unit (though this separation may be less common in smaller departments).

As with many craft units elsewhere, and in contrast to many industrial-type bargaining structures, a hallmark of police bargaining arrangements and of the police labor movement generally is the strong degree of local control. While many local police unions are affiliated with larger state and national organizations, the most important representation functions and decisions are carried out in local political and collective bargaining arenas. Consequently, police bargaining arrangements appear very fragmented when compared to the huge bargaining units elsewhere (e.g., steel, autos, communications, trucking, etc.), and the national police organizations (International Conference of Police Associations, Fraternal Order of Police, etc.) will not play a very important representation role unless most police employment conditions begin to be determined at state and national levels.

From a normative perspective I hope I do see some changes along the vertical boundaries of police bargaining units regarding the representation status of lower and middle management ranks (sergeants, lieutenants, and captains). While several cities have patrolmen-only bargaining units, the more common representation pattern seems to be for the patrolmen and one or more of the supervisory ranks to be included in the same unit. Further, most cities which have patrolmen-only units also have one or more bargaining units of supervisory ranks. My preference is for patrolmen-only units with no representation rights for superior officers, and if that is not politically feasible, for separate representation units for patrolmen and superior officers. This recommendation is based upon two major considerations: management's responsibility for the delivery of services in the event of a work stoppage, and the development of a managerial consciousness among the superior ranks.

In case of a work stoppage a union's ability to create disruptive pressures is a direct function of, among other things, the proportion of sworn officers it can persuade to withhold their services. This ability is greatly reduced if management can use supervisory personnel for patrol duty. A typical strike contingency plan calls for cancellation of all leaves and the assignment of superior officers (and nonstriking patrolmen) to alternating twelve hour shifts of patrol duty for the duration of the emergency. This strategy worked in Milwaukee and New York City in January 1971 and to some extent in Baltimore in July 1974 (the Baltimore strike also brought a visible infusion of state police).[11] While management might be able to exert pressure on superior officers in an inclusive unit to remain on the job, such a situation may create severe intraorganizational problems and ill-will.

From the more important view of developing managerial consciousness among the superior ranks, the separation of patrolmen and superior officers into different bargaining units is highly desirable. In the private sector managers enter their organizations laterally and usually do not serve an apprenticeship in the ranks they will be called upon to manage. In the police service, however, everyone enters as a patrolman and there is a tendency for supervisory personnel to identify with the delivery role rather than the management role. This inclination is aggravated by the frequent lack of supervisory training and separate reward structures for supervisors.

Hopefully, police officers, police administrators, and city labor relations officials will realize that there is an important difference in the functions of patrolmen and superior officers, that along many dimensions the relationship between supervisors-managers and employees is an adversary relationship, and that the natural affinity of all those on the same side of the "thin blue line" should be subordinate to the need for a rationalization of authority relationships and the development of professionalization among the supervisory-managerial ranks. In the near future, however, I see the representation pattern tending toward inclusive units (patrolmen plus one or more superior ranks), in large part because of union pressures for such units. In the long run, I am more optimistic that the natural differences between employees and managers will assert themselves and that the union's role in prosecuting grievances and acting as the voice of the rank-and-file will cause both the unions and management to reconsider the desirability of inclusive units.

Power and Dispute Resolution. As mentioned earlier, the key factor distinguishing police bargaining (and municipal bargaining generally) from private sector bargaining is the political context in which the parties interact. Any police union's success in using bargaining to achieve its objectives depends in large part on how well the union can manipulate the relevant local and state political influence parameters to its advantage. Consequently, the power relationships between police unions and managements should be evaluated primarily in political influence terms.

Police strikes are the most visible manifestations of these power relationships. Although police strikes are illegal, several states, recognizing that these strikes might occur anyway, have provided for various dispute resolution procedures to resolve police (and other government employee) negotiating impasses without work stoppages. The nonbinding procedures are mediation and fact-finding, and the binding procedures are one form or another of arbitration. While space limitations prevent a detailed discussion of these methods, their common feature is the presence of a neutral third party who attempts to either aid the parties in reaching their own agreement (mediation, fact-finding, and final offer arbitration) or imposes his own settlement (conventional arbitration). Each method has its strengths and weaknesses, and all have proved useful at some point or another in resolving impasses and preventing work stoppages.[12] I expect that these procedures will become more common in the rules frameworks surrounding public safety labor relations, in contrast to the current increase in the right to strike for other groups of state and local government employees.[13]

Summary. As the foregoing analysis has demonstrated, police collective bargaining relationships are very situational, pragmatic, issue-oriented, and subject to change as the actors involve change. Some observers, taking a macro-level view, may focus on the similarities across collective bargaining relationships and conclude that police bargaining is and will be very similar to the experiences elsewhere in the public and private sectors. In contrast, other observers, taking a micro view, may focus on the different or unusual features of police collective bargaining and conclude that it is unique. My own view is between these two positions. While there are many similarities between police bargaining and other collective bargaining relationships, the police bargaining systems also have adapted to the unusual or unique features of the police industry, (e.g., local control, a ban on strikes, the role of discipline, etc.) and will continue to do so.

Unionism and Professionalization

For a variety of reasons, the police do not qualify as a true profession in the same manner that such occupational groups as doctors, lawyers, university professors, and clergy do.[14] Some of the reasons include: the lack of an agreed-upon functional jurisdiction for the police, an organizational (or departmental) rather than occupational locus of specialization, the lack of an intellectual knowledge base and concomitant rigorous academic training program, and a product (ends) rather than process (means) orientation toward the delivery of police services. However, there is substantial debate about the future development of the police occupation, and many members, especially at managerial levels, are engaged in a quest for professional status in the eyes of society.

Police unions have been active over several issues that relate to the professionalization process and to the quest for professional status (these two phenomena are not necessarily the same). Some of these issues include advanced education for police officers, recruitment standards, promotions, lateral entry, civilianization, corruption, and law enforcement policy matters, and the usual direction of the unions' involvements in these issues has been discussed earlier. What can be concluded from these union postures? First, there seems to be substantial conflict between the goals police unions must pursue in their role as employee self-help organizations with elected leaders representing salaried employees in bureaucratic organizations and those objectives which would further the occupation's quest for professional status and its concomitant perquisites. This conclusion is supported by the usual police union positions on professionalization issues and also by the fact that a majority of police union energies are devoted to securing basic economic benefits and job security protections for their members. For all their talk of professionalization, the goals of police unions are *conceptually* indistinguishable from the goals of unions of auto workers, steel workers, carpenters, or railroad employees.[15] In some cases they have had to oppose management efforts to initiate changes that might lead to increased professionalization (e.g., advanced education); in other cases they have had to take positions that might be conducive to establishing the prerequisites to professionalization (e.g., no civilian review) but also may have had the effect of undermining societal willingness to grant professional status. On balance, the unions' impact upon the occupation's quest for professional status probably has been negative. However, this conclusion does not mean that police unions should be blamed for policing's historically mediocre position in this country's occupational status hierarchy, nor does it mean that there is anything "unprofessional" about a police officer's decision to be a union member.

Second, I am convinced that whatever the outcome of the professionalization debate, police unions will play a major role in the formulation and implementation of any occupational changes, and perhaps even a decisive role in selected short-run situations. Police unions have shown little reluctance to aggressively assert their members' interests on a wide range of issues, and I believe the unions have displayed considerable expertise in the strategies and tactics employed to attain their goals. Those who seek to implement occupational changes, whether or not these changes are clothed in a "professionalization" terminology, will need to secure the cooperation of the police rank-and-file and their unions if these changes are to be implemented in a successful and lasting manner. The price of this cooperation may be high, but from my perspective it seems worth paying.

Some Final Comments

Police unions are here to stay. They have become the effective voice of the rank-and-file police officer in many departments, and they have become entrenched because of the desires of the employees to correct perceived inequities and grievances rather than as a result of the temporary intrusion of "outside agitators." This permanence means that police management must devote greater resources toward dealing with these new power centers, must develop consistent personnel policies, and must insist on an effective voice in the collective bargaining process (which is likely to be controlled from city hall). Second, it is important to recognize that by representing their members' interests police unions necessarily make life more difficult for management. The unions almost always require bilateral decision-making on most personnel and some policy issues, and bilateral decisions usually are more difficult to reach than unilateral ones. Third, the unions' presence usually institutionalizes and makes more visible the employer-employee adversarial relationship that exists in almost all bureaucracies. This means that union-management relationships ultimately are power-based and have considerable potential for overt conflict. However, this conflict potential should not be equated with enduring hostility, for once the parties become accustomed to their roles and the "rules of the game," their relationships usually become routinized and businesslike.

Finally, it is worth repeating an earlier point: one's normative opinions about police unions depend primarily upon one's situational vantage point. A survey of urban patrolmen undoubtedly would produce far more positive opinions of police unions than would a survey of chiefs and high-ranking command officers. My own judgment, developed from the perspective of one who enjoys the luxuries of not having to cope with union membership pressures nor with the stresses and strains produced by the union's activities, is mixed but generally positive: police unions perform many desirable representation services and are a necessary counterweight to the traditional autocratic style of management in most police departments. I support this opinion by noting that thousands of police officers today enjoy improved employment conditions because of their union efforts, and by noting that hundreds of police superior officers are better supervisors and managers because of these same union pressures.

NOTES

1. I use the term "police union" to refer to any and all police employee organizations that systematically represent their members' interests on a full range of employment conditions. Further, the label is not limited to organizations affiliated with larger organizational groups (e.g., the AFL–CIO); it can apply to organizations formally titled "associations" (e.g., the Detroit Police Officers Association), and it is not limited to organizations that have been exclusively certified as collective bargaining agents (though most unions do enjoy exclusive bargaining rights).
2. The data and opinions expressed in this chapter reflect several sources of information and years of study of police labor relations. Most of the examples and conclusions are drawn from a 1971 study of police labor relations in twenty-two cities: Baltimore, Boston, Buffalo, Cincinnati, Cleveland, Cranston, R. I., Dayton, Detroit, Hartford, Los Angeles, Milwaukee, New Haven, New York, Oakland, Omaha, Philadelphia, Pittsburgh, Providence, Rochester, N.Y., San Francisco, Seattle, Vallejo, Ca. For a detailed description of the research design and the findings of the study, see Hervey A. Juris and Peter Feuille, *Police Unionism: Power and Impact in Public*

Sector Bargaining (Lexington, Mass.: D. C. Heath, 1973). Selected other articles which explore in more detail many of the issues discussed here include: Peter Feuille, "Police Labor Relations and Multilateralism," Industrial Relations Research Association, *Proceedings of the 26th Annual Meeting* (December 1973), pp. 170–77; Hervey A. Juris and Peter Feuille, "Police Employee Organizations," in Richard Stauffenberger, ed., *Police Personnel Administration* (Washington, D.C.: The Police Foundation, 1974, forthcoming); and Peter Feuille and Hervey A. Juris, "Police Professionalization and Police Unions," unpublished manuscript. I am deeply indebted to Professor Juris for all of his previous assistance, and he deserves much of the credit for whatever strengths this paper has. In addition, I would like to gratefully acknowledge the previous research support of the National Institute of Law Enforcement and Criminal Justice, Law Enforcement Assistance Administration, U.S. Department of Justice. This support in no way implies that the Department of Justice has any responsibility for or agreement with any of the statements or conclusions expressed herein.

3. See Juris and Feuille, *Police Unionism*, Chapter 2; and Juris and Feuille, "Police Employee Organizations," in Stauffenberger, *Police Personnel Administration*. More comprehensive treatments can be found in Donald Berney, "Law and Order Politics: A History and Role Analysis of Police Officer Organizations," (unpublished Ph.D. dissertation, University of Washington, 1971); and Philip Kienast, "Policemen and Fire Fighter Employee Organizations: A Comparative Study of Historical and Sociological Factors Affecting Employee Organizational Structure," (unpublished Ph.D. dissertation, Michigan State University, 1972).

4. Patrolman pay in large cities (over 100,000 population) has increased on average about eight percent per year for the past five years, and in several cities base salaries now exceed $14,000. For a report on police and firefighter salary levels and increases through 1973, see Bureau of National Affairs, *Government Employee Relations Report*, No. 535 (31 December 1973), pp. D1–D4.

5. While the Detroit union's efforts did not remove the judge from office, union spokesmen believed that these efforts had an "informative" impact upon the local judiciary.

6. See Jerome Skolnick, *The Politics of Protest* (New York: Ballantine Books, 1969), Chapter 7; Juris and Feuille, *Police Unionism*, pp. 159–60; and Berney, "Law and Order Politics..."

7. While some of these work stoppages may have been given different labels ("blue flu," "job action," etc.), they fit the generic definition of a strike: An organized withholding of services by some or all of the members of a particular work group.

8. See Sumner H. Slichter, James J. Healy, and E. Robert Livernash, *The Impact of Collective Bargaining on Management* (Washington, D.C.: The Brookings Institution, 1960).

9. See David T. Stanley with Carole L. Cooper, *Managing Local Government under Union Pressure* (Washington, D.C.: The Brookings Institution, 1972).

10. In contrast to the craft bargaining structures in some private industries, such as in construction and maritime where the unions regulate or control entry into the trade, police unions have no control over the labor supply (i. e., they do not control hiring or access to the craft).

11. In Milwaukee and Baltimore, management was able to put more men on the street on some shifts during the strikes than would have been on duty normally. From the disruptive pressure perspective, the Baltimore strike is the only modern police strike of which I am aware that resulted in any noticeable increase in criminal and/or disorderly behavior, and these behaviors occurred almost solely during the first night of the walkout and in selected portions of the city. See The *New York Times*, 13 July 1974, p. 1; 15 July 1974, p. 1; and 16 July 1974, p. 1. I am very grateful to Mr. Robert Bomboy, reporter for the *Baltimore News-American*, for information about the Baltimore strike.

12. A good starting point for the voluminous dispute resolution literature is Thomas P. Gilroy and Anthony V. Sinicropi, "Impasse Resolution in Public Employment: A Current Assessment," *Industrial and Labor Relations Review*, 25, 4 (July 1972), 496–511.

13. One of the newest dispute resolution procedures to come into operation is final offer arbitration. For an analysis of it, see Gary Long and Peter Feuille, "Final Offer Arbitration: 'Sudden Death' in Eugene," *Industrial and Labor Relations Review*, 27, 2 (January 1974), 186–203.

14. A much more detailed discussion of the police professionalization question can be found in Peter Feuille and Hervey A. Juris, "Police Professionalization and Police Unions," unpublished manuscript.

15. Critics may respond that most other unions have no set of interests to correspond with police union interests in and attempts to influence law enforcement policy issues. However, a close examination of these police union policy efforts reveals that they stem from rank-and-file desires to develop favorable on-the-job working conditions, and as such are directly comparable to the efforts of other unions to change working conditions in the direction desired by their members.

TOPICS FOR DISCUSSION

1. Discuss whether police unions are compatible with police professionalism.

2. Discuss the impact police unions or de facto unions have had on police management's ability to deploy manpower, discipline employees, and set policy.

3. Discuss the relationship between improved working conditions and productivity.

4. Discuss the potential for the establishment of a National Police Union.

5. Discuss the reasons why police veterans belonging to unions are more interested in increased benefits while the younger police officers are concerned more with having a voice in policymaking and programs as well as increased benefits.

8

WILLIAM J. BOPP

Organizational democracy
in law enforcement

There are certain concepts that are so deeply entrenched in the
American experience that citizens in all walks of life have a respect
for them, bordering on reverence. Two of those ideals are *due process*
and *democracy*, cornerstones upon which the country rests, virtues
that distinguish America from all but a handful of other nation states.
Succinctly defined, due process has been described as:

> The right of every person to have legal proceedings according to
> the rules and principles which have been established in our system
> of law and jurisprudence for the enforcement and protection of
> private rights. The rights are given through the Fifth and Four-
> teenth Amendments of the United States Constitution.[1]

Webster defines democracy as:

> A form of government in which power is vested in the people and
> exercised through them by their elected agents.

This chapter will not attempt to deal with due process in a juris-
prudential sense, or with the concept of democracy in a political or
social way, but will discuss them in the context of police organization
and administration. Thus, the theme herein is that modified forms
of due process and organizational democracy should be instituted in
and govern the internal affairs of police departments, especially those
serving urban areas. In short, law enforcement agencies should be
democratized so that officers will be happier and more productive in
their work, administrators will be more apt to voluntarily receive the
cooperation they now must command, and citizens will be the bene-
ficiaries of police behavior molded in a freer organizational environment. On this last point rests the foundation of another theme: that

120

police officers will be more inclined to act democratically in the field if they are treated more democratically in station houses. The following discussion will begin with a description of the traditional approach to police organization, then follow with sections on internal conflict, motivation and morale, the need for a policeman to be treated as an individual, the worth of instituting a system of supportive management, and the new role and direction of codes of conduct and disciplinary actions.

THE TRADITIONAL APPROACH
TO POLICE ORGANIZATION

The dominant approach to organizing and administering police departments is characterized by structural rigidity, management by fiat, highly formal relationships, ceremonial rather than functioning policies, and overproceduralization and red tape. In this type of environment creativity is stifled and innovativeness by anyone but those in top management is often viewed as subversive, and there is little room for individual growth and self-actualization. Some specific properties of traditional police organizations follow.

The Semimilitary Posture

The American police are generally organized in a semimilitary manner, a heritage that dates back centuries. Many early settlements were originally policed by the militia during their fledgling years. Detroit was patrolled by the militia for the first one hundred years of its existence. The story was similar in many other communities, including Cincinnati and New Orleans.[2] Historical precedents that reinforced the idea of the police as a paramilitary organization included the success of the London Metropolitan Police Force, established by Sir Robert Peel in 1829, and the American Civil War, which legitimized the wearing of uniforms by officers.

Over the years the notion of the police as a semimilitary body with civil police responsibility has been almost universally accepted in law enforcement, and this philosophy is as strongly entrenched as it ever was. Rank bears close resemblance to that of the army. First-line supervisors are sergeants, middle managers are lieutenants and captains, top managers may be designated as majors or colonels, with all the attendant uniforms, insignia, and braid. Some departments have even created corporal positions.

Disciplinary practices and departmental protocol are consistent with the military tradition. Formal firearms inspections are often held in squad rooms. Full military courtesies, such as saluting, and the repeated use of the title *Sir* to address higher ranking officers, are the rule rather than the exception. Discipline for even minor infractions reflects this authoritarian regimen. Departmental rule books usually abound with strict decrees, to the extent of containing a prohibition against "conduct unbecoming an officer." Officers are expected to subordinate their individual ambitions to the needs of the department.

The Emphasis on Hierarchical Structure

Police organizations are characterized by a formal hierarchical structure: people and activities are arranged in pyramidal form.[3] At the top of the pyramid is the chief of police, while at the bottom are the patrolmen. The rest of the structure is made up of layers of management and support personnel of various rank and authority. In this form of organization, lines of authority flow downward, from the chief to managers, and ultimately to patrol officers.[4] The aim of this system is to point up and reinforce *formal* authority-responsibility relationships among personnel.

An important element of the formal police structure is chain of command. Protocol dictates that normal communication, either upward or downward, pass from the originator to the next person in the hierarchical structure, where it is eventually forwarded to the appropriate party. It is rare that a patrol officer will communicate directly with his chief about department business. Instead, the message will usually go to the officer's sergeant, then to the lieutenant, on to the captain, and up the pyramid, until it reaches the chief (if, in fact, it ever does), who may draft his reply and forward it downward along the same route.

The Chief's Role as Director

The chief's role is to direct and to supervise the department's operations.[5] In administering the agency, certain working concepts relative to the chief's responsibility are believed to have universal application. As the top man, he is the director who is expected to orchestrate the affairs of the police department by commanding, prodding, controlling, and limiting the activities of his subordinates in the chain of command. He must also develop policies that facilitate the mission of the department. Accordingly, it is considered to be of prime importance that the institution's goals are clearly defined and understood by everyone in the organization.

The chief will try to construct his agency so that only a small number of persons report directly to him. This is consistent with a widespread belief that his effectiveness will be impaired if too many subordinates are allowed to bring all but the most important matters to his personal attention. This philosophy, called span of control, is applied throughout the organization, where it consistently presupposes that effective control has very clearcut numerical limitations.

Implicit in the chief's role as director is the dogma that each individual task in the department must be formally assigned to a person or a group answerable to a single supervisor. Doctrine dictates that under no circumstances should two supervisors be placed in simultaneous control of the same task. Traditional organizational theory has consistently underscored the folly of multiple control.

Policymaking

The police executive's function as major policymaker is considered essential to the successful achievement of departmental goals. Orthodox theory holds that the chief must articulate, publish, and disseminate throughout the agency written directives that substantially limit the exercise of discretion by line officers in the field.[6] Moreover, he is expected to draft policy that relates to discipline, work flow, tasks, image, and goals, either long- or short-term. To do this he divides policies into very specific typologies and issues several separate and distinct manuals to personnel that will hold the policy inserts that he issues from time to time. The manuals may be color coded for identification purposes. The typology usually catalogs policy as General Orders, Special Orders, Personnel Orders, or Training Bulletins, depending on their function.[7] Officers are held responsible for reading the policy directives and inserting them in the appropriate manual. When they leave the department they are expected to surrender their policy manuals, in much the same way that a professional football player gives up his play book when he is traded.

The contents of these departmental play books span the widest conceivable spectrum of activities.[8] They relate to both on-duty and off-duty conduct, the wearing of the uniform, the disbursement of report forms, use of vacation leaves, and firearms policies. Most departments have policies that limit the length of hair and specifically delineate its placement (i.e., sideburns no longer than middle of the ear; mustaches neatly trimmed to a specified point at the upper lip). The parameters of police discretion are sharply curtailed by these directives, a limitation that is completely consistent with their intent. Policy on such a massive scale tends to reinforce the other traditional aspects of police organization, including the formal hierarchical structure and the semimilitary posture, while allowing the chief to oversee and direct the department's operations. Policymaking is also viewed as exclusively a function of management.

The Allocation of Responsibilities

Traditional organization theorists contend that work on a department must be divided into component parts and closely controlled by creating a system of authority whereby the central purpose of the enterprise is translated into reality through the combined efforts of specialists. Work is allocated by 1) function or purpose, 2) process or method, or 3) clientele.[9] The type of job must be clearly defined, each task must have a commander, and the division of work must be systematic.

CONFLICT

In its most ideal form, membership in a formal organization will provide a means to accomplish individual goals while aiding the fulfillment of group objectives.[10] A police department is committed to providing very specific services to a community, and it will attempt to instill in its work force productivity values consistent with this service orientation. Unfortunately, the productivity of patrol officers is not always compatible with leadership expectations, or conducive to the achievement of a sanctioned mission. The reason is that there are human currents within the organization that are constantly in motion, fluid and dynamic tides that react to stimuli in rather predictable ways. As a result, conflict often results between those who work and those who manage the work.

Internal conflict is becoming a way of life in law enforcement. Labor and management are often adversaries, rather than members of a team galvanized toward a sanctioned end. Factionalism, class differences, and personal antagonisms abound, thereby creating an atmosphere that does not foster creative group work. There are two general causes for this: 1) class conflict, and 2) the alienating nature of the work routine.

Class Conflict

Class conflict in police departments occurs between levels of rank. In industry, traditional conflict involves line workers and management. However, in law enforcement, class antagonisms are not so clearly divided. Not only are patrol officers suspicious, and often subversive of management, but also line supervisors may be in conflict with middle and upper management, and middle managers may be aloof from top managers. The purposeful separation of ranks into a formal class structure reinforced by a semimilitary posture and a rigid chain of command contributes to isolation which, in turn, emphasizes class differences and exacerbates conflict. Students of industrial relations say that class conflict in the private sector has been largely removed as a result of an acceptance of collective bargaining and organizational democracy by both labor and management. Whether this is true, and whether it can have the same effect in law enforcement, remains to be seen. What is certain is that in the police service there is continuing conflict between those who work and those who decide the ways in which work will be carried out, heightened by traditional police administration principles that have sanctified rule by fiat and fear as a dominant management strategy.

The Alienating Nature of the Work Routine

It is indisputable that the volatile, dangerous, and frustrating aspects of police work have led to alienation between policemen and citizens, and ultimately between police labor and police management. It is inherent in the job. A few years ago Robert Blauner identified four types of alienation experienced by industrial workers which can be generalized to line policemen: 1) powerlessness, a feeling that one is controlled by someone or something other than himself; 2) meaninglessness, a belief that one is simply a cog in the wheel of an organization; 3) isolation, a sense of remoteness; and 4) self-estrangement, a loss of personal identity and selfhood.[11]

Mistaking militarism for professionalism, police managers often contribute to this alienation by encouraging their subordinates to assume an aloof, detached, impersonal stance toward citizens. A result is that line officers form "isolated masses" and live by their own codes, myths, heroes, villains, and social standards. Because so many people in a department are committed to one side or another (labor or management), there are few neutral commanders capable of mediating conflicts or diluting the "mass."[12] In point of fact, a great many departments will not allow a supervisory or command officer to retain any semblance of neutrality. Kerr and Siegel have described this phenomenon, and why it leads to strikes:

> The strike for this isolated mass is a kind of colonial revolt against far removed authority, an outlet for accumulated tensions, and a substitute for occupational and social mobility. . . . The isolated mass in a classless society, more or less permanently at odds with the community at large.[13]

Effects of Conflict

Conflict between police labor and management can be a demoralizingly disruptive force that retards mission, clouds purpose, and unnecessarily alienates the people who should be interacting harmoniously to thwart crime and violence. Certainly the kind of day-to-day conflicts that occur in the performance of one's duties do little to facilitate the formal group's mandated purpose. Yet conflict can have a positive effect on a department that has created machinery to handle it.

The existence of conflict means that accumulated tensions have risen to the surface. It can help both sides, labor and management, in separating and clarifying what is in their individual and common interests. A talented police administrator will never try to stifle reasonable dissent or rational protest, for conflict brings issues into the open where they can be made subjects of social control mechanisms. Cyril Sofer has written a line about this phenomenon that is brilliant in its simplicity: "Looked on in an organizational context, such conflict can help groups secure a share of the joint product appropriate to their contribution."[14] When conflict resolution has been institutionalized into collective bargaining procedures and grievance machinery, it permits the solution of issues and makes allowances for oganizational change without the disruptive occurrences of extreme and costly internal disputes. Law enforcement is now employing methods of crisis intervention to ameliorate conflict in the community. It should do no less to resolve internal conflict.

MOTIVATION AND MORALE

There are two incredibly important human relations principles which, thus far, have either been overlooked or somewhat misunderstood by some police administrators of the autocratic genre. Unfortunately these related forces—motivation and morale—are often the precise phenomena that go a long way toward determining whether or not an agency will consistently achieve its objectives.

Motivation

Succinctly defined, motivation is a goal-seeking drive.[15] No one can motivate another person, for each individual must make himself perform. There is a great deal of managerial dialogue over how to motivate others to work, but it simply cannot be done. What managers can do is create an in-house climate that will prompt workers to achieve established goals.

There are a great number of theories on motivation, including Abraham Maslow's theory of a hierarchy of needs. In summary, Maslow propounded that man is a striving animal and that human motivation is accomplished through five levels of needs: 1) physiological, 2) safety, 3) love, 4) esteem, and 5) self-actualization. When one need is satisfied, it will no longer act as a motivator and a person will strive for a higher need until he becomes self-actualized.

Frederick Herzberg has embraced a strikingly simple theory. Herzbergian theory holds that there are very few true motivators in a person's life, but a great many demotivators. The best motivator of all, says Herzberg, is *work itself*. Pay increases are important only in that they show workers that management believes they are doing a good job. In essence, if a person finds a job challenging, exciting, personally meaningful, stimulating, and rewarding, he will be motivated to work at an optimum level. Herzberg (and others) have analyzed 16 major studies in which 16,000 workers were asked to rank, in order of importance, various aspects of job satisfaction. The ranking, in descending order of importance, was:

1. job security
2. job interest
3. opportunity for advancement
4. appreciation by supervisors
5. company and management
6. wages
7. supervision
8. social aspects of the job
9. working conditions
10. communication
11. fringe benefits[16]

The findings are almost identical to police studies that found that job security and respect were consistently placed higher in the ranking order than pay and fringe benefits.[17]

Police departments are shocked to discover that a massive pay increase and a substantial upgrading of fringe benefits often does little to soothe a militant union for long. Of course, it does pacify them for a time, but not to a state where motivation is raised and production is increased. Herzberg equates wages and fringe benefits with daily meals. They satisfy hunger as it occurs, and they can be used to prevent serious unhappiness. They are not, however, important positive motivators in his view.

There is a clear relationship between motivation and productivity. If an officer receives rewards, either intrinsic or extrinsic, which he can gain only by producing, he will produce. On the negative side, a patrol officer may be forced to produce by threats or the actual application of punishment. This is a hazardous management tactic, for a program of repression can cause revolt.

Morale

Morale, according to a classic definition, is a "social-psychological situation, a state of mind in which men and women voluntarily seek to develop and apply their full powers to the task upon which they are engaged, by reason of the intellectual or moral satisfaction which they derive from their own self-realization, their achievements in their chosen field, and their pride in the service."[18] It is generally desirable that workers exhibit high morale for two reasons: 1) people who gain considerable pleasure from work each day will have a minimal occurrence of absences from the job, and 2) high morale usually stems from a high motivation to produce, thereby assuring that the work of an agency will be carried out.[19]

Morale is a multidimensional phenomenon that can be related to productivity. In some organizations, however, workers may exhibit high morale while productivity consistently falls below the norm. Contrariwise, morale may be low and productivity high. An explanation for this lies in the type of organization in which occupational groups labor, and in management's methods. If management has placed so much emphasis on uplifting the morale of its work force that a veritable country club atmosphere exists, workers will look forward to their on-duty time because of its social value, and the motivation to produce may be minimal. Furthermore, Victor Vroom has conducted studies that indicate that a positive relationship between morale and productivity does not exist in all types of jobs.[20] According to Vroom, in jobs which are highly engineered, such as those in assembly plants, there is little correlation between morale and productivity; low morale and high productivity can coexist. But there is a high relationship between morale and productivity in complex jobs that consist of varied work. It appears that when performance depends on the individual or on a team, and not on machinery, employees with high morale will be more likely to produce than others. Law enforcement falls within this category, so morale is an important requirement for success in a police bureaucracy.

A partial list of factors that develop high group morale includes: 1) good physical and mental health in individuals, 2) personalized supervision and management, 3) fair treatment of workers by management, 4) a sense of group security, 5) a high level of training, 6) official recognition of accomplishments, 7) elimination of rumors, 8) effective leadership, 9) shared decision making and participatory management, and 10) the use of manipulative leadership techniques instead of rule by fiat. In short, organizational democracy and due process.

Even supervisors who know little about the research findings of behaviorists are able to differentiate between high and low morale in a group. Leaders have a feeling for that sort of thing. Unfortunately, line supervisors are not always anxious to report morale problems to higher authority, lest they be blamed for them. It is therefore necessary for top managers to keep themselves apprised of agency morale. Certain barometers of low morale that allow managers to gauge the department's pulse exist. They include: 1) covert criticism of working conditions, 2) tardiness and absenteeism, 3) disloyalty, 4) willful disobedience to orders, 5) visiting (i.e., ganging up on the job), 6) drifting back to the station earlier than required to be relieved of duty, 7) gossiping, 8) waste, 9) misrepresenting overtime, and 10) laxity in equipment maintenance. Management can, if it discovers low morale, try to mandate high morale or rebuke supervisors for permitting it to happen—which will be unsuccessful. Or it can create an organizational climate that will increase the likelihood of a happier, more productive work force.

THE INDIVIDUAL IN AN ORGANIZATION

According to Douglas McGregor, traditional management dogma regarding employees is that they have an inherent dislike of work, avoid responsibility, lack ambition and feel a need for close supervision. Faced by this fundamental "truth," the only course of action open to management is to exercise close control of workers and to coerce, threaten, and intimidate them in order to force them to produce. McGregor has termed this management philosophy as "Theory X." Basic to the philosophy are the assumptions that: 1) management's authority is supreme; 2) that authority is synonymous with power; 3) decisionmaking must be centralized at the top of the hierarchy; 4) control must be exercised by fiat; 5) first-line supervisors are an agent of top management; 6) policies must clearly limit worker discretion; 7) supervisory philosophy should be production-centered, not people-centered; and 8) employees gain their major work satisfaction through pay.[21]

Maslow, Herzberg, and McGregor have proved these assumptions false, and have clearly pointed up the folly of the "Theory X" philosophy. Yet, in law enforcement, authoritarian or "Theory X" management is widespread and pervasive, and it is accompanied by a command variant: paternalism, which is a basically benevolent autocracy, in which management treats its employees well by providing good pay, security, and fringe benefits. In return, the employee is expected to be cooperative, loyal, and productive. A dependency relationship is developed whereby members are expected to be docile and perform as directed. The atmosphere is much like that of a "family," with managers functioning as parents and employees as children. In times of trouble, employees are taught that the organization will stand by them *if they have been loyal.*

Modern management philosophy is grounded on a more optimistic view of the nature of man, and it is based upon a mountain of research findings. Workers are considered to be potentially creative, innovative, trustworthy, cooperative, possess an almost unlimited growth potential, wish to make a significant contribution to the organization, and desire to work constructively with others to achieve a common end. According to behavioral scientists, such as those previously mentioned, it is the job of managers to nurture and tap man's productive drives, drives which will probably remain latent if they do not.

SUPPORTIVE MANAGEMENT

In contrast to his "Theory X" principle, McGregor has developed a "Theory Y" approach, which has been so widely accepted by his colleagues that it now represents a dominant school of behavioralist thought. Advocates of this school propound that, inasmuch as people innately possess, but do not openly display the capacity for exercising initiative, accepting responsibility, and making worthwhile contributions, organizations must create an environment that is conducive to a satisfying work experience, one in which the accent is on the individual.

Employees will actively work for organizational goals if such behavior is consistent with their own goals, and it may well be consistent if management integrates the goals of the agency with those of the individual. Insofar as possible, decisions should be more democratic, rule books should be humanized, personnel policies should be rational and functional, concerned with equity, and should have some consensus among workers; colleagueship should replace the traditional superior-subordinate relationships; the semimilitary organizational structure should be softened; the chain of command should be elasticized; the primary leadership strategy should be coordination, not direction; upward communication should be encouraged.

The role of first-line supervision is essential in supportive management. Sergeants would no longer be looked upon as part of "management's team" if for no other reason than it fosters isolationism by implying that there are two teams at work in the organization. Sergeants should be part of the departmental team, advocates of both workers and managers, synthesizers of varying viewpoints, catalysts who are people-centered and production-oriented (the two ideas are not mutually exclusive). Internal discipline and control would be minimized, and the staid personnel evaluation reports, replete with ambiguous traits and easy to score, multiple choice labels would be personalized.

CODES OF CONDUCT

Traditional departmental rules are created for the purpose of controlling behavior. They may emanate from a variety of sources, but generally are found in civil service laws, general orders, special orders, training bulletins, and in departmental manuals of rules. Of all internal publications, the rule book or manual is the most important in terms of discipline. Regardless of the comprehensive nature of statutes or the extent to which a department issues information bulletins, there is a necessity for publishing a manual of rules, which has been defined by the International City Managers' Association as a guiding document that

> ... details and defines the rules, regulations, policies, and procedures which guide the police department. It establishes a systematic plan of operations to meet overall objectives at minimum operating costs. A good manual covers all major aspects of the police department's function. It is issued to every police officer.[22]

The actual thrust of a traditional manual differs in the various jurisdictions, but it will usually serve five main purposes: 1) it informs employees of standards of conduct; 2) it assists in familiarizing new employees with the department; 3) it may be used in training employees; 4) it serves as a management control device by distributing accumulated policy to personnel; and 5) it commits chiefs of police to clearcut policies.[23]

The frequency with which courts have reversed on appeal disciplinary findings handed out by police chiefs together with the rigid operating environment they help to mold have created the necessity for a more legalistic and humane approach to drafting and enforcing codes of conduct.[24] Each sentence in a manual should be written as if it will someday be scrutinized by a judge, for it may. Police commanders often possess a great deal of expertise in their field, but it takes the practiced eye of a professional to insure that codes of conduct will be able to stand the test of appeal. Accordingly, the services of the city (or county) attorney, the district attorney and the police legal advisor will be of considerable value in this regard. Moreover, in keeping with the philosophy of due process and organizational democracy, line officers should have a hand in their articulation.

The United States Supreme Court has held that the Fourteenth Amendment applies to administrative hearings, and that other long-standing rules of law are germane to what was previously thought of as "internal affairs." When codes of conduct are drafted, they should explicitly insure that a form of due process is provided. Personnel must know in advance of the existence of the rules and what they mean. There should be provisions for hearings, both internal and external, and for advance notice of charges against accused officers. Evidence against officers should be substantial enough to support charges, especially in cases that involve dismissal. In addition to the legal ramifications of codes of conduct, certain other influences should be considered by those assigned to draft manuals of rules. Two primary considerations are the opinions of officers, and the "relevant rule": can the codes be enforced?

There may be some worth to placing time limits on rules so that administrators will be forced to review codes at specified times. The IACP has suggested that general orders be reviewed every two years to determine if individual sections should be extended, amended, or deleted. Similar time limits can be placed on manuals of rules.

There appears to be some disagreement in law enforcement over the advisability of including a scale of penalties in codes of conduct. Administrators tend to believe that every case is in some way unique, and managers and hearing boards should be given wide latitude in deciding on the facts at hand without the restrictive influence of codified penalties. This would better serve the ends of justice. Some of the sharpest criticism leveled by officers at internal disciplinary practices has been in response to the inconsistency with which penalties have been applied. The inclusion of a penalty list can eliminate this complaint and give credibility to administrative due process. Professor Raymond Dahl has drafted a model disciplinary code that employs the concept. Table 8–1 is an excerpt from Dahl's suggested code.

There is a widespread "Theory X" management belief that departmental codes of conduct should contain "catch-all" regulations that can be invoked when officers misbehave without actually violating a specific rule. Catch-all sections are broadly written prohibitions that first gained legitimacy in the military and later were transferred

TABLE 8-1 *Article I Conduct unbecoming an officer*

Section	Charge	1st Offense	2nd Offense	3rd Offense
1.01	Accepting a bribe or gratuity for permitting an illegal act	Dismissal		
1.02	Failure to report in writing an offer of a bribe or gratuity to permit an illegal act	30 days	Dismissal	
1.03	Involved in a crime of moral turpitude	30 days	Dismissal	
1.04	Knowingly and willfully making a false entry in any bureau record or report	15 to 30 days	Dismissal	
1.05	Idle conversation with known gamblers while on or off duty	3 to 10 days	10 to 30 days	Dismissal
1.06	Association with known gamblers on or off duty	5 to 10 days	15 to 30 days	Dismissal
1.07	Participating in games of chance or gambling while on duty	5 to 15 days	15 to 30 days	Dismissal
1.08	Fighting or quarreling with members of the bureau	3 to 10 days	10 to 30 days	Dismissal
1.09	Using rude or insulting language or conduct offensive to the public	1 to 10 days	10 to 30 days	Dismissal

to police work. The most commonly used catch-all terminology is "conduct unbecoming an officer." Both the IACP and the Law Enforcement Legal Unit have supported the use of "conduct unbecoming" clauses. Courts have consistently held that although the law must be clearcut and definite, it is permissible to have ambiguous provisions in rule books as long as there is some specificity to formal charges. For example, an officer may be brought up on a charge of "conduct unbecoming an officer," to wit "refusing to cooperate in an internal investigation," and the action will probably be sanctioned by an appellate court because of the legitimacy of the accompanying offense. It is not the general charge of "conduct unbecoming" that courts are interested in but the accompanying incident that gave rise to disciplinary action. There is, however, more to be considered here than just the legal ramifications of a catch-all phrase. It is *inherently unjust* to charge an officer with a vague and ambiguous rule violation. Consequently, in the interest of equity, it should be eliminated. Law enforcement in America is over 350 years old, so there is no valid reason why, based upon this long-standing experience, specificity cannot be written into police codes of conduct. Officers, as individuals, deserve no less.

DISCIPLINARY ACTIONS

During the early days of law enforcement, the maintenance of departmental discipline was a rather simple undertaking. Certain standards of conduct were expected of every officer, and deviations from the norm were treated harshly. Few written rules existed, so fledgling patrolmen were expected to discover through trial, error, and paternal advice, the expected limits of their activities. Chiefs of police ruled their agencies with iron hands, meting out punishment when and where it suited them, to whomever incurred their wrath. And when the ax fell, it landed firmly, precisely, and finally. There were few provisions for equity, as police managers wielded sovereign authority over departmental operations.

Today, the situation has changed some, but only in response to judicial fiat. Although chiefs of police still have the mandated authority to enforce internal codes of conduct, they must adhere to rather strict guidelines in the event their decisions be reversed by higher authority—civil service commissions, administrative panels, courts. Moreover, the very application of disciplinary action has become quite formal in light of the rank-and-file's recent emphasis on pursuing extradepartmental appeals. The entire disciplinary process has been complicated by the hypersensitivity of line officers and by a concomitant accent in American society on justice and the rule of law in human transactions.[25]

There are three recognized philosophies of internal discipline, each of which is dependent upon the organizational structure of the agency and the weight assigned to personal rights vis-à-vis the requirements of the department. As most convenient typologies, the three philosophical categories may also represent historical periods and evolutionary processes. These three philosophies have been termed authoritarian, anarchic, and due process.[26]

The authoritarian or "Theory X" philosophy of discipline presupposes the divine superiority of managers and recognizes the fundamental right of government to apply discipline for any or no cause. It represents the earliest and most persistent type of police disciplinary philosophy. Only now is it reluctantly passing from the scene. This traditional approach was severe, irresponsible, negative, and was, more often than some would like to recall, selectively enforced.[27]

The anarchic principle stresses individual rights over departmental requirements. Employees are given wide latitude to act as they see fit either because the agency allows it or because it lacks sufficient power to compel personnel to do otherwise. In its most acceptable form, the anarchic philosophy motivates the attainment of goals through cooperative activity. However, its existence in law enforcement usually means that chief executives have lost control of their agencies and the rank and file has embarked on a sharply competitive course.

The due process or "Theory Y" theory is based on the belief that departments should draft a body of rules and administer it through a form of judicial machinery.[28] There will be prohibitions against certain specific acts, with penalties imposed for violations. Avenues of appeal are provided to convicted parties, who are afforded the opportunity to seek relief at least one step beyond the departmental level. Legal principles such as "just cause" and "double jeopardy" are considered to have validity in the due process philosophy, even though they may not be legally required in disciplinary hearings. It is by far the most desirable of the three, and the one most consistent with the brand of organizational democracy which is the subject of this essay.

A CONCLUDING WORD

Several concepts and devices have been covered in the foregoing essay which, if implemented, would go a long way toward creating a brand of organizational democracy thus far unknown in the field. Administrators may be uncomfortable with the ideas because, inevitably, they mean a loss of power. But, in the long run, there is evidence that suggests that agencies will be more productive by putting into operation these democratic concepts. In any event, police executives must move away from the autocratic philosophy so characteristic of law enforcement, and symbolized by a quote from the manager of a New England textile mill in the latter part of the last century: "I treat my men as I treat my machines." It was not long before he, and others of his ilk, discovered the difference between men and machines: badly maintained machines break down; shabbily treated men revolt.

NOTES

1. Julian A. Martin, *Law Enforcement Vocabulary* (Springfield: Charles C Thomas, 1973), p. 71.
2. William J. Bopp and Donald O. Schultz, *A Short History of American Law Enforcement* (Springfield: Charles C Thomas, 1972), pp. 27–28.
3. William Melnicoe and Jan C. Menning, *Elements of Police Supervision* (Beverly Hills: Glencoe Press, 1969), p. 8.
4. International City Management Association, *Municipal Police Administra-*

tion, 6th ed. (Washington, D.C.: International City Management Association, 1969), p. 22.

5. A. C. Germann, *Police Executive Development* (Springfield: Charles C Thomas, 1962), p. 10.
6. The President's Commission on Law Enforcement and Administration of Justice, *Task Force Report: The Police* (Washington, D.C.: U.S. Government Printing Office, 1967), pp. 19, 27.
7. ICMA, *Municipal Police Administration,* 6th ed., p. 41.
8. An indepth discussion of codes of conduct follows.
9. ICMA, *Municipal Police Administration,* pp. 20–21.
10. Ralph M. Stodgill, *Individual Behavior and Group Achievement* (New York: Oxford University Press, 1959), p. 278.
11. See Robert Blauner, *Alienation and Freedom* (Chicago: University of Chicago Press, 1964).
12. C. Kerr and A. Siegel, "The Interindustry Propensity to Strike," in A. Kornhauser, A. P. Dublin, and A. M. Ross, *Industrial Conflict* (New York: McGraw-Hill, 1954), pp. 193–201.
13. Ibid., p. 193.
14. Cyril Sofer, *Organizations in Theory and Practice* (New York: Basic Books, 1972), p. 343.
15. Elton T. Reeves, *The Dynamics of Group Behavior* (New York: American Management Association, 1970), p. 25.
16. Stogdill, p. 258.
17. President's Commission on Law Enforcement and Administration of Justice, *Task Force Report: The Police* (Washington, D.C.: U.S. Government Printing Office, 1967), p. 144.
18. Leonard D. White, *Public Administration* (New York: The MacMillan Co., 1930), p. 446.
19. Dale S. Beach, *Personnel* (New York: The MacMillan Co., 1970), p. 462.
20. Victor H. Vroom, *Work and Motivation* (New York: John Wiley & Sons, 1964), pp. 183–185.
21. Beach, p. 50.
22. International City Managers' Association, "Preparation of a Police Manual," Report No. 206 (Chicago: ICMA, 1961), p. 1.
23. Jack B. Molden, "The Police Employee Manual," *Police* (March 1972), pp. 18–19.
24. Roger McKee, "Drafting and Enforcing Police Rules of Conduct" (a pamphlet) (Chicago: Law Enforcement Legal Unit, 1970).
25. William J. Bopp, *Police Personnel Administration* (Boston: Holbrook Press, 1974), p. 300.
26. O. W. Phelps, *Discipline and Discharge in the Unionized Firm* (Berkeley: University of California Press, 1959), p. 1.
27. Leon C. Megginson, *Personnel: A Behavioral Approach to Administration* (Homewood, Ill.: Richard D. Irwin, Inc., 1967), pp. 565–566.
28. Ibid., p. 566.

TOPICS FOR DISCUSSION

1. Discuss the impact organizational structure has on employees' ability to perform their mission.

2. Discuss the impact on organization design and administration technique of the values and expectations of the individuals making up the social

system within the organization. (For example, quasi-military design and authoritarian technique.)

3. Discuss the advantages and disadvantages of class conflict existing in an organization. Is it realistic to believe that all conflict could be removed from any organization?

4. Discuss the ranking of the various aspects of job satisfaction as stated in this chapter.

5. Discuss the element of a written policy.

9

JAN C. MENNIG
WILLIAM E. EASTMAN

The delivery of services to the community

INTRODUCTION

For the past decade, police administrators have become increasingly aware of the need for improving the delivery of service to their communities. With this increasing awareness came the formulation of a variety of delivery systems that mandated organizational modifications, the design of the organization being predicated upon the types of service to be rendered and the means by which those services would be delivered.

In 1971 the Culver City Police Department began a reorganizing process from a three-divisional structure to a model that was designed to encompass the team approach to law enforcement and to provide a more adequate means of delivering service to the community.

The following article relates demographic data concerning Culver City, discusses the background information of police organization, and concludes with an examination of the organizational design of the department with its service-oriented programs.

THE CITY PROFILE

Culver City is a community of approximately 40,000 residents. It is surrounded by the city of Los Angeles, California. Every day approximately 400,000 automobiles and occupants cross its geographical boundaries, while approximately 200,000 individuals conduct business within the community. Culver City is not unique; it feels the impact of all of the problems affecting a major metropolitan area. The city has a visible minority population, mainly composed of Mexican-Americans, Orientals, and Cubans. In the sixties, few blacks resided in the city, but this is rapidly changing with recent increases in population. The general growth taking place on the west side of the Los Angeles metropolitan area has directly influenced Culver City from the standpoint of total community expansion, with its accompanying turbulence. Surrounding areas faced a fairly high crime rate, and much of the major crime in Culver City was committed by non-residents.

Everything considered, the future of Culver City is bright. The legislative body, the city management, and the community represent a strong base of support for the police department. Local developers, working with the planning department and city administrators, have transformed much of Culver City's undeveloped areas into shopping centers, townhouses, apartments, condominiums, and chain hotels. In spite of its growth, the city has retained its humanistic and neighborly attitude.

Accordingly, the management staff of the Culver City Police Department, recognizing its obligation to the community, addressed the question of its present organization in terms of dealing with present and future problems. Since that time the department's manpower has increased slightly, and the department now has 62 sworn police personnel and 44 part-time employees.

The goals of the department were to give maximum supervisory and management support to the people doing the actual "on the street police work." Management intended to make organizational changes necessary in terms of its long-range goals, commensurate with the ability of departmental personnel to adapt to change.

Over the years the department had developed a number of innovative internal and external programs, mostly community-based citizen cooperation programs, which indicated a high degree of support between the community and its police department. An extension of these programs was seen in the expansion of community resources. In the years preceding restructuring, the department was organized along the lines of the traditional three-divisional concept, i.e., uniform, investigation, and services. The management group recognized this traditional structuring of the organization restricted the free flow of information and services that was necessary to properly accomplish an expansion of resources, ensure maximum support for the "street police officer" and to meet present and future mission requirements. As a result of police management's questioning of organizational structure the city council decided to support the police department in its quest for a more practical form of organization. The council decided to employ a consultant service to aid the police department to review the organization plans and to focus on policing goals, objectives, and requirements for the city. The consultants, working with police department personnel, were to identify departmental programs, including the goals, objectives, and policies which governed the programs. In analyzing and evaluating the planning, organization, and staffing efforts of the department, the consultant group and the department eventually determined:

1. What types and numbers of personnel would be needed, based upon growth changes and crime forecasts.
2. How personnel needs related to anticipated attrition rates.
3. How personnel needs related to the police department's organizational plan.

The process resulted in the development of an organizational model described in the following article and the enumeration of other tasks for the police personnel and consultant group.

A great deal of appreciation goes to Dr. John P. Kenney, Professor of Criminology, California State University—Long Beach, for his efforts as consultant team chief and advisor. His knowledge and research aided immeasurably in the development of the resource material and development of overall policy guidelines, program identification, and objectives. Since the report, minor changes in the original model have been made to adjust to experimental influence, based upon consultation with the personnel involved. As the team building process continues, further adjustments will evolve, consistent with the department's ability to more effectively meet its challenge.

POLICE ROLES AND ORGANIZATIONS

The control of behavior of individuals or groups acting against the safety of persons or property involves the function of policing. By custom and religion, certain acts are labeled as wrongs against society. Classes of crimes or offenses against the state have emerged from the codification of laws and regulations. This is part of the behavior of a modern, complex society. These acts are also considered antisocial in nature. Respected sources have suggested that much of the world's population is still policed in the same fashion as society has policed itself since the beginning of recorded history.

John P. Kenney, *Police Administration*, 1972, states, "It is a folk system for policing which relies on control methods established by the family, the community or the tribal leaders or councils. The prevailing customs prescribe the system."

Law enforcement history would indicate that the police task has been one of considerable difficulty. In a society such as ours, with its congestion and anonymity, it is even more obvious that the police function means different things to different people, including the police. Many practitioners as well as writers in the fields of political science and public administration have called for reassessment and rethinking of the police function in American society.

Today there are over 40,000 separate agencies for enforcing law at the federal, state, and local level. These agencies are not evenly distributed among the three levels. There are approximately 50 law enforcement agencies at the federal level, 200 at the state level, and the remaining number are distributed among the many counties, cities, villages, and towns across the nation. These local police agencies have held fast to their traditional authority and responsibility for maintaining public order. What has emerged is a vast array of decentralized organizations that comprise the bulk of law enforcement influence in the United States. To say that this represents an unwieldy problem is an understatement, as these agencies employ in excess of 420,000 full- and part-time law enforcement officers and civilians. On a distribution at the local level, in excess of 300,000 officers are divided among the county and local police agencies.

Policing practices in the United States suggest that the police have a preventive role to perform in the course of their activities. Some local U.S. police organizations have adopted a preventive enforcement philosophy that embraces the view that the police should apply their knowledge and efforts to prevent the opportunity and desire to commit crime. This is hard to identify, measure, and evaluate by traditional standards. The time-honored, peace-keeping function of the police results from laws enacted to preserve order within a community. Performing the typical tasks of police work requires a variety of skills. Emergency services must be available on a 24-hour basis. Considering the inventory of tasks required by police organizations, there appears to be an absence of well-developed policies that would guide police personnel in handling the variety of activities they are engaged in. Until recently, there have been few efforts to utilize any formal planning process to develop policies and guidelines to assist police personnel in exercising their roles. The overall criminal justice system itself is composed of a number of subsystems which, at times, appear to and do work at cross-purposes. Police administrators have an important policy-making responsibility consistent with their vital role in society. Meaningful goals and objectives must be established.

Law enforcement must be identified as a process and not a purpose. We believe the primary role or goal of police in modern society is the maintenance of ordered liberty.

The criminal aspects of law enforcement have been overemphasized, as the pure "cops-and-robbers" role covers a relatively small portion of police work that contributes to maintaining order. Recognized police authorities have indicated that approximately 98 percent of current police activity involves social service assistance directed toward prevention of crime and participation in the development of an environment of stability and security. These activities have been identified by Kenney in his writings as noncoercive, while criminal, traffic, juvenile, and regulatory law enforcement have been labeled as coercive. By recognizing another major responsibility of the police as the protection of civil rights and personal liberties as a part of the total police role in society, and when coupled with those functional areas previously identified, this understanding should give initial direction for the organization, administration, and operation of a local police agency.

In its broadest sense, police administration includes all of the activities of the federal, state, and local governments, related to accomplishments of the police function.

Historically, the Wickersham Commission, in the thirties, along with *Municipal Police Administration*, published by the International City Managers' Association, 1938, and O. W. Wilson's *Police Administration*, 1950, seem to have emerged as having been the principal influencing factors in police organization in the United States.

The succeeding editions of *Municipal Police Administration* and Wilson's *Police Administration*, have been the sources of many later police changes.

During the past decade there has been considerable progress made in police organization, personnel management, and operations. This progress has not been limited to urban departments alone. Some sheriff's departments have also modernized their activities to provide better levels of local protection. This has not been effective enough and it is evident that far more miles per gallon can be obtained by keeping apace with technological advances of other disciplines. Some agencies have taken advantage of those resources while, unfortunately, others have not.

State and local police agencies have, through the years, viewed themselves as semimilitary organizations, even looking to the military for organizational and some operational guidelines. Military ranks were also adopted to go with the police unit.

Looking at formal authority, the basic policies or guidelines for the administration and operation of the police function were derived from the federal Constitution, federal law, state constitutions and laws, county and city charters, laws, and ordinances. Administrative guidelines were developed internally through the influence of legislative bodies and administrators. The various departmental guidelines were drawn up by the departments performing the police function.

The formulation of police policy must be developed from a systematic process in which important issues regarding operational behavior of people within the organization are identified, studied, and resolved. Police organizations must engage in this process and develop guidelines covering their various operations. They must also provide for a modification of guidelines based on court decisions, public pressures, and changes in legal and administrative decisions established at a higher level. Policy should have local legislative endorsement.

An examination of the behavior of local police agencies indicates that three organizational models have generally emerged. They are the traditional, Berkeley or Vollmer plan, and the modified plan. The traditional plan uses the street, or beat policeman, performing minimal street police tasks with specialists completing any followup work required. The Berkeley or Vollmer plan involves use of the beat policeman as the heart of the operation, performing all police tasks required within his geographic area of responsibility. The modified plan has the beat or street policeman performing a wide variety of tasks, including preliminary and followup investigations, with referral in those cases requiring special expertise.

Police departments that have adopted the traditional model usually have not had a very professional view toward police work and, certainly, do not maximize their resources in terms of coordinated efforts and internal human relations. These departments have not focused on common police objectives within the various functional units. It is obvious that over-specialization would result from this model.

The structures of the Berkeley or Vollmer model and the modified model have been, basically, the same. That is, a three-divisional configuration of investigation, field, and services, supervised by an office of the chief of police, containing staff activities of personnel and training, planning, and budgeting. This organizational model plan has been easy to identify with, as the majority of the medium-sized police agencies in the United States follow it. Most of the smaller departments are organized along the pattern of being divided into three shifts or watches that are somewhat self-contained. The personnel on duty handle all situations requiring police attention. Followup requiring investigation or case processing may involve the use of specialists, designated as investigators or detectives. The chief, in this type of setting, wears many hats and, in addition to administrative functions, may serve as a followup investigator. Fairly large departments have been formed using this model, only with more internal levels in the hierarchy and far more specialization of functions. The success of this model has not been as great as expected; consequently, police administrators, police officials, and academicians in the field have sought new and better ways to organize the police, borrowing from the advanced technology of other disciplines.

Robert T. Golembiewski has introduced a structuralist application. The structuralist concept is identified in Golembiewski's *Organizing Men and Power*. He identifies the organization as a large, complex social unit, in which many social groups interact. The desirable approach to organization is to have a synthesis and integration of these group interactions in a holistic manner reflecting both management and the workers' expectations. This combines the features of both the traditional formal organization and the human relations informal organization. The model in application discards the classical models and molds the concept of the human relations approach into a new theory of formal organization. This colleague model calls for organizing assigned subunits, focusing on program activities, with integration of essential sustaining or staff activities into each subunit. The colleague model is basically a team approach to organization. Relationships are not hierarchical in the traditional sense. The top level of the organization is composed of management personnel with particular expertise in a functional or program area, working together as a team to provide direction in achieving organizational goals and objectives. Subunits of the top management units may be formed to accomplish specific functions in a program area. The program teams are responsible for accomplishing the tasks of the organization. The emphasis on programs requires participating employees to develop a new look at organization and requires a professional quality of employee at all levels. The teams require the necessary expertise to perform all essential activities of the organization. That is, an operational team response for the performance of basic field activities may consist of a number of generalist police officers for routine activities, and followup experts for the more involved types of case investigations and related tasks. The product is a self-contained unit capable of performing all essential police activities and assuring the specific responsibility and accountability for performance. This concept is designed to involve all personnel in the department in achievement of established goals and objectives.

John P. Kenney, in his book, *Police Administration*, 1972, deals with the role of police in modern society. He has developed the Golembiewski colleague model into a viable police application. His contribution is the first major input to break the log-jam of much current police thinking.

THE CULVER CITY
ORGANIZATIONAL DESIGN

The Culver City Police Department has adopted a fully integrated team policing concept, using the colleague model as identified by Kenney. A description of that plan follows.

The very recently implemented reorganization of the Culver City Police Department calls for considerable changes in the duties and responsibilities for most positions. Basically, the scope of responsibilities will be broadened and a greater degree of flexibility in assignments will take place. A capability will be developed to give greater attention to cases at the time they are reported and personnel available for field patrol will be considerably expanded.

A key change in the management of the department is the establishment of a high-level planning and coordinating staff, which will become the top management team. The team consists of the chief of police, three captains, community relations, personnel and training officers, and the necessary support personnel. Initially, the units incorporated into the top management team are as follows:

Security, Plans, and Operations
Community Relations
Personnel and Training
Controller, Service, Supply and Maintenance
Internal Audit and Special Projects

An organization chart and partial manning table are included as Figures 9–1 and 9–2.

The Security, Plans, and Operations unit is responsible for intelligence, criminal case investigation coordination, Project Culver, and traffic analytical work. A captain is in charge of the unit but will have a greater responsibility for planning and coordinating all of the departmental activities related to operations, investigations, and juvenile control work. He also will perform a control function to assure the work related to operations, investigative, and juvenile control programs is effectively and efficiently carried out.

The lieutenant in the Security, Plans, and Operations unit is responsible for the intelligence efforts of the department and will assist in the coordination of the investigative efforts and license investigations. He also is responsible for coordination of case investigations. This lieutenant will not have investigative responsibility but will audit and coordinate the investigative efforts of the investigation personnel of the operation teams.

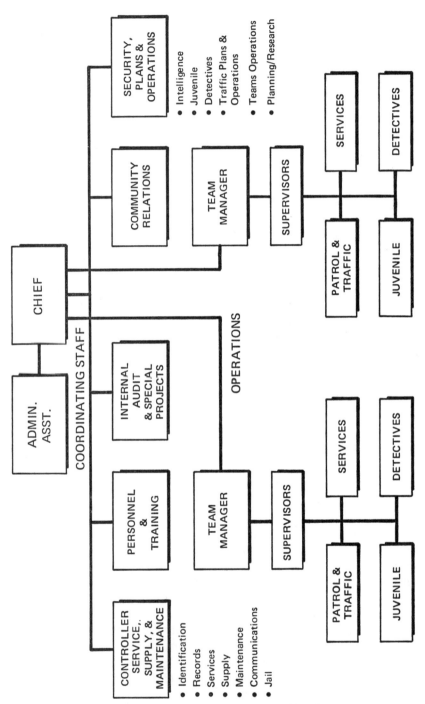

FIGURE 9–1   *Organization chart—Culver City police department.*

Two agents, one a policewoman, are responsible for the coordination of juvenile cases handled by the operating teams and have specific responsibility for Project Culver. They also provide on-sight support to the operations teams both in the station and in the field.

One agent is responsible for the traffic analytical work, traffic engineering, and traffic educational activities of the department. He

	Coordinating Staff	Staff Support Personnel	Team Personnel	Total
CHIEF	1 Chief of Police			1
CAPTAINS	1 Security, Plans, & Operations *1 Controller, Service, Supply, & Maintenance	*1 Administrative Assistant		3
LIEUTENANTS	1 Internal Audit & Special Projects	1 Intelligence & Det. Coordinator	2 Team Mgrs.	4
SERGEANTS			6 Team Supv's.	6
AGENTS	1 Personnel & Trng. 1 Community Relations	2 Juv. Coordinators 1 Traffic Coordinator	15 Operations	20
PATROLMEN			28 Operations	28
TOTAL SWORN	6	5	51	62
CIVILIAN	1 Dept. Secy. 1 Secy. (SPO) 1 Secy. (CSSM) 1 CSA (CSSM) (P)	1 Record Supervisor 1 Stenographer 2 Record Clerks 1 I.D. Officer 1 Jailer 1 Parking Enf. 1 Social Worker 1 Crossing Gd. Supv. 14 Crossing Gd. Supv. (P)	4 Comm. Oper. 1 Comm. Oper. (PEP) 1 Team Secy. 5 CSA (P) 6 CSA (PEP)	44
TOTAL DEPARTMENTAL PERSONNEL	10	28	68	106
FUTURE UNDER M.L.E. CONCEPT SWORN PERSONNEL	Chief of Police & Lts. I & II	Sgts. I & II and/or Agents III	Lts. I & II Sgts. I & II Sgts. I, II, & III Ptl. I, II, III, & IV	

* Scheduled to be replaced by a civilian employee.
(P) Part-time employees.

FIGURE 9-2 *Culver City police department personnel distribution by rank (budgeted positions as of 1/1/74).*

coordinates the work of the Traffic Commission and the departmental responsibilities for traffic engineering.

The Internal Audit and Special Projects unit performs a function similar to that of an Inspector General. The unit is headed by a lieutenant who is second-in-command of the department and is responsible for the review of planning of the field operations programs as well as investigation and juvenile control. He assures through review and analyses that the field operation efforts are continuously directed toward achievement of established goals and objectives. Emphasis is on programs, in particular the overall operations, traffic control, general crime control, crime repression, and services. The unit is responsible for the review of planning and coordination of special projects and special events for which the department has responsibility.

The Controller, Services, Supply and Maintenance unit is responsible for budget, identification, records, services, supply, and maintenance. The unit is headed by a lieutenant who, in addition to directing the efforts of the several functions, is responsible for integrating the functions with the operational programs.

The Community Relations, and Personnel, and Training units are each staffed by one agent. In addition to the normal responsibilities, they have the added task of closely planning and coordinating their efforts with other top management units and the operations team.

The operations teams are responsible for patrol, all followup case investigation, traffic enforcement and accident investigations, juvenile control, and service support activities. Each team, during its 12-hour tour of duty, is responsible for all departmental program activity required to achieve overall departmental goals and objectives. More specifically, each team consists of personnel with a capability of performing all required police tasks, including case investigations as they occur. Necessary followup investigative work required for the more involved cases is to be expected and will be accomplished by the teams.

Two operations teams, Teams A and B, are responsible for the old early morning (Watch I), day (Watch II), and evening (Watch III), watches. Each of the teams is headed by a lieutenant. Teams A and B each have sergeants and agents for supervision. Personnel assigned to the operations include detectives, juvenile officers, and all agent personnel not otherwise assigned. Currently, the two teams cover periods: 7:00 A.M. to 4:00 P.M. (Team A) and 4:00 P.M. to 7:00 A.M. (Team B).

Including the chief and his administrative assistant, eleven departmental sworn personnel are assigned to the top management team units. Thus, fifty-one sworn personnel are available for assignment at the operational level. Considering days off and vacations, this leaves approximately thirty-two sworn officers available for field duty, including the team managers and supervisors, for each 24-hour period. These are assigned to watches based upon workload evaluations.

All officers on duty are to be field available on a regular basis except for one uniformed officer in the station to support the desk communications operations and/or internal security purposes. This includes supervisors and managers. The utilization of such a requirement provides the personnel in the field with much-needed direction.

Dispatchers, records, and other service personnel are nonsworn and provide the essential station personnel complement. Each watch is adequately staffed without unnecessary sworn personnel in the station. Deployment to each watch is based on workload requirements.

In order to provide a complete police service, the Culver City Police Department engages in three broad categories of activities:

1. Programs concerned with achieving the departmental goal and objectives;
2. Activities required to support directly the primary programs;
3. Administrative activities essential for management of the department.

How well these categories are clearly defined and meshed together determine the effectiveness of departmental operations.

A program approach to operations instead of the previous functional unit approach is completely justified. As a result, a system for continuous audit and evaluation will be developed for appraising records, vehicles, communications, and field support equipment requirements. The top management team will thus be responsible for planning, coordinating, and overall audit of all implemented programs and systems. The staffing requirements will then be based on workload data and definitive policy decisions. This team approach to organization was adopted with emphasis on integration of functional activities versus unit fragmentation.

The goal of the Culver City Police Department is the achievement of excellence in the maintenance of ordered liberty. Some logical objectives are listed as the assurance that the orderly activities of the community may proceed; the protection of life and property against criminal attack; the provision of services to the individual members of the society and to other governmental units; the prevention of crime and delinquency; and, the creation of an environment of stability and security in the community.

The policy guidelines established for the Culver City Police Department are stated here for directing basic departmental operations:

1. The police shall enforce, in a reasonable and prudent manner, all federal, state, and local laws and ordinances relating to the control of crime and regulation of conduct.
2. The police shall treat all persons with dignity and respect and in accordance with the dictates of the federal and state constitutions amplified by judicial decisions as related to individual civil liberties and civil rights.
3. The police shall take such action as may be necessary and operate in such a manner as to assure the citizens of Culver City that orderly activities of the community may proceed without disruption from criminal and irresponsible elements.
4. The efforts of the police department shall be so directed as to help in the creation of an environment in the community which will prevent the occurrence of asocial and anti-social behavior.
5. The police shall be responsible for the protection of life and property from criminal attack and, in emergency situations, when the welfare of the community is threatened.
6. The police shall cooperate and assist citizens of Culver City and units of the city, county, state, and federal government with such problems in such situations as customs and traditions dictate, in matters both criminal and noncriminal.
7. The Culver City Police Department shall treat all persons equally and with fairness, irrespective of race, ethnic group, creed, or social status.

These guidelines must be complemented by the establishment of policing objectives. The guidelines represent operating policy. At its most complex level policy is behavior, and as such, the development of program guidelines was accomplished by conference with the staff and line personnel of the department in an extended series of workshop sessions. Through this process of consultation we collected a framework of guidelines. The result of the workshop sessions is attached as Figure 9-3.

Current challenges to the proprietorship of authority in organization suggest the increased desirability of recognition that management theory today is characterized by a slow but ever-present evolution of classical thinking, influenced by new or revolutionary ideas developed outside the traditional sources of public administration or management doctrine.

The department, during the past two or three years, has engaged in a series of "do-it-yourself" organizational development (OD) processes, with the established objectives of OD. OD will enable the

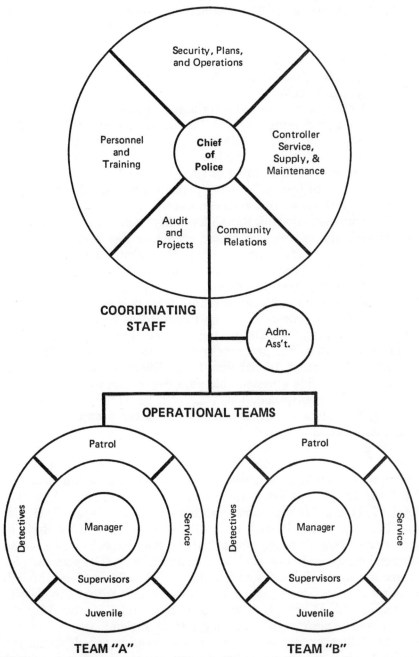

FIGURE 9-3 *This simplified characterization of the organizational model of the Culver City police department more clearly depicts the relationships that exist within the coordinating staff and the operational teams, than does the traditional, hierarchical organization chart.*

department to deal with the changes taking place in our environment.

McGregor has said, "The distinctions between line and staff are being blurred." This is recognized in our reorganization, which has embraced the colleague concept.

We also know that OD is not an end unto itself but a management tool, using behavioral science knowledge to increase organizational effectiveness and health.

This technique has proved most useful and we are expanding our program to include support from the University of Southern California's School of Public Administration in an effort to achieve greater team orientation and confidence in problem-solving.

Reinforcement and training in these skills will be undertaken on a routine basis to insure involving personnel whose roles have been changed and whose needs have been altered.

The administration of the Culver City Police Department, together with the city council, recognized long ago that in order to maximize the agency's service level, the talents and abilities of individuals within the organization should be broadened and increased. Several programs contributed to this upgrading process in the 1960s. Currently, with the advent of team policing, a continuation of the upgrading process has been identified as being imperative if departmental personnel are to function at the necessary level of effectiveness within the program approach to law enforcement. The department's concept of Mission Level Effectiveness (MLE) was developed to provide a measurable objective within each rank classification in the organization. This concept is based upon performance, training, and education at each level. It establishes requirements for each classification and grade.

Mission Level Effectiveness calls for modification of the existing rank structure. Eventually, the captain rank will be phased out by attrition. The ranks of lieutenant and sergeant will be broadened to Lt. I and Lt. II, and Sgt. I and Sgt. II. Agents will be in three skill levels: I, II, and III. Patrolmen will have a four-level span: I, II, III, and IV. Ascendancy in each rank will be based upon the criteria of performance, training, and education, and the plan calls for increased financial compensation at each level of ascendancy. The plan calls for promotion to classifications such as Lt. or Sgt. to be attained through meeting civil service requirements. Advancement within the classification, i.e., Lt. II or Sgt. II will be by merit raise approved by the Chief based on performance, training, and education.

The future impact of this plan will broaden the department's ability to more effectively utilize civilian personnel and to maximize its effectiveness by capitalizing on personnel resources without unnecessary rank/assignment restrictions.

Eventually, MLE calls for a revamping of the current organizational assignments. Eligibility for appointment to the various positions within the agency are planned as follows:

Coordinating Staff
(principal staff positions)

Ultimately, the position of Controller, Service, Supply and Maintenance Director will be filled by a civilian employee. Other positions, as principal members of the Coordinating Staff will be filled by Lts. I and II. Temporary, or transitional, assignments within the Coordinating Staff may be filled by Sgts. I and II and by Agents III.

Staff Support Personnel
(second level staff positions)

Current plans call for the Administrative Assistant position to be filled by a civilian employee. Assignment to the remaining staff support positions will be filled by Sgts. I and II, and Agents III.

Team Personnel

Team Manager positions will be occupied by a Lt. I or II. When a Lt. is assigned as Team Manager he will receive an additional 10 percent salary increment. The three skill levels of Agent and the four police officer skill levels will comprise the remainder of the operational team personnel.

With the eventual stabilizing of the classification structure, rotation of assignments for the purpose of individual and organizational growth will be accomplished with ease and will permit advance scheduling to allow for reasonable departmental planning and personal education plans.

Considering the future trends in organization, administration, and management, we believe three major points will emerge as changes to come: changes in the external environment; increasing size of organizations creating a need to focus on groups rather than individuals; informational technology that will require vastly different structures and processes.

We believe we are observing a merging of the theories of macrotheory and microtheory, where management is now regarded as a comprehensive system composed of various subsystems.

Good organization theory should explain the behavior of individuals and groups in organizations and also the collective behavior of organizations within their environment. Accordingly, our management group has identified the principal elements and components of organization to be: description of people in the organization; description of organizational goals and objectives; the role structure; and, the environment of the organization.

With these concepts it is hoped that the Culver City Police Department will be able to enter the 21st century with a degree of optimism in meeting future challenges.

CRIME REPRESSION PROGRAM

Objectives

1. To control crime.
2. To eliminate actual or suspected opportunity for wrongdoing.
3. To regulate conduct.
4. To create an environment of security and stability in the community.
5. To provide services.
6. To prevent crime.

Policy Guidelines

1. Team managers shall provide adequate number of men, at any given time, to handle official reports and maintain conspicuous patrol, consistent with our current level of service.
2. One-man patrol car operation shall be maintained except as may be required.
3. A radio car district plan will be used as a basis for distribution of the workload in terms of:
   Called-for services.
   Inspection.
   Observation patrol.
4. Field supervision will be maintained at all times.
5. District radio car officers will be responsible for the complete investigation of all cases, including preservation of evidence, making arrests, except in those cases that interfere with the performance of regular duties and those that require the attention of specialists.
6. Two or more district radio car officers will be dispatched on all calls for service wherein the nature of the situation is not readily ascertainable from the complainant and a danger may exist.

7. Field officers shall *request assistance* when making an arrest or when inspecting suspicious situations or circumstances.
8. District radio car officers will make inspections of all business and industrial establishments during hours not regularly occupied.
9. District radio car officers will constantly be available for area coverage in assigned districts and to perform tasks relating to department goals. This means appropriate action when crime is committed in the presence of the officer and appropriate processing of all requests for services, criminal and noncriminal.

INVESTIGATION PROGRAM

Objectives

1. To make a critical search for truth and information relative to all criminal and noncriminal cases.
2. To gather facts and data on criminal cases in order to effect their proper disposition.

Policy Guidelines

1. Police agents shall aid and assist district radio car officers in making investigations when required.
2. Police agents shall be responsible for the followup investigation of all criminal cases that cannot be completed effectively or efficiently by district radio car officers.
3. Police agents shall have the responsibility for the complete investigation of all criminal cases that require technical attention, such as fraud, forgeries, and extortions.
4. Police agents shall assist in the investigation of all complex cases such as safe burglaries, homicides, and forcible rapes.
5. Police agents shall apprehend offenders and recover property when such is not accomplished by patrol officers.

TRAFFIC PROGRAM

Objectives

To keep order on the streets and highways—to make their use safe and expeditious.

Policy Guidlines

1. District radio car officers shall be responsible for enforcement of all traffic violations, regulation of the movement of traffic, and investigation of accidents.
2. District radio car officers will be responsible for the complete investigation of all traffic cases including preservation of evidence and making arrests, except in those cases that interfere with the performance of regular duties and those that require the attention of specialists.
3. The principles of selective enforcement and visible patrol shall prevail.
4. All traffic accidents, injury, fatal, and noninjury, will be investigated.
5. Parking control activities shall be performed by the Parking Enforcement Detail; however, district radio car officers shall enforce those violations observed and act upon complaints received.
6. Planning for traffic control activities and liaison with the Traffic Commission shall be a staff function under the traffic coordinator.

CRIME PREVENTION PROGRAM

Objective

To aid in the correction of those factors or conditions that predispose or precipitate people's activities to antisocial behavior.

Policy Guidelines

1. District radio car officers shall be alert for conditions and circumstances that provide an opportunity for crime to occur, and to make every effort to eliminate them.
2. Continuous coordination and cooperation shall be maintained with business and community organizations to promote education programs concerned with the prevention of crime.
3. The Community Relations Coordinator shall coordinate crime prevention activities as they relate to:
   Speakers bureau
   Security inspections
   Education material distribution
4. District radio car officers shall exercise control over the conduct

of persons who engage in asocial or antisocial behavior and conditions conducive to such behavior.

JUVENILE PROGRAM

Objectives

1. To discover delinquents, potential delinquents, and conditions inducing delinquency.
2. To investigate delinquency and its causes.
3. To aid in the rehabilitation of youthful offenders through referral programs.

Policy Guidelines

1. District radio car officers shall be responsible for the complete investigation of all juvenile cases including preservation of evidence and making arrests, except in those cases that interfere with the performance of regular duties and those that require the attention of specialists.
2. Juvenile agents shall aid and assist district radio car officers in making investigations when required.
3. Juvenile agents shall make necessary background diagnostic investigation of juveniles involved in cases in order to objectively make appropriate dispositions.
4. Juvenile coordinators shall advise on final disposition of all juveniles apprehended or otherwise involved in cases.
5. Juvenile coordinators shall supervise and coordinate the activities of Project Culver with the department and the community.
6. Juvenile coordinators shall cooperate and coordinate with community agencies for the purpose of preventing crime and delinquency.

COMMUNITY RELATIONS PROGRAM

Objectives

1. To promote a spirit of trust and cooperation between the police and every segment of the community.

2. To maintain an awareness of the needs of the community and to deal appropriately with the community's needs.

Policy Guidelines

1. Every officer must demonstrate the knowledge, technique, and capacity to provide the type of police service that the people have a right to expect.
2. Superior officers shall by example demonstrate and shall instruct subordinates in proper deportment and desirable attitudes in their dealings with the public. It is not sufficient that officers do a professional job of law enforcement. It is of equal importance that everyone be convinced that such is the case.
3. Petitions, committees of protests, appeals for assistance, and letters or other forms of complaint, shall be given prompt personal attention and careful study by team managers. Every effort shall be made to correct improper conditions or, if proper, to render the assistance requested.
4. Every member of the department, individually and collectively, must recognize the principles of constitutional guarantees, and at all times, by official and personal conduct, demonstrate such recognition.
5. The planning and coordination of the department's community relations programs shall be the responsibility of the Community Relations Coordinator; however, the accomplishment of these programs rests with every member of the department.

PERSONNEL PROGRAM

Objectives

1. To provide effective and orderly management of personnel resources.
2. To endeavor to obtain the highest caliber of personnel possible.

Guidelines

1. The department shall maintain standards designed to recruit qualified personnel in accordance with POST (Police Officers Standards and Training) standards.
2. The department shall maintain adequate records of all personnel.
3. The department shall provide criteria and methods for continual evaluation of personnel.

4. Supervisors shall be responsible for the systematic evaluation of their personnel.
5. The department shall obtain the best equipment and supplies for the personnel, consonant with the needs of the department.
6. Personnel Coordinator shall maintain liaison between the department and the personnel department.

TRAINING PROGRAM

Objectives

1. To determine training needs.
2. To establish realistic training goals.
3. To develop a variety of training sources to meet these goals.

Guidelines

1. The coordinating staff shall determine criteria for minimum annual training requirements.
2. The training coordinator shall gather and assemble material to be presented to the team managers for roll-call training.
3. The training coordinator shall maintain training records on all employees.
4. The training coordinator shall examine (explore) available federal and state training grants.
5. The training coordinator shall provide liaison between the department and the educational incentive board.
6. The training coordinator shall provide coordination between the department and POST.
7. The training coordinator shall coordinate all recruit, in-service, and roll-call training programs.
8. The training coordinator shall coordinate and provide necessary training programs as specified under POST requirements.

SUPPORT SERVICES PROGRAM

Objectives

To facilitate operations of the line activities.

Policy Guidelines

Records of all police actions taken shall be made.

Records shall serve to control offense classification and completeness of investigation.

Records shall be available and shall be used to aid in all police operations.

Only bonafide agencies or persons other than departmental personnel shall have access to departmental records for reference purposes.

Facilities and equipment shall be maintained in good order at all times.

Criminalistics work shall be available for investigation support, including liaison with competent police laboratory.

ADMINISTRATIVE SERVICES PROGRAM

Objective

To provide for effective administration, management, and organization of the department.

Policy Guidelines

1. All policies shall be consonant with achievement of the objectives of the department.
2. Direction of the department shall be for the purpose of achievement of maximum coordination and control.
3. Planning shall be carried on for the purpose of coping effectively with tactical and strategic problems.

CONCLUSION

In order to successfully deliver service to its community, a police department must carefully analyze the community and its service needs, formulate programs that will act as vehicles for the delivery of those programs, and create an organizational structure that will allow for the most expeditious delivery of these programs to the community. Only when these three steps have been completed, is a department ready to attempt the delivery itself. It will always be necessary to modify program plans so as to insure the practicality of their operation. However, with these foundations firmly in place, the efficient delivery of services to the community is greatly facilitated.

TOPICS FOR DISCUSSION

1. Discuss how the traditional organizational structure restricts the free flow of information.

2. Discuss why it is necessary to make operational or organizational change commensurate with the ability of departmental personnel to adapt to change.

3. Discuss the advantages and disadvantages of each model of police organization.

4. Discuss the team policing concept as it relates to the college model and the impact this approach has on personnel problem-solving abilities.

5. Discuss the approaches being used by the Culver City Police Department to utilize the total talent of its personnel.

10

ROBERT R. J. GALLATI

Police technology
and the challenge of crime

Police technology could readily be described as having gone through three basic stages during the decade of the sixties and the early seventies:

1. The pre-President's Commission on Law Enforcement and Administration of Justice phase;
2. The pre-Law Enforcement Assistance Administration phase;
3. The SEARCH (System for Electronic Analysis and Retrieval of Criminal Histories) phase.

At the same time that police technology developed more sophisticated solutions to the challenge of crime, there slowly developed what some people believe to be a countervailing force that may be summed up as a deep concern for personal privacy. The excesses to which some law enforcement agents went in the application of technology caused a hue and cry among the citizenry and a fear of "Big Brother." With Watergate and related revelations there is today greater concern among more groups of people than ever before that police technology can lead America in the direction of a police state and ultimately erode personal liberty. We shall carefully examine these concerns in this article, but let us begin by examining the status of police technology as it has developed in recent years, as it currently exists, and its prospects for the future.

During and after World War II, American society underwent a scientific and technological revolution that radically changed our ways of doing things. However, this dramatic change had surprisingly little impact upon police agencies. The two-way radio motor patrol car and laboratory-based criminalistic techniques seemed to be the basic response of the police community to the technological revolution.

Planning, research, and development were largely ignored, and virtually no attention was given to the totality of the criminal justice system of which the police were but a single component. The courts and the correctional arms of the criminal justice system were even less progressive than the police. As crime rates continued to rise at an alarming rate, it became obvious that something was amiss in law enforcement operations, and in courts and corrections as well. The most readily apparent defect in the criminal justice system was its failure to take advantage of technology and particularly the new technology involving systems analysis, operations research, and the application of computer capabilities.

A very apt description of the situation that had existed in the past and persisted during the early sixties is to be found in the Report of the President's Commission:[1]

> In an age when many executives in government and industry, faced with decision-making problems, ask the scientific and technical community for independent suggestions on possible alternatives and for objective analyses of possible consequences of their actions, the public officials responsible for establishing and administering the criminal law—the legislators, police, prosecutors, lawyers, judges, and corrections officials—have almost no communication with the scientific and technical ommunity.
>
> More than two hundred thousand scientists and engineers are helping to solve military problems, but only a handful are helping to control the crimes that injure or frighten millions of Americans each year. Even small businesses employ modern technological devices and systems, but the Nation's courts are almost as close to the quill pen era as they are to the age of electronic data processing. The police, with crime laboratories and radio networks, made early use of technology, but most police departments could have been equipped 30 or 40 years ago as well as they are today. Hospitals and clinics draw heavily upon the most recent developments in engineering and medical science, but the overwhelming majority of reformatories, jails and prisons are, technologically speaking, a century or more in the past.
>
> This lack of contact between criminal justice and science and technology is true even in the federal government, where, as recently as 1965, the Justice Department was the only cabinet department with no share of the roughly $15 billion federal research and development budget.

Recognizing the seriousness of the situation and in keeping with its mission, the President's Commission established a task force on science and technology in April 1966. The task force gave major attention to computer technology, information systems, communications engineering and systems analysis, since these appeared to be the greatest unrealized potentials. The Commission believed that the greatest opportunity for immediate improvement was in the area of police operations, and so the task force looked particularly hard at the police, and somewhat less hard at courts and corrections. This establishment of the task force on science and technology marks the end of an era of police neglect of technology and the end of the scientific community's isolation from the challenge of crime.

This is not to say that there were no stirrings among law enforcement professionals prior to the establishment of the task force, nor that the only efforts along these lines were initiated by the federal government. As a matter of fact, state action had begun before the establishment of the President's Commission, as is typified by the programs announced as early as May 1963 by the New York State Identification and Intelligence System (NYSIIS). NYSIIS was conceived in 1963 as a computer-based central facility that would serve police and criminal justice agencies throughout the state of New York. In support of the normal daily operation of these participating agencies today, the fully implemented system provides rapid access to summary criminal history, as well as detailed criminal rehabilitative and modus operandi data on subjects; rapidly transmits graphic data, such as photographs and fingerprints, throughout the state; maintains files of personal appearance data, latent fingerprints, fraudulent checks, warrant-and-wanted notices, and provides facsimile scanning and computer-based searching of all fingerprints on file as well as arrest and disposition reports. All of these computer-based procedures are performed with greatly increased scope, accuracy, and efficiency.

The function of fact coordination, with speed, accuracy, and completeness, is the principal contribution of NYSIIS in the battle against crime. For example, many advantages are derived from the data files in one police agency being immediately available to the other 610 police agencies of the state and to additional agencies performing subsequent activities in the administration of criminal justice. All agencies enrolled in the system provide certain types of data in their possession that pertain to their activities and gain direct access to appropriate identification, criminal history, and analytical files on cases of interest.

As NYSIIS developed during the early years it worked closely with the President's Commission and its task force on science and technology. The police profession was never to be the same again, for already in 1966 the predecessor of the Law Enforcement Assistance Administration (LEAA)—the Office of Law Enforcement Assistance—began to parcel out federal grants to police departments and law enforcement agencies across the nation. It became evident that the very limited amount of money available at that time was insufficient; so in 1968, the Safe Streets Act was passed, carrying with it great promises of vast sums of money available to improve police and other criminal justice agencies in their attempts to meet the challenge of crime. The pre-Law Enforcement Assistance Administration phase was concerned with establishing the ground rules for grants and a fundamental rationale upon which massive allocations of federal funds could be properly structured. This period saw relatively small grants being given to police agencies and to special agencies serving law enforcement (such as NYSIIS). An example of the type of grant given by the Office of Law Enforcement Assistance was the Automatic License Plate Scanning (ALPS) grant to NYSIIS.

Early in 1966 NYSIIS received a $180,000 federal grant under the Law Enforcement Assistance Act of 1965, for the purpose of partially funding a NYSIIS research and development program directed towards the following goals:

1. To initiate a critical and objective research study of the stolen vehicle problem on a national and statewide basis to determine where modern technology might be applied effectively to impact the problem.
2. To conduct a limited engineering feasibility program to develop one or two conceptual approaches for the automatic mass scanning of automobile license plates, to a point where a cost-effectiveness evaluation of this method might be made on a firm basis.
3. To develop necessary prototype automatic equipment where warranted.
4. To install and operate any developed prototype equipment for a limited period to gain minimal operational experience.
5. To write a comprehensive report embracing engineering system details and operational experience. This report is to be widely distributed, and NYSIIS personnel will be made available to assist all law enforcement agencies interested in adopting the system.

A grant of $180,000 may not seem very large to us today, after several billion dollars have been spent by LEAA, but at that time it represented a substantial portion of the total federal funds available. It also represented a commitment to planning and research, as opposed to the purchase of hardware. It must be noted that the activities of the President's Crime Commission and the work on the various Reports of the Commission were also subsidized by the couple of millions of federal funds then available to law enforcement for the first time in history.

This period of groping toward the application of technology in law enforcement to meet the challenge of crime came to a climax with the passage of the Safe Streets Act and the massive infusion of federal dollars into the various components of the criminal justice system.

A whole new world opened up as consulting firms, manufacturers, technologists, inventors, authors, and vendors of all kinds descended upon the law enforcement profession en masse. Many of these people, attracted suddenly to the vast sums appropriated by Congress, were very helpful in overcoming the technological lag that had previously kept the police on the sidelines while our nation entered the space age—during the period when computers became supreme status symbols of their efficiency and progressive operation. On the other hand, many charlatans took advantage of the naivete of the police and literally sold them a "bill of goods." This was the time when police chiefs bought tanks and helicopters and gadgets and gimmickry of all sizes, shapes, and forms.

It was a trying time for all criminal justice professionals, but it was particularly challenging to the police. Some chiefs of police "goofed" badly, and, because of their inexperience with technology, poorly managed the funds made available to them; others, such as Clarence M. Kelley in Kansas City, Missouri, gained a very favorable national reputation, largely because of his effective use of the new technology to meet the challenge of crime. Henceforth, it is safe to say, no chief of police in America is likely to be entirely successful unless he can deal with law enforcement technology. It is no longer simply desirable that a police chief be sufficiently well educated to cope with advanced technology; today it is absolutely essential that the professional police executive—indeed the professional police officer—understand how to handle problems posed by the technological revolution in law enforcement.

It was very apparent to the Administrators of the new Law Enforcement Assistance Administration, which was created by the Safe Streets Act, that there had to be some mechanism to monitor funded technological developments. This was essential to assure that grants were judiciously placed where they were most likely to be effective and that duplicate grants for the same or embarrassingly similar research and development were avoided (i.e., re-inventing the wheel). It was also of vital importance that there exist a means of disseminating to all interested agencies the recommendations and conclusions resulting from grants for innovative and state-of-the-art research. Technology transfer was essential to optimize the utility of these costly grants.

Into this environment of rampant and ingenious grantsmanship the LEAA introduced a new concept in the control of technological development. Sensing that computer-based information systems and the various technologies impacting these systems were truly at the very heart of effective technology in the field of law enforcement, LEAA created SEARCH (System for Electronic Analysis and Retrieval of Criminal Histories). (It is interesting to note that LEAA came to the same conclusion in 1969 that NYSIIS had come to six years earlier—the core of police technology is based on information of one type or another.) This marked the beginning of the current era of police technology in most of its manifestations. This is not to say that some research and development has not been effectively pursued outside the aegis of SEARCH, but it *does mean* that many of the most typical and significant police technological advances have been generated by the SEARCH Project Group.

No chapter on police technology would be complete without recognition of the contributions of SEARCH, both in terms of what it has meant to the development of law enforcement science and technology, and its enormous role in awakening the police profession to the imperatives of personal privacy. The SEARCH System (and the various spinoffs that it has provided) is probably one of the greatest advances in the police profession that has occurred in this century. Project SEARCH began as a voluntary multistate effort to demonstrate the value and feasibility of a criminal justice data file and statistics system that is based on automated files created and maintained by individual states and providing for the interstate transfer of data. Originally 10 states participated in this LEAA funded demonstration project during 1970; today all 50 states are members of the SEARCH consortium. Originally the major thrust of SEARCH was to develop a compatible criminal offender record that could be exchanged between states on a nationwide basis. A secondary objective was to design a computerized criminal justice statistics system based upon the transactions (i.e., arrest, correction, court sentence, probation, parole, correctional time, etc.) which generated the "criminal offender record." Both of these goals were soon proven feasible and the FBI National Crime Information Center Criminal History Program was initiated to carry out the need for a computerized central clearing house to facilitate the interstate exchange of "criminal offender records." Transaction-based statistical systems are currently being developed in a number of states with generous financial support from LEAA through the medium of the SEARCH program.

Some of the additional projects that have been undertaken by SEARCH include:

1. Development of security and privacy concepts and standards;
2. Study of holographic fingerprint identification/verification;
3. Demonstration project involving the satellite communication of fingerprints and criminal history records;
4. Automation of fingerprint identification bureaus;
5. Standardization (nationally) of police incident reporting;
6. Development of an interstate organized crime intelligence system.

The original concept of SEARCH as primarily dedicated to the interstate exchange of "criminal offenders records" and offender-transaction-based statistics has been broadened to include all aspects of the new technology, including the testing and setting of standards for various technological equipments that are intended for the law enforcement market.

As was previously stated, there have been many very important technological advances brought about through LEAA grants. Other advances were stimulated by federal funds granted directly as categorical grants, or in the nature of LEAA revenue sharing through the various state planning agencies. Various vendors have also engaged in technological research and development in a thrust to capture a portion of the lucrative law enforcement market. As a result of all these efforts, we note a number of ingenious and effective applications of the various technologies to meeting the challenge of crime. The state of the art is daily being improved upon in all aspects of police technology.

DIGITAL COMMUNICATIONS TECHNOLOGY

Vast studies are being made to improve a number of television, radio, microwave, and land-line communications techniques. Walkie-talkies are smaller, lighter, and more effective generally. Digital receivers for police vehicles are becoming commonplace. Surveillance communications devices have become more sophisticated and more versatile. Transmission of digital data from remote stations and computer-to-computer interfaces over long distances have been achieved, and now satellite communications are being enlisted in the anti-crime effort. The National Law Enforcement Telecommmunications System (NLETS) is today a reality; the future of data exchange is limited only by the imagination of man.

IDENTIFICATION AND INTELLIGENCE SYSTEMS TECHNOLOGY

Today, some fingerprint identification bureaus are almost completely automated. Computerized fingerprint and names searches are well within the state of the art, as are computerized criminal history records. (The most resistant and elusive portion of the fingerprint identification process is the automatic scanning and classifying of the fingerprints themselves.) There have been a number of breakthroughs in the analytic identification field, including latent print, personal appearance, fraudulent check, and various other modules. Organized crime and other intelligence systems have been successfully computerized, as well as transaction-based offender statistics.

FACSIMILE TECHNOLOGY

One rapidly developing advanced communication technique involves the transmission of graphic material by facsimile over specially conditioned telephone wire on a short, medium, or long-distance basis. Fingerprints, mug shots, criminal histories, and reports may be scanned, translated to electrical form, transmitted, received and retranslated back to graphic form without the necessity of moving the original material over a long distance.

For example, a set of fingerprints may be transmitted from any part of New York State to NYSIIS in Albany in fourteen minutes or less. There, a hard copy of the set of prints is printed out, and main files are searched by a combination automatic and semimanual sequence. When the criminal history record is retrieved from the computer, it is transmitted back to the agency of origin. The originating agency now has a hard-copy facsimile of the criminal history record—and what used to take from seven to ten days is now done in a matter of *minutes*. Methods are now being developed that will greatly increase the already fantastic speed of transmission.

OPTICAL TECHNOLOGY

The science and technology of optics will be increasingly associated with police systems. Two developments are worthy of mention, in addition to the Automatic License Plate Scanning (ALPS) System previously discussed:

1. Television scanning of areas both inside buildings and on the streets, as well as open or covert television recording of crime scenes or station house bookings to substantiate drunk driving charges, refute brutality allegations, uncover corruption, etc. The manpower savings inherent in television surveillance are incredible. Coupled with night vision capabilities and laser beam potential, the possibilities boggle the mind;

2. Another development relates to in-house scanning equipment being programmed automatically to read and code alphanumeric and fingerprint data for computer processing. Automatic reading equipment (scanners) that transfer alphanumeric data from a document and directly enter such data into a computer memory have been available for some time.

A similar capability relating to fingerprints presents special problems that have not as yet been resolved. The major need is development of a compatible classification technique. Active research into the problem is being conducted by the British Home Office, New Scotland Yard, the Prefecture de Police of Paris, and the Italian National Police in Rome. In the United States, the FBI, New York State, and a host of computer manufacturers are conducting extensive research,

A new classification system based upon the characteristics of *one* fingerprint, rather than upon the characteristics of an entire set of ten fingers, will open up a dazzling era of successful criminal identification through the use of scene-of-crime fingerprints. (At the present time odd fingerprints found at crime scenes cannot as a practical matter be searched against major fingerprint files.)

CRIMINALISTICS TECHNOLOGY

Computerized methods of classifying, identifying, comparing, and analyzing physical evidence are being developed, along with medium- and long-range research not ordinarily considered the mission of the operational forensic laboratory. Facsimile and optical techniques, coupled with programmed analytical procedures are being applied to the areas of ballistics, handwriting, voice prints and trace identification, as well as to the fingerprint area.

Criminalistics research will become increasingly involved in the design and implementation of scientific modules to be incorporated within computer-based information-sharing systems.

STATISTICAL TECHNOLOGY

Not only will the computer sciences utilize new computer-compatible mathematical techniques for the analysis of detailed data developed by criminalistics testing and experimentation, but also they will place the statistical discipline into a variety of crucial roles in the police technological system. The currently maintained law enforcement data of a statistical nature relates mostly to police actions and is grossly inadequate, even for anlysis, evaluation, and decision-making feedback within the police structure. There is a vital need to add data concerning prosecution, court dispositions, probation, correctional institution, and parole. The history of statistical research in the police field is one of frustration, for unmet needs have existed—the vast storage of a variety of data, rapid search for and retrieval of data, and depth analysis of many variables—needs now capable of being satisfied by computer science and technology.

In the monumental report of the Wickersham Commission in 1931,[2] it became obvious that data about detention, prosecution, bail, release, sentencing, probation, corrections, parole, grand and petit juries, and police procedures, all necessary for analysis and evaluation, were unavailable. The ensuing thirty-six years evidenced no great amelioration of the situation, and the President's Commission on Law Enforcement and the Administration of Justice found that accurate, current, and usable data were unavailable in many areas of their inquiry.

Computer science and technology ultimately will provide for more reliable, valid, standardized, and consistent methods of statistical research in the administration of criminal justice—and perhaps even fantastic strides in crime pattern analysis, crime prediction, manpower deployment, treatment and rehabilitation methods, and a nationally coordinated approach in meeting the problems associated with crime and disorder.

CRIMINOLOGICAL RESEARCH

Undreamed-of storehouses of empirical data will become readily available for criminological research by means of computerized data banks.

The Federal Bureau of Investigation has been conducting a continuous study of the crime careers of more than 300,000 offenders whose criminal records have been computerized. In New York, NYSIIS has an extensive computer data base of criminal history relating to more than half a million persons who have been convicted of crimes for which criminal processing involves fingerprinting.

Additional computer banks are being developed in other cities, states, regional areas, and national centers which have similar potential for expediting and optimizing the resources available for criminological research.

In order to utilize this vast reservoir of information, to evaluate the activities of agencies working in the administration of criminal justice, and to perform basic research on system performance and agency effectiveness, a new host of technologically oriented research criminologists will be required. As the social sciences apply the powerful tools of computer science, greater scope will be provided for inquiry, and greater reliability will be achieved in predicting behavior. The great problems of interpersonal and intergroup conflict will be studied with a thoroughness heretofore thought impossible, and inquiry into the etiology, diagnosis, and prognosis of antisocial deviant behavior will provide insight relative to effective methods of control.

If all this sounds as if the millennium has arrived, such an understanding is premature. Great strides are being made in meeting the challenge of crime through the judicious application of police technology; however, there is still a long hard road to the summit and there are many pitfalls, many obstacles to overcome, and dangers to be met head-on. Perhaps the greatest threat to the continued viability of police technology is the very effectiveness of technology itself. As with nuclear energy, the potential of improper utilization could be catastrophic. The inherent threat to society in this apparent boon for the protection of social order has led one of our nation's most respected police chiefs to ask: *Police and Technology: Bondage or Freedom?*[3] He goes on to present his perceptive thesis:

> To say that this era will be one of technology, minimizes the point. It would be more accurate to say that technology will have a revolutionary impact upon the police. The impact will be of this magnitude because the police exist in an institutional and experiential vacuum with respect to technology. Or, put another way, the police are extremely vulnerable to technology.
>
> The police are vulnerable because they have had little experience with technology. They may have felt an acute need for technology; but, unfortunately, needing something and being able to manage it once obtained, are two entirely different matters. Consequently, the police have no actual experience to draw upon to cope with the ethical, social, psychological, political, and managerial issues technology brings in its wake.
>
> In short, when technology completes its rush into this institutional and experiential vacuum, policing will be revolutionized. Whether this revolution in policing ultimately enhances the dignity and safety of man or debases and terrorizes him, depends upon how well we manage police technology, and how well we discern its impact upon the dynamics of human interaction in a free society.
>
> That the potential is there to control rather than serve is well known. The awesome aspects of technology in the hands of those who are institutionally, experientially, and ethically unprepared to cope with it are not pleasant to behold. The imagery that must be used is that of the Orwellian specter of life in 1984.
>
> We cannot avoid that future by denying to the police the technology they must have to perform their mission, for ours is a

world of technology. If we are to avoid that future, then those who are expanding the limits of technology must tell us how imminent that future is so we might be forewarned. Those who are using technology as a means to solve technical problems must recognize that even greater societal problems can thereby be created. Those who are selling technology must temper the profit motive with a concern for its use. The police who use technology in the name of the law must do so within the letter and the spirit of that law. Finally, and most importantly, the public must insure that the law fosters democracy not technocracy.

This superbly expressed evaluation of the current situation by a truly professional police executive is unfortunately unique. Although there is a grave threat that the public may come to view the police as an alien force overwhelmingly equipped with technology, designed not to serve them but to control them, few in the police profession are aware of the impending impasse. "Big Brother" and 1984 are perhaps closer than we think.

Fortunately, in the development of SEARCH there was a recognition of the ethical and constitutional implications inherent in the development of police technology. A special Security and Privacy Committee was created as a permanent standing committee, and its output has proven to be of inestimable value in laying the conceptual and moral guidelines for the development of police technology in a democratic society. Although the work and reports of the SEARCH Security and Privacy Committee concentrate upon individual privacy as it may be placed in jeopardy by computerized information systems, they have established principles that are applicable to all phases of police technology. Of course, privacy may be invaded through electronic surveillance by various sophisticated devices and through psychological surveillance by lie detector tests, computerized questionnaires, etc., but the most pervasive threat to privacy is present in computerized information and intelligence systems. This is particularly true where interstate linkages are involved. If "Big Brother" ever arrives in this country, he will be the man (or group of men) who control the national computer net of information systems.

The work of the SEARCH Security and Privacy Committee began as long ago as 1969. One of the first efforts of the Committee was a commitment to draft a code of ethics. The Committee recognized the legitimacy of public concern about the impact of police technology upon human rights and civil liberties; it affirmed that the noblest mission of the police is to preserve the freedom of the people, and "people files" must therefore be zealously protected against misuse. It was recognized that there is a need to protect private personality as conscientiously as we protect private property, for insofar as we protect the right to privacy, we protect the right to share and communicate data. The protection of privacy implies parameters for a criminal justice data bank relating to when, where, with whom, what, how, and why information should be shared or withheld. As with all rights a paramount public interest accepted by the community and explicitly recognized should equate, in productive equilibrium, the claim of of privacy with the need to share information.

It was the opinion of the Committee that computerized criminal justice data banks may enhance rather than diminish human rights and civil liberties, if such data banks are properly developed and controlled. The Committee concluded that there need not be a conflict between the safeguarding of reasonable rights to privacy and the construction of a shared information system such as SEARCH, if the following potential problem areas are given adequate consideration:

1. The type of data that will be contained in the computerized files;
2. The persons who will receive the data;
3. The purposes for which the data will be used;
4. The relationship between the system and the people whose criminal history records comprise the data bank;
5. The organizational and administrative aspects of the system.

The committee dedicated itself to the enhancement of both individual freedom and effective criminal justice. One need not be sacrificed for the other. As new levels of progress are achieved, the delicate balance so essential to a just society will find equilibrium.

It is in this spirit, based on an understanding of the dynamics of both society and technology, that the Security and Privacy Committee, over a period of several months, developed a frame of reference for a correspondingly dynamic concept of security and privacy policy with respect to criminal history information systems. Statements of recommended policy were drawn up and officially approved by the Project Group. Some of the major policy recommendations[4] include the following:

- Data included in the system must be limited to that with the characteristics of public record.
- Participants shall adopt a careful and permanent program of data verification including systematic audits.
- Purge procedures shall be developed.
- A model state statute for protection and controlling data should be drafted and its adoption encouraged.
- Direct access to the system should be restricted to public agencies which perform, as their principal function, crime prevention, apprehension, adjudication, or rehabilitation of offenders.

- Each participating state should build its data system around a central computer, through which each inquiry must pass for screening and verification.
- Various state "public record" and "freedom of information" doctrines should be studied with a view to obtaining appropriate exemptions for the system's data.
- The use of system data for research shall involve stringent restrictions to preserve privacy.
- Users should be cautioned that reliance upon unverified data is hazardous and that positive verification of identity should be obtained as quickly as possible.
- The citizen's right to access and challenge the contents of his records should form an integral part of the system consistent with state law.
- Civil remedies should be provided for those injured by misuse of the system where not provided for by state law.
- The system participants should elect a board of directors (governing body) to establish policies and procedures governing the central index operation.
- The system should remain fully independent of noncriminal justice data systems and shall be exclusively dedicated to the service of the criminal justice community.
- A systems audit should be made periodically by an outside agency.
- A permanent committee or staff should be established to consider problems of security and privacy and conduct studies in that area.

The model state statute recommended in the original report of the SEARCH Security and Privacy Committee (SEARCH Technical Report No. 2) was soon drawn up by the Committee and has formed the basis for state and federal legislation protecting personal privacy in criminal justice information systems.[5] This was quickly followed by another seminal document providing a model set of administrative regulations to supplement the model legislation.[6]

The ultimate compliment paid to these documents (Tech. Report No. 2, Tech. Memos No. 3 and No. 4) is that they were utilized as virtually the sole source for the doctrine contained in the extremely important Chapter 8 (Privacy and Security) of the volume, *Report on the Criminal Justice System* promulgated by the National Advisory Commission on Criminal Justice Standards and Goals in January 1973. The chapter deals with the following major phases of a viable security and privacy program for criminal justice information systems:

Standard 8.1—Security and Privacy Administration

Standard 8.2—Scope of Files
Standard 8.3—Access and Dissemination
Standard 8.4—Information Review (by subject himself)
Standard 8.5—Data Sensitivity Classification
Standard 8.6—System Security
Standard 8.7—Personnel Clearances
Standard 8.8—Information for Research

For a more detailed description of the Standards, it is advisable to refer directly to Chapter 8 of the Report.[7] Suffice it to say that the theoretical basis for sound and viable security and privacy programs in criminal justice information systems has been laid. This is not yet true as it relates to intelligence systems. The Standards make a passing reference to Intelligence Files—albeit very superficially—being content to inveigh against the threat to individual rights from unrestricted intelligence operations. The two paragraphs devoted to this critical subject conclude with this injunction: "The Commission strongly wishes to discourage the retention of demonstrably inaccurate and unnecessary intelligence information and to prevent its dissemination."

It is unfortunate that the Standards did not explore the ramifications of intelligence in greater depth, particularly in the light of the Draconian provision of Proposed Federal Statute S. 2963 (Senator Ervin) Sec. 208(b) which states: "Criminal Justice intelligence information shall not be maintained in automated systems." (It should be noted that SEARCH did not deal with intelligence or analytic files in its Technical Report No. 2 and Memos No. 3 and No. 4.) There understandably now exists some confusion in the minds of alert law enforcement personnel as to the handling of intelligence files and their future status in the light, or more accurately stated the lack of light, provided by both the Standards and the proposed legislation.

Particularly ambiguous is the situation of analytical files—files that may contain both personal information and purely identification data. The definition of *criminal justice information* found in S. 2963 specifically excludes analytical files "in which individuals are not identified and from which their identities are not ascertainable." It also "defines out" analytical files and records from the remainder of the definition of criminal justice information—leaving analytical records no place to go except into the category of *criminal justice intelligence information*. The definition in S. 2963 of identification record information helps for those analytical files such as fingerprint classification, voice prints, photographs, and "other descriptive data concerning an individual which does not include any indication or suggestion that the individual has at any time been suspected of or charged with criminal activity." However, it does not help with the great bulk of special records that police agencies find it essential to maintain in order to investigate effectively—files that are not usually considered intelligence and that surely need to be automated and disseminated under controlled conditions. This problem is compounded by the absence of any discussion or recognition of the role of nongovernmental investigative agencies. There is little doubt that Senator Ervin's bill could have been a better piece of legislation had the Senator himself, or the Standards from which the Act is basically drawn, devoted more attention to the vitally important but enormously difficult problems of criminal intelligence and analytical files.

It is too late now for the Standards to provide guidance of a more profound nature to the good Senators on this critical subject. One would hope, however, that the resulting legislation reflects what is believed to be the Standards and Goals Task Force's intentions, i.e., that intelligence should be very carefully controlled but not cast into the oven. Law enforcement needs intelligence, and the liberty and freedom of the people are contingent upon the quality of available police intelligence. True—much needs to be done to control it. Objective studies of the subject by groups such as the Department of Health, Education and Welfare Advisory Committee on Automated Personal Data Systems[8] should be undertaken. There is perhaps no more urgent matter relating to personal privacy and police performance at this moment. Until such time as an authoritative study is available, one would hope that Senator Ervin reconsider Section 208(b) which would cripple the SEARCH Interstate Organized Crime Intelligence Project and the Law Enforcement Intelligence Unit (LEIU) itself, as well as many other potentially excellent systems designed to assist law enforcement. Aside from the fact that outlawing and elimination of computerized intelligence files is a nonsolution to a very, very sensitive problem, it would have exceedingly adverse effects upon the general acceptance of the Standards and Goals themselves.

It is obvious from the foregoing discussion that much remains to be done in order to assure that the benefits of technology are not denied to the police profession. There are many people who have little confidence in the police profession's ability to police itself. This social syndrome was directed at civilian review boards in the past, but today it is being targeted at abuses of the new technology, and particularly at actual and potential violations of personal privacy. The imagined horrors of the wired society, the tyranny of a national data bank containing permanent and readily retrievable derogatory data about every citizen, the prospect of no possibility of redemption from our sins of the past—all tend to increase public paranoia concerning police technology. Unfortunately, the police themselves all too often, because of mistaken zeal and lack of sensitivity to the larger issues involved, serve by words or actions to inflame this widespread distrust, and thereby confirm the worst fears of the populace.

It has been the purpose of this article to extol the current virtue and future necessity of optimizing the applications of technology in the police response to the challenge of crime. It is also the purpose of this article to alert the police profession to its grave responsibilities in the application of these powerful new tools which will, properly applied, give the "thin blue line" the necessary edge it must have to effectively deal with crime and criminals. The current thrust to encourage law enforcement officials to take advantage of the fantastic capabilities of technology needs to be carefully balanced with conscientious attempts to raise the consciousness of law enforcement officials. They need to be fully aware of the consummate necessity of protection of personal privacy in police systems.

Law enforcement officials today are unconcerned with (or even unaware of) the civil liberties aspects of their present and proposed applications of computers and the new technology. Some cynics would say there is either a conscious or subconscious drive among those few police professionals who are aware of the implications of personal privacy to sweep the issues raised under the proverbial rug and thereby avoid riling up the law enforcement consumers.

Despite the indifference (or ignorance) of most criminal justice personnel concerning individual privacy concerns, there is a tidal wave of overwhelming dimensions about to sweep in upon the police profession. Just as many police were caught unaware when the civil rights movement began to steamroller across the nation, so many police administrators have their heads in the sand once more. There is an incipient confrontation that may not cause blood to run in the streets, but, when it soon arrives, it will shake the police establishment to its roots. Those professionals who were aware of human relations, civil rights, civil liberties, and constitutional guarantees demonstrated that they could survive the blood-letting of the sixties. A similar moment of truth is sure to try the souls of police professionals before the seventies have passed into history. This time the issue will be personal privacy and at stake will be the continued availability of advanced technology to the police profession.

Since the current climate of "no concern" about privacy among criminal justice personnel is almost directly analagous to a similar lack of concern about human and community relations a decade ago, it appears that a program similar to that initiated and carried through by the National Conference of Christians and Jews (NCCJ) is indicated. Wherever the message of NCCJ was heeded, the loss of life and blood was stanched during the riots of the civil rights revolution. A similar sensitivity thrust directed towards this major issue of our times should help the police profession weather the gathering storm of protest against threats to the liberty and freedom of all the people through alleged "police state" technology.

If we can afford as a society to give the police sophisticated tools to protect us from crime, we can certainly afford the effort to assure that these same tools are not turned against our free society. For every dollar spent to increase the technological power of the police, an equivalent sum needs to be allocated for education, sensitivity training, and an entire gamut of conditioning techniques on a system-wide basis. Freedom is too precious a heritage to be placed at the mercy of those who are not sensitive and dedicated to individual liberty and personal privacy.

NOTES

1. President's Commission on Law Enforcement and Administration of Justice, *The Challenge of Crime in a Free Society*. Washington, D.C.: U.S. Government Printing Office, 1967.
2. The National Commission on Law Observance and Enforcement, popularly known as the *Wickersham Commission*, published its report in 1931.
3. An address by Bernard L. Garmire, Chief of Police, Miami Police Department, to the 1973 Carnahan Conference on Electronic Crime Countermeasures at the University of Kentucky, Lexington, Ky.
4. The Code of Ethics and the full list of twenty-three major policy recommendations with detailed references is contained in Project SEARCH Technical Report No. 2, July, 1970. California Crime Technological Foundation, Sacramento, Cal.
5. Project SEARCH. *A Model State Act for Criminal Offender Record Information, Technical Memorandum No. 3*. Sacramento, California Crime Technological Research Foundation, May 1971.
6. Project SEARCH. *Model Administrative Regulations for Criminal Offender Record Information, Technical Memorandum No. 4*. Sacramento, California Crime Technological Research Foundation, March 1972.
7. National Advisory Commission on Criminal Justice Standards and Goals, *Report on the Criminal Justice System* (Washington, D.C.: Law Enforcement Assistance Administration, January 1973).
8. See United States Department of Health, Education and Welfare, *Records, Computers and the Rights of Citizens: Report of the Secretary's Advisory Committee on Automated Personal Data Systems* (Washington, D.C.: July 1973).

TOPICS FOR DISCUSSION

1. Discuss why there are so few scientists and engineers helping to solve crime problems.

2. Discuss how important it is for today's police administrator to understand the nature of scientific inquiry.

3. Discuss the Kansas City, Missouri Police Department's preventive patrol study.

4. Discuss how television surveillance could save money for a police department.

5. Discuss the reasons why citizens should be concerned about the technology-privacy issue.

11

A. C. GERMANN

Police power vs. citizens' rights: a delicate balance?

INTRODUCTION

The writing of this chapter has been difficult for me. Originally, the title of this chapter was "Police Power vs. Citizens' Rights: The Delicate Balance." Such title implies that there is a balance, and that unjustly applied police power is balanced by the presence of Constitutional protections. At one time I would have accepted the idea without question; now, I am not so sure, and see an ever more independent police, equipped with computerized space-age technology, heavily weaponed in paramilitary style, ever more distanced from large segments of the American community.

As both practitioner and academician, I have studied the police with great interest for twenty-five years, and my observations have made me most cynical, indeed. I know policemen—in differing ranks and age groups—who daily exemplify the greatest amount of sensitivity and professional commitment. However, I believe that for the most part our police are led by narrow, ignorant, well-meaning men who are incapable of rising above the repressively conditioned approach of traditional law enforcement. And I believe that for the most part the working police (dealing directly with the general citizenry) are simple mercenaries who, for regular pay and pension, dumbly perpetuate the inane and wasteful procedures of past ages, however disguised with a veneer of science and technology.

I know that civil liberties attorneys have obtained court decisions, from time to time, that enhance personal liberty; but I also know that police can and do ignore, violate, or circumvent the strictures of the courts. I know that some unjustly treated citizens have had access to brilliant legal talent and investigative reporting; but I also know that many citizens have not had that access, and to their disadvantage. I do believe that our police agencies operate, for the most part, as an occupying army in our ghettos and barrios, and willingly accept the idea of harassment of the nonconforming minorities. Police power vs. citizens' rights: a delicate balance? *No way!* I do not believe that there is any *real* recourse for an aggrieved citizen who is a genuine victim of unjustly applied police power. If there were, we would be conscious of policemen who were fired and prosecuted, of substantial awards for damages, of many changes in police policy and procedure, of increased citizen trust in police, and of police interest in due process. And if the current Neanderthal incumbents maintain their power and position, and choose their replacements, I see no change in attitudes or practices, and ever greater alienation of police from the citizenry.

THE CRIMINAL JUSTICE NONSYSTEM

Criminal justice, notwithstanding the billions of dollars in LEAA grants, the substantial addition of facilities, equipment, and manpower continues to act as an ineffective institution. How else can we categorize it? Some 8,600,000 crime index offenses were reported in 1973 uniform crime reports, and a 21 percent clearance rate. Yet national crime surveys consistently indicate that crime is two to five times higher than that reported to, or observed by, police. If such is the case, we probably have over 25,000,000 index offenses, in reality, for 1973, and a true clearance rate of 7 percent. And if that is so, about 93 percent of the offenses—some 24,000,000—are unaffected by the actions or nonactions of the police! Would this not tend to indicate that our police are really dealing with the unlucky, or inept, or mentally retarded antisocial offender who represents that 7 percent that are identified and charged? No wonder that police feel frustrated and angry—they suspect or intuit or know that they have been, are, and will be almost totally ineffective in controlling antisocial behavior, no matter how many times deployment is doubled, no matter how advanced the computers, no matter how lethal the firepower, no matter how militarized the organization, no matter how manipulated the statistics.

The general public labors under the media-spawned and agency-assisted stereotype that the handsome white supercop, occasionally accompanied by a token minority assistant, aided by technology and weaponry, making unilateral determination of all means used, will be successful in winning out over the unkempt, dark and ugly supercriminal. Such claptrap philosophy does not assist our nation one whit. It causes many people to turn to the police with unrealistic expectations, demanding action, offering unqualified support, instead of organizing fellow citizens to work closely together and using trusted police assistance to develop a safe and secure neighborhood. The outcome is a frightened citizenry and a separated police agency. The agency, pressured to perform miracles, continues to utilize the traditional approaches, grows in arrogance and supercilious omniscience, moves toward paramilitary approaches with much more regard for firepower and gadgetry than for sensitive social concern, and becomes a police force which lends itself, in ignorant enthusiasm, to minor and gross violations of human dignity, and has no greater success than when half the size and budget.

POLICE ATTITUDE

There exists a very special problem that relates to police power and citizens' rights: the problem of police attitudes. The American policeman is identified with conservative, ultra-conservative, and very right-wing mental sets. If such mental sets are negatively biased toward minority groups, liberal and progressive groups, youth, pacifistic, academic and humanistic groups, such mental sets can affect police decisions, particularly if made unilaterally, and by the top-level traditionalists. Many of our police agencies exhibit, not a variety of social postures, but an almost unanimous mental set that identifies with that *singular part* of the community that has regularly supported the application of immediate massive force to solve local, state, and national problems. To such an extent that the agency is unrepresentative of the community as a whole, it becomes a predictable engine of destruction, rather than a helping community adjunct. Thus some citizens suggest that the "Protect and Serve" motto is but "PR" and that it should be changed to "Search and Destroy."

This right-wing identification makes it difficult for the police to identify with many citizens who have worked with peace groups, with civil rights groups, with liberal groups, with people of unconventional lifestyles, and many avenues of public cooperation are foreclosed because the traditionalist is frightened of, and hateful toward, the nonconforming minorities. Such attitudes stultify recruitment efforts, and prevent many motivated people from affiliating as careerists, or cooperating as concerned citizens.

THE SENSITIVE CAREERIST

A young man, sensitive and aware and humane, becomes a policeman. He is bright, knows how to play all the games (societal, academic, institutional, etc.) and takes his place in the ranks. Within a few months he sees the police picture very clearly, not only in his own department, but in the others nearby. He sees that the docile and unquestioning officer (who thinks and does what he is told to think and do) is given the better assignments, shifts, and performance ratings. He sees that the questioner of independent mind and humanistic inclinations is *persona non grata* in the police family and must wait for police practices to consistently operate within the U.S. Constitution. He realizes that most of the people working directly with the public are at the lowest ranks—and with a shock he notes that they constitute either green new officers, like himself, or bitter, cynical senior officers who could not achieve promotion and who are, for the most part, traditionalists and firepower-oriented. He notes that the bright and energetic people move up in rank within three-seven years. He reads the police literature and senses an incredible preoccupation with mechanical matters, with organizational structure, with records and communications and weaponry, and being curious, he studies ever more seriously, and slowly recognizes a pattern—a party line—becoming clear to him. In time, after study and demonstration of an ability to do the work of policeman well, he is promoted and learns even more about the police hierarchy. He sees that the independent minds are continuously in conflict with the top-level administration, so much so that they often leave policing, very frustrated, to affiliate with a peripheral criminal justice activity —or they remain, waiting for retirement, taking up a specialty of one sort or another. He sees that the way to the top is to echo the party line—which he may or may not be able to do. And he muses to himself about needed change, and wonders how it can be achieved when those doing the work at the lower levels are green recruits or cynical traditionalists, those in middle management are either traditionalists going up in the organization or independent-minded mavericks going nowhere in the organization, and those in the top levels are rigid, narrow traditionalists who have learned to play all sorts of "professional" games and sing all sorts of "professional" tunes, but are incapable of change, clinging to a repressive orientation and demanding slavish commitment to the status quo. Our sensitive careerist is in a bind. If he stays in policing, he will be relegated to lower or middle ranks; if he leaves policing, he won't be able to help make the changes he knows must come. Give him your sympathy and your hand; he is marking time on most police agencies. He is waiting for citizens of good heart to give him needed support. If he tires of the waiting game and leaves, this nation may well find itself with a police establishment indistinguishable in attitude and deed from the "green berets" of military fame. And when that happens, there will not be a "delicate balance" between police power and citizens' rights—there will be policing more fit for a dictatorship than for a democracy, and police power will be supreme.

This is not to say that there have not been, nor are, very sensitive and aware chiefs of police. It is to say that they are anomalies—irregulars—in the panorama of policing. But remember, reader, that the constructive work of making radical changes in policing will be done by a very small percentage of careerists. Most will be indifferent, or reluctant to challenge the status quo, or only interested in fattening their wallets or resumes. It is my hope that some of the sensitive and aware and humane careerists will stick it out, no matter how difficult, without selling their souls, their liberty, their conscience—and wait for a better day.

POLICE LITERATURE

Take up the representative journals of policing. I suspect that you will scan a multiplicity of advertisements for police gear and come to some understanding of the police-industrial complex. I suspect that you will find many footnoted articles, complete with graphs and tables, on police administration, management, technology, and operational procedure. I suspect that you will find editorials stressing the need for more facilities, equipment, and personnel, and for more (unquestioning) public support.

Read those journals for their philosophy of social control, for their humane and compassionate expressions, for programs that involve genuine public partnership, participation, trust, and co-equal respect—and you will, for the most part, look in vain. Do not look for sympathetic understanding of social unrest; do not look for enthusiastic dedication to civil rights and civil liberties; do not look for open and spirited debate relative to philosophies, policies, and motivations; do not look for critical comment relative to illegal, immoral, unjust, self-defeating applications of police power—for you will, for the most part, look in vain.

You will know that real change is afoot when you find professional police careerists launching the attack upon unprofessional police careerists. You will know that real change is afoot when you find nonpolice joined with police against unworthy police. You will know that real change is afoot when you pick up a police journal and find letters to the editor from policemen who are civil libertarians. You will know that real change is afoot when you find police leaders who insist upon public scrutiny of police agencies. You will know that real change is afoot when women and minorities appear as top-level administrators. You will know that real change is afoot when there are as many readers of *Ramparts* and *The New Republic* in police ranks as there are readers of *American Opinion* and *Human Events*. You will know that real change is afoot when nonconforming minorities begin to trust and welcome the appearance of a police officer. You will know that real change is afoot when criminal justice leaders make open admission that the billions of public dollars now expended for social control measures really relate to a tiny fraction of offenses and offenders. You will know that real change is afoot when police academy instructors spend as much time on unprovoked assaults *by* police as on unprovoked assaults *on* police. You will know that real change is afoot when sensitive civil libertarians and sensitive police are working cooperatively and productively on due process-oriented crime control. You will know that real change is afoot when the college and university criminal justice programs are open arenas for debate and formulation of new constructs rather than disguised police academies sniffing about for fat grants. You will know that real change is afoot when LEAA begins to fund as many consciousness raising programs for police as it funds technical projects. And you will know that real change is afoot when there really is some balance between police power and citizens' rights, and everyone in the nation is proudly conscious of the fact.

Until then, continue to scan the police literature for hopeful signs. I have perused it for twenty-five years, and it is my current judgment that policing has not undergone *real* change. The Neanderthal is still in the driver's seat, the party line continues to reflect a firepower-oriented gadget-ridden emphasis, and the sensitive, aware, humanistic police remain outnumbered and quiescent.

PUBLIC INVOLVEMENT

Our police are closely inbred, suspicious of the general public, and fearful of change. Recent events have increased police paranoia, as more and more investigative reporting continues to expose governmental decay. Watergate may have been a beginning of a new type of public education, and we may be entering an era that will have hundreds of Watergates at the state, county, and municipal levels. We are witnessing the exposure of agency excesses by former members of governmental agencies—and this may be expected to continue, particularly with respect to police, as more and more educated people enter police ranks, become disenchanted with the realities of current policy and procedure, and leave to avoid the compromise of all principle. I would expect many more books and articles, and, as a result, some desire on the part of the general public for change-oriented involvement—aroused citizens demanding a responsible decision-making role in policing.

Should the people *and* the police decide on policy and procedure, or should the police unilaterally decide? Most traditionalists mistrust the public and believe that police matters should be decided by police. Some independent-thinking working police and middle management people believe that the public should be part of the act, to a much larger degree than present, for they sense that to involve people in decision making is to develop public trust and cooperation.

Should *all segments* of the community be involved in major policing decisions? The traditionalist would rather deal with captive politicians or with docile commissions. (Sometimes the intelligence dossiers or police files assist in maintaining control and docility?) The traditionalist will desire that only true friends of police (read: unquestioning supporter) be admitted anywhere behind the booking desk, or given any agency data. The innovative careerist would like to involve people from every segment of the community—including the nonconforming minorities—but is constantly queried by the police Neanderthal: "whose side are you on?"

I believe that until there is public involvement in police decision making (Shall we discontinue field interviews? Shall we leave domestic intelligence to the FBI? Shall we move to .32 weapons? Shall we enforce gambling laws at the Elks Club? Shall we increase our consumer fraud unit to 20 percent of the agency? Shall we eliminate present uniforms? Shall we fire and prosecute abusive policemen? Shall we elevate salaries of working police to middle management levels? Shall we eliminate many middle management positions so that we have mostly professional working police and very few supervisors? Should we concentrate attention on crime prevention? Should we allow the university to educate and train our police? Should we revise our goals? our priorities? Should we obtain community referendums on controversial policies? Should we replace civil service tenure with a contract system? Should we budget a firing range or a consciousness raising program?) it will be difficult to obtain citizen trust and cooperation.

CONCLUSIONS

We are in an age of change; one era is coming to an end; all of our institutions are affected. You know and I know that the balance between police power and citizens' rights depends, in final analysis, on attitude. The traditional police attitude has been simplistic, moralistic, self-righteous, puritanical, hypocritical, punitive, repressive, and narrow as a laser beam—such attitude is now an anachronism, an impediment, a scandal. You know and I know that people are more important than computers; that all citizens deserve humane treatment by police; that violence breeds violence; that contempt breeds contempt. You know and I know that the current leadership is blind to the real world, and as out of place today as one of the robber barons of old, but wielding great influence.

As I look to the future, I see the possibility of two scenarios. One scenario extends the current police philosophy into the future—with a continuance of the reliance on science and technology, with a continuance of paramilitary emphasis, with a continuance of current police-public alienation. This scenario involves the identification of all members of the nonconforming minority, and with times of unrest, their neutralization—by infiltration of their organizations, by incitation to violence by agents provocateurs, by preventive detention, by contrived arrest, and, if necessary, elimination of their leadership by any fashion deemed useful. Such scenario involves a continuance of police identifications and affiliations and involvement with conservative, ultra-conservative, and very right-wing movements and philosophies. In this scenario any and all sensitive citizenry slowly but surely remove themselves from police affiliation, or are purged by the police, leaving the police Neanderthal in total control. The scenario develops the idea of the coldly efficient police machine, aided by all the science and technology, and a ruthless elimination of the nonconformist, complete with cooperative prosecution and judiciary, and a prison institution charged with the long-term custody of millions. The police, in such scenario, would become as hated as the German Gestapo (or more so, because the Gestapo never had the use of space-age technology).

But there is, hopefully, another scenario. The second scenario involves the development of citizen pressure for humane policing. It involves the replacement of current leadership with people-oriented men. It involves a large-scale change of program and priorities; a de-emphasis of force, a development of neighborhood concern, and the policeman as ombudsman of the weak, ignorant, confused, frustrated, unemployed, cold, hungry, sick, and those who have lost hope. It involves the policeman as community organizer, community counselor, community helper. It involves the policeman as a warm and trusted and approachable friend. It involves the policeman as example for the youth, and as teacher of the community. This hopeful scenario would present the policeman, not as heavily armed mercenary, not as cold and indifferent bureaucrat, but as an educated and well-trained member of the community family.

There may be other scenarios; I have a hunch, however, that they would resemble, in essence, one or the other of these two. At any rate, we all bear some responsibility for the future police who will help or "bust" our children and grandchildren. It is my considered judgment that only with the second scenario is there a faint chance for balance between police power and citizen rights in this nation. And it is my considered judgment that the second scenario is possible only with large-scale changes of attitude by both police and citizen.

TOPICS FOR DISCUSSION

1. Discuss the relationship between policemen and the right-wing or conservative.

2. Discuss the kinds of leadership existing in police agencies today.

3. Discuss the need for police to be civil libertarians in order to cause change in policy philosophy.

4. Discuss the relationship between police power vs. citizens rights, and personal liberty vs. community security.

5. Discuss the second scenario as it applies to the "safety-welfare generalist" depicted in *Administrative Behavior and Police Organization,* by Jim L. Munro. (Cincinnati, Ohio: W. H. Anderson Publisher, 1974).

12

PAUL F. CROMWELL, JR.

Issues in police-community relations

In these times of social upheaval, much is being written about the relationship of the police to the public they serve. The need for strengthening police relationships with the community is a major and critical problem facing law enforcement and the criminal justice system. For the past decade in America we have been faced with momentous social change and a population growth that has produced an enormous amount of strain on the very fabric of our society. People and groups have grown apart and have become polarized through lack of communication, prejudice, discrimination, disparate philosophy, and outright alienation from each other. Members of minority groups, students, and others are taking action to acquire rights and services which they feel have been historically denied them. As the most visible representative of the society from which these groups are demanding fair treatment and equal opportunity, police are faced with an unprecedented mandate requiring they develop policies and practices governing their actions and their relations with all the groups with whom they come into contact.

In 1967, the President's Commission on Law Enforcement and Administration of Justice stated:

> Even if fairer treatment of minority groups were the sole consideration, police departments would have an obligation to attempt to achieve and maintain good police-community relations. In fact, however, much more is at stake. Police community relations have a direct bearing on the character of life in our cities and on the community's ability to maintain stability and to solve its problems. At the same time, the police department's capacity to deal with crime depends to a large extent upon its relationship with the citizenry. Indeed, no lasting improvement in law enforcement is

likely in this country unless police-community relations are substantially improved.[1]

In order to do this, the cooperation and assistance of each institution, group, and individual citizen must be stimulated and sustained. Police-community relations can provide a major step in this direction. It has a potential for creating and strengthening bonds of communication and participation between the police department and the community so that they both are supported in fulfilling their responsibilities in law enforcement and honorable citizenship.

HISTORICAL PRECEDENTS

As early as 1829, Sir Robert Peel recognized the need to command public respect and support when he organized the London Metropolitan Police. Peel was convinced that police must be dedicated, trained, ethical, and paid personnel of local government. His police faced many of the same problems as do the police of today. Riots, unemployment, strikes and poor economic conditions had prevailed for over a decade prior to the passage of the act establishing a London Metropolitan Police. The people feared the establishment of a police force as a representative instrument for the benefit of the privileged classes. The government was unpopular, there was fear of the mob and apprehension for the security of property. The people of London showed their fear and resentment by attacking and injuring the first police contingent to patrol the streets.

Peel recognized that it was essential that the police gain public acceptance and from the beginning placed emphasis upon public service, self-control, and gaining the public trust. In *Instructions* and *Police Orders* for 1829, issued to the personnel of the Metropolitan Police Department, Peel stated:

> ... The constable must be particularly cautious not to interfere idly or unnecessarily.... He must remember that there is no quality more indispensable to a police officer than a perfect command of temper, never suffering himself to be moved ... by any language or threats...; if he do his duty in a quiet and determined manner, such conduct will probably induce well disposed bystanders to assist him....[2]

Police Orders for October 17, 1829 warned that "Some instances of rudeness on the part of the police toward persons asking civil questions has been reported to the Commissioners," and called upon the superintendents to warn and instruct their men.[3]

It took many years; however, through courteous but firm enforcement of the law, the police won the respect of the British people. In England, Sir Robert's policemen became known affectionately as "the bobbies." Yet even Peel had his problems with community relations, for while the English people accepted and respected their police, in Ireland, where a substantially identical organization was imposed upon a people who were hostile to all English authority, policemen were known as the "Bloody Peelers."

As an issue then, police-community relations is nothing new in law enforcement. Nor is it a new idea that a police department can take steps to improve its image in the community: broadly defined, such programs have been in existence at least 40 years. When, in the 1930s, uniformed police officers visited schools to assure children that "the policeman is your friend," they were practicing police-community relations in its most basic form.

In 1957, St. Louis became the first police agency to actually organize a Police-Community Relations Division. Since that date, virtually all large police departments in the United States have developed Police-Community Relations Divisions. A good many of these have been poorly organized, lacking in constructive programs and adequate guidelines for community action, and are ineffective in creating and maintaining positive relationships between the police and the public.

In discussing the need for a positive program of police community relations, we should consider the effects of poor community relations. The 1967 President's Commission on Law Enforcement and Administration of Justice reported deleterious effects in four areas of concern:[4]

The Effect on the Police Department as an Organization

1. Recruiting suffers: young men generally seek occupations that are less dangerous and that have the respect and support of their families and friends.
2. Morale suffers: police officers become less enthusiastic about doing their job well.
3. Dissatisfied citizenry do not support police enthusiastically on issues such as police salary, sufficient numbers of officers, equipment, and buildings.
4. Police become isolated from the public and become less capable of understanding and adapting to the community and its changing needs.

Direct Effects on Police Operations

Poor community relations adversely affect the ability of police to prevent crime and apprehend criminals.

1. People who are hostile to police are not so likely to report violations of law, even when they are victims. They are less likely to report suspicious persons and to voluntarily testify as witnesses.
2. Public hostility may make officers reluctant to act; it may also induce the use of unnecessary force, verbal abuse, or other improper practices.

Effect on Individual Officers

1. Poor police-community relations increases the danger of police work. Statistics compiled by the FBI reveal that 37,523 officers were assaulted, 14,625 seriously injured and 112 killed during 1972. Many of these assaults resulted, at least partially, from general hostility toward the police.
2. Poor police-community relations places a serious personal burden upon a police officer. Like any other person, the officer resents having to work day in and day out, frequently for low pay and in danger, for people who verbally abuse him or silently dislike him.

Effect on Community Stability

1. Poor police-community relations, together with poor housing, unemployment, and oppressive commercial practices were basic underlying causes to the riots in the mid 1960s and to innumerable tensions prevalent in the urban areas of our country today.

Acknowledging the ruinous effects of poor relationships between the police and the community brings forth the logical question: What are the causes? and, What are the solutions? There is no dearth of information, speculation, nor research into these vitally important questions. Police science journals are replete with scholarly prose addressed to the subject, and each year several new books speak entirely to the topic of police-community relations. Police administrators, police professors, lawyers, judges, leaders in the minority community, psychologists, and social workers have all brought their knowledge and talents to bear on the problem, yet the problem still exists and, to many, appears to worsen.

Police agencies throughout the country have instituted positive programs to ameliorate the situation. A few have proven somewhat effective, others mere "eyewash" with negative or no results at all.

POLICE-COMMUNITY RELATIONS
PROJECTS

A variety of special programs have developed across the country, and they are as diverse in approach as the problem is in complexity. Johnson and Gregory (1971) reported several projects that lend further insight into the problem, as well as point toward solutions.[5]

New York City.   Begun in the late 1960s, a project was developed to demonstrate the possibility of training police as specialists in family crisis intervention. Research has shown that much of the police work both in New York and other metropolitan areas involves family crises in the form of marital fights.[6] Some eighteen policemen were chosen to work in a largely disadvantaged, racially mixed neighborhood and were trained to operate as police crisis intervention specialists. The men received training from members of the psychology department at City College of the City University of New York. The officers learned how to walk in on family crises, to talk to each individual separately, to disarm people if armed and when they have calmed the family members, to refer them to a counseling center.

Houston, Texas.   A group of businessmen formed an organization to aid in bringing together "police and community for mutual exchange of attitudes and images." The program involves T-group and sensitivity training approaches. A series of human relations laboratories were devised, each laboratory lasted six weeks, meeting three hours each week. Each group contained an equal number of police officers and community members.

Group leaders were doctoral level psychologists and their assistants were graduate students in psychology. In initial meetings, the police and community members used an exchange of images model. Police were asked to develop a list of images of the community and of themselves. Community people were asked to do the same. The two subgroups then confronted each other with these images. After that, other methods were used depending upon the group leader— techniques such as psychodrama, role reversal, and role mirroring.

At the completion of the program, group members were asked to evaluate and analyze the program and to indicate in what ways the course had changed their attitudes. In answer to the question about attitude changes, community people said they had gained 1) better awareness of the policeman's role, his problems and the scope of his responsibility; 2) recognition of their responsibility as citizens to enforce law and order, to become involved, and to work with, not against or apart from, the police; 3) greater respect for the police as individual human beings rather than being classed into one un-differentiated group, the blue minority; and 4) hope that some of the police will change their attitudes and behavior toward minority group members. At the same time, policemen said they were gratified that 1) the community had gained some appreciation of the police-man's role, and what he can do and cannot do; 2) the recognition that police may provoke situations and aggravate feelings by verbal abuse; 3) an awareness and a shocked revelation by some of the in-tensity of the hatred for police held by some community members; and 4) some awareness of the need to control personal feelings and emotions.

Boston. Thirteen police districts have a community relations work-shop that include the police captain and about twelve representative citizens from the area. They meet on a regular basis. Some of the programs set up by these workshops include 1) preparing minority members for police entrance examination; 2) a city-wide community relations conference; 3) familiarizing grade school students with the police; and 4) a three-day institute conducted by the National Con-ference of Christians and Jews.

Covina, California. An eight-week course was designed to provide greater knowledge of values and ethics, individual human behavior, interpersonal and group relations, organizational behavior, intergroup or race relations, and the nature of the community for the twenty members of the Covina Police Department who participated. This course is held under the direction of the City of Covina officials. The program is conducted by Creative Management Research and Devel-opment, a nonprofit organization. Included in the program was an open-ended two-day retreat, a series of seven discussion sessions, a field experience in Riverside County Jail, research and evaluation, and a closing banquet.

One of the more unique aspects of this program was the field ex-perience referred to as "operation empathy." Policemen from a nearby county came into one of the class meetings and arrested the entire class. They were handcuffed and transported to Riverside County Jail. Each member of the class was booked and sentenced to spend the night in jail. Afterwards, the members of the class reported they had learned a great deal from the experience. Because of the success of that experience, the Covina Police Department planned additional field experience. Policemen were dressed up as skid-row bums, given the appropriate paraphernalia, and asked to spend a day in the Los Angeles skid-row district. Again the experience was found to be very valuable. Police claimed that they had learned the importance of certain techniques for handling people, such as telling a man exactly how he is going to be searched before searching him and using respectful names in talking with people rather than words that would trigger hard feelings.

Newark. A police-community relations training program developed by the Newark Police Department involved police and poor people in a dialogue. The sample of citizens selected included probationers and parolees. They planned on five classes of 50 persons each, including 30 law enforcement officers and 30 poor citizens from Newark. Programs would include lectures, case discussions, field experiences, and open discussion. Attitudes and behavior patterns both would be evaluated and the follow-up study designed to determine effectiveness of the program.

Tampa. The Tampa Police Department has developed a program to help prevent crime. Through police talks, films, radio announcements, and educational television programs, the project is supposed to educate the public about law enforcement, to improve the image of the policeman, to discuss responsibilities of the public for law enforcement, and to enable the crime prevention division to listen to public opinion and thereby design prevention programs to fit the need.

Kansas City. A program was set up whereby a team of policemen, including one white officer and one black officer visited fourth grade classes in some 80 elementary schools. They spoke to a total of 6,000 children. On a secondary level, eleven schools were visited with a total of 5,500 ninth graders involved. The role of the police department and obligations of policemen to protect people and property were explained to these young people. Apparently, no evaluation was carried out on this project.

Detroit. The new Chief of Police, Johannes Spreen, issued a St. Valentine's Day appeal for a 100-day public love-in toward the police —an era of good feeling to enable him to make certain needed reforms. It worked. Almost overnight bouquets of flowers and "Cops are tops" valentines began flooding his office. He followed this by asking Detroiters to help the police by $1 donations for new equipment. Ten thousand donations were made. Spreen had other brainstorms which included motor scooters for use instead of squad cars, which he claimed "isolate the police and citizenry"; an information center to

keep relatives informed of the status of prisoners; review boards; and
$1,000 raises for police with college degrees.

A LOOK AT THE BASICS

Despite well-intentioned and sincere efforts by police agencies to
improve their community support and rapport, it cannot be done
through programs such as those described. These and most other
police-community relations projects involve a small percentage of the
total manpower of the agency and to paraphrase a cliche, "One man
in five minutes can undo a year's work of an entire police-community
relations division." The problem of police community relations is the
problem of the individual police officer. No program can be effective
unless developing positive police community relationships becomes
a priority for every officer.

The President's Commission on Law Enforcement and Administration of Justice stated:

> A community's attitude toward the police is influenced most by
> the actions of individual officers on the streets. No community re-
> lations or recruiting or training program will avail if courteous and
> cool-headed conduct by policemen in their conduct with citizens
> is not enforced.[7]

The Commission observers in several cities saw incidences of
physical abuse, verbal abuse, and rudeness. They reported that
officers too seldom used polite forms of address to members of
minority groups and juveniles. Observers saw a certain amount of
harassment in the use of such orders as "move on" and "break it up."
They found that in some instances high crime neighborhoods are used
as "punishment" assignments for ineffective or misbehaving officers.

Most of the solutions to such problems as reported by the President's Commission can be found in the Principles of Law Enforcement
first enunciated by Sir Robert Peel. They are ancient, but principles
do not change and many of the solutions to the problems of community relations can be found here.

PHILOSOPHY AND ROLE
OF LAW ENFORCEMENT

Los Angeles Chief of Police, Edward M. Davis, once said, "Anyone
going into a business is well advised to understand the philosophy of

that business."[8] This observation leads to asking questions of our own law enforcement business. What are the objectives of the police? What are the major functions of law enforcement?

The American Bar Association project on Standards for Criminal Justice, *Standards Relating to the Urban Police Function*,[9] have identified the major responsibilities of police as:

1. To identify criminal offenders and criminal activity, and where appropriate, to apprehend offenders and participate in subsequent court proceedings.
2. To reduce the opportunities for the commission of some crimes by preventive patrol and other measures.
3. To aid individuals who are in danger of physical harm.
4. To protect constitutional guarantees.
5. To facilitate the movement of people in vehicles.
6. To assist those who cannot care for themselves.
7. To resolve conflict.
8. To identify problems that are potentially serious law enforcement or governmental problems.
9. To create and maintain a feeling of security in the community.
10. To promote and preserve civil order.
11. To provide other services on an emergency basis.

Whether or not the police respond to these objectives and priorities for police services is determined in a large measure by a police department's self-concept of its role. This is especially true with regard to the handling of those matters due to "social problems," for it is generally assumed by police officers that such problems require the attention of a "social worker." Social work in turn is generally thought of as involving a commitment to working with individuals on a continuing basis and employing a "permissive" approach, which many people see as being inconsistent with efforts at achieving effective control. On the other hand, there are indications that the police want very much to be used in a helping role and therefore welcome the opportunity to perform these functions that require speed, courage, and resourcefulness.

Elmer Johnson[10] attempted to delineate the various roles played by the police officer in the course of performing his duties. He found the roles falling onto various points along a continuum ranging from control functions to supportive functions.

Toward the control end of the continuum, Johnson identified the *guardian of society* role. In this role the officer views himself as a sentry manning the battlements in a war on crime. This role centers about search, chase, and capture as a typical sequence of activities. Johnson found that when in this role, the policeman is most likely to have high morale and a favorable self-image because he is engaged in what he regards as "real police work." Under these conditions, the police goals are rather clear cut: apprehend the offender, bring him before the court, and bring the case to a satisfactory close.

At the supportive end of the role continuum is the *public servant.* Here police attempt to meet the needs of individuals in crises. These include finding lost children, recovering drowning victims, referring individuals for emergency services, receiving complaints about rubbish, etc. Because other community agencies usually do not provide round-the-clock services, the law enforcement agency fills an institutional vacuum. The police are particularly likely to be called upon to assist the poor, ignorant, and the stranger without resources whose needs are not met by social service agencies. In situations where the middle-class member of the community is likely to call on the family physician, clergyman, or attorney, the lower status person becomes a "client" of the policeman.

The other roles fall somewhere between the control and the supportive ends of the functional continuum. In the course of their duties, officers are drawn into situations that call for mediating human relationships. Tending toward the control function is the *peace keeper.* In preserving order in the community, the policeman fluctuates between coercion and mediation as he performs a variety of tasks from the enforcing of traffic regulations, through settling of a family dispute, to dealing with a riot.

In his role as *instrument of the law,* which falls somewhere near the center of the continuum, the mediation activities of the police officer are more dominant. Through regulations not directly concerned with crime in the popular sense, the policeman frequently becomes a third party in disputes in which his arrest decision fixes liability in civil cases and extends the social stigma of criminal status to such incidents as automobile accidents, labor disputes, and racial unrest.

Johnson states, "The popular view is that the *guardian of society* is the most frequent role, but the daily work of a policeman places him most frequently in the roles of *peace keeper, public servant,* or *instrument of the law.*" One study monitored 800 incoming telephone calls at a police complaint desk in a metropolitan police department. Of the 800 calls, 652 were for police services. Thirty-nine percent of the calls involved the control function of law enforcement, while the remainder involved requests for assistance outside the control function. Thirty-five percent of the calls were in regard to personal problems which persisted over a period of time: health services, children's problems, incapacitated people, and nuisance problems usually related to noise. The other 26 percent concerned periodic personal problems such as disputes, violence, protection of the individual, missing persons, youth gangs, and hot-rodders.[11]

To achieve optimum police effectiveness and to achieve a personal sense of worth, police officers should recognize that they have complex and multiple tasks to perform in addition to identifying and apprehending persons committing criminal offenses. The recognition and acceptance of this public service role is the first step toward creating the attitude necessary for improvement of relations between the public and the police.

The diverse and complex role of the police officer has led to a professional code of ethics for law enforcement officers, developed in 1957 and since adopted by all major police associations and agencies in the country. It reads as follows:

LAW ENFORCEMENT CODE OF ETHICS

As a law enforcement officer, my fundamental duty is to serve mankind; to safeguard lives and property; to protect the innocent against deception, the weak against oppression or intimidation, and the peaceful against violence or disorder; to respect the constitutional rights of all men to liberty, equality and justice.

I will keep my private life unsullied as an example to all; maintain courageous calm in the face of danger, scorn, or ridicule; develop self-restraint; and be constantly mindful of the welfare of others. Honest in thought and deed in both my personal and official life, I will be exemplary in obeying the laws of the land and the regulations in my department.

Whatever I see or hear of a confidential nature or that is confided to me in my official capacity will be kept ever secret unless revelation is necessary in the performance of my duty.

I will never act officiously or permit personal feelings, prejudices, animosities or friendships to influence my decisions. With no compromise for crime and with relentless prosecution of criminals, I will enforce the law courteously and appropriately without fear or favor, malice or ill will, never employing unnecessary force or violence and never accepting gratuities.

I recognize the badge of my office as a symbol of public faith, and I accept it as a public trust to be held so long as I am true to the ethics of the police service. I will constantly strive to achieve these objectives and ideals, dedicating myself before God to my chosen profession ... law enforcement.

Developed from the principles of law enforcement as stated by Robert Peel, the Law Enforcement Code of Ethics provides a guideline and a framework of action and behavior which, if followed diligently by every officer in the course of his duty, would eliminate the need for police-community relations divisions and special PCR projects, as well as create for a department as a whole the image of the law enforcement officer as both a protector and friend.

The philosophy of law enforcement as set out in the Law Enforcement Code of Ethics demands action of a sincere and positive nature. As Gourley put it,

> The policeman ... must always remember that law enforcement is not an end in itself; but is, rather, a means to an end—and that end is the maintenance of an orderly society.[12]

It is important for policemen and police agencies to recognize that responsibility for creating an atmosphere of respect for peace officers in the mind of the public has as a base, individual police-public contacts. As noted earlier, a high percentage of police-public contacts are nonrelated to the enforcement function. Herein lies an area where police can take positive, effective action to improve their relations with the public. Respect for the law is a shared responsibility of the public and the police, but the police must never fail themselves, if they are to collectively and individually merit respectful treatment by the citizens whom they contact daily. Police administrators and training officers must imbue each officer with a challenge to foster truly a personal attitude of cooperation with the public. If this is to be accomplished on a continuous basis, it means more than training programs and lip service; it means each officer must willingly accept a challenge for professional exhibition of the attitudes and qualities that spell good law enforcement to the layman. It is more than having regulations and codes of ethics. It is the acceptance by each law enforcement officer of his own responsibility to see to it that he willingly exerts every effort to conform to all these highly important qualifications, while exhibiting an attitude that shows that he is not just "doing a job," but he is engaging in the professional execution of his police responsibilities.

Each police officer must accept a role in both the development of and the adherence to a philosophy of professionalization. In the course of his field assignments, he may deliver babies, arbitrate marital disputes, cite a speeding motorist or pursue an escaping criminal through back alleys and over fences. The point is, that law enforcement today requires a professional approach to each and every such incident, and that is what the philosophy of the individual police officer is all about.

The earlier suggestions regarding formal police-community relations programming cannot and should not be ignored by the police administrator who desires to better his relations with the community he serves. Neither can the individual officer afford to be recalcitrant in his duty to further the profession. This means that police agencies as a whole have a vital role to play in improving police-community relations, and it presents a highly individual challenge to every working policeman. Law enforcement demands the same type of devotion and professionalization as does medicine, teaching, the ministry, and the law.

CONCLUSIONS

A 1967 Task Force report on police by the President's Commission on Law Enforcement and Administration of Justice,[13] sought to establish basic principles to underlie any meaningful community relations program.

1. No police-community relations program can be effective without the full and complete support of the top administrative officers.
2. Improved community relations is not merely the job of police community relations units or of citizens' organizations. Instead, as a distinguished group of New York citizens advised Mayor Lindsay:

    Community relations is not a part-time task of the police department, or a mere postscript to its traditional work. We believe that community relations is essential to all law enforcement and therefore an integral part of all police work. Improving community relations is a full-time assignment of each man on the force. Healthy community relations can only be achieved by inculcating an attitude—a tone—throughout the force that will help facilitate a creative rapport with the public.[14]

3. The commitment of the chiefs of police must result in more than honest, hard work to improve community relations. Many things that may need to be done will seem to interfere with other objectives and needs of the department. For example, harsher penalties for officers who engage in serious misconduct, increased promotion for qualified black officers to higher ranks, and even discussion with more aggressive civil rights leaders may alienate some police officers and perhaps, at least temporarily, lower morale. However, if these measures help to improve community relations, the result will probably be to improve considerably the ability of the police to control crime.
4. An effective police-community relations program requires simultaneous efforts in many areas. Otherwise, any individual effort, no matter how well conceived, is likely to be ineffective. For example, neighborhood advisory committees will work well only if, in response to committee discussions, the police department is genuinely willing to reevaluate its policies concerning the activities of officers on the streets and its method of handling civilian complaints.
5. Police-community relations will probably not improve sub-

stantially unless policing as a whole improves. More educated policemen are essential, which means, in turn, higher salaries and better working conditions. Police morale must be raised.

6. Police-community relations is not merely a problem of a particular police department. The public tends to see the police as one group just as they view lawyers, doctors, or members of any other profession. Consequently, when the police in one area are abusive, for example, to peaceful demonstrators, respect and support for police officers everywhere is weakened.

7. The problem between the police and the community, particularly the minority community, is not merely a product of lack of communication or information. It will not be solved merely by having the police and the community talk together or by having the police educate the community concerning their role and activities. Instead, the conflict concerns real points of disagreement, such as how police treat the citizens on the street, whether they discriminate in applying the law, and how citizen complaints are handled. Discussion and education can only help if the police address the serious problems and attempt, where necessary and possible, to change their policies and activities to meet citizens' objections.

8. Police officials and officers often adopt a defensive attitude toward those who criticize and are hostile to them. Many of the people most hostile to police are ordinary citizens acting honestly out of firm belief. It is therefore essential that the police explore problems openly—that, indeed, the police seek out their critics so that problems can be met together.

9. The movement toward professionalization of the police must include a professional approach toward community relations problems.

Further recommendations for effective police-community relations should include:

1. Police agencies should recruit, train, and promote only those men with a sound respect for people.

2. They should insure that greater numbers of minority group members seek careers in police work by improving recruitment programs and by preventing discrimination, whether conscious or not, against such applicants.

3. Personnel from the community relations unit and human relations experts should have considerable responsibility for providing recruit and in-service training, and the amount of time given specifically to human and community relations must be dramatically increased. The training should be given as a combination of basic and in-service training over a period of time.

4. In-service training should provide special instructions on the culture of the various neighborhoods in which the police must

work and, in some areas, courses in basic Spanish should be taught for officers working in communities with a substantial Spanish-speaking population.

5. Every police department should establish formal machinery for the investigation of complaints against police activity or employees and for the determination of whether departmental policy is carried out. No department can be expected to operate without some misconduct; however, every department can be expected to attempt to discover its faults, correct them, and learn from them.

There can be little hope for improved relations between laymen and lawmen until every police officer views himself not simply as an enforcer of the law but as a professional with complex and diverse duties of public service. He must be a *part of* not *apart from* the community he serves. It is only in effective partnership of police and citizenry that the myriad problems of American law enforcement will be ameliorated.

NOTES

1. President's Commission on Law Enforcement and Administration of Justice, *Task Force Report: Police* (Washington, D.C., 1967), p. 144.
2. Public Bills, I, 1829, pp. 409–415.
3. Ibid.
4. President's Commission, pp. 145–149.
5. D. Johnson and R. Gregory, "Police Community Relations in the United States: A Review of Recent Literature and Projects," *Journal of Criminology, Criminal Law and Police Science,* March 1971, pp. 94–106.
6. Ibid., pp. 101–102.
7. President's Commission on Law Enforcement and Administration of Justice, *The Challenge of Crime in a Free Society* (Washington, D.C., 1967), p. 102.
8. Edward M. Davis, "Professional Police Principles," *Federal Probation,* March 1971.
9. American Bar Association, *Standards Relating to the Urban Police Function* (Chicago, Illinois, 1972), p. 53.
10. Elmer Johnson, "Police: An Analysis of Role Conflict," *Police,* Jan.–Feb. 1970, pp. 47–52.
11. Cummings, et al., "Policeman as Philosopher, Guide and Friend," *Social Problems* (Winter 1965), pp. 276–286.
12. Douglas Gourley, *Public Relations and the Police* (Springfield, Ill., 1963), p. ix.
13. *Task Force Report: Police.*
14. Ibid.

TOPICS FOR DISCUSSION

1. Discuss the differing expectations of a heterogeneous community regarding the police role.

2. Discuss the following (From Victor G. Strecher, *The Environment of Law Enforcement: A Community Relations Guide,* Englewood Cliffs, N.J.: Prentice-Hall, Inc., 1971, p. 96):

   A fundamental matter for every police officer is coming to grips with his role in the community and arriving at a self-concept. If a man persists in identifying himself as primarily a crime fighter when in fact his function has never been more than 20 percent crime fighting and when his daily experiences do not support his self-concept, it is inevitable that he will experience cognitive dissonance.

3. Discuss how each student would improve police service.

4. Discuss the definition of community, neighborhood. How would you identify the needs of your community regarding justice administration?

5. Discuss the ways each student would explain the role of the police to the community.

6. Discuss a list of priorities for the police role.

3

Law and the Courts

What, in fact, do law and our courts have to do with the administration of justice? Does the law of our land allow the court to determine guilt or innocence of an accused person? Does the adversary system really work, or does the court usually concern itself mostly with sentencing? What should I do with this person is usually the question, but more specifically the question is what should I do with this person before me who has been arrested previously—once, twice or three times? The adversary system usually comes into play when there is a trial, and each year a trial is less likely to occur. This leads one to ask what is the role of the court, the prosecutor, the defense attorney? Are we facing reality when we think in terms of a trial to insure due process and justice? How many members of the legal profession feel the criminal justice system needs to be reorganized or revolutionized?

We are a law-minded people and have an impulse to correct by passing a law. Should we have more police, judges, courts, and attorneys to maintain our justice system or should we have fewer laws and, consequently, fewer laws broken and less need for police, judges, courts, and attorneys? Anyway, criminal defendants are adjudicated today (approximately 90 percent plead guilty) by private negotiation between actors. The disposition of any case must allow for a working relationship between judge, prosecutor, defense attorney, and also do justice to the defendant and the community.

The role of the criminal lawyer in this process is the topic of chapter 13. It is the law of the land that each accused person have the right to be defended by competent counsel because freedom and liberty are at stake. Professor Cole discusses the two models of the criminal justice process, first, the "due process model," often referred to as the "combat or adversary model," and secondly, the "crime control model," which de-emphasizes the adversary nature of the judicial system. It is within these two models that the American criminal lawyer must find his role. In reality, most criminal lawyers are not highly thought of as professionals by their colleagues. To a great extent, this is due to the environment in which the criminal lawyer finds himself when practicing his profession. Most criminal defendants are poor; consequently, the criminal lawyer must try to receive payment for his services in advance.

It is important that the criminal lawyer understand people, as must the entire system of justice administration. There must be a good working relationship among judges, prosecutors, defense attorneys, police, parole, probation, and corrections. If the crime control model continues to be utilized to the extent it has been in the judicial process, then the understanding of people will continue to be an important talent for the participants to possess. Criminal justice education has the tools to assist in this understanding and in cooperative relationships. I believe this to be true, even if standard 3.1, *Abolition of Plea Negotiation,* of the National Advisory Commission on Criminal Justice Standards and Goals is implemented because the alternatives of careful screening, diversion, and streamlining the trial process require similar talents. For the criminal lawyer, their understanding of, and favorable relations with, people are not only important aspects but essential talents.

As the title of chapter 14 indicates, more and more scholars and practitioners agree that traffic violations should be made infractions subject to administrative regulations except in certain serious offenses. One statement epitomizes their belief, "You sure shouldn't pay a police officer fifteen thousand dollars a year and have him stand on street intersections and direct traffic all day." Another economic view regards the expense of providing judges, prosecutors, and possibly a public defender, or even a jury for traffic related offenses as absurd. There is another potential problem for the total traffic/criminal approach to traffic regulations and that is that combining traffic cases and criminal jurisdiction in one tribunal endangers the quality of the administration of the criminal jurisdiction. A review of most traffic courts would reveal many mechanical sentencing practices.

Discriminalization, however efficient and effective it may be, or justice reformation has two basic obstacles. First, public apathy, and second, the average citizen's fear. Too many people believe that dis-criminalizing conduct is equivalent to governmental approval, since the law in the community represents the view of the community, much the same as if it were a statement of social policy. These two basic views may be extended also to the attitudes of legislators, who make changes in the law. Finally, there are always those with a vested interest in the status quo. Can the quality of justice administration be improved without some type of reformation? Should the reform include dis-criminalization of certain offenses? Is it possible to overcome the obstacles through a compromise between discriminalization and total enforcement? What is the cost of discriminalization and total enforce-ment? What is the cost of discriminalization in terms of money and morale? What is the cost of increasing the responsibility, authority, and accountability of local law enforcement regarding the enforcement of white collar crime, such as tax evasion, embezzlement?

The court administrator is important to the viability of the adminis-tration of justice. Our poorly managed judicial system will decay even further if this administration of justice tool is not fully implemented.

Mr. Chamelin emphasizes this fact by pointing out ten categories of management responsibility for the court administrator. Chief Justice Burger proclaims the need for a business and public administration background in the selection requirements for court administrators. The scope of responsibility includes the full spectrum of personnel management, an area of special significance for any public administrator today.

Generally speaking, the qualifications for court administrator include: knowledge of the justice system, the individual attitude toward problem service, understanding modern management techniques, human relation skills, and appreciation of the role of the court administrator. If court reform is to be effective, top priority must be given to the quality of the individual selected for the very important position of court administrator. With the right personnel, the administrative arm of the court system may be able to reduce the caseload of judges, especially in the area of administrative hearings for specified traffic violations. In any case, the concept of court administration seems to be valid, accepted, and approved by all in the justice system.

In chapter 15, Judge Moylan presents a realistically clear picture of the controversies facing the administration of justice in our country today. He points out that there are no simple, easy solutions and suggests a few principles that should be applied. What constitutes an adequate day in court? How much and where should plea bargaining be allowed? Should plea bargaining be abolished? Should we follow the English system for juries which convicts or acquits by a vote of 10–2 or 9–3? Is the grand jury approach nothing more than a duplication of the prosecutor? Should the grand jury be abolished or should the role be re-defined? What about bail vs. release on recognizance? Is capital punishment a deterrent? I will not elaborate on these questions in this introduction since the honorable Judge Charles E. Moylan has so aptly captured the issue-problem concept of the text in this comprehensive chapter.

13

GEORGE F. COLE

The american criminal lawyer: a role definition

Most Americans have not seen a criminal lawyer in action. The vast majority have never visited a courtroom and only a tiny proportion have ever been defendants in criminal actions. Yet most Americans can probably describe the role played by lawyers in the criminal justice system. Through television, motion pictures, and literature, images of the great defense attorneys—Clarence Darrow, Perry Mason, Jerry Giesler, Edward Bennett Williams, and Melvin Belli— have been portrayed. Criminal lawyers are understood to be involved, by their investigative proficiency prior to trial, verbal skills in the courtroom, knowledge of the law, and ability to knit these talents together in a constant searching and creative questioning of decisions at every stage of the judicial process. As "Sam," a "moderately successful" thief, told social scientist Bruce Jackson:

> If I'm going to trial, actually going in to have one, you know what I like to have? I like to have me a little bitty young lawyer, a fire-burner. You know, one that will go up there and really argue the case. *But then I also want a real good old appeal lawyer to get the reversal.*[1]

Counsel is essential for the defense of a person accused of a crime. The stakes are high not only because his freedom is at issue, but also because the essence of the adversary system depends on the assumption that well-qualified and active defense counsel keep the system honest. Even though his various procedural tactics will undoubtedly slow the disposition of a case, an attorney is important as a conflict-causing agent in the administration of justice. Under ideal conditions, according to due process values, the defense counsel's activity will spur the other actors to "keep on their toes" so that they do not relax into the lethargy often associated with the criminal justice bureaucracy.

If "Sam" is correct in his appraisal of the legal talent needed for a trial, why does he assume that he will be convicted and need to appeal? Perhaps "Sam" has a more accurate perception of the criminal justice system (he's been through it many times) than does the general public. In another portion of his theory he says:

> When you want a lawyer, you don't want a trial lawyer, you want a fixer. You don't care how good he is in a courtroom, you want to fix it; you don't want to go to trial. You're hiring him *not* to go to trial. And if you *have* to go to trial, you're hiring him so whenever you walk into the courtroom you already know what you're going to get because he's already dealt out what.[2]

As "Sam" indicates, what he is looking for in a criminal lawyer is not someone who is skilled in the adversarial techniques of the courtroom but rather someone who knows his way around, who is on friendly terms with the prosecutor, police, and judges, and who is able to negotiate an agreement so that there will be little uncertainty as to the outcome.

These differing conceptions of the role of defense lawyer reflect assumptions about the nature of the criminal justice process and its supporting values. The "due process model," often referred to as the "combat or adversary model," is the image reflected in Perry Mason and the great advocates of the law. This view stresses both the adversary nature of courtroom proceedings and the rights of the individual as the truth is discovered. Herbert L. Packer has compared the "due process model" to an obstacle course, since a determination of guilt may be affirmed only by following certain procedures.[3] Although it does not deny the social desirability of repressing crime, the due process model stresses the problem of errors committed during the fact-finding stages. Because of the weight placed upon the individual's freedom, the deprivation of which could result from the judicial process, every effort is made to protect the accused from the consequences of mistakes in the system. Hence, this model assumes that a person is innocent until proved guilty, that he has an opportunity to discredit the case brought against him, and that an impartial judge is provided to decide the outcome.

Compared with the due process model, the crime control model de-emphasizes the adversary nature of the judicial system. Rather than stressing the combative elements of the courtroom, this model notes that bargaining between the state and the accused occurs at several points. The ritual of the courtroom is enacted in only a small number of cases; the rest are disposed of through negotiations over the charges, usually ending with the defendant's plea of guilty. An assumption of this model is that law enforcement officials do not have the resources for the practices extolled by the combat model. To operate efficiently, the crime control model must be based on a high rate of apprehension, the sifting out of the innocent, and the conviction of the offenders; this demands speed and finality, which depend upon informality and minimized occasions for challenge. Hence, probable guilt is administratively determined primarily by the results of the police investigation and a screening process in which those cases that may not terminate in conviction are filtered out of the system. At each successive stage—from arrest to arraignment, preliminary hearing, and courtroom trial—a series of routinized procedures is used by a variety of judicial actors to determine if the accused should be passed on to the next level.

The reality of the day-to-day administrative practices of the criminal justice system calls attention to the values of the crime control model. Particularly in the courts of large cities, disposition of criminal cases is made with lightning speed by overworked judges who seem more interested in moving the steady stream of cases than in weighing the facts on the scales of justice. Cases are disposed of through negotiation: defendants trade their admission of guilt for reduced charges, dismissal of multiple counts, and/or a lesser penalty. Because of the central role played by plea bargaining, trials are rare.

Although the opinions of the Supreme Court and the values of the due process model may be based on an idealized conception of the defense attorney as a combative element in an adversarial proceeding, it is of fundamental importance that we ask if this conception squares with reality. Reinforcement of the adversary thrust will be realized only if the social and organizational setting enhances the role of the criminal lawyer. Rather than act as the adversary challenging the decisions made at each step in the process, defense counsel may, in fact, be a broker among the defendant, prosecutor, and judge. It is possible that a defendant with an attorney who is attuned to the administrative system would be less of an impediment to its smooth operation than would be a defendant without counsel and whose notion of criminal justice had been formed by Perry Mason. The latter defendant would be unwilling to cooperate because he would not understand the ropes. The assistance of counsel may help the prosecutor and judge to "pull the loose ends together" so that a bargain can be worked out. In whose interest the bargain is made remains an open question.

ROLE: A CONCEPT FOR ANALYSIS

Two different conceptions of the part lawyers play on the criminal justice stage have been described: adversary and negotiator. When we think of the position of criminal law in American society we recognize that its practitioners have a particular function to carry out and in general possess similar occupational characteristics. All have been to law school, all are members of the legal profession, and all are expected to abide by a code of ethics, yet it is obvious from the comments of "Sam the thief" that there are important differences in the ways they perform. Perry Mason and a "fixer" both occupy the same socially defined *position* (that of criminal lawyer), yet each conceives his *role* (the way he acts on a daily basis) differently.[4] The playing of a role, therefore, is not only a function of the formal aspects of the position but also a product of such other important factors as the individual player's personality, the environment within which he operates, and his expectations of the attitudes of the "others" with whom he interacts.

Role emphasizes the relationships among people and recognizes that individuals activate somewhat different behaviors depending on the "other" in the interaction. A defense attorney behaves one way toward his client and another way toward the prosecutor. The same attorney may work very hard for a paying client, yet cut corners on the case of an indigent assigned to him by the court. The comradeship existing between fellow lawyers may melt away once a prosecutor and defense attorney enter the courtroom. Throughout the trial they may play their roles as advocates to the hilt, yet renew their friendship over a drink once the trial is ended.

Society has defined the position of criminal lawyer and has stipulated certain behaviors that are either prescribed or prohibited. Between these extremes of what a defense attorney *must do* and what he *must not do* there is wide latitude for him to determine the role he would like to play. But there are also aspects of his position that are not clear, and certain of society's expectations are contradictory. For example, although the adversarial stance is emphasized, the general public seems to feel that defense attorneys are somehow "soiled by their clients" and are engaged not so much in the practice of freeing the innocent as in letting the guilty escape by way of "technicalities" in the law. Additionally, because most defense lawyers are continuously on the losing side, they must suffer the discontent of their clients, who may feel that they did not work hard enough. The public defender is the special focus for such complaints. In some prisons "PD" is an abbreviation not for public defender but for "prison deliverer."

CRIMINAL PRACTICE

The professional competence of many of the lawyers who regularly take criminal cases has come into question. Surrounding most courthouses in large cities are the offices of attorneys such as those called "Fifth Streeters" in the District of Columbia and the "Clinton Street Bar" in Detroit. These designations refer to that group within the legal profession often found prowling the urban criminal courts searching for clients who can pay a modest fee. As Blumberg so well describes, these criminal defense "regulars" are:

> ... highly visible in the major urban centers of the nation; their offices—at times shared with bondsmen—line the back streets near the courthouses. They are also visible politically, with clubhouse ties reaching into judicial chambers and the prosecutor's office. The regulars make no effort to conceal their dependence upon police, bondsmen, jail personnel, as well as bailiffs, stenographers, prosecutors and judges.[5]

Rather than prepare their cases for disposition through the adversary process, they negotiate guilty pleas and try to convince their clients that they have received exceptional treatment. Such lawyers cease to be true professionals, but instead act as fixers for a fee. They exist in a relatively closed system where there are great pressures to process large numbers of cases for small fees, and they depend upon the cooperation of judicial personnel. These few practitioners usually are not as well educated, work harder, and are less secure financially than are their brothers in corporate practice.

It is true that there are some nationally known attorneys such as Melvin Belli, F. Lee Bailey, and Percy Foreman who have built reputations by adhering to the Perry Mason model. But they are few and expensive, and usually take only the dramatic, widely publicized cases; they do not frequent the county courthouse. Between the polar types of a Melvin Belli and a "Fifth Streeter" are many private practitioners who are willing, on occasion, to take criminal cases. Often they are members of, or connected to, a large firm whose upper-status client has run afoul of the law. Although this group is fairly substantial, its members have little experience in trial work and do not have well-developed relationships with the actors in the criminal justice system. Lacking this inside know-how, they may find that their client is better served if a courtroom regular is given the case.

It should be emphasized that we have been describing the practice of the criminal bar in big cities. In middle-sized and small cities it appears that a greater proportion of the legal profession does criminal defense work as part of general practice. Despite this fact, criminal law is not of major importance either in terms of time spent or as a principal source of income in the smaller communities. As a larger portion of the accused come to be represented by public defenders, the number of marginal private criminal lawyers may decline.

With the increased specialization and urbanization of the bar, it would seem that those persons engaged in the practice of criminal law have been relegated, both by their profession and by the community, to a lower status. As in other professions there is a ranking of members relative to the "cleanliness" and remunerativeness of the functions performed. To perform as the brilliant advocate in court, the criminal lawyer must engage in duties (gathering evidence, dealing with informants and criminals, negotiating with the prosecutor's office) where guile and force are needed but not admired. These characteristics of criminal practice, in addition to the fact that such service is poorly paid, mean that most defense specialists are given little professional status.

The membership of the urban bar appears to be divided into three parts. First, there is an inner circle, which handles the work of banks, utilities, and commercial concerns; another circle includes lawyers representing interests opposed to those of the inner circle; and, finally, an outer group scrapes together an existence by "haunting the courts in the hope of picking up crumbs from the judicial table."[6] With the exception of a highly proficient few who have made a reputation by winning acquittals in difficult, highly publicized cases, most of the lawyers dealing with criminal justice belong to this periphery.

Recognizing the place of criminal practice within the legal profession, we might ask who it is who takes criminal cases. What are the qualifications of the practitioners? How were they recruited to the lower rung of the bar? Social scientists interested in the bar say that the average criminal lawyer is a solo practitioner and is likely to be an immigrant's son who has "worked his way up," has gone either to a proprietary or a night law school, and still maintains close ties with his old neighborhood. Jerome Carlin examined solo practitioners in both Chicago and New York and found that criminal lawyers had to rely upon a wide range of religious or ethnic organizations as well as court officials for business contacts.[7]

When the background characteristics of this portion of the bar are tied to the recruitment patterns, certain dilemmas are bound to follow. For many upwardly mobile individuals law provides the easiest and cheapest avenue to professional status, yet once they become members of the bar, they may find that access to the higher ranks of corporate practice is all but closed to them. This means that the positions they do manage to achieve are often marginal, and their role in the profession precarious. In a real sense members of the criminal bar may not feel that they are true members of the legal profession since they rarely interact with their colleagues in the large firms, and their practice does not conform to the adversary work style taught in law school.

Environment of Criminal Practice

Other aspects of the criminal lawyer's profession help to explain his lower status within the bar. In general, we may stipulate that the unpleasant phases connected with his practice are not overcome by monetary or status inducements. For example, criminal cases, as well as those concerned with matrimonial problems, tend to involve the lawyer in emotional situations. Much of the service that he renders is preparation of the client and his relatives for the possible outcome. This means that the client's troubles are an emotional drain. Even the lawyer's exposure to "guilty knowledge" may be a psychological burden having an impact on his lifestyle. Lawyers have explained that they may easily become emotionally entangled, since they are the only judicial actors to view the defendant in the context of his social environment and family ties; overidentification with the client is too high a psychological price for many.

The criminal lawyer must also interact on a continuous basis with a lower class of clients, and with police officials, social workers, and minor political appointees. He may be required to visit such depressing places as the local jail at all hours of the day or night. If he wins the case he may find himself unable to collect his fee. Even an appearance in court may be viewed as a disadvantage. As Washington, D.C. attorney Thomas M. O'Malley wrote,

> It is also more comforting to work in the friendly atmosphere of one's office than in an unfriendly court where otherwise discerning people sometimes miss the subtle distinctions between the criminal and the defense attorney.[8]

The milieu of most criminal lawyers is a far cry from the mahogany panelling, plush carpets, and stimulating conversation of the upper-status law firm.

Criminal business when it does pay does not pay well. This is probably the key variable of the defense attorney's environment, influencing most other aspects of criminal practice. For the most part criminal defendants are poor. In addition, the loss of a case is likely to reduce even further the earning capacity of the defendant. Most attorneys must make every effort either to secure their fee in advance or somehow tie the defendant and his family financially to the law firm.

> "The lawyer goes out and tries to squeeze money from the defendant's mother or an aunt," explains Judge Charles W. Halleck, of the local trial court in Washington, D.C. "Sometimes, he asks a jailed defendant, 'You got $15 or $25? Here, let me hold it for you.' And later that becomes part of the fee."[9]

Although professional norms may emphasize the right of every person to a defense, practical monetary considerations may dictate that the attorney insist upon a formula for payment in advance. The search for a fee may, on occasion, occupy much of the time a lawyer spends with his client. Martin Mayer tells the amusing story of the fictitious "Mr. Green": when a fee has not been received, a common practice is for attorneys to ask the judge for a continuation or recess on the grounds that his key witness, "Mr. Green," has not yet arrived; this code is well known to judicial actors and the request is usually honored.[10] As one Seattle lawyer said, "More people don't take criminal cases because there is just no money in it."

The impact of the financial circumstances of criminal defense generally means that most attorneys are forcer to handle a multitude of cases for small fees. This heightens the incentive to bargain with the prosecutor rather than bring the case to trial. The same fee may be received for a fifteen-minute conference with the prosecutor and a five-minute appearance in court to render a guilty plea as may be collected after a three-day trial with its risks for the attorney. A frequently heard statement from criminal lawyers is, "I make my money on the phone or in the prosecutor's office, not in the court-room."

DEFENSE COUNSEL
IN THE ADMINISTRATIVE SYSTEM

We have seen that most of the criminal lawyers in metropolitan courts are persons whose professional environment is precarious; they work very hard in unpleasant surroundings for small fees and are not recompensed by professional or public acclaim. In a judicial system where bargaining within an administrative context is a primary method of decision making, it is not surprising that defense attorneys find it essential to maintain close personal ties with the police, prose-cutor, judges, and other court officials. Thus the ability of the attorney to establish and continue a pattern of informal relations with these individuals is essential both for his own professional sur-vival and for the opportunity to serve the needs of his clients.

> Getting along with people—salesmanship. That's what this young lawyer in my office right now doesn't know anything about. He's a moot court champion—great at research. But he doesn't know a damn thing about people.[11]

At every step of the criminal process, from the first contact with the accused until final disposition of the case, the defense attorney is dependent upon decisions made by other judicial actors. Even such seemingly minor activities as visiting the defendant in jail, learning the case against him from the prosecutor, and setting bail can be made difficult by these officials unless there is cooperation by the defense. A lawyer's concern with preserving his relationships within the criminal justice system may have greater weight for him than his more transitory interest in his client. Long-run objectives may be more important than short-run, and he may be able to rationalize that, although an occasional client must suffer, his clientele as a whole benefits from his standing in the system.

We should not assume that counsel is at the complete mercy of judicial actors. At any phase of the process, the defense has the ability to invoke the adversary model with its formal rules and public battles. It is this potential for a trial with its expensive, time-consuming, and disputatious features that the effective counsel can use as a bargaining tool with the police, prosecutor, and judge. A well-known tactic, certain to raise the ante in the bargaining process, is for the defense to ask for a trial and to proceed as if he meant it.

Not only does a public trial create additional uncertainties for all the actors, but the requirements of evidence and procedure make the work of both sides more difficult. Besides, the justice system operates like a small town: because judicial personnel must "live and work together," they seek to avoid friction. The introduction of adversary tactics is disruptive of harmony; thus, for the benefit of the participants and to avoid possible detriment to the clients, every effort is made to temper possible animosities.

Some attorneys are able to play the adversary role with skill. They have developed a style that emphasizes the belligerent behavior of a professional who is willing to fight the system for his client. Such lawyers are experienced in the courtroom and have built a practice around defendants who can afford the expense. Further, there may be clients who demand and expect their counsel to play the combatant role; they feel they are shortchanged otherwise. The costs of this kind of practice are not only financial. There must be a willingness to gamble that the results of a trial will benefit the accused and counsel more than a bargain arranged with the prosecutor would. Having once broken the informal rules, the combative attorney may find that he has jeopardized future cooperation from the police and prosecutor.

Even when verbal fireworks occur, one cannot be certain that the adversaries are engaged in a meaningful contest. It has been shown that in some cities attorneys with clients who expect to get a vigorous defense may engage in a courtroom drama commonly known as the "slow plea of guilty." Although negotiations have already determined the outcome of a case, a defense attorney with a paying client who expects to get his money's worth may arrange with the prosecutor and even the judge to stage a battle even though it culminates in a previously agreed upon sentence.

> We had to put on one of these shows a few months ago. Well, we were all up there going through our orations, and the whole time the judge just sat there writing. Finally the D.A. reduced his charge, and the judge looked up long enough to say "Six months probation." Afterwards in the coffee shop my partner told the judge, "Jesus man, can't you try to look a little more interested while you're filling out your docket sheets?" The judge said, "What in the hell am I supposed to be interested in? You come to me with this scheme all planned out, you tell me exactly what you're going to do, then you tell me exactly what I'm going to do—and now you expect me to have acted interested."[12]

For the criminal lawyer who depends upon a large volume of petty cases from clients who are poor and who he assumes are probably guilty of some offense, the incentives to bargain are strong. To sustain his ability to secure cases, serve his clients' interests, and maintain his status as a practitioner, the criminal lawyer has found that friendship and influence with judicial officials are essential. There are specific benefits that he can obtain from these sources: informal discovery and plea bargaining from the prosecutor, fact finding and favorable testimony from the police, sentencing discretion and court-room reception by the judge, and the influence of all three on the bail decision. But for these courtesies there is a *quid pro quo:* information elicited from the client, a less than vigorous defense, the cultivation of active social relationships, political support, and a general degree of cooperativeness. During each step of the crminal justice process the defense attorney has professional and interpersonal problems that must be resolved. Defense attorneys interviewed in a number of studies have overwhelmingly stated that they could act most successfully for themselves and their clients when they were able to maintain a cooperative posture.[13]

Securing Cases

As is necessary in other professions where the potential for client exploitation exists, the American bar has erected rigid strictures against the solicitation of clients. Lawyers are not allowed to advertise their services, and those with reputations as "ambulance chasers" soon find that their conduct is held in low regard by colleagues. Though people often have ties with members of the medical profession—which has similar canons—they are much less likely to have such connections with the legal profession; most citizens do not have a "family lawyer" and when the exceptional occasion arises must seek out legal services. This means that for both the practitioner trying to make a living and the accused who is in need of counsel, the difficulties of establishing contact may be severe.

There may be criminal lawyers who chase patrol wagons, but most depend on a broker—a person who by a variety of circumstances is in a peculiarly advantageous or sensitive position for identifying and channelling potential legal business to the attorney. The broker may be a bondsman, policeman, fellow attorney, prison official, or clergyman. The criminal lawyer seeking clients has the problem of making himself known to the broker and creating a climate so that cases will be referred. Participation in social or political groups is one way the attorney makes contact with brokers. Favors, such as free legal advice on personal matters to law enforcement actors, can bring about an "indebtedness." These arrangements for the funneling of clients can lead to the lawyer's becoming more obligated to his broker than to his client. A police captain is probably going to be less likely to hand the attorney's business card to a prisoner if, on the basis of past experience, he has found that the lawyer is not cooperative.

Relations with Clients

If the criminal lawyer is not an advocate, using technical skills to win a case, what is the service that he performs for the accused? We have shown that one of the assets that he sells is his influence within the judicial system: his ability to telephone the sheriff, enter the prosecutor's office, and bargain for his client with judicial officials. Based on his knowledge of the accused, the charge, the evidence, and the possible sanctions, the defense attorney may view his role as getting his client's penalty set at the lowest end of the range provided by statute. All of the activities are played so that the defendant believes that he is getting his money's worth; a feeling of professional confidence, an aura of influence, and "inside dopesterism" are essential. Neubauer quotes a prosecutor in Prairie City as pointing to the first arraignment as the greatest boon to the defense bar. In this proceeding, the accused is told what the maximum penalty is for the charges made. When his lawyer secures a bargain in which three to five years in prison will be the price, his client is grateful that he has been spared the multiple charges with a potential of sixty-five years outlined in the law.

> The lawyer's fee is money charged for getting his client the normal penalty, which is substantially less than the maximum penalty under the law. Clients have no way of knowing what to

expect from the system and one imagines attorneys do not go overboard in stressing "I did what any attorney could do."[14]

A second device performed by the defense attorney is labeled by Blumberg as the "agent mediator" role.[15] Not only is the criminal lawyer an advocate for his client, he is also an adviser, explaining the judicial process and letting the accused know what to expect. This facet of the attorney's role may evolve into a confidence game in which he prepares the accused for defeat and then "cools him out" when it comes, as it is likely to do. Toward this goal the attorney helps the accused to redefine his situation and to restructure his perceptions, and thus prepares him to accept the consequences of a guilty plea. In the process of "cooling out" the accused, the lawyer is often assisted by the defendant's kin, probation officer, prosecutor, and judge. All try to emphasize that they want him to "do the right things for his own good." Thus the defendant finds himself in a position analogous to that of a patient with various treatments urged upon him by those proclaiming that they are working in his behalf.

The public defender has a special problem of client control. Since the defendant has not selected his counsel, he may dig in his heels and not accept the bargain, insisting that a trial be held. Because the public defender may fear a charge of misleading his client, he may have to invoke the formal procedure. The extent to which the defender *represents* the accused is open to question. Judicial actors may use the trial as an opportunity to impress upon other defendants that a cooperative attitude is important.

The criminal lawyer acting as an agent-mediator may in fact be viewed as a double agent. With obligations to both his client and the court, he is a broker seeking to effect a satisfactory outcome. The position is fraught with conflicts of interest. As Blumberg notes:

> Too often these must be resolved in favor of the organization which provides him with the means of his professional existence. Consequently, in order to reduce the strains and conflicts imposed in what is ultimately an overdemanding role obligation for him, the lawyer engages in the lawyer-client "confidence game" so as to structure more favorably an otherwise onerous role system.[16]

Plea Bargaining: Relations with the Prosecutor

Of the many criminal justice officials with whom lawyers must interact, the prosecuting attorney is most crucial for the defense. From the time of arrest to the final disposition of the case the prosecutor is in a position to make decisions that will determine to a great extent whether the case will be prosecuted, the charges to be brought into the courtroom, the bargains to be agreed upon with the defendant, and the level of enthusiasm with which the case is pursued and new evidence developed until a conviction may be obtained. Defense counsel may attempt to influence each of the prosecutor's decisions, but plea bargaining is the most prevalent of their interactions.

Plea bargaining is essentially a game in which the prosecutor, defense attorney, defendant, and sometimes the judge participate. Each enters the contest with his own objectives. Each attempts to structure the situation to his own advantage, and comes armed with a number of tactics designed to improve his position. Each will judge the success of the exchange. The game may be deemed successful by the prosecutor if he is able to convict the defendant without trial, by the defense attorney if he is able to collect his fee with a minimum of effort, and by the judge if he is able to dispose of one more case from a crowded calendar. Yet Casper found that defendants felt that they could not win. As he comments, "It is a game in which they can, should they choose to play and be skillful or lucky, lose less than they would if they failed to play at all."[17]

Defense counsel may approach these negotiations by threatening to ask for a jury trial if concessions are not made. His hand is further strengthened if he has filed pretrial motions that require a formal response by the prosecutor. Another stratagem is to seek pretrial continuances with the hope that witnesses will become unavailable, public interest will die, and memories of the incident will fade. There are other attorneys who believe that rather than resort to legal maneuverings it is important to keep a low profile and dicker on the basis of friendship. As one Oakland attorney said:

> I never use the Constitution. I bargain a case on the theory that it's a "cheap burglary" or a "cheap purse-snatching" or a "cheap whatever." Sure, I could suddenly start to negotiate by saying, "Ha, ha! You goofed. You should have given the defendant a warning." And I'd do fine in that case, but my other clients would pay for this isolated success. The next time the district attorney had his foot on my throat, he'd push too.[18]

Since negotiations are primarily between the prosecutor and the defense attorney, the interests of the public and even the defendant may become secondary to the needs of these principal actors. This becomes an aggravated ethical problem when the defense attempts to bargain on a package basis, agreeing to trade the guilty pleas of some clients for promises of less severe treatment for others. Referring to a fellow lawyer, one Seattle attorney said:

> You should see _____. He goes up there to Carroll's [the prosecutor's] office with a whole fist full of cases. He trades on some,

bargains on others and never goes to court. It's amazing but it's
the way he makes his living.

Discriminatory treatment of defendants may not always be
purposeful, especially when one negotiating session covers several
cases. There appears to be a natural tendency for the prosecutor to
remain firm when considering the first cases so that he will not
diminish his bargaining strength on later cases.

Plea bargaining between counsel and prosecutor bears a striking
resemblance to a formal ritual in which friendliness and joking mask
the forceful advancement of antagonistic views. The pattern is a
familiar one: initial humor, the stating of each viewpoint, resolution
of conflict, and a final period of cementing the relationship. Throughout the session each tries to impress the other with the confidence
he has in his own case, while indicating weaknesses in his opponent's
presentation. All during the discussion there appears to be a norm of
openness and candor directed toward the maintenance of the relationship.

Neither the prosecutor nor the defense attorney is a free agent,
since each must count on the cooperation of the defendant and judge.
Attorneys often cite the difficulty that they have convincing a client
that he should uphold his end of the bargain. Experienced criminals
have expressed the opinion that they are better off without a lawyer
because they can then deal directly with the prosecutor.

The bargaining system also depends upon acceptance of the
negotiated plea by the judge. It means, too, that the judge must
consummate the agreement by sentencing the accused according to
the recommendation of the prosecutor. Although the judge's role
prescription requires that he give the public interest its full due, he
may be reluctant to intervene and repudiate an agreement acceptable
to the litigants. Thus, it is common for both the prosecutor and defense attorney to confer with the judge regarding the sentence to be
imposed. At the same time, the credibility of the myths surrounding
the process mandates that he hold in reserve his power to reject the
agreement. To diminish the element of uncertainty that is one of the
hazards of the administrative system, observers look to the judge's
decisions for indications of his future behavior.

SUMMARY

The role of the defense attorney is structured by his occupational
environment within the criminal justice system. Recruitment into
criminal practice, financial considerations, interpersonal relations,

and the demands of the system for a speedy disposition of a huge caseload create needs that are met through a process of bargaining. As a result, criminal lawyers participate in a number of interpersonal relationships that influence case disposition. A primary focus for decision making is plea bargaining, where the various perspectives of the defendant, prosecutor, defense lawyer, and judge are brought to bear. "Sam" is probably right. What a criminal defendant needs is a "fixer"! As one judge told the author, "Lawyers are helpful to the system. They are able to pull things together, work out a deal, keep the system moving." But we must ask, "Is that the role that should be played by criminal lawyers?"

NOTES

1. Bruce Jackson, *A Thief's Primer* (New York: The Macmillan Company, 1969), p. 131. (Italics added)
2. Ibid., p. 130.
3. Herbert L. Packer, *The Limits of the Criminal Sanction* (Stanford: Stanford University Press, 1968).
4. The concept of role is well developed in: Theodore M. Newcomb, Ralph H. Turner, and Philip E. Converse, *Social Psychology: The Study of Human Interaction* (New York: Holt, Rinehart and Winston, 1965). For applications of the concept see: John H. Kessel, George F. Cole, and Robert G. Seddig (eds.), *Micropolitics* (New York: Holt, Rinehart and Winston, 1970).
5. Abraham S. Blumberg, "Lawyers with Convictions," *Transaction,* 4 (July, 1967), 18.
6. Jack Ladinsky, "The Impact of Social Backgrounds on Lawyers on Law Practice and the Law," *Journal of Legal Education,* 16 (1963), 128.
7. Jerome Carlin, *Lawyers on Their Own* (New Brunswick: Rutgers University Press, 1962).
8. Leonard Downie, Jr., *Justice Denied* (New York: Praeger Publishers, 1971), p. 172.
9. Ibid., p. 173.
10. Martin Mayer, *The Lawyer* (New York: Harper and Row, 1966), p. 162.
11. Jackson B. Battle, "In Search of the Adversary System—The Cooperative Practices of Private Criminal Defense Attorneys," *University of Texas Law Review,* 50 (December 1971), 66.
12. Ibid., p. 108.
13. Ibid.; Jerome Skolnick, *Justice without Trial* (New York: John Wiley, 1966); Arthur L. Wood, *Criminal Lawyers* (New Haven: College and University Press, 1967).
14. David W. Neubauer, *Criminal Justice in Middle America* (Morristown, N. J.: General Learning Press, 1974), p. 75.
15. Abraham S. Blumberg, "The Practice of Law as Confidence Game," *Law and Society Review,* 1 (1967), 11–39.
16. Ibid., p. 38.
17. Jonathan D. Casper, *American Criminal Justice* (Englewood Cliffs, N.J.: Prentice-Hall, Inc., 1972), p. 78.
18. Albert W. Alschuler, "The Prosecutor's Role in Plea Bargaining," *University of Chicago Law Review,* 36 (Fall 1968), p. 86.

TOPICS FOR DISCUSSION

1. Discuss the realities of the functions of the courts in America today.

2. Discuss the possibility of reducing the number of laws which now exist. Identify in order of priority which laws should be repealed first.

3. Discuss how each student views the criminal lawyer/defense attorney/ public defender.

4. Discuss the dissenting view of Mr. Stanley C. Van Ness, page 319–20 of the National Advisory Commission on Criminal Justice Standards and Goals Report on Courts as it applies to the criminally accused and the criminal lawyer.

5. Discuss the local situation regarding criminal lawyers, ambulance chasers vs. highly professional.

6. Discuss the impact "politics" has on the "role" of the criminal lawyer.

14

CHARLES E. MOYLAN, JR.

Traffic courts and the retreat from criminalization

In the far-ranging debate over the problems and the future of the American criminal justice system, no single problem looms quantitatively more significant than that of the nation's traffic courts. The volume of cases flowing through this one arena is more massive than the aggregate moving through all of the other criminal courts combined. The average citizen gets his one and only impression of his criminal justice system in the course of an embarrassed and apprehensive visit to a traffic court. The sight he sees is an appalling one and the impression it leaves is darkly dispiriting.

Some of the troubles are obvious and others more deep-seated. In many of the traffic courts, vestigial corruption still lingers from the days when those courts were the exclusive preserves of the big city political machines. Ill-trained and very part-time magistrates qualified for their sinecures by loyally working their precincts and managing their wards. The clerkships were a regular reward for the party faithful. The most corrosive problem was not simply the process of selection of the personnel but the resulting quality of the justice they dispensed. Massive ticket fixing was, and in some places still is, a characteristic feature. If the right politician or the right lawyer stood with a defendant in front of the judge, the verdict was not guilty however overwhelming the evidence of guilt may have been. Frequently the politician or the lawyer simply "fixed" the matter in advance in the judge's chambers. The crooked practices were by no means confined to parking violations or the running of red lights. Significant drunken driving offenses were frequently the object of the political, or otherwise corrupt, "fix." Sometimes cash was the consideration in straight *quid pro quo* briberies. More frequently, political favoritism and cronyism were the corrupting influences. In either event, the air of the typical station house reeked with petty graft.

Massive court reforms of the last decade or two have gone a long way toward cleaning the Augean stables of the nation's traffic courts. More and more metropolitan centers are recognizing that only legally trained, highly professional, adequately compensated, full-time judges can be permitted to operate a judicial system. The judges themselves are increasingly merit appointees, with secure tenure in office, rather than political hacks. Civil service, or its equivalent, is providing a healthy antidote to what once prevailed in the supporting staffs and clerks' offices.

The obviously needed reform in the selection of court personnel is revolutionizing the quality of justice in the lower tier of the court system around the country. In the traffic courts, however, this solution (necessary as it is in many regards) does not solve the entire problem. Judicial competence and judicial integrity are indispensable, of course, but they are not sufficient. The underlying problem may be with the system itself. We must ask ourselves the basic question of whether the regulation of traffic and the processing of traffic violations ought to be the business of the criminal law. In the traffic court, as in the criminal court, the proceedings are in the name of the state. The process is titled "State versus," "The People versus," or "Commonwealth versus." We maintain a fiction called the trial process, but obviously there may be nothing resembling an adversary proceeding when a typical traffic court hearing is expected to take two minutes and when five minutes is an intolerable filibuster. Massive volume has aggravated the problem, of course, but the root condition was always there.

The hour may already have long since arrived when some administrative agency should take over from the courts the whole business of processing traffic charges. If we persist in calling these hearings criminal trials, the day may soon be upon us when an assistant district attorney and an assistant public defender, both at public expense, will be doing battle over every parking ticket before a robed judge, with a court reporter transcribing every word and a twelve-man jury in the box. The criminal trial, as it is being polished and perfected (and consequently protracted) through constitutional decisions, may no longer be a viable institution to handle a hundred thousand or a half million traffic violations per year. To do the job of trying cases, as they are now theoretically supposed to be tried, would require for any good-sized American city a hundred new judges, two hundred new assistant prosecutors and two hundred new assistant public defenders, even to begin to cope with the unimaginable caseload. The machinery is just too cumbersome for its function, and the whole structure seems as if it could some day, in the not-too-distant future, collapse of its own weight.

Traffic violations are grouped with crimes, but are obviously a genus apart. An appeal from a decision in the traffic court entitles the defendant, as a matter of right, to a trial *de novo* in the circuit court. When the full majesty of Old Bailey is invoked so that a dozen of his peers may decide unanimously over days or even weeks whether John Q. Public overparked, something in our system is sadly out of joint. We are swatting flies with thermonuclear hammers.

Initially, it is highly questionable whether the basic criminal process is even appropriate to traffic violations. But for the distinguishing feature that almost one hundred million people drive cars every day, traffic regulation would be recognized as philosophically akin to health regulation, zoning regulation, sanitary regulation, the regulation of the sale of stocks and bonds, or the regulation of the practice of law or medicine.

Any complex society needs its building codes, electricians' codes, plumbers' codes and banking codes. We license and regulate bars and barbers, dentists and beauticians, carpenters and taxicab drivers. Such regulation is essential, but breaches of the regulations are not in a traditional sense criminal. Those who do not always abide by the conditions of their licensing unquestionably have violated regulatory laws and must be made to conform. They are not, however, outlaws or enemies of the state in the sense that a thief, a rapist, a robber, a burglar, or a murderer may be. Violations of rules and regulations can generally be dealt with by civil suit, equitable injunction, or administrative sanction. Licenses can be suspended or revoked. Every unlawful act is not necessarily a criminal act. There is a basic qualitative distinction between the kinds of unlawful acts. The difference is sometimes referred to as the difference between a *malum prohibitum* and a *malum in se*—the thing which is wrong simply because it is prohibited and the thing which is wrong because it is evil by its very nature.

Many commentators feel that traffic violations should, like their less numerous counterparts, be handled administratively. A few of the more extremely antisocial forms—manslaughter by automobile, drunken driving, etc.—could appropriately continue to be handled by traditional criminal process. The great mass of the traffic infractions, on the other hand, could almost certainly be handled much more efficiently by motor vehicle administrations. The person charged today with a typical moving violation is less concerned with a $25 fine than with the accumulation of "points," leading to the possible suspension or revocation of his driver's license. Administrative procedures are far more streamlined and far less cumbersome than a criminal trial in assessing such "points." A vehicle's speed as clocked by a radar machine, the blood alcohol count of a driver, the running of a red light, or a parking meter violation are observations sufficiently scientific and precise to make it perfectly appropriate for a person charged with them to carry the burden of establishing either a defense or extenuating circumstances. To require the state to go through the motions time after time of proving its case "beyond a reasonable doubt" is a senseless waste of time and effort for the sake of form. The regulation of those licensed to use the highways is not a deprivation of life, liberty, or property and need not invoke the manifold protections of the due process clause.

The robotlike unformity in our traffic court sentencing practices reveals in part the inappropriateness of applying traditional criminal sanctions. We do not, and of course should not, ask for pretrial sentence reports for traffic violators. To place the entire phenomenon in perspective, we might ask why we punish in traffic cases. Immediately apparent is the fact that neither rehabilitation nor retribution play any significant role in our rationale. We do not generally tailor the sentence to the peculiarities of the man sentenced. Sentences in traffic cases serve almost exclusively the function of deterrence. Everyone who exceeds the speed limit by five miles per hour will pay $25 and court costs in order to deter other potential speeders. When deterrence is virtually our sole purpose and when the assessment of the sentence is so essentially automatic, an administrative decision may be just as effective and efficient as the discretion of a judicial officer.

A growing awareness of the inappropriateness of handling traffic infractions within the context of the traditional criminal law raises the spectre of overcriminalization in general. Perhaps other areas of social regulation have also been inappropriately engrafted onto the criminal process.

One such area is that of alcohol-related offenses. Arrests for drunkenness outnumber those for any other crime but traffic violations. Should, however, this entire category of antisocial behavior or harmful conduct be treated as crime? Built into this area of criminal law enforcement are some perplexing juridical problems that the legal profession has hardly begun to address, let alone to answer. Should an alcoholic—considering the essentially involuntary nature of his conduct, which the doctors say is but a symptom of his disease— logically and fairly be held criminally responsible for the involuntary act of getting drunk, even assuming he does it in public? Should an alcoholic logically and fairly be held criminally responsible for any crime committed while he is involuntarily drunk? May a voluntary drunk who is not an alcoholic at least have the degree or severity of his crime mitigated by his condition at the moment of perpetration? Some crimes such as first-degree murder, burglary, and larceny have special mental elements—a "specific intent" or "special *mens rea*"— that a drunken brain simply cannot form. Should mere drunkenness aggravated by no other factor even be a crime at all? Should safekeeping in a detoxification shelter be an alternative to thirty days in jail? Should some sort of civil commitment to a hospital for alcoholics replace the treadmill of the Saturday nights in the tank at the local lockup? How should an enlightened society deal with the phenomenon of alcohol and alcoholism? But if an alcoholic cannot logically and fairly be held criminally responsible for getting drunk, how can an addict logically and fairly be held criminally responsible for taking dope? Or a kleptomaniac, for stealing? Or a pyromaniac, for burning? We are only beginning to ask the questions and do not yet have any intelligent answers to them.

As we rethink the whole problem of alcohol and its effects, our thought inevitably must turn to such allied "crimes" as those involving narcotics, marijuana, amphetamines, barbiturates, hallucinogenic drugs, and, while on the subject, why not tobacco? If we could stand off on a mountaintop and view ourselves with panoramic perspective we might suddenly appreciate that what we are doing in this area is asking ourselves, as a people, a very fundamental question: to what extent are we going to permit people, even when they know what they are doing and even when they want to do it, to inflict harm not upon others but upon themselves? If after listening to all of the medical testimony, we ultimately conclude, a decade hence, that marijuana does indeed induce sexual promiscuity or other forms of permissive behavior and that tobacco does indeed induce cancer of the lungs and arteriosclerosis, then where does the criminal law step in and where does it stay out? To whom, if anyone, should the criminal sanction be applied? The manufacturer? The distributor? The advertiser? The consumer? Should it be placed upon all equally?

If we look for a moment at the causes for this sort of "crime," we will realize that causation here is of a very different species from the causation of street violence. The ghetto dweller who robs or yokes (mugs) or steals may be doing those things, the sociologists tell us, because he has been denied, among many other things, entrance into the American mainstream. On the other hand, the middle-aged woman who drinks too much, the young person from the well-to-do family who persists in smoking pot, or the busy executive who despite the warnings chain-smokes three packs of cigarettes a day—these people may be doing those things just because they are too intently and intensely involved in that American mainstream.

Another area where overcriminalization—on the books at least, if not in actual practice—may be thrusting the criminal law and its processes into inappropriate matters is with regard to "sexual crimes." Involved here is governmental regulation of moral behavior, once perhaps appropriate in a Puritan theocracy but now quaintly anachronistic in a pluralistic twentieth-century democracy. These "crimes" represent transgressions of our nominal national morality—

the flouting of our ancient tribal taboos. These "crimes" came late into the criminal law, out of the ecclesiastical courts of medieval England. The handwriting is upon the wall that they, via the 1st or 9th Amendment, will soon be leaving the criminal law.

The efforts of enforcement in this arena are understandably ineffective. By way of example, the crime of adultery has been on the books in the state and the proprietary colony of Maryland since 1714; yet no one in the history of that state has ever been convicted of, or even charged with, adultery. No self-respecting prosecutor would think of indicting someone for adultery, with its maximum penalty of a $10 fine, any more than he would think of indicting someone for blasphemy.

A revolution, recently spurred by the Supreme Court, is taking place on a nationwide scale with respect to abortion laws. It is rapidly being recognized that the decision of whether to continue or to terminate a pregnancy should be a personal decision made by the pregnant woman (or, at most, something between her and her God, as opposed to something between her and her civil state). Great Britain has paved the way for taking out of the criminal law homosexual relations between consenting adults. Any thoughtful observer must wonder how long the criminal law can continue to condemn, frequently hypocritically and almost always ineffectually, so-called "perverted practices," even of a heterosexual variety, and even, indeed, between husband and wife in the privacy of a marital bedroom. What of incest? What of solicitation? Mrs. Warren's profession may remain under the interdict a time longer because of its potential for organization and corruption and because of its threat to public hygiene. Looking ten years into the future, however, one would have to predict that the criminal law will be getting out of the business of even attempting to regulate sexual behavior, except perhaps where children are debauched or where conduct is so open and notorious as to offend the sensitivities of a public that cannot shield its eyes or get out of the way.

Involved inevitably in this particular area of possible over-criminalization is the attempt to regulate criminally traffic in pornographic and allegedly obscene literature. Here again, it is the morals of the community which are looking to the criminal law for support. The moral transgressions here are, to be sure, vicarious rather than direct, but to the puritan, the evil thought is tantamount to the evil deed. The dilemma here for the courts and the judicial process is one of definition—how to draw lines. What does the censor answer if he is asked a series of questions, "If you would ban a Danish nudist magazine, would you ban *Playboy?* If so, would you ban *Esquire?* If so, would you ban *Ulysses?* If so, would you ban the Venus de Milo?" Conversely, what does the civil libertarian answer when asked an equally perplexing series of questions, "If one may write in most graphic terms in a novel of an act of sexual intercourse, may one portray it with still photographs? If so, may one portray it in moving pictures, in technicolor, with stereophonic sound? If so, may one portray it upon the live stage? If so, may amateur troupes perform in the back yard? If so, may they perform upon the public street?"

Ultimately, the hard conclusion dawns that on the continuum between those things that are clearly for the proscenium and those things that are equally clearly for the obscenium, there are no great discernible leaps but only a series of little steps, each one leading imperceptibly into the next. As a result, any demarcation line we attempt to draw between the legitimate, upon the one hand, and the illegitimate, upon the other, must, perforce, be very arbitrary in relation to its immediately adjacent points. One cannot help but wonder whether this is an appropriate mission for the criminal law. Might not trash sink to its own level in a free marketplace? Does not a criminal prosecution or a "banned in Boston" notice sometimes create an artificial bull market for a product that otherwise might, on its own lack of merit, fail commercially? Is the regulation of morals the proper business for the criminal law?

The root problem is that the criminal law, essentially by default, is being called upon to deal with many social problems for which it was not devised. Another of these inappropriate areas is the regulation of domestic relations. This is a totally new responsibility to the criminal law. In a more leisurely and rural society, the community supplied its own sanctions, and resort to the courts was unknown. Time was when a gentleman's code of honor or, in the more difficult cases, a father's shotgun were the only sanctions needed to make "that fellow marry the gal." Today, however, we utilize the judicial process, and largely the criminal aspect of that process, to handle yearly thousands upon thousands of cases of bastardy and of non-support of wives, children, and aging parents. A subspecialty within this area deals on a full-time basis with "uniform reciprocal nonsupport," just to help local wives or mothers collect from delinquent out-of-state husbands or natural fathers and to help out-of-state wives or mothers collect from delinquent local husbands or natural fathers.

Here again, it is highly questionable whether the full superstructure of the criminal law should be erected around such procedures. Should we proceed in the name of the state instead of having the aggrieved party bring his or her own private action? Is proof beyond a reasonable doubt the appropriate burden? Should public defenders or court-appointed attorneys be available for those who have been domestically errant? Is incarceration an appropriate ultimate sanction? We should be facing such issues squarely and making basic policy decisions. Instead, we sometimes fall into judicial patterns almost by chance.

There is another area where the appropriate decision may be not to retreat from past criminalization but to forbear future criminalization. This involves the wide new horizon of environment "crimes." Regulation, and regulation with strong sanctions, is unquestionably needed. We are just beginning, as a people, to appreciate that our classic notions as to what criminals look like are out of touch with new realities. We are beginning to recognize that a seventeen-year-old black running out of a store with a stolen flashlight or can of beans is not necessarily more dangerous to us than someone who would steal from us the air we breathe and the water we drink. The new conceptualization comes hard when the new brand of criminals are residents of well-to-do residential suburbs, graduates of Ivy League colleges, members of the country club and pillars of the church, whose criminality consists of devotion to the economic principles of Adam Smith. We are, however, recognizing the new reality. The question is whether local law enforcement and the local judicial process are capable of handling the problem. Investigation is quite obviously beyond the capacity of local sheriffs and policemen. Prosecution is quite obviously beyond the capacity of local district attorneys. In this arena, perhaps only the federal government or the attorney general's office of a larger and more sophisticated state is equipped to move, with its broad arsenal of civil, criminal and equitable weapons. Before we venture into such new areas, long thought is called for as to what the sanctions should be and as to who the enforcers should be. It is too important a decision to be left to the hand of chance.

A problem somewhat allied to that of dealing with the environmental crimes is that of local tax evasion. No one doubts that criminal sanctions are appropriate for such violations. There is a real question, however, as to whether local law enforcement in its present mold is structured or tooled up to handle such problems. For years we have had state income taxes. Many cities now have a municipal earnings tax. It would be naive to assume that on the local level no one ever files a fraudulent return or fails to file a return at all. Why would individuals risk, as many of them obviously do, the wrath of a vigilant Internal Revenue Service at the federal level, yet shrink from stirring up local law enforcement? Yet no one is ever locally prosecuted, for the simple reason that there is nobody to catch him. It is just not economically feasible for a state comptroller's office or a city department of finance to establish an intelligence division trained to stalk suspects in and out of Swiss banks or to estimate net worth. Local police are neither structured nor staffed for this type of long-term, sophisticated investigation. As a result, another species of criminal sanction has been established, while its enforcement goes by default. No institution at the local level has yet been devised to handle this brand of lawlessness, and existing institutions are not readily adaptable to that purpose. Again, we as a society have to make basic decisions as to where we are going and as to what vehicles are appropriate to go there in.

A great deal of debate is currently being generated nationally on the question of whether our law is overcriminalized when it comes to gambling offenses. This, like the sexual "crimes," is essentially a question of morals. The anti-gambling laws are a throwback to our Puritan yesteryears. The practical problems are somewhat different, however, from those concerning regulation of sexual offenses. Gambling is a crime of commercialized vice—one of the so-called victimless crimes. These are the crimes that attract the affluent society as well as the destitute society, and are profitable enough to corrupt government and sophisticated enough to flout even honest but unimaginative law enforcement. The insidious effects that the backers of underground gambling have had upon government at all levels—the weekly $10 bill to the beat patrolman or the massive unseen contributions to statewide political campaigns—have recently been seen in city after city and state after state across the nation. The effect upon police departments can be deadening. Corruption scandals, growing almost exclusively out of gambling, have wrecked one otherwise good department after another. There is the additional question of whether the deployment of quantitatively significant squadrons of highly trained detectives to police vice is strategically economical considering the many fronts upon which the war on crime must be fought.

In terms of society's making a moral judgment, even the moral basis of the anti-gambling laws has been seriously eroded. When wealthy businessmen may fly to Las Vegas but poor blacks may not "shoot craps" in the alley, the question arises, "What's the difference?" Morally, there is none. With many states now sponsoring lotteries, with pari-mutuel betting permitted at the racetracks, with church bingo games a part of our life, it is difficult to summon up moral outrage against unregulated street gambling. Our efforts in this area are reduced from the question of what conduct is permitted to the much lesser question of what group of people may indulge in certain conduct. It is an area that demands, whatever the ultimate conclusion, profound rethinking.

Another area that calls for a fundamental reappraisal, not so much in terms of whether it should be criminal but rather in terms of who shall police it, is that of commercial or white-collar crime. Traditionally in the United States and in England before that, the role of the law enforcement officer was to keep the King's peace. The job of the policeman, the sheriff, the constable on patrol, and the night watchman was to deter and to detect the thief, the rapist, the murderer, and the burglar. The nature of the offenses was clearcut. The roles of the policeman, the prosecutor and the judge were equally clearcut. This is not the case, however, with today's highly sophisticated and exasperatingly subtle white-collar crimes. Society is increasingly aware of being plagued by such crime but has not yet faced the basic issue of who shall police these crimes.

By way of example, even in terms of the relatively traditional crimes, where can a businessman go who suspects that he has been made by an employee the victim of a subtle embezzlement? He cannot go to the district attorney's office, because the district attorney, contrary to popular belief, basically has no independent investigative capacity whatsoever. His responsibility is to the trial table. He enters the criminal process only when an investigation has been essentially completed and when a package has been prepared by someone else for presentation to a grand jury. The district attorney depends for his investigation upon the local police department, but that policeman, in turn, is not prepared to begin to investigate a complex embezzlement. He is recruited, trained, and paid as a conservator of the peace and not as an auditor. He is prepared to pursue his man, when duty demands, to the ends of the earth, but he would be lost in an instant in a set of account books or balance sheets. At the local level in this country today, there is simply no arm of law enforcement that has the necessary specialist on its staff, or that has the budgeted funds to contract with such a specialist, to handle this type of investigation. The embezzlement victim is, in short, left to his own investigative devices. He must, out of his own pocket, hire his own auditor and his own private investigator just to see if a crime has been committed, let alone see if a case can be made. This is perfectly feasible, of course, if and when the bank president with all of his resources suspects the cashier. But how does the system work if the cashier suspects the bank president? It simply does not work at all.

In the wider arena of general consumer fraud, whole vistas are opening up today that were once totally irrelevant to the criminal law. The criminal law and the agencies that enforce it have never been restructured or retooled to meet the new demands. Back in the golden day when our law was formed, when English yeomen and Yankee farmers grew their own food and manufactured their own clothing, a few well-considered purchases got the average family by for the entire year. The law's only pronouncement was the purely negative "Buyer, beware!" The cases and commentaries coming down to us from the formative period of the common law reiterate the underlying philosophy that it is not the function of the criminal law "to protect a fool from his folly." The wily peddler and the wary farmer stood on a par with one another in a one-to-one bargaining confrontation. "May the better man win!" Indeed, for most of our history, the shrewd, Yankee horse trader was very much a folk hero for a self-reliant frontier.

Madison Avenue is not the county fair, however. With urbanization, we all depend on the marketplace for a million products that we can no longer kick or pinch or measure. The criminal law is now called upon to shield a latter-day consuming public from such new phenomena as false labeling, misleading advertising, inept manufacturing, and subliminal suggestion. Unfortunately, the legislatures that invoke the criminal sanction in the commercial field seldom think to provide any investigative machinery. As a result, outside of the federal government and perhaps New York City and Los Angeles, there are thousands of new crimes upon the books with no one to enforce them. When a victim yells, "Help, I'm being robbed!" there is, in theory at least, a patrolman somewhere to come running; but when a victim yells, "Help, the used car salesman turned back the speedometer," there is no one anywhere to come running. In a few states, consumer protection bureaus are being founded, generally under the aegis of the attorney general's office. These are in their infancy, however, and will have to grow a hundredfold to meet the mushrooming need.

Commercial fraud and white-collar crime constitute a crime wave all their own, just as massive as, though less melodramatic than, that of street violence. It has a causation all of its own; the education that may cure crimes of violence may only aggravate and make more subtle crimes of greed. It requires an army all of its own to combat it. Even a vastly expanded police department can probably never serve as that army.

The police, the prosecutors, the courts that enforce the criminal law—and indeed the criminal law itself—have fallen heir to many of these responsibilities simply by default, if not by dumb luck. As institutions, they were never structured nor staffed to handle many of these responsibilities. They are ill equipped to do so today. Instead of simply attempting "to bumble through," what is required is that bar associations and legislatures and constitutional conventions and the public itself begin to rethink fundamentals. Just what shall our institutions of government and of law enforcement be? What shall they do? What shall we ask of our police? If not everything, then to whom shall we look to fill the vacuum? Which of our rules to govern ourselves should be part of the criminal law and which should not? Some long thoughts are overdue.

TOPICS FOR DISCUSSION

1. Discuss the expense of the local traffic court procedures. Would an administrative process be more efficient and effective?

2. Discuss ways in which the local police agency could improve the use of police officers for traffic enforcement, vis-à-vis talent vs. task or use of civilian personnel.

3. Discuss whether the local procedure of handling traffic offenses has an effect on the quality of the administration of justice.

4. Discuss the possibility of reviewing the disposition of traffic cases for the local jurisdiction for the past year to determine similarities, differences, and possible conclusions.

5. Discuss the definition of legal terms used in this chapter.

6. Discuss the comparative cost of the following:
   a. Decriminalization in terms of money, morals.
   b. Increased local law enforcement responsibility for white collar crime.
   c. Increased responsibility in the private sector for their own security e.g. computer fraud, embezzlement, etc.

15

NEIL C. CHAMELIN

The court administrator concept:
  let the judges judge

INTRODUCTION

Much attention has been given to the criminal justice system in the past decade. Such notable studies as the President's Commission on Law Enforcement and the Administration of Justice (1965–1967), the American Bar Association Project on Standards for Criminal Justice (1964–1973), and the National Advisory Commission on Criminal Justice Standards and Goals (1971–1973) have focused national concern on the problems of the administration of justice. The apparent decline in respect for "law and order" in the 1960s was a major factor influencing this widespread interest in examining the problems of the justice system. Virtually no aspect or component of the system has escaped the scrutiny of either the study groups or the public at large. Numerous problems have been identified and many solutions proposed. The establishment of the Law Enforcement Assistance Administration in 1968, as a federal agency created to assist in the reduction of crime and the improvement of the criminal justice system, has also contributed to the examination of problems and the attempts to provide viable alternatives for improvement.

The judiciary has not escaped its share of attention. Appropriate emphasis has been given to the problems of the courts. In fact, with the exception of the recognition of the need for revised delivery mechanisms of police services, the cry for court reform has received the most emphasis. Many suggestions have been made to bring about needed change. Among them have been recommendations for: unifying state court system structures, improving state-federal judicial relationships, revamping court procedures, improving the quality and quantity of court personnel, and instituting modern management techniques in the administration and operations of court systems.

Traditionally, courts and court systems have been totally administered by judges. As a result, two problems immediately surface. First, few judges have any formal training in management. This results in court systems being administered on a sometimes haphazard and unorganized basis. Many courts are operating using the same methods of budgeting, maintaining calendars, assigning personnel, and the myriad of other necessary administrative tasks as did the courts of one hundred years ago. Such procedures have been proved inefficient.

Second, those judges expected to perform administrative duties are, for the most part, not overly enthusiastic about this responsibility. After all, their primary responsibility is to dispense justice in their role as judges. Often, this diversity of roles requires judges to make a choice as to which function they will give greatest attention. Usually, the choice is an obvious one. Most judges will tend toward functioning efficiently and effectively in their judicial roles, for it is in this capacity that their backgrounds, training, and interest lie. There is little management-oriented training in law schools. Thus, the administration of the courts is often neglected or at least relegated to a position of lesser importance. Whether the choice is a conscious one or not is relatively academic. The fact is that the problems of managing courts have not been squarely faced until recently.

Courts are business enterprises. True, they are not profit-seeking enterprises, but they are businesses that require the application of sound management principles. Police departments, correctional institutions, and courts are public business agencies with a different purpose from profit-making private firms, but requiring no less administrative direction.

HISTORY OF COURT
ADMINISTRATION

As suggested by the title of this chapter, a solution to this dilemma is operative. The employment of professionally trained people to handle the administrative affairs of the courts, thus freeing the judges of this responsibility and allowing them to perform their judicial functions, is not a new concept, but its widespread application is of recent origin. The first attempt at establishing an administrative office can be traced to the federal court system in 1922. The Conference of Senior Court Judges was created in that year to survey "the condition of business in the courts of the United States and prepare plans for assignment of judges to or from circuits or districts where necessary and submit suggestions to the various courts in the interest of uniformity and expedition of business."[1]

The Conference had difficulty functioning because of insufficient administrative staff to collect data and make recommendations. Yet a significant step forward had been taken; there had been an effort to define the administrative needs of the courts.

In 1939, the Administrative Office of the United States Courts was created in an effort to bring about some release of judicial manpower from administrative duties for judicial work. Beginning in 1937, states began creating statewide administrative offices under the chief justices of the supreme courts of the states. From that time until 1966, twenty-nine states had established such offices to study and respond to the problems of court administration on a statewide basis.

Although surveys indicate that there were some attempts to establish court administrative positions as early as 1950, the first effective attempt to apply the court administrator concept to trial courts on the state level occurred in 1958. Prior to this time, the administration of the Los Angeles Superior Court represented a familiar pattern across the country. The court system had a presiding judge who was elected and responsible to the other judges in the system. He was charged with: controlling the calendars of the court, coordinating trial calendars, caring for the physical plant, managing judicial and nonjudicial personnel working for the courts; and many other nonjudicial tasks.

On July 21, 1958, the Los Angeles Superior Court became the first and largest trial court system in the country to take steps toward the employment of a separate, nonjudicial administrative officer, whose responsibility was to handle the internal administration of the court system—to let the judges judge. As stated later by Edward C. Gallas, appointed as the first executive officer (court administrator) of the Los Angeles Superior Court, "this was an important development—not because I was that first person—but because the focus was finally directed at the place where the real problem of court administration must be solved—the trial court."[2]

Although the Los Angeles experience was not all peaches and cream—the new executive officer was immediately confronted with the chore of convincing authorities to free the court of county budgetary domination as an essential prerequisite to effective management and to judicial independence, as well as convincing the judges of the desirability of instituting efficient management practices—it furthered the understanding that court reform does not depend solely on dollars or on the quantity of judges. Efficiency in court administration can be promoted by more effective use and greater productivity of manpower through improved methods, improved machinery, improved management, and trained administrative personnel.

The big push nationally for the employment of court administrators came in the latter part of 1969, following a breakfast address delivered by Chief Justice Warren E. Burger to the Institute of Judicial Administration in Dallas on August 12. The chief justice made the following remarks:

The courts of this country need management which busy and overworked judges, with vastly increased case loads cannot give. We need a core of trained administrators or managers ... to manage and direct the machinery so that judges can concentrate on their primary professional duty of judging.

Such administrators do not now exist—except for a handful who are almost entirely confined to state court systems. We must literally create a core of court administrators or court managers and we must do so at once. I propose a program to do this—at once—because the need is now, not at some distant future date ....

Courts with few judges can perhaps continue to function reasonably well with what they now have; but at some point—whether it is four, six, or eight judges, I am not sure—highly skilled management is needed. We should not use "judge time" to accomplish tasks that others with less training can do at less expense to the public.

Law makers who control the appropriations are already harassed with overwhelming demands for more money and more personnel. It will do no good simply to ask for more money. We must demonstrate the need and make out a solid case that court managers will be effective and economical in the long run.

... An immediate step is to find out how to supply the potential demand for court management specialists. It is surely a paradox that our space program, which is barely a dozen years old has produced more astronauts than we have genuine specialists in court management. Most of them are now employed in state court systems.

The Committee on the judiciary ... has had a sub-committee ... studying the problem and legislation has been drafted to provide administrators for the federal courts. If that legislation were passed at once we could not begin to fill the positions. We should indeed pass the legislation, but we must also take immediate steps to insure a supply of administrators. We cannot legislate court administrators any more than we can legislate astronauts; they must be trained.

I therefore propose that we call together a dozen or more of the best informed people in this country and ask them to plan a program to train the large number of managers we need. I know this can be done and it must be done at once. It should begin in the next sixty or ninety days. We have not demonstrated great imagination or skill in this area, and hence I would ask that the planning conference be composed of perhaps six court managers of established standing, four experts in public administration, and two in business administration, and perhaps a few progressive trial judges and experienced litigation lawyers ....

I hope the American Bar Association will take the leadership and call on the Federal Bar Association, the Institute of Judicial

Administration and others. They in turn can draw on the skills and experience of the best brains in public administration and in business administration. This planning should ultimately draw universities which have a demonstrated capacity to train public administrators.[3]

The American Bar Association responded rapidly and affirmatively to the challenge posed by the Chief Justice. Within weeks a task force composed of leaders in business, government, law, and education was convened to study the proposal. The initial purpose of the task force—to design a training program for court administrators—was soon broadened to encompass a complete development program for court administration. The task force realized that the program had to serve a dual purpose. It had to prepare people to work in the court systems as they presently exist. At the same time, these people had to be change agents prepared to bring about innovations in court administration. The development program could not be justified simply to convey information or to maintain existing levels of stagnation. Individuals who would be developed into court administrators had to be reformers, knowledgeable about the law and the operations of court systems so as to be able to recognize problems and understand the environment in which they were to function but also able to draw upon the disciplines of business, government, education, and many others to influence the development of modern court administration.[4]

Within a year of Chief Justice Burger's Dallas address, the Institute for Court Management opened its doors at the University of Denver in Colorado under the joint sponsorship of the American Bar Association, the American Judicature Society, and the Institute for Judicial Administration. Thirty-one students with varied backgrounds in law, systems analysis, corrections, public administration, and court administration comprised the first class to spend six months in the complex training program including formal study, and internships. Since its inception, the Institute has produced a number of well-qualified court administrators working in various court systems throughout the country at salary ranges from $15,000 to $25,000 in smaller systems and from $30,000 to $40,000 in large state and metropolitan court systems.[5]

DEFINITION AND FUNCTIONS OF THE COURT ADMINISTRATOR

Court administrator is the most popular title given to individuals who serve as behind-the-scene, nonjudicial administrators responsible for the efficient management of the nonjudicial activities of the courts. They are also known by such titles as executive officer, executive officer and jury commissioner, deputy county clerk, administrative assistant, administrative director, clerk administrator, superior court secretary and jury commissioner, and administrative assistant to the chief justice. Just as the titles vary greatly, so do the duties and responsibilities of court administrators based on such variables as size of the court system, complexity of the problems, willingness of the judiciary to delegate authority and responsibility, and need for the services and expertise of a professional manager.

Ten major categories of management responsibility can be identified as falling within the scope of court administration.[6]

1. *Personnel.* Personnel management and administration principles can be as broadly applied to the courts as they are to other public agencies and private business. The organization of court systems is composed of people. This alone justifies the need for personnel management. But the diversity of functions of both judicial and nonjudicial personnel requires that the administrator be cognizant of his roles and responsibilities as well as his need to apply sound personnel management practices.

The court administrator is an executive in the court system. He is not a clerk. Yet although he may function in a supervisory capacity over the nonjudicial personnel in the court—clerks, reporters, bailiffs, secretaries—personnel matters affecting the judges will generally be beyond his sphere of influence. Judges, as elected or appointed officials are responsible to the public and/or the appointing authority.

A newly appointed court administrator is likely to be confronted with both internal and external forces influencing his decisions as a personnel manager. He may have to deal with civil service or merit systems on the outside and employees of long standing, desirous of continuing the "old ways," internally.

His responsibilities may include preparing or revising position and pay classification systems; recruitment, selection, promotion, motivation, discipline, and evaluation of nonjudicial employees; and maintaining personnel records of court workers. In addition, he may be given responsibility for terminating unsatisfactory employees.

2. *Finance.* One of the most sensitive yet most crucial area of management responsibility for the court administrator is budgeting and budget management. Here again, he must be cognizant of the financial needs for the effective operations of the court system and at the same time be sensitive to the priorities of the budgeting authority, be it county or state. Specific responsibilities might include: preparing the budget, gaining approval for fund expenditures, approv-

ing vouchers, collecting and maintaining receipts and records on financial matters, and maintaining accounting records.

3. *Space and Equipment.* This task entails: overseeing management and maintenance of court facilities, securing and disbursing supplies and equipment for both judicial and nonjudicial personnel, conducting space management studies, and maintaining property control records.

4. *Liaison.* The court administrator must assume some of the judges' burden of attending meetings, making speeches, and keeping interested and concerned public and private agencies informed of relevant court matters.

5. *Public Information.* Closely related to the liaison function of the court administrator is his defined role as a public information officer. His primary responsibility in this regard is to provide information to the news media and other groups. Gallas perhaps summed this up best:

> Another skill requirement is in the field of public relations. Unlike an industrial organization, a court does not have to win favor from the public to stay in business. However, though the court sells no product but justice, and its judges and employees will be paid regardless of public attitudes (at least for a time), and its customers will continue to knock at the door, it too must have skilled counsel in the public relations area. Without public support the court will not be able to make the management improvements we all seek unless laws are changed that limit or reverse the trend to usurpation of court powers by local government. Without public support, resistance to efficiencies emanating from bar associations and lawyers with narrow and selfish interests, and from minority groups who wish to use the court for their own ends, cannot be overcome.[7]

6. *Jury and Witness.* Even though jurors and witnesses are considered participants in the judicial side of court operations, there are recurring managerial and supervisory services that precede and accompany their appearance in the courtroom. Examples include supervising methods for selection of jurors and assuring adequate procedures are established and accommodations are available when sequestration of jurors and/or witnesses is required.

7. *Report.* Much administrative paperwork is attendant to the nonjudicial work of the court. The court administrator may assume the task of preparing annual reports, statistical analyses and reports, and documents pertaining to recommendations for improvements in the business practices of the courts.

8. *Data Processing and Systems Analysis.* As in any modern organization, the heart of the dynamics of change in the courts lies in the collection, analysis, and use of data, both quantitative and qualitative. A court administrator who has the ability to apply the techniques of data processing and systems analysis is in a position to better evaluate the administrative practices and procedures of the courts with a view toward recommending modifications and improvements.

9. *Calendar.* Expediting the flow of judicial work that comes to the attention of the court can have a major effect on the overall improvement of the justice system. In this regard alone, the administrator can easily earn his salary if he can improve on the methods by which cases are docketed and litigation is processed in the courts.

10. *General Management.* This is a catchall category that includes those responsibilities not listed above, including arranging meetings, preparing agendas, taking minutes or notes at conferences and generally organizing and administering the nonjudicial affairs of the court. In this category must be added the planning function of the court administrator.

All the functions described above, except for personnel management, illustrate the technical, scientific aspects of court management. But success in court administration also must be founded in the art of management—the people side.[8] The decision-making functions of an administrator in any organizational setting must take into account the behavioral aspects of organization and management. The court administrator must deal with the same principles that apply to other organizations. But he is in a highly complex structure; his success depends on the degree to which he and his ideas are acceptable to the judges and other court employees, and to external sources. He can easily become the center of conflict, some of which he may not be able to resolve, all of which he must recognize. His effectiveness is based not solely on his skills for changing mechanical and physical aspects of the organization but also on his ability to change the perceptions and attitudes of the people with whom he must directly and indirectly work.[9]

Effective planning spearheads the bringing about of change in any organization. It is the foundation of reform. The success of any plan, however, is in its built-in flexibility, and the success of the court administrator is in his ability to ascertain the climate for change. Planning is an imperative and ongoing part of the court administrator's job. He must be able to take into account the climate in which he must accomplish plans, and the influences that are generated by the judicial, political, legislative, professional, community, and employee side that makes up the power structure in the court picture. He must be open-minded enough to work with this structure yet ready to make demands when necessary and willing to compromise when appropriate.[10]

QUALIFICATIONS OF A COURT ADMINISTRATOR

As can be deduced from the information presented thus far, court administrators must be highly qualified generalists with many specialties. Expertise in management is the essence of court administration, for it is in this area that the executive must function—leaving judges free to function in the legal arena.

The one issue that has received the most attention by individuals concerned with court administration has been the controversy as to whether court administrators should be lawyers. There are still those who argue that doing any kind of important administrative work in a judicial setting requires legal training, hence, a lawyer. Gradually, most judges, lawyers, bar associations, and others who deal with the courts on a regular basis are beginning to appreciate the role in court administration of management expertise rather than legal expertise. This is not to say that lawyers cannot function as effective court administrators. Many are highly skilled at it, but if they do not already possess the requisite management skills for court administration, they must receive the necessary additional training to become truly effective. Approximately one-half of the students in the first class at the Institute for Court Management were lawyers seeking the additional skills required for effective court management.

A court administrator does not need a background in law. What he must have is an understanding of the legal environment in which he will work, court organization and procedures, and the adversary process. The development program at the Institute for Court Management provides this kind of background through formal classroom instruction and internships during its comprehensive six-month program. Other classroom work is concentrated in such management specialities as accounting and finance, personnel, information systems, operations research, public relations, and general management.[11]

THE NEED FOR COURT ADMINISTRATORS

Thus far, this chapter has examined what court administration is about. The issue must now be faced as to whether it is needed. There appears to be little doubt that court reform will occur largely by changes brought about in the nonjudicial administrative practices of the courts. Somebody must initiate these vast changes. Meyer notes four reasons why court administrators are needed:

1. Courts have become large, complex organizations requiring the services of management specialists.
2. Time devoted by judges to administration is time they cannot spend in adjudication.
3. Many judges are not trained in management skills, and many are not interested in administrative functions.
4. Present methods of court operation require modernization and the application of businesslike procedures.[12]

ACCEPTANCE OF COURT ADMINISTRATION AND ADMINISTRATORS

The focal point for concern over the acceptability of court administrators lies mainly with the judiciary. When the court administrator concept was first introduced on a national scale in trial courts, the two main fears of judges were the potential loss of judicial independence and the potential loss of policy-making authority. The manner in which court administrators have approached their missions, however, has allayed these fears for the most part. The significant increase in the number of court systems employing administrators over the past several years attests to the fact of their acceptability and contributions. Court administrators serve the judiciary. They work for the judges.

PROGNOSIS: THE FUTURE OF COURT ADMINISTRATION

Although there is not yet a great deal of literature on the topic of court administration, the tendency toward growth is most apparent. The repeated emphasis placed on the need for more effective court administration by national study commissions and various noted authors lends credence to the development of the field as a profession.

The creation of education and training programs to develop court administrators is showing signs of expansion. Besides the Institute for Court Management, there are now three other institutions offering degree programs in the field. They are American University in

TABLE 15-1   *The breakdown of administrators of courts of appellate*
jurisdiction by state

State	Total Courts of Appellate Jurisdiction	Court Administrators[13]
Alabama	3	1
Alaska	1	1
Arizona	3	3
Arkansas	1	1
California	6	2
Colorado	2	1
Connecticut	1	1
Delaware	1	1
District of Columbia	1	1
Florida	5	2
Georgia	2	0
Hawaii	1	1
Idaho	1	1
Illinois	6	2
Indiana	2	2
Iowa	1	1
Kansas	1	1
Kentucky	1	1
Louisiana	5	3
Maine	1	1
Maryland	2	2
Massachusetts	1	1
Michigan	2	2
Minnesota	1	1
Mississippi	1	0
Missouri	4	1
Montana	1	0
Nebraska	1	0
Nevada	1	1
New Hampshire	1	0
New Jersey	2	1
New Mexico	2	2
New York	8	6
North Carolina	2	2
North Dakota	1	1
Ohio	89	69
Oklahoma	5	2
Oregon	2	2
Pennsylvania	3	2
Rhode Island	1	1
South Carolina	1	0
South Dakota	1	1
Tennessee	3	2
Texas	16	2
Utah	1	0
Vermont	1	1
Virginia	1	1
Washington	4	4
West Virginia	1	1
Wisconsin	1	1
Wyoming	1	0
Total	203	136

Washington, D.C., the School of Business and Administration at Duquesne University, and the University of Southern California. In addition, a number of other schools offering graduate and undergraduate degree programs in criminal justice have instituted courses and concentrations in court administration.

There has been formed a nationwide professional organization and voice called the National Association of Trial Court Administrators, and processes for certifying court administrators on both federal and state levels are underway.

All of these factors indicate the presence of those elements inherent in the rise to professionalism. But what of the need and demand for more qualified court administrators? A study released by the Law Enforcement Assistance Administration revealed that for the 206 total courts of appellate jurisdiction on the state level (including the District of Columbia), there were 136 court administrators as of July 1, 1971. Thirty-six served single courts while the other 100 were shared by two or more courts. These figures indicate that court administrators are employed by two-thirds of the appellate courts. The breakdown by states is shown in Table 15–1.

At the trial or general jurisdiction court level only 15 percent of the courts in the states employed court administrators as of July 1, 1971. The figures reveal a total of 533 administrators. Three hundred and one of these served more than one court while 232 worked for single courts. The total number of courts of general jurisdiction identified in the study was 3,630. The placement by states of these administrators is reflected in Table 15–2.

The 3,630 trial courts of general jurisdiction comprise a total of 1,569 court systems served by 4,929 judges.[15] A court system is a judicial agency established or authorized by constitutional or statutory law and may consist of a single court (with one or more assigned judges) or a group of two or more courts in a particular judicial district. The significance of these statistics is that various noted authorities recommend the need for court administrators to serve every multijudge trial court with more than seven judges. Others have gone so far as to suggest that courts served by three or more judges require the services of a court administrator.

To those figures indicated above must be added the eleven United States Courts of Appeals and the ninety-three United States District Courts, many of which are or should be staffed with qualified court administrators.

In summary, the prognosis for the future of the court administrator concept looks very bright. The elements of professionalism are present, the value of administrative services to the courts has been shown without question, the resources for producing the quality of personnel required to perform these management functions exist, and

TABLE 15-2   *The breakdown of administrators of courts of general jurisdiction by state*

State	Total Courts of General Jurisdiction	Court Administrators[14]
Alabama	73	9
Alaska	4	2
Arizona	14	2
Arkansas	172	14
California	58	13
Colorado	63	44
Connecticut	12	12
Delaware	6	3
District of Columbia	1	1
Florida	67	8
Georgia	159	9
Hawaii	4	4
Idaho	44	18
Illinois	102	28
Indiana	129	10
Iowa	99	5
Kansas	105	22
Kentucky	120	6
Louisiana	65	3
Maine	16	1
Maryland	24	11
Massachusetts	14	1
Michigan	84	10
Minnesota	87	7
Mississippi	184	17
Missouri	117	12
Montana	56	2
Nebraska	93	6
Nevada	17	1
New Hampshire	10	1
New Jersey	42	21
New Mexico	32	32
New York	119	23
North Carolina	100	0
North Dakota	53	8
Ohio	88	18
Oklahoma	77	19
Oregon	36	4
Pennsylvania	67	31
Rhode Island	4	4
South Carolina	46	6
South Dakota	64	5
Tennessee	196	16
Texas	254	18
Utah	29	5
Vermont	14	3
Virginia	140	4
Washington	39	6
West Virginia	66	4
Wisconsin	142	23
Wyoming	23	1
Total	**3,630**	**533**

there is enthusiastic interest and support for this concept. It appears that court administration as a profession is here to stay. Judges are and should be pleased, for the introduction of the court administrator concept will truly let the judges judge.

NOTES

1. U.S. Code, Title 28, sec. 331.
2. Edward C. Gallas, "The Profession of Court Management," 51 *Journal of the American Judicature Society,* 334 (1968).
3. "Court Administrators — Where Would We Find Them?", 53 Journal of the *American Judicature Society* 108–110 (1969).
4. Herbert Brownell, "A Development Program for Court Administration," 54 *Journal of the American Judicature Society* 100 (1970).
5. Bernadine Meyer, "Court Administration: The Newest Profession," 10 *Duquesne Law Review* 220, 222 (1971).
6. This list of categories was taken from Meyer *supra* footnote 5 at 224–225.
7. Gallas, *supra* footnote 2 at 335.
8. Edward C. Gallas, "The Planning Function of the Court Administration," 50 *Journal of the American Judicature Society* 268 (1967).
9. Ibid., at 269.
10. Ibid., at 268.
11. Meyer, *supra* footnote 5 at 226.
12. Ibid., at 230–231.
13. Source: *National Survey of Court Organization,* U.S. Department of Justice, Law Enforcement Assistance Administration, National Criminal Justice Information and Statistics Service, U.S. Government Printing Office, Washington, D.C., October 1973. p. 61.
14. Ibid., at 62.
15. Ibid., at 13.

TOPICS FOR DISCUSSION

1. Discuss the effectiveness of the state and local court administrator in your jurisdiction. When was the concept introduced?

2. Discuss five projects, in order of priority, that might improve the administration of the state and local court system.

3. Discuss the need for the court administrator to be a lawyer.

4. Discuss the possibility of the court administrator managing a system which contains a regulatory arm to handle certain traffic offenses administratively.

5. Discuss the impact the court administrator has made on local court-community relations, if any. If there is no local court administrator, discuss the potential improvements in court procedures if one were appointed.

16

CHARLES E. MOYLAN, JR.

Legal controversies

As the United States enters the last quarter of the 20th century, the words of Charles Dickens have telling appropriateness for its criminal justice system: "It was the best of times; it was the worst of times. It was a season of despair; it was a time of hope." In the early summer of 1961, the Supreme Court decided the landmark case of *Mapp v. Ohio*, applying the federal exclusionary rule of evidence to the criminal courts of the various states. That decision triggered the so-called Warren court revolution, the reverberations of which are still being felt in our law and in our courts today.

No facet of the system has been left unexamined. Practices and institutions dating back to the formative period of early English common law are now in profound transition. New rules are being applied. Roles are being drastically altered. As in any period of dynamic change, dislocations are being suffered and stresses are being felt. Notwithstanding the discomfort of those who liked things the way they were and wanted them always to remain the same, the very fact of change reveals the vital health of a living organism. We are re-examining long-standing practices in terms of fundamental fairness. We are asking whether age-old institutions still have a role to play. As a society, we are asking basic questions, and that, in a democracy, is the indispensable attribute of healthy growth.

PLEA BARGAINING

As the Supreme Court has revolutionized the practice of the criminal law since 1961, the inevitable by-product has been the almost thermonuclear explosion of negotiated guilty pleas. The criminal trial is unquestionably a fairer and more searching process today than it was in the years before the due process clause of the 14th Amendment applied most of the protections of the federal Bill of Rights to trial procedures in state courts. A price, however, has very definitely been paid. The cost in dollars we have managed to absorb. The cost in hours we have not yet begun to absorb.

In the wake of *Mapp v. Ohio*, we insist that searches and seizures touch all 4th Amendment bases before their fruits may be admitted into evidence. The result is good, but it entails lengthy pretrial and in-trial suppression hearings. In the wake of *Gideon v. Wainwright*, we insist that a criminal defendant have the benefit of assistance of counsel, privately retained or court-appointed. Untutored defendants are no longer "railroaded" to jail, but full and fair trials consume four or five times as many hours as a "railroading." In the wake of *Duncan v. Louisiana*, we encourage resort to jury trials. With jury selection, opening statements, trials within trials over questions of admissibility, closing arguments and instructions, however, jury trials inevitably involve at least twice the hours involved in a court trial. In the wake of *Miranda v. Arizona*, we quite properly scrutinize confessions more closely, but the scrutiny involves lengthy hearings, the calling of numerous witnesses and the utilization of much legal and judicial manpower. In the wake of *Wade, Gilbert and Stovall*, we analyze more closely line-up procedures, but again we expend finite trial resources in the process.

The catalogue of enhanced rights could go on almost indefinitely. Each one, however, protracts that much more the time required to move an individual through the process. As a classroom model, the end product is a vastly improved individual trial. As a statistical reality, however, the end product may be one showcase trial plus eleven backroom "deals." We are moving unquestionably in a right direction, but in a finite system of finite resources, grim questions must be asked. If the question could be asked in a quantitative vacuum, we would all agree that it is better that a criminal defendant receive fully "his day in court" than that he be shortchanged with but half a day. Relatively, however, would we rather give ten defendants a truncated half-day in court apiece or give one defendant a full week in court at the price of denying nine others any court time at all? Realistically, our system is facing just such choices.

Some national studies in recent years have estimated that 90 percent of American criminal cases are disposed of by plea bargaining. In the four major boroughs of New York City, the figure for negotiated pleas is between 97 and 98 percent of the total number of cases. There is hardly a major metropolitan area in the country where the figure runs less than 50 percent. A defense attorney sits down in an office with an assistant prosecutor and hammers out a "deal" in what is now the typical scenario for resolving the grave charges of the state against an individual. There is no court reporter.

There is no glare of publicity. There is no supervising judge. The process takes place in a back room.

The loser in such an inadequate and expedient procedure is sometimes the criminal defendant. He may be intimidated into "copping a plea" to some lesser count to avoid the risk of a conviction and proportionately longer sentence under some greater count. Assembly line, small-time criminal defense attorneys and overworked public defenders, both of whom deal inevitably in volume, may well have an eye out more to their pending backlogs than to the optimal defense of any single client. On the other hand, the charity defendant may not be entitled to an optimal defense, but only to an adequate defense. The saving factor, in terms of the criminal defendant, is that with very rare exceptions the truly innocent don't plead guilty. The worst that can be said for the system is that some significant number of persons may be induced to plead guilty who might be found technically "not guilty" if they could afford to play out the string. Regret for such lost opportunity is more intellectual than visceral and is tempered by the belief that there may be at work in such a loss a higher justice than transcends mere legal justice.

The real loser when it comes to plea bargaining is the public. With a massive expenditure of limited public dollars, we might conceivably double our courtroom capacity in a decade. Involved, of course, are not merely building and judges, but almost unimaginable support facilities and support personnel. There are bailiffs, secretaries, deputy clerks, deputy sheriffs, court reporters, and security guards for the courtroom alone, not to mention maintenance and more remote administrative considerations. There are prosecuting staffs and public defender staffs and their secretaries, investigators, and other back-up personnel. Even this multiplication does not begin to calculate the chairs, desks, telephones, typewriters, and postage stamps. In any event, a doubling of facilities is at least conceivable, even if astronomical in cost. There is simply no way, however, for courtroom capacity to expand ninefold or tenfold, or in New York City fiftyfold. The hard reality is that there is no way to take most criminal charges to the trial table. The prosecutor knows this and, therefore, must settle a significant proportion of his cases out of court. The defense attorney also knows this and can, therefore, bargain from strength.

Plea bargaining in moderation, of course, can combine approximate justice with judicial economy. The American Bar Association endorses the notion in principle. The key word, however, is moderation. When a defendant has perpetrated thirty burglaries and enters full guilty pleas to two or three of them, in return for which the state dismisses the other twenty-seven, essential justice is done. A range of up to thirty or up to sixty years does not unduly hamper a judge's discretion any less than Draconic sentencing does. When an armed robbery defendant, facing a twenty-year felony charge, agrees to plead guilty to an also felonious simple robbery, carrying a possible penalty of ten years, approximate justice is again done. A defendant, probably foredoomed in any event, receives some break in sentencing. In return, he spares the state significant trial time and expense as well as the risk that the prosecution will somehow miscarry. Both sides give a little and both sides take a little.

The rub comes when, in jurisdictions like New York, where crushing caseloads overwhelm the system, twenty-year armed robbery felonies are compromised down not to ten-year simple robbery felonies but to one-year simple assault misdemeanors. Cold-blooded potential killers will be "on the bricks" again within three to four months, and criminal justice has become a hollow mockery. Too great a price is being paid by society when such travesties occur in the name of plea bargaining.

In the laboratory of fifty state court systems, some method must be devised to get more cases tried with the resources realistically available. Perhaps it will be, if not the elimination of the jury trial, at least the elimination of lengthy jury selection. The three-day or the three-week voir dire examination may have become a luxury we can no longer afford. Perhaps it will be a drastic curtailing of the exclusionary rule, eliminating lengthy suppression hearings. Perhaps it will be a dropping back from unanimous jury verdicts to permit conviction or acquittal by majorities of ten to two or even nine to three. The incidence of hung juries and costly retrials would be dramatically reduced. In any event, as long as we have finite trials resources, attention needs at long last to be paid to the intelligent and economical deployment of those resources so as to get the maximum return of at least adequate justice. Heretofore, we have been heedless profligates and may have been selling the farm to save the cow. Our thinking must be strategic in terms of the entire system and not simply tactical in terms of the individual trial.

Another troubling aspect of plea bargaining is more qualitative than quantitative in nature. When "respectable" criminals who commit white-collar crimes occasionally get caught, a guilty plea to a minor count carrying a token sentence, frequently suspended, is the standard scenario. To the sophisticated analyst, the disbarring of a lawyer, the social disgracing of a prominent doctor, or the consigning of a proud man who might have been President to the long immortality of being another Benedict Arnold may represent far more punishment than weeks or months of imprisonment could ever represent. To the millions of John Does, however, "Mr. Big" got a break which they would not have gotten, and the apparent inequity does not sit well. In a democracy, the appearance of equal justice is as vital as the fact of equal justice, if faith in the system is to be maintained. The negotiated plea, as an institution, should be calling for long thought and deep debate in terms of its broad social implications.

THE GRAND JURY

Another venerable fixture of Anglo-American law now undergoing serious reevaluation is the grand jury. It would seem to have outworn its original purpose, but during the course of centuries, it may have taken on additional reasons for being. The grand jury can be better understood if we disabuse the myth that it is somehow supposed to be neutral, judicious, and evenhanded. It is not a judicial arm; it is a prosecutorial arm. Its deliberations are secret and it is bound by no rules of evidence. It may even act upon the private knowledge of its own members. It hears but one side of the controversy and it is not concerned with an accused's version of the story. Its function is only to hand down charges and not to render verdicts.

The grand jury began when King Henry II promulgated the Assize of Clarendon in 1166. When royal justices would make their periodic visits to various English counties, grand juries of twenty-three knights of the shire were to present to the itinerant justices a list of charges against all felons who had perpetrated misdeeds in the vicinity since the last judicial visit to the county. The twenty-three knights were local and were expected to know, by personal knowledge and neighborhood gossip, what misdeeds had been going on and who had been doing them. There were no policemen or state investigators to bring charges. Common knowledge in the local community was the means by which the entire criminal process was set in motion.

Over the years, the *modus operandi* of the grand jury changed. In larger communities in later centuries, grand jurors seldom had personal knowledge of the felons who deserved to be indicted. Witnesses became essential to bring information to the grand jury. Sheriffs, then police, then prosecutors assumed responsibility for mustering those witnesses. The grand jury, in the process, became more deliberative and did less of its own leg work. As this happened, the function of initiating the process passed from it to the sheriffs, the police, and the prosecutors. Although in a rare case the grand jury may still act solely upon its own initiative, it came to exist largely to place society's formal imprimatur upon the policeman's or prosecutor's tentative decision to place charges. In doing so, it became by definition a bit of a screen for filtering out certain charges.

Even though it remained indisputably a prosecutorial arm, the grand jury began to be viewed by many as a more reliable initiator of the criminal process than either the policeman or the prosecuting attorney. Those law enforcement officials were, after all, single individuals; the grand jury represented the collective wisdom and judgment of twenty-three persons, who could act only upon majority vote and who had, furthermore, the objectivity of not having been involved in the investigative chase. To compel a man to stand trial for his life or freedom was a grave step. A grand jury would only take such a step if the case presented to it represented a *prima facie* case of guilt. Mere suspicion or unsubstantiated accusation would not suffice. The 5th Amendment of the federal Constitution included the provision that no one could be compelled to stand trial in the federal courts for a serious crime except upon a grand jury indictment. The constitution or statute laws of more than one-half of our states provided a similar screen through which the accusation would have to pass before a man could be called before the bar of justice.

In the 20th century, however, the rapid evolution of the committing magistrate and the preliminary hearing has served largely to supersede the grand jury function. The policeman or prosecutor must now present his evidence, at least partially, before a hearing judge. The judge, moreover, is most definitely a judicial arm and, unlike the grand jury, not a prosecutorial arm. That judge must be persuaded that there is a *prima facie* case of guilt or charges will be dismissed. As a result, two screens are now interposed between the accusation and the trial table. The natural question is, "Are both necessary?" As a screen, quite clearly either could do the job alone. The British, more inclined than we to ask fundamental questions, abolished in 1933 the grand jury, which they had invented in 1166. They concluded that the metropolitan police court had rendered the grand jury superfluous. In terms of the superfluity of the screen, the same case could now be made throughout the United States. One judge is more efficient than twenty-three laymen. He is legally trained and they are not. He is judicial in character while they are prosecutorial in character. In terms of the grand jury's more ancient function of initiating prosecution, that role is now handled more efficiently and properly by trained criminal investigators whose job it is to respond to citizen complaints of crime. In terms of traditional function, the case for the abolition of the grand jury is a strong one.

Living organisms, however, adapt to altered environments. If over the centuries the grand jury became more quasi-judicial and less prosecutorial in nature and if in this century the quasi-judicial function has been preempted by the committing magistrate, the end product may still be not abolition but rather the return to a more truly prosecutorial role. That role, to be sure, will not be a mere return to 1166. As a statistically significant initiator of the criminal process, the grand jury has forever yielded up the field to the police investigator. The grand jury may, indeed, have no significant role to play in 99 percent of the criminal charges. Routine cases will be made by the police and will be screened by the committing magistrates. However, a new and significant prosecutorial role has begun to emerge for the grand jury.

It may, in response to public opinion, initiate long-term investigations that a politically timid or unimaginative prosecutor for some reason, fair or foul, does not initiate. More frequently, however, the grand jury can work hand in glove with the prosecutor in the long-term sophisticated investigation. White-collar crimes, governmental corruption, broad abuses in a police department or other agency, circumstantial tracing of widespread gambling or narcotics conspiracies—all are more amenable to grand jury investigation than to routine police investigation. The grand jury and the prosecutor together can do things, furthermore, that the prosecutor alone cannot do. The grand jury has the power, which the prosecutor frequently does not have, to summons witnesses and to summons documentary evidence. Testimony once perpetuated under oath in front of the grand jury can form the basis for later perjury charges and, as a practical result, generally precludes later perjury. The investigative grand jury, as opposed to the routine grand jury, has assumed a uniquely valuable role in the American criminal justice system.

The vestigial power of the grand jury to bring criminal charges on its own remains a healthy curb on ineptitude, and even sometimes corruption, at the committing magistrate level. In the gambling and vice areas particularly, cases have frequently been thrown out in lower courts while a prosecutor stands there objecting helplessly. A later review of all the circumstances at the executive level of the prosecutor's office may cause the prosecutor to present the case to the grand jury and obtain an indictment, notwithstanding the earlier dismissal. Double jeopardy is not involved, and the public may be well served. In short, although old functions may long since have languished, new functions may keep the institution of the grand jury vitally alive. We will be concerned with the things a grand jury may be able to do in 1986 and not with the things it was invented to do in 1166.

BAIL AND RELEASE ON RECOGNIZANCE

A revolution of its own, triggered by the equal protection clause of the 14th Amendment, has taken place in our attitude toward the bail bond. The run-down bondsmen's offices on the side streets surrounding a police station and the ubiquitous and sleazy bail bondsmen themselves haunting the halls and corridors of those station houses had become a Runyanesque feature of American urban life. Because of the intense reevaluation of the bail bond system, those familiar features may be passing from the scene.

Bail is an outgrowth of the Anglo-American dilemma about the presumption of innocence. Sheriffs of yore and policemen today charge people because they have done something wrong, possibly in full view of the sheriff or policeman. Our mythology insists that such a person be presumed innocent (although perhaps not quite so innocent as someone not charged). Our dilemma is over what we do with a person whom we must presume to be innocent but who we know is probably guilty. On the one hand, we cannot incarcerate presumably innocent people for days, weeks, or even months pending trial. At the end of the long wait, which is getting longer all the time, that person may be found not guilty, with no way for us to make recompense to him for the unfair and unwarranted incarceration. A more likely consequence is that he will be found guilty, but of an offense calling for a $10 fine or at worst probation, but certainly not calling for days, weeks, or months behind bars. We simply cannot, as a society, permit a policeman's charge alone to subject a citizen to such a deprivation of liberty.

On the other hand, it is not satisfactory simply to take the name and address of the charged person and send him blithely upon his way, reassured that he will be notified of his trial date. If the procedure were that informal, the names and addresses would more often than not be total fictions. The person charged would never be seen again. In addition to the false identification problem, there is the real problem of what to do with the stranger to the jurisdiction. Check passers and confidence men are nomadic by nature. Once they have left a jurisdiction, even after having furnished proper identification, the chance that they would return for trial is slim and the costs of extradition are more often than not prohibitive. Summer resort areas and winter ski meccas are flooded with teenage drug violators and with adults who commit simple assaults or are drunk and disorderly. Favorite convention cities suffer the same problem. The nature of the offense does not warrant full-scale extradition, but neither does it warrant a cavalier dismissal of the charges.

Some method had to be devised to secure the presence of the person charged at his ultimate trial. Early in the formative period of the common law, the method arrived at was to insist that the person charged post collateral. He would put up goods or cash, the value depending on the seriousness of the charge. The common experience was that a person would appear to face his reckoning in court rather than suffer the forfeiture of his valued collateral. This posting of one's or one's family's personal collateral still prevails throughout most of the common law world. The exceptions are the United States and, by way of inheritance from us, the Philippine Islands. In these two jurisdictions alone has grown up the institution of the professional bail bondsman. These are persons who post collateral for people charged with crime. For that service, they collect a premium—a percentage of the amount posted. If the accused fails to appear for trial, the bondsman's collateral is forfeited. The bondsman, to insure the return of that collateral, then becomes his own private detective force and traces the absconding defendant.

At the same time that the Warren court was looking at the inequity of the well-to-do defendant having the benefit of privately retained trial counsel while the destitute defendant was "railroaded" into jail with no attorney to help him, attention also began to focus on the inequities in the bail situation. The net result of the bail system was that the financially well-to-do remained free pending trial, while the financially destitute awaited trial from inside their cells. Under the auspices of the Vera Foundation in New York, a bold and innovative program was begun in 1963 to test whether our familiar bail patterns had any validity. The working hypothesis was that the financially destitute person was no more likely to flee the jurisdiction because of an impending trial than was a person with greater financial means. If that were so, there was no justification for incarcerating the former while allowing the latter to roam free. Many commentators on the American scene were concerned that a price tag was being put upon justice. Such discriminatory treatment between rich and poor could not be reconciled with the clause of the 14th Amendment guaranteeing "the equal protection of the laws."

With the cooperation of the New York authorities, the Foundation began a broad experiment with the use of release on recognizance (R.O.R.). It soon found that when certain criteria were used to select the R.O.R. candidates, the percentage of R.O.R. candidates who appeared for trial was even greater than the percentage of those on professional bond who appeared for trial. After several years of experimenting with some tens of thousands of R.O.R. candidates, the percentage of "no shows" was running significantly less than two percent. Bail reform was in vogue overnight and within the decade, measured from 1963, hardly a major American metropolitan area was without one or another type of bail reform.

The general results were predictable enough for those who might have had vision to look. One key factor in an R.O.R. decision is residence and family. A person with roots in a community generally lacks either the means or the inclination to pick up and make a new life elsewhere. It is easier to stand trial and even to undergo moderate incarceration. When such ties are found by R.O.R. investigators, affirmative points are registered for the R.O.R. decision. A "drifter," on the other hand, is far more likely to flee and does not qualify for R.O.R., at least on the basis of this criterion. The length of time one has been in a community is also a definite factor. A lifelong resident has deeper roots than a more temporary resident. The holding of a job is a significant criterion, as is a history of job stability. A prior criminal record is also a factor. With such criteria in mind, the R.O.R. investigator makes a quick check on a person who has been locked up in the station house. If enough of the signs point to the strong probability that that person will appear for trial rather than flee the jurisdiction, the decision is made, and ratified at a higher level, to release that defendant upon his own recognizance. Most bail reform programs also maintain continuing communication with their R.O.R. defendants. They check upon them periodically and make sure that trial notification is received. The experiment nationwide has been an unqualified success.

The outlook for the professional bail bondsman is hard to picture. If a person meets all of the qualifications for release on recognizance, that person has no need to resort to the bondsman. If, on the other hand, a person is incarcerated who is well-to-do but who does not meet the R.O.R. criteria, the question arises as to whether that person should be released even upon the posting of bond. If the collateral were personal, the guarantee of trial appearance would be more secure. As it is, our only assurance is that the bail bondsman, if the collateral is large enough, will track down the absconder and bring him back.

Although we may hesitate to follow our principles to ultimate conclusions, the picture is clear. As long as we are talking about a guarantee of trial presence and not preventive detention, one factor and one factor alone is determinative—the likelihood that a defendant will appear at his trial. Let us pose the hypothetical extreme situations. Defendant A is charged with murder. We somehow acquire enough information about and insight into him to know that, pending his trial, he may well rob a dozen banks, set a dozen fires and kill a dozen victims. We know of some quirk of his character that assures us, however, that he will definitely be at the trial table when his case is called. If we are true to our criteria, we must release him upon his own recognizance. Contrasted to Defendant A is defendant B. Defendant B is charged with a much more minor offense. We have enough information about and insight into Defendant B to know that, pending his trial, he will lead an exemplary life. He will save a life or two and he may even discover the cure for cancer. Some quirk in him, however, will send him into a panic the night before his trial and will cause him to flee. If we are true to our criteria, we cannot release him upon his recognizance. The potential killer is a good risk and the potential lifesaver is a bad risk. The ultimate question is the like-lihood that an individual will show up for his trial. All other con-siderations are extraneous.

The type of social problem posed by the foregoing hypothetical examples gives rise, however, to the question of a very different brand of pretrial detention and one that is the subject of much current controversy. This is the highly questionable tactic of preventive detention. Preventive detention would permit an individual to be incarcerated pending his trial not because of the likelihood that he will flee but because of the likelihood that he will engage in violent or other antisocial conduct if released. The jurisdictions beginning to experiment with preventive detention recognize that some type of hearing may be called for and some type of judicial ruling may be required to declare a person so potentially dangerous as to require incarceration. The state may well have a real burden of proof to carry to make such a charge stick. The potential problems involved in such a hearing are manifold. The hearing would have to concern itself, unlike a criminal trial, not with the fact of past conduct but with speculation about possible future conduct. Logistically, a large num-ber of such hearings would only aggravate the already overwhelming problem of untried case backlogs. If counsel were to be appointed for such a hearing and if witnesses were required, the situation would soon develop where it would be virtually as easy to try the pending criminal charge as to hear the case for preventive detention.

The whole premise, furthermore, rests upon a shaky philosophical base. If we may incarcerate someone not because of what he has done but because of what he may do, why should the preventive measure be limited to those awaiting trial on other charges? Why not incar-cerate any potentially dangerous individual if, according to our criteria, he is likely to commit a crime? If A and B have equally bad records and equally bad socio-pathological profiles, but A is awaiting trial for an automobile theft and B is not, how do we justify incar-cerating A (assuming he is a good risk to show up at his trial) because of a crime he may commit tomorrow and not incarcerating B, who is just as likely to commit a crime tomorrow? The whole notion of preventive detention is going to call for a great deal of searching examination.

CAPITAL PUNISHMENT

No controversy has been more heated or more enduring than that which swirls about the question of capital punishment. Much of the debate is in terms of moral values and is, therefore, beyond the purview of this article. The moral argument against capital punishment stresses the essential barbarism of taking a life for a life (or for kidnapping or for rape). It points out that capital punishment debases and brutalizes the very society that resorts to it. It cites the overwhelming precedent of the rest of the western world, which has long ago outlawed capital punishment. The ultimate moral judgment on the question is essentially personal and not the food for academic discussion. A second and sociological argument, which is also beyond the scope of this brief survey, is made for abolition. That point is the statistical conclusion that capital punishment is inflicted in the United States almost exclusively on blacks. The inordinate percentage of black over white executions had a pivotal bearing on the decision of the Supreme Court in *Furman v. Georgia* to restrict severely the constitutionality of capital punishment.

A number of peripheral questions that arise in, and sometimes confuse, the debate are worthy of observation. The abolitionists have the benefit initially of the high ground, morally and sociologically. To obtain a clear majority, however, they still need converts of a more pragmatic bent. Many fence-straddlers could be persuaded to enlist in the cause of abolition if they could be assured that the alternative to the death penalty was life imprisonment, by which they mean the fact of life imprisonment and not the current fiction. Many citizens would be willing to forego the killing of even a first-degree murderer if they knew that he would remain behind bars for life. They will not, however, accept the possibility, if not the probability, that a killer will be free after fifteen years. In cases where death might otherwise have been the appropriate sanction, perhaps some special form of life imprisonment "without parole" could be placed upon the statute books. Civil libertarians who recoil at the thought might well be advised to fight one battle at a time and to accept the lesser setback to achieve the greater and more immediate victory. Such a strategic ploy may be necessary to win over the critical "swing vote."

Another approach to capital punishment hard-liners that might sell better than the moral value judgment is that the death penalty is uneconomical even in terms of old-fashioned "law and order." As a statistical reality, capital punishment was de facto eliminated in the United States in the early 1960s. When executions nationwide are numbered in terms of one or two per year, or even one every two or three years, the great debate about abolition is over something quantitatively meaningless. Capital punishment retains significance only as an emotionally charged symbol. The hard-liners might be made to realize that for the retention of the symbol, they are paying a terribly inordinate price. The grim irrevocability of death prompts many juries to return verdicts of not guilty on proof on which they would convict if the spectre of death were not hovering over their deliberations. Many a first-degree murderer stands convicted only in the second degree because juries, otherwise convinced of full guilt, shrink at leaving within the discretion of the sentencing judge what seems to them, perhaps subconsciously, the possibility of inordinate retribution. Criminals who go free or who escape with convictions upon lesser charges are only one of the prices paid for the preservation of the grim symbol.

Even appellate courts, in their splendid isolation, frequently cannot escape the awful impact of the sentence of death. When the feeling that the penalty is brutally inappropriate intervenes, reversal is not permitted on that personal judgment itself. What happens, however, is that other reasons are frequently found to accomplish the merciful end. The reasons articulated have ramifications and spinoffs that ripple out across the whole body of the criminal law, affecting thousands of trials for non-capital felonies and even petty misdemeanors.

One can only speculate as to how many trial procedures, administered fairly in New York and Oregon, have been needlessly struck down as unconstitutional because the Supreme Court simply could not countenance, in fundamental fairness, southern blacks at times almost cavalierly sentenced to the gallows by unfeeling judges. When appellate courts have to accomplish humane purposes by indirect means, those indirections shape the law itself, frequently inappropriately but always with universal application. That the symbol of capital punishment has again been grossly counterproductive would be evident if only more of the debaters could coolly assess its dividends and its costs even in terms of hard-line law and order. Intelligent strategists don't want pyrrhic victories.

The great debate gets fuzziest, however, over the question of whether capital punishment is effective in accomplishing its purpose. The unspoken question is, "What purpose?" For some strange reason, the only purpose generally considered is that of deterrence, although deterrence is but one of three or four of the generally accepted ends of the criminal law. In terms of deterrence, the debate is generally reduced to emotional and highly amateurish speculation. Empirical data simply is not available and never will be. Everyone who has committed a capital crime was, by definition, undeterred. They represent the failures of deterrence. What we lack is any figure for comparison. There is no way to measure those people who have never committed capital crimes but have refrained only for fear of the death penalty. The most innocent-looking stranger passing us on a crowded street corner may or may not be someone who has been so deterred. We may wonder even about our friends and relatives. We simply cannot know. Even if we could go into every brain, we don't know what to measure. Do we count every irate husband or distraught business partner who in a weak moment entertained fleetingly the thought of doing in his wife or his associate, or do we count only those who stopped at the last possible moment and stopped only for fear of death alone? We would have to factor out somehow those who refrained because of fear of prison or fear of social disgrace. The psychologists and the penologists tell us that the thing that deters criminals is the sureness and the swiftness of punishment, not its severity. It is not reasonable to believe that a bank robber would not be deterred if he knew that he would be caught within the hour or within the week and would spend twenty years in prison. Whoever is capable of being deterred by the fear of death could surely be deterred also by the sure knowledge that he would spend a life behind bars.

An ironical wrinkle in the great debate is that the capital crimes, by and large, are those least susceptible to the effects of deterrence. The threat of capital punishment could probably wipe out overnight income tax cheating and parking violations. Those are crimes particularly susceptible to deterrence. The crimes presently defined as capital, on the other hand, are more typically the "crimes of passion" where the perpetrator simply does not coolly assess the possible consequences to himself. Rape, almost by definition, is an illogical act of passion where strong temporary emotion has utterly beclouded reason. At a particular moment, a rapist wants to take a woman and yields to an irresistible impulse, virtually blinded to the possible cost. His motivating hope, to the extent to which he thinks ahead at all, is that he will not get caught, not that he will simply spend his life in prison if convicted. Most murder is also a crime of passion. Jealous husbands kill promiscuous wives; girlfriends kill faithless boyfriends; passions flare when business partners fall out or feel betrayed; drunken arguments between friends escalate lethally; junkies kill because they are frenzied over the next fix. These situations are, by their very nature, barely vulnerable to deterrence.

Forgotten, however, are the other purposes of the criminal law. One is to rehabilitate those who have gone wrong. In terms of rehabilitation, of course, capital punishment is singularly ineffective. We cannot rehabilitate those we have killed. Another end of the criminal law is isolation. We take the dangerous outlaw and segregate him from society for the protection of society. The net effect of capital punishment is totally effective isolation from society. The flaw in the use of capital punishment to achieve isolation is that we are probably less in need of protection from convicted murderers than we are from convicted bad-check passers or confidence men. The recidivism rate for murderers is notoriously low, whereas for bad-check artists (paper hangers), it is notoriously high. We presumably need to isolate only those who are likely to repeat their crimes, where isolation as such is our aim. The isolation period for rape need not, therefore, be for more than a decade or two, since its incidence flags dramatically as male rapists pass the milestone of thirty years of age.

The best argument that can be made for capital punishment, in coldly logical as opposed to humanitarian terms, is that predicated upon the theory of punishment as straight punishment. The most ancient, and still current, rationale for a criminal law is in terms of the theory of retribution—or vengeance. The great advance in the common law of King Henry II in the twelfth century was the emergence of organized public vengeance, according to uniform rules of order, in place of random and haphazard private vengeance. Although we shrink from the term vengeance, its spirit pervades the atmosphere whenever we speak of wrongdoing. "Mommy, Billy ate my candy. What are you going to do *to* him?" "If anyone hits me, I will hit him back." "An eye for an eye; a tooth for a tooth; a life for a life." Some such primitive sense of retributive balance lingers just below the civilized surface in most of us, and it slips out in moments of great stress.

When a Lee Harvey Oswald or a John Wilkes Booth hurts us all deeply, we are totally unconcerned with rehabilitating the poor wretch or even with deterring other possible presidential assassins, who are in any event probably psychiatrically immune from deterrence. We all demand vengeance, even if we wince at acknowledging the term. Even the soft-hearted who might oppose the death penalty would nevertheless demand some imprisonment at least, even if they were convinced that it could serve no purpose either in terms of rehabilitation or deterrence. They would insist that some punishment, even as straight punishment, be exacted from the heinous transgressor. Vengeance is just another word for punishment. Once the presence of vengeance in our repertoire of purpose is acknowledged, there is a sound logical, even if barbaric, predicate for capital punishment. If our purpose is to wreak vengeance, the death penalty is indisputably an effective way to do it. The semantic hang-up is that even the vengeful hesitate to acknowledge their own vengefulness. Politeness compels them to base capital punishment upon a theory of deterrence, whereto it is an illogical and ineffective means, and to foreswear the theory of vengeance, whereto it is a means that is coldly logical and deadly effective. Perhaps, despite the price in semantic clarity, this very sensitivity to acknowledging, even to ourselves, more primitive motives is itself a sign of advancing civilization. Even hypocrisy may have ennobling aspects.

TOPICS FOR DISCUSSION

1. Discuss the "day in court" concept as it relates to local jurisdiction. What has been the impact of plea-bargaining?

2. Discuss the possibility of having the local prosecutor present to the class the pros and cons of pleas bargaining as it exists in the local jurisdiction.

3. Discuss the statement "plea-bargaining in moderation can combine approximate justice with judicial economy."

4. Discuss the definition of the role of the grand jury if it is to remain a viable concept in today's and tomorrow's system of justice. Discuss the part politics would play in this role definition.

5. Discuss pretrial release programs, criteria for release on recognizance, and the need for professional bail-bondsmen.

6. Discuss capital punishment as a valid deterrent.

4

Corrections

There is a tendency on the part of the thinkers involved in the field of justice administration to speak only in terms of what should or could be. There is a real need to continue this kind of thought, but realism has to be included if progress is to occur. There has to be a willingness to deal with what is before confronting what ought to be. For example, what is rehabilitation, can it be defined, and if so, are we defining it in a way that has total applicability or will the definition change when relating rehabilitation to the institutional facility as opposed to the community approach? Also, what is the role of rehabilitation in corrections, criminal justice process, or the administration of criminal justice? What is the impact of rehabilitation on the ability of practitioners to reduce crime? These are appropriate questions and an attempt to answer them validly must be made. To do this, objectives and measures of effectiveness must be determined. Must a criminal be completely transformed for us to say that success has been achieved, or should success be a matter of degree depending on the individual?

Therefore, what is, could be, or should be must be dealt with in terms of the expectations of each component of the criminal justice system, and each component's relationship with the other, the system as a whole, and the community.

It appears that most people agree that juvenile offenders should not be incarcerated with "hardened criminals." Diversion is the word or concept of the day. Since the causes of juvenile delinquency are many and sometimes difficult to define accurately, the remedy is not so easily forthcoming. The problems of social control, a lack of a sense of belonging, a feeling of being manipulated, inability to attain goals, or even an inability to identify legitimate goals are only a few factors among the many that make up the complex world of the juvenile offender. Other factors include: a setting of subcultures vis-à-vis the professional criminal; the peer group or youth gangs; the physical environment, and a lack of positive family input. Finally, in approaching a remedy, the complex problems of abuse of drugs and alcohol by juveniles must be confronted. Once more, we must begin to face the situation as it exists, not as it should or could be. This does not mean that approaches with potentially measurable positive payoff should not be researched.

Prisons have, for the most part, been the facility to which convicted criminals were remanded. What happens to the individual after he arrives is worthy of consideration. Is society taking vengeance or retribution? Is society attempting to incapacitate or rehabilitate? Possibly, America does not really know what is meant by corrections. Many police officers believe that it is a revolving door. Questions about the relationship of or the difference between deterrence and rehabilitation are certainly relevant to consider for future planning in the corrections field. There must be some kind of central direction for corrections to achieve objectives that are achievable. There must be administrators capable of administering the corrections component in a manner that achieves stated multiple objectives. Today, research indicates that long-term sentences are detrimental to correctional objectives. But what about long-term sentences for multiple offenders or career criminals? What effect would the isolation of repeat offenders have on society? Can correctional facilities be "all things to all people"?

The impact of sentencing on the behavior of the correctional client may best be described by an attitude of "what do I have to lose?" Many prisoners with this attitude are the leaders of the internal organization of the prison facility. The ability of the correctional administrator to operate a facility is certainly affected by the relationship between the nature of the prison population and the objectives of his administration. To some degree, these must be at least not contradictory. Additionally, there should be an appropriate amount of resources (treatment personnel) if the objective of rehabilitation is to be achieved. There is some question about this equation in existing corrections facilities.

The humanitarian approach used by the judiciary in fulfilling their responsibilities has been probation. Parole has been more related to the administration process. What is common to both is the supervision of the offender and the imposition of conditions of behavior. The philosophical question posed by John Stuart Mill in his essay "On Liberty" regarding interference into the life of the individual by the state leaves an opening by arguing against the state allowing a man to sell himself into slavery, "for selling himself as a slave, he abdicates his liberty: he foregoes any future use of it beyond that single act." Any attempt at rehabilitation must include interference and control by the state. How much interference and control is the crucial issue, and this issue should be addessed according to objectives to be achieved.

In addressing objectives, Eugene Czajkoski identifies the mission of parole and probation as being composed of four basic elements, none of which enjoy universal acceptance over a sustained period of time. These four basic elements are: (1) humanitarian goals, (2) protection of society, (3) rehabilitation, and (4) a blend of the need to provide incentives and the need to maintain power.

As they do with other areas of the administration of justice, the issues of change, role definition, and environment evolve as central questions in the discussion of parole and probation.

The evolution of these central questions brings into focus a clear picture of "community-based corrections" and the "how" of handling the corrections client. The concepts, relevancy, and effectiveness of community-based corrections deal with two philosophical mandates: 1) the reduction of institutional isolation and the intensification of social ties in the community for correctional clients, and 2) the relationship to the appropriate standards in the report "Corrections" of the National Advisory Commission on Criminal Justice Standards and Goals. Dr. R. Paul McCauley addresses the specific issues of correctional research, planning, policy, adaptability, priorities, idealism vs. realism, budgets, and alternatives in chapter 20 that should be thought-provoking and interesting for the students of justice administration.

Finally, it is imperative that students think about the issue: If the money spent by the federal government up to this time (mostly on police) in the attempt to reduce crime has not achieved that goal, what will closing prisons, emptying jails, and supporting community-based programs achieve?

17

MICHAEL SCHWARTZ
MARY ANNA BADEN
GORDON F. N. FEARN

Toward a workable theory
of rehabilitation

Determining a workable theory of rehabilitation is difficult in the
extreme. All sorts of attempts have been made at this, from having
prisoners pray to current work release programs. What is most
notable about these attempts at rehabilitation is *not* their failure.
Success or failure of any program is very difficult to demonstrate.
Rather, the extraordinary lack of understanding of the data and
theory of the social and behavioral sciences in rehabilitative program
design is most notable. For too long, we have tried our hands at rehabilitation by basing our ideas on personal ideologies and political
considerations. Rarely are programs based on what we know. That is
to say, when we have had to choose between what we know *in fact*
and what we believe (or would like to believe), we have had an overwhelming propensity to act in terms of the latter, not the former.

The point of departure for this chapter then, is what social
psychologists call "role theory." This is a critical theoretical position
to take in a discussion of rehabilitation because it is, in reality, a
scientific discussion of identity. After all, rehabilitation is about the
acquisition of real and legitimate identities that are not stigmatized
in society as a whole. To ask about a person's identity is to ask many
questions at once. It is to ask first, however, about the nature of the
society in which one lives. Those complex organizations of human
relationships that we call societies are composed of all of the roles
that people must play in order to "make things work." Husband,
father, mother, wife, worker, friend, doctor, teacher, and so on—all of
these are roles or the building blocks of society. Identity refers to all
of the roles occupied by any individual *plus* the way that individual
feels about himself or herself as the player of those roles.

Whatever the reason, there are people in all societies who have difficulty in constructing a rewarding and satisfying identity from the roles available to them. That problem is no small one; no one can persist over a long period of time without being able to answer the question, "Who am I?" Moreover, there are an enormous number of people who can indeed answer the question, but the answer given is one that they find dissatisfying, unpleasant, and even punitive. A major aspect of rehabilitation in this sense is to provide help in finding satisfying answers to the "who am I" question. That is not a simple therapeutic task, and the fact that it is accomplished through various therapeutic techniques as often as it is, is most remarkable.

For an increasing number of people, however, the solution of the identity problem does not come so easily. Many find themselves achieving identities in deviant or "abnormal" ways (that is, finding identities in stigmatized roles as delinquents. alcoholics, addicts, criminals, or the roles of the mentally ill). Once an individual has developed a deviant identity, the problem of rehabilitation becomes far more severe and difficult to manage. Such deviant or abnormal roles represent methods of coping which have proven to be satisfactory—even rewarding—to the individuals who play them out in day-to-day interactions with others. In such instances, the rehabilitation process requires that an individual give up an immediately satisfying answer to the problem of identity and to begin to learn alternative answers. There are no immediate guarantees that these new answers will be as satisfying and rewarding as the old ones. The clear implication of this is resistance—behavioral change does not come about easily.

The ways in which the processes of behavioral and identity change are initiated must be thoroughly understood. They cannot be based upon a vague philosophy or an untested (or untestable) theory. We should then, turn to a discussion of one modern social psychological view to see what it portends for the rehabilitative process. Essentially, this is the view of "identity" or "self-concept" formation. Self-concept is a crucial notion because human action takes place from a base. This base is the way in which the individual perceives and feels about himself or herself.

Beginning with Mead and Cooley and continuing into current role theory and symbolic interactionism, researchers have moved toward a conceptual integration of personality variables with social structural variables. Goffman (1961:148) has noted that ". . . the self arises not merely out of its possessor's interactions with significant others, but also out of the arrangements that are evolved in an organization for its members."

Cohen (1965:12) has indicated the need ". . . to establish a more

complete and successful union with role theory and theory of self."
His suggested starting point

> ... is the actor engaged in an ongoing process of finding, building,
> testing, validating, and expressing a self. The self is linked to
> roles, but not primarily in a locational sense. Roles enter, in a very
> integral and dynamic way, into the very structure of the self.
> They are part of the categorical system of a society, the socially
> recognized and meaningful categories of persons. They are the
> kinds of people it is possible to be in that society. The self is con-
> structed of these possibilities, or some organization of these possi-
> bilities. One establishes a self by successfully claiming membership
> in such categories.
>   It is the concept of role which ties the individual to society.
> Roles are conceptualized dramaturgically as parts which people
> play and also as systems of expectations which serve to structure
> social interaction.

Kai Erikson has noted that the acquisition of roles involves the
process of role-validation ("when a community 'gives' a person certain expectations to live up to") and the complementary process of
role-commitment ("a person adopts certain styles of behavior as his
own, committing himself to role themes that best represent the kind
of person he assumes himself to be").

It is through this process of validation, commitment, and revalida-
tion/recommitment that the self develops. Erikson further suggests
that sociologists

> ... have generally been more concerned with the process of valida-
> tion than that of commitment, concentrating on the mechanisms
> which groups employ to persuade individuals that roles validated
> for them deserve their personal commitment. In doing so,
> *sociologists have largely overlooked the extent to which a person
> can engineer a change in the role expectations held in his behalf,*
> rather than passively waiting for others to "allocate" or "assign"
> roles to him. This he does by being so persistent in his commit-
> ment to certain modes of behavior, and so convincing in his
> portrayal of them, that the community is persuaded to accept
> these modes as the basis for a new set of expectations on its part.
> (1957: 263-274)

This comment implies the concept of "self-engineered change"
where the person is actor as well as reactor, an active participant in
the development of self. Using this concept as a catalyst, we turn to
a discussion of how the process of role acquisition and the development of self may be utilized to develop a behavior change model.

ROLES, LABELING, AND
SELF-CONCEPT

The process whereby individuals come to enact certain kinds of roles has been of major concern to students of social deviance. Initial research has focused on the way in which persons are cast into deviant roles by the larger community. Freidson has noted that the individual does not enter into or play a deviant role until he has been so defined by others. The extent to which others respond to the deviant will depend on such variables as the time the behavior is committed, who commits the behavior, and the consequences of the behavior (Becker, 1963). Labeling, of course, may occur both formally and informally.

Formal control agencies such as mental hospitals and prisons hold tremendous power to make identifications of deviance. Institutionalization (and its inherent processes of labeling and degradation) has the effect of segregating from the larger community those individuals with similar problems of adjustment or disability. Given that the institution attributes to individuals certain meanings about themselves (evaluations and expectations), it seems logical that such imputation over time would provide the individual with the necessary material to "... organize and stabilize deviant behavior into special roles." Erikson noted that

> ... such institutions gather marginal people into segregated groups, give them the opportunity to teach one another the skills and attitudes of a deviant career, and often provoke them into enjoying those skills by reinforcing their sense of alienation from the rest of society. (1964:16)

Freidson, speaking specifically of the crystallization of the deviant career, notes the relation between role involvement and commitment:

> ... the career consists in a progressive narrowing of alternatives until none but the deviant role remains. ... The most important point of the career of the prospective deviant lies in the events that establish his new role beyond any doubt—when he is trapped and cannot turn back—one suddenly discovers that the cost of turning back is greater than that of continuing and that he is committed. (1966:89)

This narrowing of alternatives is facilitated by others who unite the deviant role to the individual. Oftentimes only a few behavioral indicators are necessary for application of the label. The hardware and the technical skills associated with the deviant role will be assumed by the individual (Lofland, 1969).

In support of the interactionist framework, Scheff states that ". . . a stable role performance may arise when the actor's role imagery locks in with the type of 'deference' which he regularly receives." Role behavior becomes stabilized when the individual's expectations and feelings for his own self approximate those which have been attributed to him by significant others and the society at large. Scheff, like Freidson, notes the importance of the labeling process as the precipitating and reinforcing factor in the early stages of role playing.

The imagery, then, is not one whereby the individual is catapulted suddenly into a deviant role (although this *may* occur, particularly with arrest), but rather it is one of a gradual process. The actor may try to test certain parts of a deviant role. Others in turn come to impute a deviant role to actor. This interaction may eventually eliminate for the actor any immediate possibility of performing a nondeviant role.

THE SOCIAL PSYCHOLOGY
OF REHABILITATION

Just as social interaction will be a crucial determinant in the acquisition of a deviant role, so social interaction will influence movement out of a deviant role. In both instances, the central research question is what form the interaction must take to move the individual in either direction. All relational contacts between people are potentially therapeutic in nature; that is, there is the ever present potential that interpersonal contact will have the effect of defining, in one way or another, the self-meanings of those involved in the interaction. The shaping of self through relational contact is associated with the selection of and involvement in social roles. While the clinician usually comes on the scene when there is confirmed maladjustment, it is deemed much more important that the consequences of interaction prior to maladjustment be recognized, studied, and adapted to the rehabilitative model being used.

There is a growing sociological awareness of the structurally generated dilemmas which make institutional and community living, in part, incompatible. The harm occurs when we note that virtually millions of people who are or have been subjected to institutional care have had their illness or deviance reinforced rather than eliminated, substantiated rather than reduced. Medical hospitalization is perhaps a frequent exception, since, as Parsons has noted, society shelters the medically ill person while he functions in the sick role.

By setting role expectations for the ill person (exempting him from his usual social duties and assuring that he will return to them as soon as possible), society effectively neutralizes the onus his failure to perform would otherwise imply (Erikson 1957:268)[1]. But society is not as kind to other deviants, whether they are self-motivated or the product of societal reaction or labeling. We think here of the aggressive child, the delinquent, the adult criminal, the institutionalized psychotic, even the stigmatized orphan, or the otherwise disabled person.

The therapeutic environment of the mental hospital and the prison may, from the perspective of the officials of these institutions, provide the optimal setting for treatment. However, society tends to view entrance into one of the institutions as indicative of altered status, i.e., movement into the role of deviant. Thus, while the patient or inmate my emerge from the institution "cured" or "rehabilitated," society is singularly reluctant to accept these labels.

Emotional maladjustment is something other than physical illness; whereas society legitimates the "sick role" and permits its encumbent to return to normal living upon regaining health, the mentally disturbed person or the prison inmate is the subject of society's more uncertain attitudes about psychiatric and prison practices, and therefore he is looked upon with more ambivalence. He is perceived as somehow still "impulsive," still functioning at a level different from that usually handled by the standard informal processes of social control.

A social psychological approach to rehabilitation would stress resocialization into the larger society. It should be noted that the prison or mental hospital does not fit this prescription, nor does the patient's one-hour-per-week contact with the psychiatrist. The resocialization must involve participation in an environment which supports behavior that is in accord with the values of society at large.

Milieu therapy, a frequently employed philosophy of treatment, utilizes community-type settings to stimulate personality adjustment.[2] The physical vastness and restrictiveness of most custodial institutions precludes the possibility of using such treatment. Thus, milieu therapy is employed most often in permissive settings catering to adolescent behavior problems, and in more inclusive rehabilitation-oriented organizations such as the California-based Synanon—a private organization catering to drug addicts and operated by its past graduates. In the case of childhood emotional disturbance, the assumption behind milieu treatment is that illness becomes stabilized; it becomes a defense against environmental forces perceived by the child as rejecting and hostile. The institution tries to develop a rapport with the child, through controlled interpersonal contact with staff, which is nonthreatening and which is supportive of an emerging self-identity. The therapist meets the child at his own level of communication and tries to work through, on the spot rather than in the office, the child's behavior problems. The "reality" of a particular situation is not lost as the child is forced to confront issues as they occur, before time permits their distortion or forgetting.

While the psychologists in these programs may in fact be dealing with resocialization, they speak of the process in terms of a reintegration of ego processes. The first stage in therapy is to take the child back to the point where there first occurred a developmental deviation from normalcy. Whereas the concept of regression usually denotes retreat to an earlier stage of development, the taking back of the child in treatment is a programmed step which lies as a prerequisite to personality redevelopment. This redevelopment commences after regression is completed. The actual time of this change-over may be noted, in some institutions of this type, where the child is physically moved from a dependency child-caring unit to a new unit oriented toward ego support.

Milieu therapy is a clinical procedure of considerable merit because of its permissive, community-like atmosphere. But there are at least four deficiencies which suggest that as a treatment model it *may be contributing toward the accomplishment of undesirable, unanticipated, and perhaps harmful ends.* First, it encircles the child in a prescribed and intensive psychotherapeutic relationship with a staff model, without due regard for the child's voluntary involvement with others. It would seem more advantageous *to provide a variety of role opportunities to the child for selection,* rather than to *commit the child involuntarily to a limited role relationship with a single other.* In short, the milieu model exhibits little sensitivity to the structural reality of the society from which the child has temporarily been taken and to which the child must return. From this, an important principle emerges: any resocialization must involve the possibility of playing new roles which will be meaningful to the individual and which allow participation upon release into the larger society.

This suggests a second deficiency of the milieu model, one which may be called the institutional halo effect. This in part is caused by the noncomparability of institutional and community roles; behavior that is acceptable within the institution will be blocked when engaged in after release into the community. But the halo effect is largely the result of institutionalization itself (i.e., of having been the recipient of treatment of uncertain value to the members of the community). The once-institutionalized person fears the unknown and is constantly reminded of his past illness or past incarceration—problems, it will be said, which have no strict cure as in physical problems. While strictly speaking prison inmates are not necessarily mentally ill, there is a tendency on the part of both prison officials and the general public to view them as "emotionally disturbed." Rehabilitation programs are directed toward helping the inmate to solve personality problems (Irwin 1970:46). However, psychiatrists and psychologists must deal with clients and patients in an atmosphere of general public uncertainty. Unlike physicians, they cannot be certain that in naming persons to sick roles the community will substantiate the claim (Erikson 1957:269). Furthermore, the label of "sick" is acquired at a considerable emotional price for the "patient," as withdrawal from the label is extremely difficult. The public has a tendency to believe that mental illness cannot be completely cured (Erikson 1957:269–270).

The patient's or inmate's dilemma may be attributed to an institutional halo effect. The milieu therapy itself does not cause the effect—it is the product of the social uncertainty associated with the psychiatric profession and rehabilitative programs. These are perceived more as ideologies rather than as objective sciences. The halo effect is a significant factor when gauging treatment effectiveness at the time of readjustment to the community. Unless the institution has provided the patient with realistic parallels regarding what can be expected upon re-entrance into the community, it is suggested that treatment effectiveness will be retarded and further maladjustment will ensue.

A third difficulty with regard to milieu therapy lies in its assumption that rehabilitation is best served with the establishment of one-to-one therapeutic relationship between client and therapist. The therapist enacts a role that is clinically designed to serve as a model of socially adjusted and valued behavior. While this is the assumption, there is some evidence to suggest that children effectively rehabilitated do not identify with the therapist-model to the degree that they identify with and relate to other nonclinical models in the environment.

In a study dealing with emotionally disturbed children in milieu therapy, Schwartz, Fearn, and Stryker (1966) found that children in the good prognosis category (i.e., those least committed to the deviant role) tended to be anxious about themselves and to have developed significant relations with peers. They further note that often good prognosis patients develop friendships with nurses aides, janitors, etc. Those in the poor prognosis category were less anxious about themselves and had developed significant relationships only with their therapists. The researchers suggest that the therapists are, in fact, reinforcing the very behavior they wish to eliminate. Their support for the patient removes anxiety about the deviant role and thus leaves little possibility for the reward of alternative behavior. Why should the patient alter his behavior if the deviant behavior is being rewarded by the most significant person in his life, namely, the therapist? The effective therapist should act as a buffer—an absorber of the clients' emotions enabling him or her to more effectively relate to peers and others.

Individuals who withdraw from social relations within the larger society provoke anxiety reactions in others. This withdrawal may take several forms: 1) narcissistic withdrawal, where the individual withdraws from all social relationships; 2) dyadic withdrawal, where the person dissociates from larger collectivities to the dyadic relationship; and 3) familial withdrawal, where disassociation from larger collectivities into the family occurs. Whatever form withdrawal may take, the structure and stability of the collectivity are perceived to be threatened. Furthermore, the person who withdraws is likely to be labeled "sick." Yet institutionalization in general and milieu therapy in particular are conducive to exactly this type of withdrawal. The individual inmate or patient is encouraged into excessive dependency on the therapists and/or on atypical groups.

The initial socialization process is based in large part on the dependency needs of children. Children must learn to interact and in essence to please others in order to have these needs met. At the same time, in learning to please others they come to please themselves because they are "learning to do what is 'right'." Slater (1964: 168) has noted that resocialization may depend on exactly these same processes.

Recall that milieu therapy institutions arrange their clients into two groupings: one fosters regression through dependency and the other resocializes. One would expect that both units would experience failure unless clients were encouraged and rewarded for maximizing relations with those who play nondeviant roles. The client, of course, must be provided with the opportunity for such interaction.

One might wonder how it is, given such theoretical difficulties, that the milieu model seemingly works so well. John and Elaine Cummings (1966) dwell upon their clinical applications of milieu treatment. Speaking of such centers as Synanon, they discuss therapeutic communities as facilitating increased role opportunities. Patients are placed in "...a milieu in which every antisocial act is subject to discussion and sanction by the whole therapeutic community." The mainstay of their argument centers upon crisis resolution as a therapeutic tool, this being directed toward ego growth ("...ego growth is essentially a series of disequilibriums and subsequent reequilibriums between the person and the environment."). And this amounts to saying that residential centers bring about change more through creating opportunities for interpersonal (particularly peer) contact, than through any particular structural arrangement.

From the social psychological perspective, the general aim of rehabilitation must be somewhat more than the integration of the individual into the larger society. The fact of the matter is that delinquents, emotionally disturbed adolescents, young criminal offenders, drug addicts, and any other cohort of deviants must be perceived in relation to their role standards. Their rehabilitation must be attempted within the context of their already internalized standards of behavior and the resultant effect these standards have had upon their conceptions of self. To dissociate these aspects of past experience from the rehabilitation design is to defeat the purpose of rehabilitation.

Most new members of society will, at one time or another, find themselves with diffuse and unstable conceptions of self. This, in turn, may be associated with a relatively low level of self-evaluation. While in the early teens the individual may be expected to be motivated toward obtaining a more stable and positive conception of self. Playing the roles which are offered or which are available, whether deviant or conventional might be expected to enhance self-evaluation. Schwartz and Stryker (1973) have documented this notion of a variable self-concept in the context of becoming a delinquent or a nondelinquent. Both may possess positive, stable self-concepts depending upon their commitment to the role based on support from significant others.

If the potential, but not yet committed, delinquent is institutionalized as, let us say, an adolescent behavior problem, his or her treatment should be based on stabilizing the self-concept and building the identity around normatively acceptable behavior. But, the uncommitted adolescent is probably a better candidate for rehabilitation than the committed delinquent. The committed delinquent has been confirmed by others and has confirmed himself in the deviant role. Ordinarily the conception of self will be high and role-playing will be of a stable type. Adolescents of this group would be expected to hold the poorest treatment prognosis. The job of the institution is to first reduce the salience of the delinquent role as a focus of identification. To do this is to lower their self-evaluations, to see them as more amenable to change. Then they should be directed toward involvement in conventional roles, again accruing a positive self-evaluation through nondelinquent role activity.

Two questions which arise from this discussion must be the focus of attention for both theoretical and empirical study. First, how does the institution reduce the salience of the deviant role as a focus of identification? Whereas this phase is accomplished through a regressive-dependency group in the milieu model, it might be best accomplished through the establishment of model communities which differentially reward conduct valued by conventional society. But to be effective, such a model community would have to excite the initiative of the clients themselves so that the voluntary introduction of new roles could be facilitated. Second, in the rehabilitation of the committed deviants, given successful institutional treatment, how does one overcome what was before called the institutional halo effect? Provision must somehow be made for a smooth transition to the community. It is suggested further that changing public attitudes coupled with mass information programs will aid in reducing the uncertainty associated with nonmedical institutional settings. Both of these questions may be boiled down to the problems in and the means of release from roles—for those who seek such release.

NOTES ON THE CONCEPT
OF ROLE CHANGES

Role-commitment may be conceived in terms of the time, energy, and personal resources invested in playing a particular role or set of roles. Commitment will vary both according to the options available for alternate roles and to the extent to which these roles are rewarding. In order for a person to change roles, new options must be perceived. Even when roles are structurally available, if the individual does not perceive them as such, they will not constitute realistic alternatives. Furthermore, if these roles are not rewarding or if the cost of achieving them is too high (or even simply unknown), then commitment to them is unlikely.

With the exception of some forms of extreme mental illness (such as autism), total commitment to any one role is not probable. However, roles that approach total commitment for their incumbents are those that exist in Goffman's "total institutions." These are the various prison and sick roles.

From the growth and developmental perspective, increased stability and commitment tends to come with age. Society expects this to occur and labels those who are unable to commit themselves as "immature." One aspect of role acquisition that is frequently ignored is the recognition that there are times when it is culturally acceptable to play at roles. Adolescence, for example, is a time that provides vast opportunities for young people to opt in and out of various roles activities; most adolescents utilize the mandate given them to do just this in preparation for later stability. The stability which eventually comes is likely to center around several roles. These might include occupation, marriage, and parenthood.

In dealing with deviants, however, a false unidimensionality about the nature of the role is frequently assumed. A single deviant role is no doubt a rarity; it will seldom describe all the life experiences of one individual. Most deviants are deviant in a few areas, leaving other aspects of their lives undisturbed by deviant behavior. But we tend to accept the idea that a singular deviant role embraces all life activities. It is reasonable, and probably accurate, to postulate that from a developmental point of view, the process of becoming deviant is slow moving like all other processes of socialization. For the most part, individuals gradually come to assume a deviant role only after other alternatives have closed off. Even when the deviant role becomes the most salient role, other normatively acceptable roles may be in the individual's repertoire. Thus we may expect that under the proper conditions, commitment to deviant role activity can be terminated even when the strength of the commitment is relatively strong.

In various rehabilitative procedures, deviance is usually conceived of in terms of near total commitment, even when the commitment may only be partial. To overlook the fact that actual deviance may be only a fraction (albeit a large fraction) of one's total role set is to overlook the fact that the remaining segments of the role set can and should be tapped as catalytic to change.

Rehabilitation too frequently centers upon the provision of new and acceptable roles to the neglect of working with the role remnants already present. Instead of prodding the patient toward a new self, perhaps an old self could be refurbished.[3] Regardless of whether we are concerned with the treatment of the drug addict, the delinquent, or the emotionally disturbed child, incarceration seems not to be the most appropriate response to deviance and maladjustment. To be institutionalized means to be categorized as a particular type of person, thereby stressing the salience of the deviant role to the neglect of many other role activities. In effect, opportunities to play normatively acceptable roles are removed and the deviant role may come to be perceived as rewarding. In many cases, institutionalization probably cannot be avoided, and so the basic issue revolves around the problem of the avoidance of the attribution of total commitment to deviance and the provision of adequate opportunity and reward for playing acceptable roles.

While much of the literature is concerned with entrance into roles, little deals with the reversibility of roles or the process by which individuals exit from given role activities. Assuming that role-commitment is a reversible process, we should perhaps focus on the structural and psychological contingencies that facilitate or impede exit from some roles and entrance into others.

The idea of role changes is at least implicit in some recent social psychological literature. Those who have discussed brainwashing, or the more substantive topics of attitude and behavior change, usually do so from the perspective of goals, processes, and techniques. They are, for example, concerned more with what the new attitude will be rather than with the original attitude and its relationship to other variables. They emphasize the processes and techniques appropriate to facilitate change, and tend to leave to implicit interpretation the fact that for a new element to replace an older element it is necessary not only for the new element to be brought in, but also for the *old element to be given a means of escape.*

The balance theories of social psychology are appropriate to such an analysis in that when dissonance develops between new and old elements, it is reduced most frequently through some form of manipulation of these elements. Anxiety is thought to be an agent of change for any role player; relationships that do not provide comfort and security will be relationships that may be tapped to facilitate role change. Relationships involving anxiety can provide the justification for role exit and thus role change, i.e., if the relationship does not "feel good," perhaps something else should be tried. This justification is needed for the ego to "maintain face" and for various alters to relinquish their previous role demands and obligations.

The cultivation of anxiety is the aim of the dissonance milieu. That which is to be avoided at all costs is the re-enforcement of members in their deviant roles. Utilizing the assumption that a deviant role is but a part of the more global role set for most individuals, attempts at role manipulation might facilitate shifting the salience from the deviant role to others already established in the client's role vocabulary. The strategy is to stimulate the deviant to think in terms of a whole role set problem rather than in terms of one particular categorized role. While pushing the deviant to define herself or himself in terms other than those associated with the deviant role, dissonance is being induced, creating the need for a choice to be made. In choice situations, dissonance will be greatest (1) where other roles that are more attractive than the deviant role can be offered or refurbished, (2) where negative consequences of deviant role involvement can be made more apparent to the individual, and (3) where other nondeviant role opportunities are greater in number and attractive in quality (Brehm and Cohen, 1962:303). This strategy must be exerted as early as possible in the life of the deviant, for, as the individual becomes more involved in deviant patterns and associations, he or she might reasonably be expected to derive an increasing proportion of self-meanings from these deviant activities. To create a dilemma of dissonance is to cut into this process of deviant socialization.

The dissonance milieu must be particularly sensitive to the response of others within the milieu. It must deal with the individual who wishes to exit from a role *and* with the structural system which must be made capable and ready to release the individual. Both of these perspectives are rooted in the system of role-others, those others who impinge upon both individual actions and upon the structure to permit, block, or make difficult the individual's movement into or out of a particular role.

Role complementarity may be the major mechanism for the induction of both dissonance and change. The idea of complementarity comes from the great volume of literature on dyadic interaction, particularly with regard to marital relationships and psychotherapeutic relationships. Noting almost as many exceptions as there are statements of confirmation, Swensen indicates that ". . . members of the dyad are most likely to have a satisfying relationship if they 'complement' each other (i.e., are opposites)" on certain dimensions (1967:7). Research presently in progress provides the following if only tentative conclusion:

> The basis of therapist-patient compatibility may be of a complementary rather than a similar variety. For example, if the therapist, when undergoing psychological difficulty, behaves as the client would (e.g., each turns against himself or herself in a depressive, distress-sensitizing manner—the therapist probably has *blind spots* in the same areas as a turning-against-the-self patient. Thus, similarity between client and therapist might be a hindrance, and the client had best see someone whose solution to the problem is complementary, or of a different sort. Similarly if a therapist undergoing stress tends to avoid other people, he or she, even in good times, may be less responsive to a client who sports the same line of retreat.[4]

Thus, in considering client-therapist relations, those that are secure, comfortable, and static are also quite likely to be reinforcing and frustrating. The relationship is reinforcing because the therapist perceives the client's problems and reacts to them in the same way as the client. There may be much empathy but no place to go. And that is why the similarity is so often frustrating. When the deviant, who is in reality only a partial deviant with respect to total role set, is placed in an environment where complementarity is the motif, alternative modes of relating and achieving are perceived for the first time. The structure provided by the dissonance milieu manufactures choice situations for role change.

The treatment design being advocated here is not dissimilar to what in fact occurs in the milieu model. The differences are mainly in two areas. First, the dissonance milieu is established with cognizance of the pairing procedures which best promote personality and behavioral change, noting in particular that the provision of complementary role opportunities facilitates role exit—the first major step in the change to new role behaviors. However, pairing cannot be accomplished as deliberately as it may be in the psychotherapeutic relationship, because it would mean making the milieu structure more rigid than is really necessary in order to stimulate choice through dissonance. Second, the institutional arrangement should seek to develop and utilize roles that parallel those available in the larger community. To this end, frequent movement of individuals from milieu to community and vice versa should be encouraged in an attempt to demonstrate or display to those in treatment the nature and availability of varying kinds of roles. While institutionalization probably cannot be avoided, its degree of totalism can be lessened. The dissonance milieu will likely work best where differences between institution and community are minimized.

NOTES

1. A qualification is in order for those who are legitimately sick in accordance with medical diagnosis. Society expands its rules in cases of medical deviation. See Talcott Parsons, "Illness and the Role of the Physician," *American Journal of Orthopsychiatry,* 21 (1951) 452–460. But psychiatric deviation is another question. See Kai Erikson, *"A Dilemma of the Mentally Ill," Psychiatry,* 1957. This is discussed in slightly more detail later in the article.
2. For basic theoretical statements, see Bruno Bettelheim, *Love Is Not Enough* (Glencoe: The Free Press, 1950); Fritz Redl, *When We Deal With Children* (New York: The Free Press, 1966); Fritz Redl and David Wineman, *The Aggressive Child* (Glencoe: The Free Press, 1963); Heinz Hartmann, *Ego Psychology and The Problem of Adaptation* (New York: International Universities Press, 1958).
3. We are indebted to Philip Weinberger for pointing this possibility out to us.
4. Private communication with Juris I. Berzins, University of Kentucky. For related research, see Barbara J. Bentz, "Experiences in Research in Psychotherapy with Schizophrenic Patients," in H. H. Strupp and L. Lubrsky (eds.), *Research in Psychotherapy,* Vol. 2 (Washington: American Psychological Association, 1962), pp. 41–60.

REFERENCES

BREHM, J. W., and COHEN, A. R. 1962. *Explorations in Cognitive Dissonance.* New York: John Wiley & Sons.

COHEN, A. K. 1965. The Sociology of the Deviant Act: Anomie Theory and Beyond. *American Sociological Review.*

CUMMING, J. and CUMMING, E. 1966. *Ego and Milieu.* New York: The Atherton Press.

ERIKSON, K. T. 1957. A Dilemma of the Mentally Ill. *Psychiatry.*

————. 1964. Notes on the Sociology of Deviance. In *The Other Side,* ed. H. S. Becker. New York: The Free Press of Glencoe.

FREIDSON, E. 1966. Disability as Social Deviance. In *Sociology and Rehabilitation,* ed. M. B. Sussman. Washington: American Sociological Association.

GOFFMAN, E. 1961. *Asylums: Essays on the Social Situation of Mental Patients and Other Inmates.* Garden City, New York: Anchor Books.

HALL, P. M. 1966. Identification with the Delinquent Subculture and Level of Self-Evaluation. *Sociometry.*

SCHEFF, T. J. 1963. The Role of the Mentally Ill and the Dynamics of Mental Disorder. *Sociometry.*

————. 1966. *Being Mentally Ill: A Sociological Theory.* Chicago: Aldine Publishing Company.

SWENSON, C. H. 1967. Psychotherapy as a Special Case of Dyadic Interaction: Some Suggestions for Theory and Research. *Psychotherapy: Theory, Research and Practice.*

TOPICS FOR DISCUSSION

1. Discuss ways of determining measures of effectiveness in rehabilitation.

2. Discuss a successful rehabilitation program.

3. Discuss the rehabilitative (or reformation) theory of corrections vs. the deterrence or incapacitation theory.

4. Discuss the following statements individually and collectively.

   a. Individuals incarcerated in correctional institutions should be deemed rehabilitated on an individual basis in terms of degree of reform, (minimum standard).

   b. A social-psychological approach to rehabilitation would stress resocialization into the larger society.

   c. The psychologist speaks of the process of resocialization in terms of reintegration of ego processes.

   d. If rehabilitation is an objective, and persons differ in their capacity to be rehabilitated, then two persons who have committed precisely the same crime under precisely the same circumstances might receive very different sentences, thereby violating the offenders' and our sense of justice. The indeterminate sentence, widely used in many states, is expressive of the rehabilitation ideal: A convict will be released from an institution, not at the end of a fixed period, but when someone (a parole board, a sentencing board) decides he is "ready" to be released. Rigorously applied on the basis of existing evidence about what factors are associated with recidivism, this theory would mean that if two persons together rob a liquor store, the one who is a young black male from a broken family, with little education and a record of drug abuse, will be kept in prison indefinitely, while an older white male from an intact family, with a high school education and no drug experience, will be released almost immediately. Not only the young black male, but most fair-minded observers, would regard that outcome as profoundly unjust.

18

GARY B. ADAMS

The juvenile offender

JUVENILE DELINQUENCY IN THE UNITED STATES

Crime by young offenders has increased alarmingly during the period 1960–1971. Violent crime by persons under 18 jumped 193 percent. Over the same period, property crimes such as burglary, larceny, and auto theft by youths under 18 increased 99 percent. Persons under 25 account for 59 percent of all crimes of violence and for 81 percent of all property crimes each year. Thus, young people remain proportionally the most important contributors to the crime problem.

Approximately one million juveniles will enter the juvenile justice system this year. Although 50 percent will be informally handled by the juvenile courts' intake staff, 40 percent will be formally adjudicated and placed on probation or other supervisory release. Approximately 100,000 young people, or 10 percent, will be incarcerated in juvenile institutions.

The cost of maintaining the juvenile justice system is enormous—nearly $1 billion a year—and it is increasing at a rate of $50 million a year. By far the most expensive and wasteful parts of this system are the institutions in which juveniles are incarcerated on a long-term basis. The average annual cost per youth is $5,700—far higher than the average cost of halfway houses or group homes ($1,500 per youth) or probation services ($500 per youth). Yet it is in these larger institutions that most young people are placed, and most damage is done. This is made clear by the startling fact that recidivism among juveniles is far more severe than among adult offenders. (Recidivism among adults has been variously estimated at 74 to 85 percent.)

Juvenile crime comprises only a part, although the most dramatic part, of all delinquency offenses. There is an entire range of "juvenile status offenses" which subject children to the juvenile court process.

The most common juvenile status offenses include ungovernability, truancy, and running away. The distinguishing characteristic of these offenses is that if they were committed by an adult there would be no legal consequences at all. While the effect of these offenses on society is not as serious as that of a criminal offense, the child often suffers permanently damaging legal and emotional consequences. It commonly is acknowledged that at least half of the children currently in our institutions have been incarcerated for these juvenile status offenses (14:12–13).

MAGNITUDE OF THE JUVENILE DELINQUENCY PROBLEM

In proportion to their numbers in the national population, young people are the largest contributors to the crime problem. Criminal involvement of young people, as measured by police arrests, is increasing at a rate of four times their percentage increase in the total population. They commit more crimes and have a higher rate of recidivism than adults. In the period 1960 to 1971, arrests for serious crime increased 71 percent; adult arrests increased 57 percent and juvenile arrests increased 99 percent. Adult arrests for violent crime increased 54 percent; while juvenile arrests for violent crime increased 148 percent in the same period. Seventy-four percent of offenders under 20 released from institutions in 1963 were re-arrested by 1969.

Figure 18–1 illustrates the rapid rise in juvenile court cases during the last 35 years.

The national cost of crime committed by juveniles is greater than $16 billion annually. This estimate is summarized in Table 18–1. The table shows the total cost of crime-related activities and losses and the portion of these costs attributed to juveniles. Other indirect costs and the costs related to problem youths not in contact with the justice system are not included (9:11–12).

CAUSATION OF JUVENILE CRIME AND DELINQUENCY

Social Control Theories

The individual deviant was singled out for examination. If individual deviants could be proven constitutionally different from law-abiding men, then the reasons for their behavior would be known along with implications for their treatment. One of the first men to supply evidence was a medical doctor of Italian birth, Cesare Lombroso. He described the physiology of the deviant or "criminal" as one of "enormous jaws, high cheek bones, extreme size of orbits, prominent

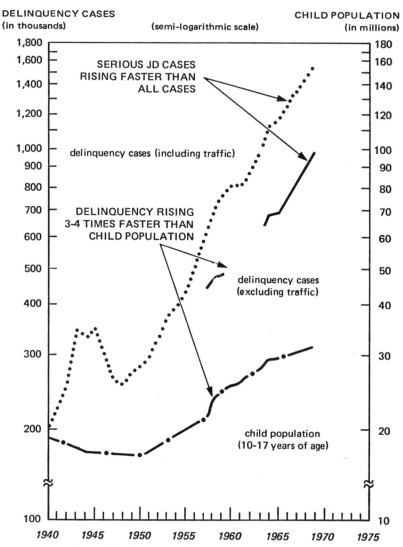

FIGURE 18–1 Trend in juvenile delinquency cases and juvenile population. Source: *Directory of Federal Juvenile Delinquency and Related Youth Development Programs: A Handbook for Juvenile Delinquency Planners* (Washington, D.C.: Government Printing Office, January 1973), p. 10.

TABLE 18-1   Cost of juvenile-related crime, Fiscal Year 1969

Item	Total Cost (Millions)	Juvenile Related Cost (Millions)
Economic Loss	$20,980	$10,784
Business Loss	3,049	1,567
Corrections	1,462	751
Indigent Defense	78	40
Prosecution	360	190
Judicial Activities	1,002	515
Police Protection	4,430	2,277
Total	$31,370	$16,124

superciliary arches, handle shaped or sessile ears" (19:361–391). Lombroso explained the criminal as a throwback to a former stage of evolution. The criminal type was an inferior development stage of man. Hence he could not respond to the control mechanisms that society had set in motion to provide guidance for the general population. Since Lombroso's explanation resided in genetics and the inherited traits of criminality, it was as applicable to the offspring of deviants as to adults.

Operating on the same sociogenetic premise as Lombroso, his disciples attempted to further refine the art of explaining crime and delinquency causation. The result was the positive school of criminology (19:361–391).

A more recent and sophisticated sociogenetic theory of social control maintains that the propensity for criminal behavior rests not only in the physiochemical properties of the individual but in his personality and temperament as well. From this perspective, physical traits are not solely responsible for delinquency or crime. Rather, when a disadvantageous environment is offered to certain physical types of persons, delinquency merely becomes highly probable. More specifically, Sheldon reported that hard, rectangular persons were more likely to become criminals because their physical and personality traits favored active assertion of themselves in competition (5:119). This explanation may apply to the hyperactive child who is usually eager to assert himself in active competition. If his energy is channeled in the wrong direction, he may become classified as delinquent. A similar conclusion can be drawn from recent research on chromosomal types (6:411–418).

Sheldon and Eleanor Glueck refined the sociogenetic assumptions with a sociological explanation of delinquency (3:190). Although maintaining that the delinquency potential may reside within the particular child, they conceded that the way in which other people react to him is important. This may be especially true of children with problems of being either overweight or underweight; they may become delinquent because of their own feelings or the reactions of others to them.

If in fact these theories of sociogenetic causation were correct, the remedy would be relatively simple. Those afflicted with the traits could be sterilized, and within one generation we would have a crimeless society.

Rejecting physique as a causative factor, some theorists conducted studies to see if social control fails to deter delinquents because they have abnormal psychological makeups. Generalizing from Freudian concepts of personality structure, theorists taking a psychoanalytic approach to delinquency adhered to the theory that a faulty superego is the explanation for juvenile delinquency. The passions and instincts of the id are not controlled by the superego; the result is an inflated ego and deviant behavior. The superego has not held the id in check; the individual is not controllable by the usual forces set up by society (5:54).

The psychodynamic theories have received much attention within society even though they are generally considered untestable. This does not mean they will be discarded as irrelevant. In fact, they appear to be gaining in popularity. One of the most widely cited works utilizing psychodynamic theories has been that of Bandura and Walters, *Adolescent Aggression*. Basically, their report states that boys who are subjected to harsh and aggressive discipline at home are more likely to exhibit antisocial, aggressive, and destructive behavior (5:210).

Most theories of social control focus upon the individual and attempt to explain the inadequacies of internal factors. Recently some theorists have asserted that delinquency results from the dynamics of social interactions which isolate the adolescent from societal norms. The most acknowledged of these theorists is David Matza, who has characterized much of juvenile delinquency as drifting behavior. That is, lacking strong social attachments to conventional adult society, the youth becomes a more likely candidate for delinquency. Matza finds that delinquency occurs in interaction with peers; and he questions a youngster's total commitment to delinquency. But, according to Matza, society has stereotyped the child's reactions as delinquent, and the youth is kept permanently in that category. In any case, delinquency follows from the absence of social bonds between the society and the adolescent.

Theories of Strain

Whereas theories of social control consider delinquency to be the inevitable reaction by youth to a society that lacks sufficient control mechanisms to prevent undesirable acts, strain theorists see delinquency as a reaction by the young against failures of society to provide adequately for acceptable goal-seeking. Strain theories of delinquency are based upon the assumption that society has failed to create realistic motivations for youth. Strain results from the failure of inadequate means to reach goals, i.e., perceived goals and obtainable goals are two different situations. When the youth realizes that the desired goal is unobtainable through legal or moral means, he turns to deviant behavior to reach the goal.

The best known of the strain theorists is Robert Merton, who described several forms of behavior which follow from differential access to goals and means. Merton subdivided society into five distinct groups of persons. The conformist, according to Merton, is one who has access to socially approved goals through socially approved means. The ritualist has the means but lacks the goals. The retreatist has neither goals nor means. The innovator lacks conventional means for obtaining his goals. The rebel has mixed access to both goals and means. Delinquency can be expected to emerge in the retreatist, the innovator, and the rebel. Merton provided the foundation for several other theories of delinquency.

Albert Cohen built one such theory on Merton's innovator type. Cohen described the innovator as the social type most responsible for lower-class and working-class delinquency (2:16). He explained that the youth, who is aware of the criteria for success but also is acutely aware that he will probably not be able to achieve the goal, develops other means, most of which are illegal, to reach the desired state. In the school environment, the lower-class boys feel they are being judged by middle-class standards and they react by appearing unmotivated and being inadequately prepared. Cohen relies upon the Freudian concept of reaction formation to explain how the lower-class boys, feeling alienated by middle-class values, band together to form gangs (2:16–31).

Without a doubt, the greatest impact on social policy for the control of deviance has been created by the strain theory as expressed by Cloward and Ohlin (1:111). Expanding upon Merton's concept of differential accessibility to goals, Cloward and Ohlin divided the opportunity structure into two parts. The legitimate opportunity structure provides legitimate access to conventional goals. Juveniles in those portions of the social system offering access to approved goals through legitimate means will not be expected to become delinquent nor to interact with gangs (1:111–124). However, many juveniles are immersed in segments of society in which illegitimate means are easily available and in which common causes exist to support gangs. This environment is termed the illegitimate opportunity structure. Cloward and Ohlin subdivide it into three subcultures: criminal, conflict, and retreatist (1:65). The criminal subculture is an environment of professional criminals. The juvenile in this setting can be expected to join youth gangs for both financial security and prestige. The conflict subculture contains youth living in an environment of small-time criminals, slum housing conditions, and adults who provide no positive role models. The activities of youth gangs in conflict subcultures are those of competition for local recognition for toughness and bravado. The third subculture is the retreatist. Members of this group live in a world where "kicks" are the prime motivation, and drugs are the typical outlet.

The strain theorists agree that if the strains could be removed from society, the problem known as delinquency would cease.

Cultural Deviance Theories

Among the oldest theoretical perspectives is the notion that delinquents are behaving in subculturally accepted ways, although contrary to the laws of the larger society. Theorists have spent many decades examining why adolescents of disadvantaged ethnic and social status are more likely to be delinquent than advantaged adolescents. Shaw and McKay, on the basis of their work, explained that the high percentage of delinquent youth in slum areas occurs as a result of the social norms of that area (4:21–40). Walter Miller, in a more recent publication, sees the normal focal concerns of the lower class to be deviant only from the perspective of middle-class mores (16:102). According to Miller, the cultural concerns of toughness, smartness, trouble, fate, autonomy, and excitement typify the lower class, but can lead to behavior that is antisocial in terms of middle-class values and institutions.

Edwin H. Sutherland was the most prominent theorist within the cultural deviance school, and his theory of differential association is the most comprehensive example of cultural theories of delinquency (5:78–105). He maintained that criminal behavior is learned in the same way that noncriminal behavior is learned. That is, interaction with a criminal peer or primary group, if early and long lasting, will produce criminal behavior. The central thesis of the theory of differential association is that if interaction teaches a person more social definitions favorable to criminal activity than definitions unfavorable to law violation, then he will be criminal. The criminal learns not only the mechanics of crime but also the motivations and justifications for his participation. Early and constant exposure to criminal behavior of others will instill the learned trait within the adolescent, and he will take on the characteristics of the criminal (5:79–80).

Theories of labeling are products of the subcultural thought. Recently, a few theorists of delinquency have found causal factors of delinquency within the judicial and treatment processes. In effect, they say the judicial and correctional processes label adolescents as delinquents, and the stigma never is removed. The subcultural environment is not entirely to blame; the criminal justice system itself must accept part of the blame. In the same sense, aggressive law enforcement can be blamed as one of the causal factors of delinquency. As the law enforcement officer attempts to enforce what he feels are the general societal norms he may, in fact, be discriminating against the lower-class adolescent, or what is termed the "delinquent-prone" subculture. Moreover, the differential application of the law in favor of the middle class may polarize the subculture against what they may define as institutions of oppression and police brutality. In this manner, labeling may actually generate delinquency under certain conditions. Irving Piliavin is one who contends that the making of laws and the enforcement of laws are responsible factors for delinquency (17:56–97).

Behavior: Delinquent and Official Delinquency

The distinction between deviant behavior and official delinquency has been a problem for the juvenile justice system and officers engaged in the prevention of delinquency for many years. Delinquent behavior is norm-violating behavior of a juvenile, which if detected by a law enforcement officer will result in some legally prescribed sanction. Official delinquency is the identification of and response to delinquency by the police and courts (18:210).

Whether the policeman chooses to ignore the delinquent behavior may be contingent on such factors as sex, age, race, social status (as perceived by the policeman), and citizen complaint. The policeman's response to the detected delinquent behavior is only the first stage in a lengthy filtering process from informal notice through formal arrest to court referral to incarceration in a reformatory.

The often cited finding of official delinquency as a lower-class phenomenon is a product of the above filtering process. The attitudes of the police officer and the citizen complainant are the all important factors. Official identification of and response to delinquency behavior show a strong relationship to lower-status juveniles; however, it does not necessarily mean that lower-status youths are involved in more delinquent behavior than any other social status group (18:210).

An analysis of self reported delinquent activities conducted by Hindelang (1968) tends to indicate that although the males generally had engaged in 24 activities with a greater frequency than females, the patterns of involvement were quite similar for both sexes (see Table 18-2).

The sample used by Hindelang was composed of 72 percent Caucasians, 14 percent Mexican American, 10 percent Negroes, and 4 percent Orientals (12:522).

For each of the 24 activities listed in Table 18-2, the respondents were asked to report the number of times in the last year that they had engaged in the act. Response frequencies were given a weight

TABLE 18-2   *Percent engaging in act one or more times* (12:525).

		A Male	B Female	C Ratio
1.	Theft less than $10.00	53.45	26.27	2.03
2.	Theft greater than $10.00	19.02	4.58	4.15
3.	Property destruction (<$10)	51.31	16.35	3.13
4.	Property destruction (>$10)	23.78	7.72	3.08
5.	Drinking alcohol	63.61	42.79	1.48
6.	Getting drunk	39.42	17.44	2.26
7.	Individual fist fights	56.03	21.64	2.58
8.	Gang fist fights	25.82	6.27	4.11
9.	Carrying a concealed weapon	33.23	10.13	3.28
10.	Individual weapon fights	11.08	4.10	2.70
11.	Gang weapon fights	8.47	2.90	2.92
12.	Gambling	16.34	3.86	4.23
13.	Using marijuana	26.15	14.50	1.80
14.	Sniffing glue	10.75	6.75	1.58
15.	Using LSD, Methedrine, or Mescaline	7.50	4.86	1.54
16.	Using Heroin	4.27	2.90	1.47
17.	Shaking down others for money	9.45	3.15	3.00
18.	Promiscuous sexual behavior	58.22	11.96	4.86
19.	Drag racing on street	45.17	22.49	2.01
20.	Driving under the influence	21.20	6.36	3.33
21.	Hit and run accidents	9.73	7.00	1.39
22.	Cheating on exams	71.76	59.67	1.20
23.	Using false ID	23.86	15.29	1.56
24.	Cutting school	40.56	24.75	1.63
		N=319	N=444	

equal to their numerical value for responses of zero through eight times; frequencies of greater than eight were given a weight of nine. This procedure was followed so that extreme scores would not distort the mean values which were calculated by the various computer programs used. Table 18–2, in part, shows the percentage of males and females who report engaging in each activity at least once (columns A and B).

It can be seen from this table that the percentage of respondents who report engaging in each activity—especially among the females—is generally not large. A typically shaped distribution of respondents was that for getting drunk; the percentages of respondents falling into categories zero through nine were 61, 14, 7, 4, 3, 3, 1, 0, 0, and 7 respectively for the males, and 83, 9, 4, 2, 1, 1, 0, 0, and 0 respectively for the females. The distributions of the 24 delinquent activities were generally J-shaped, which has been found to characterize self reported delinquent involvement in previous research (Gold, 1970; Hindelang, 1969). Among the males, more than half of the respondents report having engaged at least once in cheating on school examinations, drinking, promiscuous sexual behavior, fist fighting, theft of items worth less than $10.00 in value, and vandalism doing less than $10.00 damage; among the females, more than one-fifth of the respondents report having engaged at least once in cheating on school examinations, drinking, theft of items worth less than $10.00 in value, cutting school, drag racing, and fist fighting.

By examining the ratio of the percentage of males who report involvement to the percentage of females who report involvement, the discrepancies between male and female delinquencies can be examined. In column C of Table 18–2, it can be seen that for all activities the percent of males involved exceeds the percent of females involved; the ratios are largest for promiscuous sexual behavior, gambling, theft of items worth more than $10.00, and group fist fighting; the ratios are smallest for cheating on school examinations, hit and run accidents, heroin use, drinking, using LSD, methedrine, or mescaline, using false ID, and sniffing glue. This column shows that nearly five times (4.86) as many males as females have engaged in promiscuous sexual behavior at least once, but only about one and one half times as many males as females have used heroin (1.47), used LSD, methedrine, or mescaline (1.54), and sniffed glue (.158) at least once. Across all 24 activities, the mean male to female ratio was 2.56—less than the figures from official sources (12:524–26).

Age. National figures indicate that persons under 15 years of age made up 9 percent of the total police arrest; for those under 18, the percentage figure was 26 percent; under 21, 39 percent. In the suburban areas, the involvement of the young age groups in police arrests is markedly higher than the national figures, with the 15 age group represented in 12 percent; 18 age group was 33 percent, and the under 21 age group 49 percent. In the rural areas, the distributions were lower for the younger age group, with the under 15 group being involved in 5 percent; under 18, in 18 percent, and under 21 in 35 percent (8:34).

Table 18–3 shows the number of youth arrested for specific offenses and age group breakdown.

Problems of runaway youth. The runaway problem is extremely serious and it is growing. The Subcommittee first examined the problem in 1955. At that time, it was estimated that 200,000 young people ran away from home each year. When the problem was re-examined in Subcommittee hearings in January 1972, testimony indicated that an estimated 1 million children run away each year (Committee on the Judiciary United States Senate).

Equally as serious as the numbers involved is the developing trend toward younger runaways. Although a few years ago the typical runaway was 16 or 17, today's runaway is probably no more than 15 years old. Moreover, there has recently been a marked increase among very young runaways. New York City has reported that 43 percent of its runaways are in the 11 to 14 age category. Further, available evidence indicates that the majority of runaways are female. In some cities, such as San Diego, the ratio is as high as two females for every male.

Since running away is a juvenile status offense, it has serious legal consequences for the young people involved. While the applicable age varies somewhat from state to state, a runaway under 18 years old is subject to arrest, detention in a jail or juvenile hall, and even incarceration in a juvenile institution. According to the FBI, 232,000 runaways were arrested last year. Running away (which applies only to those under 18) is the seventh most frequent cause of arrest out of the 21 categories of arrest recognized by the FBI.

Many runaways are placed in detention. For example, during the last 3 years, 4,700 runaways were detained on an average of 8 days each in the San Diego juvenile hall. Many runaways, especially females, are eventually incarcerated in juvenile institutions. It was reported last year that half of the inmates in both the Indiana and Illinois Training Schools for Girls were runaways.

Even more serious than the legal consequences of running away are the dangers faced by young runaways on the street. Most runaways flee their suburban family life to go to the city. Being young, unfamiliar with the urban scene, and often without money, they are easy marks for the drug pusher, the hustler, or the street thug. Testimony developed at the Subcommittee hearings linked the runaway incident to the use of dangerous drugs and to petty theft, especially shoplifting. Runaways often have to sell drugs or steal to support themselves. In this way, the runaway incident often serves as the

TABLE 18–3 Total arrests of persons under 15, under 18, under 21 (6,195 agencies; 1972 estimated population 160,416,000) (8:128).

Offense charged	Grand total all ages	Number of persons arrested		
		Under 15	Under 18	Under 21
TOTAL	7,013,194	665,887	1,793.984	2,753,814
Criminal Homicide:				
(a) Murder and nonnegligent manslaughter	15,049	221	1,634	3,700
(b) Manslaughter by negligence	2,986	33	282	778
Forcible rape	19,374	818	3,842	7,752
Robbery	109,217	11,387	34,823	59,005
Aggravated assault	155,581	9,094	27,256	47,095
Burglary–breaking or entering	314,393	68,087	160,376	219,377
Larceny–theft	678,673	165,360	336,983	442,828
Auto theft	121,842	16,711	65,255	87,155
Violent crime[1]	299,221	21,520	67,555	117,561
Property crime[2]	1,114,908	250,158	562,614	749,360
Subtotal for above offenses	1,417,115	271,711	630,451	867,699
Other assaults	307,638	25,237	60,322	98,068
Arson	10,645	4,251	6,203	7,248
Forgery and counterfeiting	44,313	690	4,311	12,320
Fraud	96,713	1,069	3,705	13,227
Embezzlement	6,744	112	379	1,054
Stolen property; buying, receiving, possessing	71,754	6,932	21,988	36,736
Vandalism	129,724	57,490	91,586	103,697
Weapons; carrying, possessing, etc.	119,671	4,928	18,656	35,612
Prostitution and commercialized vice	44,744	127	1,399	10,132
Sex offenses (except forcible rape and prostitution)	51,124	4,037	10,977	17,471
Narcotic drug laws	431,608	12,865	98,308	227,048
Gambling	70,064	267	1,728	4,668
Offenses against family and children	52,935	270	1,034	7,855
Driving under the influence	604,291	168	7,568	50,749
Liquor laws	207,675	7,609	76,894	150,948
Drunkenness	1,384,735	4,064	40,625	127,898
Disorderly conduct	582,513	46,446	127,756	218,297
Vagrancy	55,680	1,060	5,547	14,337
All other offenses (except traffic)	966,722	96,954	256,815	412,258
Suspicion	41,475	3,784	12,421	21,181
Curfew and loitering law violations	116,126	33,610	116,126	116,126
Runaways	199,185	81,306	199,185	199,185

1. Violent crime is offenses of murder, forcible rape, robbery and aggravated assault.
2. Property crime is offenses of burglary, larceny and auto theft.

young person's initial contact with the police and the world of criminal activity. The longer the community ignores the underlying problems that cause it, the greater the likelihood that future behavior will be far more serious.

On the basis of its investigations, the Subcommittee developed S. 2829, the Runaway Youth Act, which provides federal assistance to local groups to establish temporary shelter/care facilities, counseling services, and research on the nature and scope of the runaway problem. S. 2829 was favorably reported from the Subcommittee on January 26, 1972, and from the Committee on the Judiciary on July 27, 1972. This bill was passed by the Senate on July 31, 1972. At the time of congressional adjournment, S. 2829 had been favorably reported by the General Education Subcommittee of the House Education and Labor Committee on October 3, 1972 (14:5–7).

Drug abuse. (Prepared Statement by Dr. Thomas T. Noguchi, Chief Medical Examiner-Coroner, County of Los Angeles, Calif.)

The drug abuse problem among youth, based on availability of drugs and their "fashionable usage among peers," presented a much different picture in the sixties than in the fifties. Even in the early sixties, the problem had not yet spread alarmingly into school, home and everyday life.

Author Andrew Weil advocates in his book entitled *The Natural Mind* that, in essence, we not be so scared that drugs are being used; that this may be one way in which we can explore the possibilities of the natural mind and development; that drug culture is here to stay, and he stated it is a part of our lives.

May I concentrate on street drugs—barbiturates, narcotics, or the combination of both. It is felt that street narcotic use in teenaged youths is now somewhat restricted because of the criminal resources that must be employed, the high cost, and the limited channels of availability. A general assumption exists that very few new teen addicts will be added in the community, and thus the death statistics will not increase, but will, in fact, decrease. On the contrary, our studies tend to indicate that the next 5 or 6 years will show an upswing in deaths due to, or associated with, overdose of drugs including heroin, and of methadone. As we keep looking for ways in which to substitute, new procedures and manmade products are being introduced; in this area, abuse is probable, and we can expect to see the effect in fatalities.

Combined medico-legal investigation, including toxicology, and behavioral scientific analysis of young people fatalities show many similarities. Most victims have a history of severe emotional stress, including family disturbances, loss of important supportive figures, stays in juvenile homes, mental hospitals, and a more or less continuous contact with juvenile courts, probationary and community agencies. Most have a long history of criminal contacts by an early age; crimes are basically burglary, auto thefts, petty theft, pickpocketing, and prostitution. It is important to note that this history is no longer limited to the black and Mexican-American—it is now found in increasing numbers among Caucasians, and is expanding to middle-class America (10:1930).

*Alcohol.** Among junior high school, senior high school, and college students, alcohol is by far the drug of choice. Figures extrapolated from student surveys show that by 1972, approximately 56 percent of the junior high school students, almost three-fourths (74 percent of the senior high school students and 83 percent of the college students have used alcohol at least once. (See Figures 18–2, 18–3, and 18–4.)

The trends (percentage change) in use (ever) of alcohol among the three student groups between 1969 and 1972 are shown in Table 18–4. The data reveal a small percentage decrease (−7 percent) in use of alcohol among college students but significant percentage increases for the secondary school students, particularly those in the senior high school grades (+ 33 percent and + 90 percent, respectively).

Examination of the figures on the growth rate of alcohol use relative to the incidence of other drug use for the period 1969 to 1972, reveals three separate and distinct patterns. (See Table 18–4.) Among junior high school students, although alcohol maintained its substantial lead over all other drug types in the incidence of use, the gap was beginning to close. Over the four year period, the percentage increase in the incidence of use of all drugs, except tobacco and inhalants, was equal to or greater (in several cases much greater) than the percent increase in the incidence of alcohol use.

TABLE 18–4 Percentage change in student ever use of drugs, 1969–72 (in percent).

Drug category	Junior high school	Senior high school	College
Tobacco	+24	+8	−6
Alcohol	+33	+90	−7
Marihuana	+60	+74	+56
Inhalants	+10	−18	(1)
Hallucinogens	+50	+133	+133
Stimulants	+80	+36	+9
Depressants	+33	+23	+17
Opiates	+118	+58	+18

(*Major portions of the following are taken from: *Drug Use in America: Problem in Perspective.* Second report of the National Commission on Marihuana and Drug Abuse.)

	1969	1970	1971	1972
tobacco	41%	41%	44%	51%
alcohol	42%	53%	48%	56%
marihuana	10%	9%	11%	16%
inhalants	10%	11%	11%	11%
hallucinogens	4%	4%	3%	6%
stimulants	5%	8%	6%	9%
depressants	6%	7%	5%	8%
opiates	2.2%	3.55%	2.1%	4.75%

FIGURE 18–2 Mean percentage of junior high school students who have used drugs (ever used) by type and year of survey. Source: *Drugs in America: Problems in Perspective*. Second report of the Commission on Marihuana and Drug Abuse (Washington, D.C.: Government Printing Office, 1973), p. 81.

	1967	1968	1969	1970	1971	1972
tobacco	50%	34%	61%	49%	45%	66%
alcohol	62%	47%	39%	65%	72%	74%
marihuana	15%	23%	23%	23%	25%	40%
inhalants	4%	5%	11%	8%	7%	9%
hallucinogens	6%	9%	6%	7%	8%	14%
stimulants	4%	10%	14%	12%	11%	19%
depressants	3%	4%	13%	12%	10%	16%
opiates	0.4%	1.7%	3.3%	3.3%	4%	5.2%

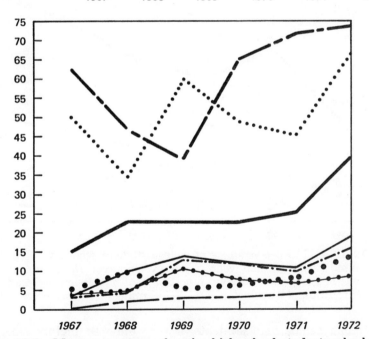

FIGURE 18–3   Mean percentage of senior high school students who have used drugs (ever used) by type and year of survey. Source: *Drugs in America: Problems in Perspective*. Second report of the Commission on Marihuana and Drug Abuse (Washington, D.C.: Government Printing Office, 1973).

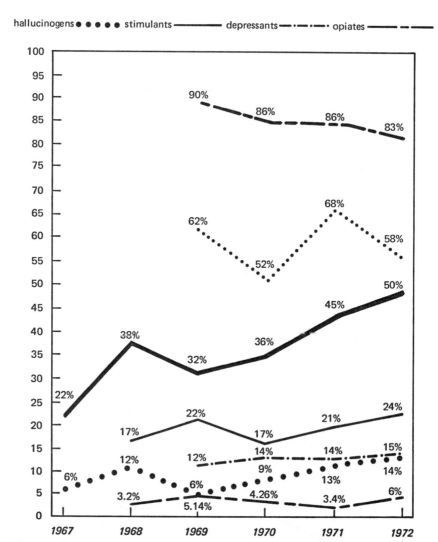

FIGURE 18-4 Mean percentage of college students who have used drugs (ever used) by type and year of survey. Source: *Drugs in America: Problems in Perspective*. Second report of the Commission on Marihuana and Drug Abuse (Washington, D.C.: Government Printing Office, 1973).

Among senior high students, a very different picture emerged. The large increase in the incidence of alcohol use (+ 90 percent) over the four year period was surpassed only by the larger percent increase in hallucinogen use (+ 133 percent), but was trailed closely by the increase in marihuana (+ 74 percent). All other drug types show percentage increases far below that of alcohol, and the incidence of tobacco use actually decreased.

For the college students, yet a third pattern emerged. Relative to the incidence of alcohol, which showed a percentage decrease, use of all drug types except tobacco and inhalants increased. The incidence of hallucinogen use showed the highest rate of growth (+ 133 percent), followed by marihuana (+ 56 percent), and still farther behind were the opiates, depressants, and stimulants, in that order.

In sum, although the incidence of drug use has generally increased among secondary school students, percentage increases in the number of students who have tried marihuana, hallucinogens, stimulants, depressants, and the opiates have begun to approach, equal, or surpass the percentage increase in the incidence of alcohol use among students at the secondary school level. At the college level, the proportion of students who reported ever use of alcohol in 1972 declined somewhat while ever users of other drug types, particularly the hallucinogens and marihuana, continued to increase.

Marihuana. Data from the student surveys show that next to alcohol, marihuana is the most popular intoxicant among both secondary school and college students. By 1972, approximately 16 percent of the junior high school students, 40 percent of the senior high school students, and 50 percent of the college students in the United States reported using marihuana at least once. (See Figures 18–2, 18–3, and 18–4.)

Between 1969 and 1972, the percentage of junior high school, senior high school, and college students reporting ever use of marihuana increased by 60 percent, 74 percent, and 56 percent respectively. (See Table 18–4.) For the secondary school populations, the largest percentage increases occurred between 1971 and 1972 (junior high: 46 percent; senior high: 74 percent). At the college level, however, the largest percentage increase occurred one year earlier, between 1970 and 1971.

The fact that the 1971–72 percentage increase for ever use of marihuana among college students (11 percent) dropped below the corresponding figure for 1969–70 (13 percent) suggests that at least for college students, the magnitude of yearly increases in the percentage of students who have tried this drug has begun to decline. This finding suggests that the incidence of marihuana use in this population may have reached its peak and may be leveling off, as was suggested by this Commission in its 1972 report and is indicated in the findings of two Commission-sponsored national surveys.

Further, because many more students in junior and senior high school have tried marihuana before they go on to college, we may expect to reach a saturation point on the incidence (ever use) of marihuana among the college populations in the not too distant future. This hypothesis finds additional support in the survey data on patterns of use and projected future use of marihuana. These data, to be discussed in detail later on, show that most of the students who have not tried marihuana do not plan to do so in the future; and that most of the ever users experimented with the drug only a few times, terminated its use, and did not plan to use it again. If this is the case, we should not expect that those who tried marihuana and terminated its use in junior high school will repeat the process in either senior high school or college. Consequently, one might suggest that the point in time at which the percentage increase in the incidence of marihuana use reaches its peak at the junior high school level will signal the beginning of a decline in total use of marihuana among future generations of secondary school and college students.

This is not to suggest that marihuana use will be totally eliminated or terminated, as there will probably always be a certain number of ever users who continue to use marihuana with varying degrees of frequency and intensity. It does suggest, however, that the proportion of students who may be expected to experiment with and to continue use of marihuana will stabilize and possibly decline within the foreseeable future.

Inhalants. The survey findings suggest that experimentation with inhalants occurs primarily among junior high school students, begins to wane among senior high school upperclassmen and disappears almost entirely once a student enters college. Surveys undertaken during 1972 show that 11 percent of the junior high school students, 9 percent of the senior high school students, and only about 2 percent of the college students have tried inhaling volatile solvents at least once. (See Figure 18–2 and 18–3.)

The data also show that the percentage of secondary school students who try inhalants has remained relatively stable since 1969, when the popularity of the practice seemed to have reached its peak, and that use of these volatile substances, once initiated, is quickly extinguished; on the average, two-thirds of the junior high school students and 70 percent of the senior high school students terminated this practice after experimenting with these substances once or twice.

Hallucinogens. In direct contrast to the inhalants, experimentation with hallucinogens is generally limited to high school upperclassmen and college students. Also dissimilar to the inhalants is the trend line of hallucinogen use; although the practice of sniffing glue and other volatile solvents began to wane after 1969, experimentation with LSD and other hallucinogens did not increase significantly until after that time.

The greatest percentage increases in the incidence of hallucinogen use among secondary school students were not experienced until about 1971; for college students, however, the significant yearly increases began about 1969. (See Figures 18–2, 18–3, and 18–4.) For the four year period, 1969-1972, the numbers of junior high school, senior high school and college students reporting use of hallucinogens at least once increased by 50 percent, 133 percent, and 133 percent, respectively. (See Table 18–4.)

Despite these large increases in the ever use of hallucinogens, the number of students who reported in 1972 that they had tried these drugs remained far below the ever users of marijuana among all three student populations, and considerably below inhalant ever users among junior high school students. Hallucinogen ever users also trailed, although by a much smaller margin, ever users of stimulants among senior high and college students and ever users of depressants in senior high school. In 1972, 6 percent of the junior high school students and 14 percent of the senior high school and college students reported having tried hallucinogens at least once. (See Figures 18–2, 18–3, and 18–4.) If this trend continues, we can expect these figures to climb over the next several years.

Stimulants. As of 1972, 9 percent of the junior high school students, about one-fifth (19 percent) of the senior high school students, and approximately one-fourth (24 percent) of the college students had taken stimulants at least once. (See Figures 18–2, 18–3, and 18–4.) Similar to the trend for hallucinogen ever use, the proportion of college students who tried these drugs began to increase significantly in 1970 and continued upward in 1972 (an increase of 41 percent over these two years). The significant percentage increase among secondary school students followed by about one year the percentage increase for college students, but the magnitude of this one-year increase for both groups of secondary school students exceeded the two-year increase noted above for the college population (50 percent for the junior high school students and 73 percent for the senior high school students).

Depressants. Among junior high school students, the specific incidence figures and the trend line for ever use of depressants closely parallel those noted for the stimulants; the proportion of students reporting ever use of depressants rose from 6 percent in 1969 to 9 percent in 1972, a four-year increase of 33 percent.

Among the senior high school students, the magnitude of the four-year percentage increase was somewhat smaller (23 percent), but by 1972, 16 percent claimed to have taken depressants at least once, a 60 percent increase over the preceding year.

Among college students, the four-year percent increase to 1972 was smaller (17 percent) than that of either group of secondary school students, but by 1972 a sizeable 14 percent of the college student population reported having used depressants on at least one occasion. Unlike the pattern for stimulant use among these students, however, the percentage of ever users has remained stable since 1970, when the ever use figure jumped two percentage points over the corresponding 1968 and 1969 figures.

These data suggest that although experimentation with depressants among college students may have levelled off, the relatively high incidence of ever use is likely to be surpassed by future generations of college students. The level of ever use of depressants among senior high school students is already approaching the college level, and junior high school students are well on their way to catching up.

Opiates.   In contrast to survey findings drawn from samples of inner city populations, school drop-outs, or minority groups, the incidence (ever use) of heroin and other opiate use among secondary school and college students as a whole is comparatively low, increasing from about 2 percent to 6 percent between 1969 and 1972. (See Figures 18–2, 18–3, and 18–4.)

This is not to suggest, however, that these figures are insignificant or that the phenomenon of opiate use among students is stabilizing or diminishing. Rather, all three student populations have experienced significant increases in the proportions of those who have at least experimented with one or more of the opiates (junior high school: 118 percent; senior high school: 58 percent; and college: 18 percent). (See Table 18–4.) Contrary to prevalent public opinion, however, the largest majority of these opiate ever users terminate use of these drugs after experimenting with them once or a few times. Only a small proportion of the ever users in the student population go on to become frequent users or reach dependent status.

SUMMARY

In sum, the incidence data drawn from secondary and college student surveys demonstrate a substantial, significant, and rapid increase in the number of young people who have tried various types of drugs at least once, thereby entering the pool or population at risk. These figures, however, tell us nothing about the prevalence or patterns of drug use in these student populations; they provide no indication of the proportion of ever users who terminate use after one or a few experimental trials, nor the relative proportion of either the total student body or the ever users who go beyond their initial experiences and adopt patterns of more prolonged, frequent, or intensive drug use. In order to determine the extent to which such conversion takes place and to identify the usage patterns which emerge, one must examine data relative to the frequency, intensity, and duration of drug use.

REFERENCES

Books

CLOWARD, R. A., and OHLIN, L. E. 1966. *Delinquency and Opportunity: A Theory of Delinquent Gangs.* Glencoe, Ill.: The Free Press.
COHEN, A. K. 1955. *The Culture of the Gang.* Glencoe, Ill.: The Free Press.
SHAFER, S. 1969. *Theories in Criminology.* New York: Random House.
SHAW, C. R., and McKAY, H. D. 1942. *Juvenile Delinquency in Urban Areas.* Chicago: University of Chicago Press.
SUTHERLAND, E. H., and CRESSEY, D. 1970. *Principles of Criminology.* Philadelphia: J. B. Lippincott.

Articles and Government Publications

BAUMILLER, R. C. 1969. XYZ Chromosome Genetics. *Journal of Forensic Sciences* 14:411–418.
California Council for Criminal Justice. 1973. *Synopsis of the 1973 Comprehensive Plan.* Sacramento, Calif.
Crime in the United States. 1972. *Uniform Crime Report,* Washington, D.C.: GPO.
Directory of Federal Juvenile Delinquency and Related Youth Development Programs. 1973. *A Handbook for Juvenile Delinquency Planners.* Washington, D.C.: GPO.
Select Committee on Crime, House of Representatives. 1972. *Drugs in Our Schools.* Washington, D.C.: GPO.
National Commission on Marijuana and Drug Abuse. 1973. *Drug Use in America: Problem in Perspective.* Washington, D.C.: GPO.
HINDELANG, M. J. 1971. Age, Sex and the Versatility of Delinquent Involvement. *Social Problems* 18:522–35.
————. 1973. Causes of Delinquency: A Partial Replication and Extension. *Social Problems* 20:471–87.
Report of the Committee on the Judiciary, United States Senate. 1973. *Juvenile Delinquency.* Washington, D.C.: GPO.
MERTON, R. K. 1938. Social Structure and Anomie. *American Sociological Review* 3:672–682.
MILLER, W. B. 1959. Preventive Work with Streetcorner Groups: Boston

Delinquency Project. *Annals of the American Academy* 322:97–106.

WELLER, B. 1966. The Police Role in Prevention. *Police Chief* 33:54–60.

WILLIAMS, J. R., and GOLD, M. 1972. From Delinquent Behavior to Official Delinquency. *Social Problems* 20:209–29.

WOLFGANG, M. 1961. Pioneers in Criminology: Cesare Lombroso (1835–1909). *Journal of Criminal Law, Criminology, and Police Science* 52:361–391.

TOPICS FOR DISCUSSION

1. Discuss the reasons for the more recent upsurge in youth gangs.

2. Discuss the amount of discretion police officers should possess in handling juvenile offenders.

3. Discuss the relationship between increased discretion for police in handling juvenile offenders and the central thesis of the theory of differential association, i.e., if interaction teaches a person more social definitions favorable to criminal activity than definitions unfavorable to law violation, then the person will be a criminal.

4. Discuss the relationship between legalization of marijuana and other drugs, and increased criminal offenses committed by juveniles.

5. Discuss the effectiveness of using the juvenile offender as a correctional manpower resource.

6. Discuss the following statements taken from *A 1976 Preliminary Report* by Robert D. Vinter, George Downs, and John Hall, University of Michigan:

   During fiscal 1974, the states spent $300 million on institutions for juvenile offenders; only about one-tenth as much was spent on community-based programs such as halfway houses.

   "Nothing we learned in this study challenges the criticism leveled against traditional institutions for the handling of juvenile offenders, or the argument that community-based corrections are more economical and probably at least as effective."

   "On any 'average day' in 1974, there were 28,001 juvenile offenders reported in state-run institutions and 5,663 in community-based residential programs. Even fewer were in day programs."

   The President's Commission on Law Enforcement and Administration of Justice in 1967 recommended that correctional authorities develop more extensive community programs providing "special, intensive treatment" for both juvenile and adult offenders.

   The report said, however, that while there is continuing "widespread interest" in such programs, only four states—Massachusetts, South Dakota, Minnesota and Utah—send even as many as half of their juvenile offenders to them.

   The rest of the children are placed in such institutions as state training schools and camps. Six states have no community-based programs for juveniles.

Nearly four out of five state agency administrators surveyed agreed that most delinquents do not belong in institutions at all, the report said. Fifty-four percent said community-based programs are better than even the most effective institutions.

Yet, the report concludes, "there has been little actual progress in shifting from the traditional to alternative correctional methods."

19

VERNON FOX

Institutional confinement: countdown to explosion

Prisons emerged between 1773 and 1799. For more than 200 years prior to this development, major offenders were transported to distant lands and minor offenders and sturdy beggars were confined in workhouses, which had first developed at Bridewell in 1557. The workhouse developed at Ghent in Belgium in 1773 was managed by Jean Jacques Philippe Vilain (1717–1777) who developed businesslike methods that became significant in later prison management. At the same time, in 1773, the first prison in America was at Simsbury, Connecticut, about 40 miles north of New Haven, when administration buildings were constructed over the shaft of an old abandoned mine, which served as a prison. The first prison riot was there in 1774.

It was John Howard (1726–1790) who first suggested a penitentiary system, and two bills passed the Parliament in 1774 correcting some of the abuses in jails and providing a foundation for a prison system. Impressed by the Hospice di San Michele in Rome, constructed by Pope Clement XI in 1704 for the treatment of wayward youth, and by Vilain's management of the Maison de Force in Ghent, Howard pressed for further reform. With the assistance of Sir William Blackstone and Sir William Eden, Howard drafted the Penitentiary Act that was passed by Parliament in 1779. No penitentiaries were constructed immediately, however, and England sent offenders to Australia until 1856. A prison was designed by Jeremy Bentham in 1799 as a circular Panopticon covered by a glass roof, with cells on the outer circumference, and apartments for the keepers or guards in the center. Only three Panopticon-style institutions were ever built, all in America, in Virginia at Richmond in 1800, the Western State Penitentiary at Pittsburgh in 1821, and at Stateville in Illinois between 1916 and 1925.

In the meantime, the Quakers in Philadelphia remodeled the Old Walnut Street Jail in 1790 to formalize the beginning of the penitentiary movement with humane treatment, solitary confinement, labor within the cells, and religious counseling. In 1815, New York opened a more economical prison at Auburn which featured silence, congregate labor during the day, solitary confinement at night, and corporal punishment. The American prison had been invented.

Sentencing has been the traditional beginning of society's response to crime, whether vengeance, retribution, incapacitation, rehabilitation, or other forms of the social institution today known as corrections. Ancient and medieval court dispositions were based on compensation and vengeance for personal wrongs against individuals (well enunciated in Exodus 21 and 22 in the Old Testament). While the ancient Greeks in the sixth and fifth centuries B.C. introduced the abstract concept of "justice" as a mitigation of strength with some wisdom and a limited protection of the weak from the strong, the introduction of "justice" in the due process model awaited the maturity of model law between 1650 and 1820. The criminal law was included last in this "justice" system about the time of the American and French Revolutions and before the War of 1812. Sentencing in the criminal justice system then became more equitable, following Beccaria's famous slogan (1764), "Let the punishment fit the crime."

It was in 1928 when Robert Park of the University of Chicago wrote that the criminal trial and sentencing procedure had become a ceremonial ritual with little meaning and of almost no effect, and "we might as well dance!"[1] The court procedure after arrest, with its prosecution and defense, had become a ceremony with primary concern for procedure and the due process model through which substantive information concerning the offense is processed according to constitutional procedure and the court decisions and laws of criminal procedure pertaining to it. It was only after a verdict of guilty that the personality and social situation of the offender might receive consideration. Even then, the personal and social orientation and philosophy of the sentencing judge frequently became more important than the personality needs and social situation of the offender. This is why the American Law Institute recommended in 1939 that a separate board, such as a Youth Authority or an Adult Authority, determine the disposition and program according to the needs of the convicted citizen-offender. California was the only state to adopt the Adult Authority in part and about a dozen states have adopted some variation of it for juveniles and youthful offenders.

OBJECTIVES OF SENTENCING

The objectives of sentencing are still in flux and have not been completely defined. Rather, sentencing becomes a result of many pressures of public opinion that range from complete vengeance and retribution to almost complete forgiveness. The traditional objectives of sentencing have been (1) retribution, (2) restitution, (3) incapacitation, and (4) rehabilitation. The objective or combination of objectives used in any specific case must depend upon the philosophy of the judge and the public he serves. As a public servant, either elected or appointed, the judge must be aware of community attitudes. As an individual person, the judge brings his own philosophy and social orientation to the sentencing procedure. Within the bounds of discretion afforded by the law, three patterns of the sentencing behavior emanate as the philosophies of (1) punishment, (2) sentimental and lenient approaches, and (3) treatment and rehabilitative approaches.

The punishment or retributive approach appears frequently in conservative groups and manifests itself in vitriolic attacks against lenient judges and "bleeding-heart" parole boards who let loose vicious criminals on society. Many calls for "stiffer penalties," capital punishment, and other punitive approaches reflect this view. Closer examination divorced from emotional responses, however, indicates that the punitive approach in criminal justice aggravates the problem and makes big resentments out of little ones, so that the individuals subjected to such approaches become worse than they were when they entered the criminal justice system. When sentencing consisted of a one-way trip to Siberia, Australia, Devil's Island, or other distant lands that resulted in permanent exile, the punitive approach was not harmful to society. In modern America, however, the fact that 3 to 5 percent of prisoners die in prison means that 95 to 97 percent of them are returned to the community. The average stay in American prisons is 21 months. This means that the punishment approach is counterproductive, both for the rehabilitation of the individual and for the protection of society.

The sentimental, "bleeding-heart," or "sob-sister" approach simply does not attack the problem. If the criminal behavior itself is rewarding, then the sentimental or "forgiveness" approach may even reinforce criminal behavior. There is reason to believe, however, based on the experience of many juvenile court judges, that the sentimental approach does less damage than does the punitive approach. At least the sentimental approach does not make big resentments out of little ones and aggravate the problem by creating hostility and aggression in a growing personality that is already caught up in the criminal justice system.

The treatment or rehabilitative approach incorporates an attempt to diagnose and treat the offender on the basis of his psychological and social needs without emotional involvement. It takes experience, sensitivity, and competence to view a person with the same discretion an engineer looks at a steel girder, assessing its strengths and weaknesses and determining where it should be buttressed in order to carry the load expected of it. Like the medical doctor, an effective practitioner in the criminal justice system has to diagnose and treat a client without loving him and without hating him. As soon as a criminal justice practitioner becomes emotionally involved, either by becoming punitive or sympathetic, he loses his treatment effectiveness. How many punishment-oriented people view treatment-oriented judges as "lenient" and "soft." On the contrary, the studies of sentencing behavior on the part of punishment-oriented judges as compared with treatment-oriented judges does not support this myth. For example, David Fabianic's study in 1963 of federal judges revealed that the treatment-oriented judges gave longer sentences than the punishment-oriented judges did in an effort to give the institutions to which the convicted offender was sent time to do the expected job.[2] Consequently, it is an error to equate treatment with leniency. The treatment approach is the only practical, commonsense, businesslike approach to working with people who have been brought into the criminal justice system and will be released to the community again at some time in the future.

Long sentences have been consistently seen by correctional administrators and by research criminologists as detrimental to the correctional objective.[3] When a person lives in a prison long enough to acquire the values and customs of the prison culture, his chances of adjusting to the outside society are reduced even more than they were when he arrived in prison. He surely did not have much adaptive capability or he would not be in prison—and long sentences imposed by society's agencies of social control are subtracting from it! More information about the person is needed as opposed to the crimes he committed, and more needs to be known about what prisons do before any prediction can be made as to the efficacy of correctional institutions. Thus far, the evidence of their success is disappointing, according to a survey of 100 studies in this area.[4] At present, it appears that the maximum security prison may be counterproductive and maybe even dangerous.[5]

THE CORRECTIONAL CLIENT

While there is no such thing as a "criminal personality" or "the criminal mind," there are some general characteristics of correctional caseloads that are dissimilar to those caseloads carried by other public agencies and services. Crime is a sociopolitical event, rather than a medical or clinical condition; however, encroachment on the rights, lives, and property of others has resulted in attracting the attention of social authority and criminals have been processed by the courts into the criminal justice system. The welfare client is generally characterized as inadequate, not capable of coping with the economic environment, and a poor manager. Social workers engaged in income maintenance programs spend their counseling time assisting their clients in learning personal and household budgeting, and limit their use of client accountability. Incidents of aggressiveness on the part of welfare clients have been limited to a few isolated irate clients raising havoc in the local welfare office or a peaceful demonstration like the one in New York City in 1968. Patients in mental hospitals are frequently psychotic, although any number of clinical diagnoses may be represented. Insanity, of course, is a legal status that does not necessarily mean psychotic, though most psychiatrists serving as expert witnesses for the courts and staff members of state hospitals concentrate on the psychoses. In any case, only a small percentage of these patients are violent or are criminally insane. Those who are considered criminally insane were insane first and criminal second.

Public and private mental health clinics, psychiatrists, and marriage counselors generally have caseloads characterized by neuroses. Most neurotics are too concerned about their own welfare to engage in criminal behavior but, rather, internalize their hostilities and develop ulcers or psychosomatic symptoms. A few neurotics, particularly obsessive-compulsive patterns, do engage in criminal and delinquent behavior such as auto theft, forgery, larceny, compulsive drinking, drug use, and some other minor offenses. A few have committed violent offenses, but the proportion of this type of behavior among neurotics is small.

The correctional client is different from all these other clients because he "acts out" his tensions, frustrations, and problems. He has an acting out disorder and the average correctional client uses the mechanisms of projection and denial, rather than the internalization of hostility. A minority of correctional clients are psychotic and neurotic and their behavior is a compensatory and reactional product of these conditions, but the majority are normal in terms of clinical grouping and medical condition. The clinical group that appears more frequently in correctional caseloads and prisons than in any other group receiving governmental services has variously been called psychopath, the sociopath, or antisocial personality disorder. The confusion in this terminology results from the change of name from psychopath to sociopath by the American Psychiatric Association in 1952, and then to antisocial personality disorder in 1968. Whatever the terminology, it refers to a group that has been recognized by psychiatrists for at least two centuries (known as "moral lunacy" until the early 20th century).

The psychopath does not internalize the value system of the

culture, does not develop guilt and anxiety, nor does he have the deep emotional responses that permit long term stable relationships, appreciation of art and religion, and other values considered to be normal in American society. Hervey Cleckley's *The Mask of Sanity*,[6] Robert Lindner's *Rebel without a Cause*,[7] and many other contributions to the literature constitute attempts to explain and describe this psychopath. The *Archives of Criminal Psychodynamics*, Fall, 1961, incorporated one of the best collection of papers taken from a symposium on Psychopathy presented in the 1959 meeting of the American Psychiatric Association in Philadelphia. Most of the contemporary "experts" in the field of psychopathy contributed to this symposium. The behavior of the psychopath (sociopath, antisocial personality disorder) is an acting out individual who has not developed anxiety, guilt, or remorse and is not bound by ethics and social values.

Many studies have indicated that the intelligence of the correctional client is the same as the rest of the population, but in terms of achievement, he is retarded, both in the number of grades he completed in school and in his ability to perform on academic achievement tests. Consequently, the average correctional client is an individual of average ability who has not assimilated the tools and values of the culture to which he has been exposed. He is an "underachiever." He is not only academically retarded, but he is retarded in the internalization and assimilation of all phases of the culture, including the value system, work habits, and ability to deal with his environment.

In a large city, such as New York, little children of seven or eight can left hook and kidney punch with the best of them. The influence of Hell's Kitchen, the lower East Side, and similar neighborhoods has scrambled the traditional value system in favor of survival-of-the-fittest. People growing up there learn to deal with people "at arm's length," never trusting anyone and never having a meaningful relationship with an adult. A person growing up there is likely to see other people either as a threat or as an opportunity. This is one reason that correctional caseloads and prison populations are made up of a majority of people from the inner city and relatively few from rural areas. The "pressure cooker" of the urban ghetto is not conducive to producing stability, confidence, and trust. Rather, it is likely to produce a defensive and aggressive personality struggling for security.

There have been many explanations for the aggression found in the acting out disorders in the correctional plan. Lombroso in 1883 pointed out that the "criminal man" was an atavistic "throwback" to previous savagery, which made him a "born criminal." In the late 1960s, some Australian and English geneticists pointed out that there were more males with XYY chromosomes in prison populations than would be expected based on their numbers in the general population. The normal male is XY, while the "super male" is XYY, and he becomes more aggressive than others. The brain has been viewed as the source of aggression.[8] Psychosurgery and lobotomies have been used to reduce aggressive and violent behavior, but some legal concerns have arisen resulting from the observation that people turn into "vegetables" if too much psychosurgery takes place. Castration is used in Scandinavian countries to reduce the sex drive in aggressive rapists. Differential androgen levels produced by the testes are associated with different levels of aggression in the males of all species. In the American system of criminal justice, however, there are procedural difficulties associated with psychosurgery, electroconvulsive therapy, behavior modification, and other types of "treatment" surgery and intervention.[9]

Whatever the cause—social, psychological, or biological—the correctional client tends to be more aggressive than the rest of the population. He is involved in more fights. He runs out of ideas faster and is more willing to resort to physical force. Prison populations, then, have a higher proportion of aggressive people than would ordinarily appear in the general population.

PRISONS AND
CORRECTIONAL INSTITUTIONS

The prison is a closed society characterized by lack of privacy, constant presence of authority, segregation, controlled movement of inmates, regimentation, and deprivation of all sorts. The walls, towers, and armed guards are penetrated only by newspapers, radio, television, and letters from home, all supervised and controlled—even the basic bodily functions in the daily toiletries are supervised.

Prison staff in America, whether administrative, custodial, or treatment-oriented are too frequently deficient in both quantity and quality. To control a large organization with a limited staff, regimentation is necessary. Some of the rules needed to maintain this regimentation appear to be trivial and annoying. The correctional officers who enforce these rules vary from too lenient, to reasonable, to the strict and meticulous officer who writes citations for minor violations of institutional regulations.

The inmate's world is with the other inmates. In many institutions, the inmate has to make up his mind whether he is going to get along with the administration or get along with the other inmates, since he cannot reconcile the differences and get along with both. It is only the inmate who is serving a very short term who can afford to get along with the administration. If the prison is going to be his residence for any significant length of time, he soon discovers that the pressures from fellow inmates tend to overwhelm pressures from the administration. He soon learns to get along with his fellow inmates and "play the nods" with the correctional officers and staff. His getting along with inmates and courteous but minimal, relationships with the staff result in his "doing his own time." He learns to do his time one day at a time, without much reflection on his past or much planning for the future. Over a long period of time, inmates tend to become "institutionalized," characterized by apathy and dependency on the system. Unfortunately, many prison personnel are also "doing time;" they become institutionalized and develop the same characteristics.

Other prisoners become frustrated, angry, and hostile in response to prison restrictions and control. It was these prisoners about which Robert Lindner wrote in his *Rebel Without a Cause* in 1944. Most of these people are, in fact, without "causes" and they are unable to articulate or define what they are angry about, except that they are angry about the "system" and their situation in it. For their own ego protection, they do not accept the blame themselves. Hostility, then, legitimately can be directed outward. The attitude of many persons in prison can be expressed well by this doggerel:

I'm walking about a prison,
What do you think I see?
A lot of dumb-bells doing time,
While all the crooks go free.[10]

In the middle 1950s, Schnur surveyed the number of prisoners in state and federal prisons and reformatories, and surveyed the personnel hired to keep and care for them. There were 161,587 inmates and 17,280 prison personnel.[11] Of the 17,280 hired to keep prisoners in prison, only 1,377 or 7.7 percent were classified as people who were "there to get them ready to go out and stay out," and many of these were clerical. There were 23 full-time psychiatrists, 67 psychologists and psychomatrists, 96 institutional parole officers, 155 chaplains, and 257 caseworkers. Assuming that all these people were in contact with inmates at all times (which is a false assumption because of paper work and other functions) they could provide an average of 82 seconds of psychiatric help each month, about 4 minutes of psychological attention, about 6 minutes of parole counseling, about 10 minutes of religious counseling, and 16 minutes of casework per month. At the same time, there were 739 academic, vocational, and trade school teachers that averaged about 45 minutes per month for each inmate. In comparison, a caseworker or therapist in a mental health clinic generally has 12 or 14 cases, works with them one hour a week, and spends more time consulting with the psychiatrist about each case, sometimes a "staffing," where the entire clinic staff works in consultation on the case, on the diagnostic effort, and on recording the progress of each case. This type of approach would be impossible in prison, where the most aggressive and dangerous people are located. It can be readily concluded that any significant treatment process would not be even coincidental—it would be accidental!

When the reports of the President's Commission on Law Enforcement and Administration of Justice were published in 1967, the same type of survey was made ten years after Schnur's survey. By that time, the inmate population had increased to 201,220, which means that the treatment personnel would have had to increase to slightly over 2,000 in order to maintain the same level of service. The number of "treatment" persons employed in 1965 had increased to 2,199.[12] This means that there was little change in the ratio of treatment personnel to prisoners during that decade. In the competition for state and federal funds through legislators and through Congress, it is apparent that the situation in corrections seems to have become stabilized.

Prison society is further complicated by a built-in three-way conflict between custody, treatment, and the inmates. In most cases, a three-way conflict grows into more complex conflicts because of factions within each group. At the minimum, the three-way conflict produces strain in the prison community. Custodial and the administrative personnel are interested in preventing escapes and maintaining order, which is accomplished by strong security. On the other hand, treatment personnel prefer a relaxed atmosphere because casework and counseling function best when the clients are not defensive and "on guard." Further, they are interested in preparing inmates to get out and stay out. The inmates also want to get out and stay out, and they want a relaxed atmosphere while they are in the prison. The result is that the treatment people and the inmates want the same situation, if for different reasons. As far as custody and administration are concerned, then, the treatment personnel are "on the side" of the inmates. Even though chaplains are the oldest and most secure of treatment-oriented personnel in the prison, they remain suspect as far as custodial personnel is concerned because of their personal interest in inmates.

THE SETTING FOR EXPLOSION

It is not difficult to understand the incompatible components of the modern maximum security prison. A bomb is composed of a strong outside with high pressure on the inside. Pushing a volatile substance into a strong shell can cause it to explode. This is what prison is all about. A prison has high walls or fences with armed guard towers manned by security-oriented custodial officers, and internal order is kept by regimentation and segregation of inmates by uniformed correctional officers. The inmates are basically aggressive, acting out, and angry people who project the blame for their situation on "the system." The social distance and different viewpoints and goals pit officers against inmates. There are not enough "treatment" people to counteract the hostility. Treatment people are generally in untenable positions in a maximum security prison and many correctional officers think that they do not know what their responsibilities are. In the setting where there is mutual suspicion and conflict among the staff (built-in because of immediate objectives that could be mutually exclusive), the correctional caseload is characterized by aggressive, acting-out people. The ingredients for explosion are present in all maximum security prisons.

DEFUSING THE BOMB

The objectives of sentencing are hardly consistent with the performance of the prisons. The situation just does not permit any of the intended objectives to be implemented. The punishment objective is the most nearly achieved objective because of the material and psychological deprivation to which all prisoners are subjected. The motto adopted by the United States Bureau of Prisons a few years ago, "People are sent to prison *as* punishment, *not* for punishment," is a statement of intent that treatment should prevail within the prisons. The treatment approach is subverted, however, because of the unfavorable ratio of treatment personnel to inmates. Those few treatment personnel who are there have to explain their presence to both custody and administration in many instances. There is no prison with a sentimental and kind approach, even though some people consider this approach to be an objective of sentencing.

A medical model of treatment was attempted after World War II and throughout the 1950s, undoubtedly a vestige of the emergence of clinical psychology in the military services and in the Veterans Administration. The medical model is characterized by casework, counseling, and psychotherapy. By the 1960s, it was obvious that the medical model had to be abandoned, not because it was ineffective, but because correctional institutions and agencies simply did not have the manpower to implement it. When prisons exist with nearly 4,000 inmates and one part-time psychiatrist, perhaps a psychologist, there is no way to implement the medical model. Probation and parole agents frequently have in excess of 100 persons in the caseloads, and institutional treatment personnel generally have many more. In child guidance clinics, mental health clinics, or private psychiatrists' caseloads, they are generally limited to 12 or 14, as previously mentioned. The standards of the American Psychiatric Association hold that no consulting psychiatrist can advise or provide consultation with caseworkers or therapists handling more than 20 cases—and the psychiatrists do not see the patients in these settings, but only consult with the caseworkers. Dr. Benjamin Karpman told this writer at an annual meeting of the American Psychiatric Association in 1959 in Philadelphia that a competent psychiatrist realistically influences the lives of 125 to 130 people in a professional lifetime! He may see many more, as many do in professional settings, but they are only for evaluation and diagnosis, rather than for treatment. Thus, there is no way to obtain the necessary manpower to implement the medical model in corrections, however effective it may be in other settings.

A recent trend has been to select correctional officers who have demonstrated empathic capability by getting along effectively with inmates, give them supplementary training, and to use them as correctional counselors. This has been successful in several states and the United States Bureau of Prisons. By using available psychiatrists, psychologists, and social workers in a training capacity, rather than working with inmates, some treatment can be implemented by capable correctional counselors who then become available.

The peer pressure approach in the 1950s in Guided Group Interaction proposed by Dr. Lloyd McCorkle and Dr. F. Lovell Bixby of New Jersey was reported in their *The Highfields Story* in 1958.[13] In this system, responsibility for the inmate was placed upon the other inmates. The system was fully developed at the Minnesota State Training School at Redwing, in the New York State Youth Services, and throughout the Florida Division of Youth Services. It has possibilities with some juveniles and has been successfully demonstrated at the adult level.

There are several group approaches that make use of fellow inmates and diminish the role of the leader.[14] This is helpful, too, since the resentment against authority could be diffused a little when a competent and sensitive leader is "outnumbered." In some approaches, the leader is not even present, but leadership is assumed by an inmate who has been in the institution a long time, is responsible, and is acquainted with the method. Positive Peer Culture is another new approach that involves less aggression than some approaches.[15] Reality Therapy has also been helpful.[16] There are many new and innovative approaches, but they are generally combinations of old concepts. Many clinicians have observed that the success or failure of any treatment approach depends more upon the competence of the therapist than on the specific method. In any case, *some* effort must be made to bring treatment programs into correctional institutions.

Environmental changes reducing the size of prisons would reduce the unfavorable ratio between the custodial forces and inmates. Very few riots have been reported from institutions for 300 persons or less, and almost none from prisons of less than 100 inmates, though there have been disturbances in some jails. Further, disturbances do not occur in minimum custody institutions. This indicates that breaking down the large maximum security prison into one or two small maximum security psychiatric-oriented institutions for the more dangerous offenders, and having a series of smaller medium and minimum custody institutions for property offenders and other offenders who do not pose security risks would reduce the possibility of mass violence.

The social surgery of removing people from the community intensifies the alienation of an individual from society. Consequently, sentencing should be reserved for most compelling reasons related to the safety of society, rather than the punishment of the individual. Punishment is expensive in terms of implementation and in what it produces.

The "sound barrier" between prisons and the rest of society seems to have been broken. The two factors responsible are (1) the aggressive and sophisticated reporting by newspapers, radio, and television that has emerged since World War II and (2) greater activity by the courts in civil suits by prisoners for violation of constitutional and civil rights that developed in the 1960s and early 1970s. While many previous riots have received news coverage,[17] the first major riot in which newsmen representing all the forms of the media saturated the prison and its personnel was the major riot at the State Prison of Southern Michigan at Jackson, April 20–24, 1952. This was the largest riot in prison history, involving 2,600 men in the yard, 179 men holding twelve hostages in the disciplinary cellblock, and $3.5 million worth of damage done in three hours on Monday, April 21. The vast amount of reporting and analysis over a period of years in newspapers, books, radio serials, and television marked the beginning of public interest in prison conditions. That type of aggressive and sophisticated reporting has continued. The most recent major incident was the riot at the State Correctional Facility at Attica, New York, September 9–13, 1971. Incidents between these two major riots included disturbances at Soledad and San Quentin in California, and various incidents in Massachusetts, Maryland, Ohio, Oklahoma, and elsewhere.

As a result of media interest and court interest, there have been outlets for the pressure other than violence. New and innovative treatment methods have helped. Certainly, there will be considerable relief from the pressures found in maximum custody prisons and correctional institutions if the recommendations of the National Advisory Commission on Criminal Justice Standards and Goals are implemented.[18]

CONCLUSIONS

The prison experiment had begun as a humane gesture, both in England and America. Nearly two centuries later, the Quakers who started the Penitentiary Movement in 1787–1790 now called the American Friends Service Committee have written:[19]

> The horror that is the American prison system grew out of an eighteenth-century reform by the Pennsylvania Quakers and others against the cruelty and futility of capital and corporal punishment. This two-hundred-year-old experiment has failed.

The old doctrine of least eligibilities has contributed to the failure. No society has been willing to give to offenders more than the least of its law-abiding citizens. Yet, for adequate rehabilitation, the law-breaker's problems are greater and the needs for remedial assistance are, too. This was no problem when offenders were executed, banished, or whipped, but when the humanitarian philosophy of John Howard and the Quakers developed the prison, a new setting emerged. Humanitarian philosophy without the resources to implement it has been damaging and, consequently, has failed. The entire question of "justice" arises; equal treatment to unequals is as great an injustice as is unequal treatment to equals. The modern prison does not have the resources to make the distinction.

The primary conclusion that can be made regarding the outcome of sentencing is that nothing happens. "We might as well dance!" Prisons and correctional agencies have not received sufficient funds to implement any type of treatment program. When an institution or agency remains understaffed and underfunded, the treatment approach is crisis-oriented and superficial, and the implementation of a sentence becomes a matter of warehousing, or deep freezing. The result is stagnation or rebellion, depending upon the adaptation mode of the inmates who are subjected to this process.

Perhaps the best approach to prison reform would be the destruction of most of the facilities that are antiquated and the construction of smaller institutions around urban centers, staffed by personnel adequate in quality and quantity. The news media, the courts, the unions, and other associations interested in the correctional process will make the facility move somewhere. Prison facilities have already changed the caliber and social orientation of wardens and correctional administrators. A realistic criminal justice process in which law enforcement, the courts, and corrections communicate in a meaningful way appears to be a first step. The humanitarian values are strong enough so that there is a chance of making headway toward effectiveness. Consequently, administrators and practitioners dedicated to serving as their brother's keeper must maintain their efforts toward improvement of corrections in quality and in quantity in whatever way may be open. Otherwise, criminal justice, whose success and failure rate is measured by the productivity of corrections, is quite obviously in a countdown to explosion!

NOTES

1. Edwin H. Sutherland and Donald R. Cressey, *Principles of Criminology,* 7th edition (Philadelphia and New York: J. B. Lippincott, 1966), p. 10.
2. David Fabianic, *A Study of the Relationship Between Race and Length of Sentence in a Northern Correctional Institution,* unpublished master's thesis, Florida State University, 1963.
3. James V. Bennett, *Federal Prisons*—1957 (Washington, D.C.: United States Bureau of Prisons, 1958), p. 3; Paul Tappan, "Habitual Offender Laws in the United States," *Federal Probation,* Vol. 13, No. 1, March, 1949, pp. 28–31; Harry Elmer Barnes and Negley K. Teeters, *New Horizons in Criminology,* 3rd edition (Englewood Cliffs, N.J.: Prentice Hall, 1959), p. 567; Ross V. Randolph, "Are Long Sentences Necessary?" *American Journal of Correction,* Vol. 21, January–February, 1959, pp. 3ff; Elmer Hubert Johnson, *Crime, Correction, and Society* (Homewood, Illinois: The Dorsey Press, 1967), pp. 435–437.
4. Walter C. Bailey, "An Evaluation of 100 Studies in Correctional Outcomes," in Norman Johnston, Leonard Savitz, and Marvin E. Wolfgang (eds.), *The Sociology of Punishment & Correction,* 2nd Edition (New York: John Wiley and Sons, 1970), pp. 733–742.
5. Sheldon B. Peizer, "What Do Prisons Do, Anyway?" in Clyde B. Vedder and Barbara A. Kay (eds.), *Penology: A Realistic Approach* (Springfield, Ill.: Charles C Thomas, 1964), pp. 292–298.
6. Hervey Cleckley, *The Mask of Sanity,* 2nd edition (St. Louis: C. V. Mosby, 1950). Originally published by same publisher in 1941.
7. Robert M. Lindner, *Rebel without a Cause: The Hypnoanalysis of a Criminal Psychopath* (New York: Grune & Stratton, 1944).
8. Vernon H. Mark and Frank R. Ervin, *Violence and the Brain* (New York: Harper and Row, 1970).
9. David B. Wexler, "Token and Taboo: Behavior Modification, Token Economies, and the Law," *California Law Review,* 1973, pp. 81ff. Also Nicholas N. Kittrie, *The Right to Be Different: Deviance and Enforced Therapy* (Baltimore: The Johns Hopkins Press, 1971), especially chapter 9, "Liberty in the Therapeutic State: Reducing the Dominance of the Savers," pp. 372–410.
10. Quoted by Albert Morris in "Criminals' Views on Crime Causation," *The Annals,* Vol. 217, September, 1941, pp. 138–144. Also, Barnes and Teeters, *New Horizons,* p. 57.

11. Alfred C. Schnur, "The New Penology: Fact or Fiction?" *The Journal of Criminal Law, Criminology and Police Science*, Vol. 49, November–December, 1958, pp. 31–334.
12. *Task Force Report, Corrections,* The President's Commission on Law Enforcement Administration of Justice (Washington, D.C.: Government Printing Office, 1967), p. 97.
13. Lloyd E. McCorkle and F. Lovell Bixby, *The Highfields Story* (New York: Holt, 1958).
14. James K. Whittaker, *Social Treatment: An Approach to Interpersonal Helping* (Chicago: Aldine, 1974).
15. Harry H. Vorrath and Larry K. Brendtro, *Positive Peer Culture* (Chicago: Aldine, 1974).
16. William A. Glasser, *Reality Therapy* (New York: Harper & Row, 1965).
17. Vernon Fox, *Violence Behind Bars* (Westport, Conn.: Greenwood Press, 1974), originally published in New York in 1956.
18. *Corrections,* Report of the National Advisory Commission on Criminal Justice Standards and Goals (Washington, D.C.: United States Government Printing Office, 1973).
19. American Friends Service Committee, *Struggle for Justice* (New York: Hill & Wang, 1971), p. v.

TOPICS FOR DISCUSSION

1. Discuss the new correctional philosophy which is based on at least two major considerations: first, society, in addition to the offenders, needs changing; and second, more emphasis should be placed on the offender's social and cultural setting if we are to obtain any substantial relief from recidivism.

2. Discuss the attitude profile of a person entering prison in America today. Does length of sentence affect the attitude? How?

3. Discuss the potential for an "Attica" style prison revolt occurring in your state prison(s).

4. Discuss ways to reduce the gap between possible mutually exclusive objectives of correctional officers and treatment personnel.

5. Discuss the statement: Prisons should be built to self-destruct in twenty years.

6. Discuss the part news media plays in assisting or hindering police and corrections officials in handling prison riots.

20

R. PAUL McCAULEY

On community-based corrections

INTRODUCTION

> *The Doctrines of the quiet past*
> *are inadequate to the stormy present.*
>
> —Abraham Lincoln

The subject of community-based corrections has received increased attention in the last decade. Federal, state, and local governments are emphasizing community-based corrections, i.e., alternatives to *corrections*. Ostensibly, this "new direction" is to utilize services available in the community rather than to attempt to reproduce those services in the traditional centralized, and normally isolated, correctional institution. The fact that some state prisons are located in the "downtown area" of major cities (the community) does not necessarily qualify it as a community-based correctional program; likewise, it is not automatically excluded as a community-based correctional service because it is a centralized state prison. Community-based corrections is to be viewed as a philosophical concept upon which administrative policies, treatment programs, and physical facilities are developed. The question which must be addressed is not *where* can we best handle the correctional client, but rather *how* can he best be handled with maximum safety and success?

For years probation and parole, for all practical purposes, have been the extent of community-based correctional services. However, in addition to these services being expanded, other community-based efforts are being implemented. Community-based corrections includes halfway houses, prerelease programs, community service centers, vocational rehabilitation programs, work-furlough and other community settings, and resources that can benefit the correctional client—adult and juvenile.

Most authors claim, in one form or another, that the growing interest in community-based corrections is due to "the realization that isolation in institutions does not accomplish the job of intensifying the social ties in the community for the correctional client."[1] The concept of community-based corrections then is:

- reduce institutional isolation
- intensify social ties...
- ...in the community...
- ...for correctional clients.

These four philosophical mandates are stated rather simply and "as a matter of factly." The truth is each of these is complex and interrelated.

Reduce Institutional Isolation

Experience has shown that, as opposed to isolation and punishment, community-based corrections which permit a person to live in his own community and maintain normal social relationships, while providing control, guidance, and access to rehabilitative resources and services, is a more efficient, economic, and more humane approach to the treatment of the offender.[2]

The ingredients necessary to reduce institutional isolation for the correctional client then are to:

- live in *his own* community
- maintain *normal* social relationships
- be subject to control, guidance, and access to rehabilitative resources and services.

This is another series of over-simplified, but obviously worthwhile objectives.

Without addressing a substantial and diverse body of penological literature while stimulating thought, the following questions are being submitted. Should a correctional client be returned to his own community if that community is a "bad" community? If the client's community is "bad," is it ethically, legally, and morally right to place him or her in some other community? Who determines normal social relationships? What are the rehabilitation resources and services in a community? What are the limits—frequency, duration, quality— of control, guidance, and rehabilitation resources and services? These are questions which need to be addressed. These questions and others are the reasons that research must be increased (and improved).

Intensify Social Ties

The maintenance of normal social relationships can only be achieved, after the "normal social relationships" are defined. Intensifying social ties, on the other hand, raises the question of quality versus quantity of social bonds, i.e., is reintegration of the offender into a functional, noncriminal life better achieved through his having many "weak ties" or fewer "strong ties?" The ultimate question is in which environment, the institution or the community, can he be provided the necessary mechanisms to achieve these social ties?

In the Community

Whose community? It was previously stated that the correctional client should be placed in his own community. It was also mentioned that some offenders may have come from "bad" communities and that attempts at "correcting" them in this "bad" community may not be desirable for various reasons.

The concept of community is subject to definition and, consequently, it can be tailor-made, more or less. Correctional clients on probation, parole, or in some other community-based program have restrictions placed upon them in the form of rules and regulations— the conditions of probation for example. These restrictions can include persons, places, and things clients may or may not do or associate with. These restrictions, in essence, define the client's community. The greater the restrictions the less access he has to the community. The reciprocal of this statement is threatening to many, i.e., reducing these restrictions increases the client's access to the community. By increasing this access, do we increase or lessen the client's chances of maintaining normal social relationships, and to what extent is control and guidance of the client affected? Likewise, will the quality and availability of resources and services be enhanced or abridged?

Correctional Clients

Should community-based corrections be available to *all* correctional clients? Should client participation in community programs be voluntary or mandatory?

For some reason simplistic answers are attractive and actively sought. Unfortunately, the questions asked are often far too complex to be responded to in a single sentence or in a page or even in a lifetime. Corrections is dealing with extremely complex problems and one-sentence answers are inappropriate.

The term correctional client really doesn't tell us much except to provide a general category into which we can easily lump burglars, rapists, check forgers, and other offenders. But correctional clients are not all the same. The characteristics to be considered when defining correctional clients are far too numerous to list here. However, the following factors are the more obvious: offense committed, adult or juvenile, male or female, first offender or repeat offender, pre-institutional (probation) or post-institutional (parole). Scores of less obvious but equally relevant factors must also be considered in defining correctional client; these basic facts must be considered in the classification of offenders and in the treatment program, whether it is institutional or community-based.

In conclusion, if the correctional client is taken from the institutional setting and placed in a community-based program, it can be assumed logically that institutional isolation will probably be reduced and that the opportunities to increase social ties exist. However, is the reduction of institutional isolation a prerequisite to intensifying social ties for all offenders?

A NATIONAL INTEREST

In 1967, the President's Commission on Law Enforcement and the Administration of Justice published its *Task Force Report on Corrections*. This report described the "new corrections"—the reintegration of offenders into the community—and the role of community-based corrections. The Commission, with regard to re-integration of the offender, stated:

> The general underlying premise for the new directions in corrections is that crime and delinquency are symptoms of failures and disorganization of the community as well as of individual offenders. In particular, these failures are seen as depriving offenders of contact with the institutions that are basically responsible for assuring development of law-abiding conduct: sound family life, good schools, employment, recreational opportunities, and desirable companions, to name only some of the more direct influences. The substitution of deleterious habits, standards, and associates for these strengthening influences contributes to crime and delinquency.
>
> The task of corrections therefore includes building or rebuilding solid ties between offender and community integrating or reintegrating the offender into community life—restoring family ties, obtaining employment and education, securing in the larger

sense a place for the offender in the routine functioning of society. This requires not only efforts directed toward changing the individual offender, which has been almost the exclusive focus of rehabilitation, but also mobilization and change of the community and its institutions. And these efforts must be undertaken without giving up the important control and deterrent role of corrections, particularly as applied to dangerous offenders.[3]

The Task Force prophesied that there would be increased use of community treatment.

The main treatment implication of reintegration concepts is the value of community-based corrections. Most of the tasks that are now carried out by correctional officials would still be required if the goal of reintegration were adopted: diagnosis and classification, counseling, application of necessary controls and sanctions.

But probation and parole would have wider functions than are now usually emphasized within their case work guidance orientation. They would have to take much more responsibility for such matters as seeing that offenders get jobs and settle into responsible work habits: arranging reentry into schools and remedial tutoring or vocational training; giving guidance and counseling to an offender's family; securing housing in a neighborhood without the temptations of bad companions; or getting a juvenile into neighborhood club activities or athletic teams.... Obviously it will require more complex probation and parole organization, with specialists concerned with various areas of help and treatment. In many cases it will clearly require that community treatment officials take an advocate's role in fighting against such barriers as rules prohibiting readmittance of offenders to their former schools or employment of those with convictions. And it will require that corrections officers have funds with which to purchase needed services, such as special training or medical attention, that cannot otherwise be obtained.[4]

The report went further and stated eight recommendations regarding community-based corrections. The eight recommendations are summarized as follows:[5]

- Make parole and probation supervision available for all offenders
- Provide for mandatory supervision of released offenders not paroled
- Increase number of probation and parole officers
- Use volunteers and subprofessional aids
- Develop new methods to reintegrate offenders by mobilizing community institutions
- Make funds available to purchase services otherwise unobtainable for offenders
- Vary caseload size and treatment according to offender needs
- Develop more intensive community treatment programs as alternatives to institutionalization.

So it was written; and strangely enough so it began to happen. The acceptance of these recommendations was stimulated by a flood of money and a new federal agency—the Office of Law Enforcement Assistance (OLEA), which later became and is currently the Law Enforcement Assistance Administration (LEAA).

The point being developed here is quite simple but often overlooked, i.e., why should a national priority or emphasis be placed on community-based corrections? Further, how did the Commission arrive at its conclusions; what information did it have? A very important question remains—who is to benefit from such efforts?

It has been said that the Commission's recommendations were stated and money made available to buy the recommendations, whether they were good, bad, or indifferent. And the "worst" recommendations often have been allocated the most money, in the long run, in an attempt to head off a failure or to cover one up. Nevertheless, community-based corrections is gaining momentum in the United States.

A NATIONAL REAFFIRMATION

The federal commitment to community-based treatment has survived, and the Report of the National Advisory Commission on Criminal Justice Standards and Goals indicates that commitment is going to continue. The evidence which has become available concerning the "success" of community-based treatment looks promising in many respects. This is not to say there are not problem areas or even outright failures. However, to many, the advantages appear to outweigh the disadvantages.

The National Advisory Commission listed twenty-four recommendations regarding community-based corrections. These recommendations, which are listed below, can provide some meaningful insight as to the direction and priorities of community-based corrections.

The following are the recommendations of the National Advisory Commission as they pertain to community-based corrections.[6]

STANDARD 7.1

DEVELOPMENT PLAN FOR COMMUNITY-
BASED ALTERNATIVES TO
CONFINEMENT

Each state correctional system or correctional system of other units of government should begin immediately to analyze its needs, resources, and gaps in service and to develop by 1978 a systematic plan with timetable and scheme for implementing a range of alternatives to institutionalization. The plan should specify the services to be provided directly by the correctional authority and those to be offered through other community resources. Community advisory assistance (discussed in Standard 7.3) is essential. The plan should be developed within the framework of total system planning discussed in Chapter 9, Local Adult Institutions, and state planning, discussed in Chapter 13, Organization and Administration.

Minimum alternatives to be included in the plan should be the following:

1. Diversion mechanisms and programs prior to trial and sentence.
2. Nonresidential supervision programs in addition to probation and parole.
3. Residential alternatives to incarceration.
4. Community resources open to confined populations and institutional resources available to the entire community.
5. Prerelease programs.
6. Community facilities for released offenders in the critical reentry phase, with provision for short-term return as needed.

STANDARD 7.2

MARSHALLING AND COORDINATING
COMMUNITY RESOURCES

Each state correctional system or the systems of other units of government should take appropriate action immediately to establish effective working relationships with the major social institutions, organizations, and agencies of the community, including the following:

1. Employment resources—private industry, labor unions, employment services, civil service systems.
2. Educational resources—vocational and technical, secondary, college and university, adult basic education, private and commercial training, government and private job development and skills training.
3. Social welfare services—public assistance, housing, rehabilitation services, mental health services, counseling assistance, neighborhood centers, unemployment compensation, private social service agencies of all kinds.
4. The law enforcement system—federal, state, and local law enforcement personnel, particularly specialized units providing public information, diversion, and service to juveniles.
5. Other relevant community organizations and groups—ethnic and cultural groups, recreational and social organizations, religious and self-help groups, and others devoted to political or social action.

At the management level, correctional agencies should seek to involve representatives of these community resources in police development and interagency procedures for consultation, coordinated planning, joint action, and shared programs and facilities. Correctional authorities also should enlist the aid of such bodies in formation of a broadbased and aggressive lobby that will speak for correctional and inmate needs and support community correctional programs.

At the operating level, correctional agencies should initiate procedures to work cooperatively in obtaining services needed by offenders.

STANDARD 7.3

CORRECTIONS' RESPONSIBILITY FOR CITIZEN INVOLVEMENT

Each state correctional system should create immediately: (a) a multipurpose public information and education unit, to inform the general public on correctional issues and to organize support for and overcome resistance to general reform efforts and specific community-based projects; and (b) an administrative unit responsible for securing citizen involvement in a variety of ways within corrections, including advisory and policymaking roles, direct service roles, and cooperative endeavors with correctional clients.

1. The unit responsible for securing citizen involvement should develop and make public a written policy on selection process, term of service, tasks, responsibilities, and authority for any advisory or policymaking body.
2. The citizen involvement unit should be specifically assigned the management of volunteer personnel serving in direct service capacities with correctional clientele, to include:
   a. Design and coordination of volunteer tasks
   b. Screening and selection of appropriate persons
   c. Orientation to the system and training as required for particular tasks
   d. Professional supervision of volunteer staff
   e. Development of appropriate personnel practices for volunteers, including personnel records, advancement opportunities, and other rewards.
3. The unit should be responsible for providing for supervision of offenders who are serving in volunteer roles.
4. The unit should seek to diversify institutional programs by obtaining needed resources from the community that can be used in the institution and by examining and causing the periodic reevaluation of any procedures inhibiting the participation of inmates in any community program.
5. The unit should lead in establishing and operating community-based programs emanating from the institution or from a satellite facility and, on an ongoing basis, seek to

develop new opportunities for community contacts enabling inmate participants and custodial staff to regularize and maximize normal interaction with community residents and institutions.

STANDARD 7.4

INMATE INVOLVEMENT IN
COMMUNITY PROGRAMS

Correctional agencies should begin immediately to develop arrangements and procedures for offenders sentenced to correctional institutions to assume increasing individual responsibility and community contact. A variety of levels of individual choice, supervision, and community contact should be specified in these arrangements, with explicit statements as to how the transitions between levels are to be accomplished. Progress from one level to another should be based on specified behavioral criteria rather than on sentence, time served, or subjective judgments regarding attitudes.

The arrangements and procedures should be incorporated in the classification system to be used at an institution and reflect the following:

1. When an offender is received at a correctional institution, he should meet with the classificaton unit (committee, team, or the like) to develop a plan for increasing personal responsibility or community contact.
2. At the initial meeting, behavioral objectives should be established, to be accomplished within a specified period. After that time another meeting should be held to make adjustments in the individual's plan which, assuming that the objectives have been met, will provide for transition to a lower level of custody and increasing personal responsibility and community involvement.
3. Similarly, at regular time intervals, each inmate's status should be reviewed, and if no strong reasons exist to the contrary, further favorable adjustments should be made.
4. Allowing for individual differences in time and progress or lack of progress, the inmate should move through a series of levels broadly encompassing movement from (a) initial security involving few outside privileges and minimal contact with community participants in institutional programs to (b) lesser degrees of custody with participation in institutional and community programs involving both citizens and offenders, to (c) partial-release programs under which he would sleep in the institution but have maximum participation in institutional and outside activities involving community residents, to (d) residence in a halfway house or similar noninstitutional residence, to (e) residence in the community at the place of his choice with moderate supervision, and finally to release from correctional supervision.

5. The presumption should be in favor of decreasing levels of supervision and increasing levels of individual responsibility.

6. When an inmate fails to meet behavioral objectives, the team may decide to keep him in the same status for another period or move him back. On the other hand, his behavioral achievements may indicate that he can be moved forward rapidly without having to go through all the successive stages.

7. Throughout the process, the primary emphasis should be on an individualization—on behavioral changes based on the individual's interests, abilities, and priorities. Offenders also should be afforded opportunities to give of their talents, time, and efforts to others, including other inmates and community residents.

8. A guiding principle should be the use of positive reinforcement in bringing about behavioral improvements rather than negative reinforcement in the form of punishment.

What Does This All Mean?

It appears, first of all, that the interest in community treatment programs has increased since the 1967 Commission Report was issued. In 1967, the Commission's recommendations were extremely broad, but by 1973 the Advisory Commission's report was more specific and more comprehensive.

The earlier report was based primarily on the principles of human decency, and although little supporting scientific evidence was available it set the trend. The specificity of the second report may, in many instances, indicate an attempt to remedy an earlier problem which had been determined through evaluation of functioning community programs. The recommendations of the 1973 report hopefully give direction to the concept of human decency via scientific evidence. The development, implementation, and evaluation of many community-based programs has provided us with considerable information.

Recognizing the problems involved in social and behavioral research, collected and analyzed data have indicated both successes and failures in the community corrections scene. Some programs are receiving praise and are expected to show positive results; some programs are being modified, while others are being discontinued. Modifying or discontinuing programs as a result of research is not to indicate a reduction in human decency but prioritizing decency. Simply, they are asking what methods and approaches can be used to achieve the greatest success. For example, the emphasis the 1973 report placed on citizen involvement is a specific recommendation based on experience, of how to achieve the earlier Commission's recommendation to develop more intensive community treatment programs as alternatives to institutionalization.

Recommendation or Mandate

Both national reports, 1967 and 1973, make several recommendations. However, are these recommendations in fact recommendations, or are they mandates? The federal government (LEAA) does not say "you will develop and implement community-based correctional programs." But they may not provide federal dollars for programs that are not community-oriented. The facts are clear. Money is available to those agencies that engage in those activities and programs supportive of the national commitment.

The federal dollar (with restrictions) that flows to the states can be perceived as a compromise to the "new federalism" and a threat to the states. If correctional authorities view the federal dollar with skepticism, and refuse the funding, as some law enforcement agencies have done, the community-based programs will be delayed. In addition to viewing the federal dollar negatively and with resentment, the state reaction could engulf the basic philosophy that the dollar supports. Should this become the case, the national strategy will be counterproductive and it will deal a devastating blow to community-based corrections and to the criminal justice system. The questions to be answered are: To what degree are the states resisting federal funding for correction programs? Is this resistance a response to the potential threat of excessive federal supervision or is the resistance against the fundamental philosophy of community programs? If federal money, rather than correctional philosophy, is inhibiting the advancement of community correctional programs, what alternatives does corrections have?

Something very basic must also be addressed here, that is, the implementation of a national community-based corrections policy in a nation of vast geographical and social differences. Is such a policy realistic and how do we plan for its implementation?

Total correctional planning is vitally important if we are to "treat" rather than "contain" offenders in the future. The corrections profession must understand that treatment has implications for institutions and community-based programs. Obviously, correctional policies will be formulated and implemented on the basis of our understanding of the interrelationships between the various components of the correctional system. Therefore, in order to develop and implement sound policies for community treatment programs, we must examine their relationship to the other components of corrections, specifically, and to the total criminal justice system (including the community) in general.

The corrections profession must clearly acknowledge the fact that the offender population, at any level of government, is not homogeneous, that different treatment approaches will be necessary because "programed treatment" cannot be equally applicable to all types of offenders. Further, treatment cannot be regarded as standard and having "canned" application. Treatment modalities are not constant for all offenders in all geographic areas. One must consider just how universally applicable the National Advisory Commission's recommendations are. In essence, the Commission's recommendations must be subjected to the qualifying questions—where and for whom?

Community-based treatment programs are designed to meet the needs of a variety of clients. Many practical considerations determine the design of a community-based corrections program, such as costs, facilities, community resources, and need for the program. It is obvious the community in which a program is developed determines the nature of the resources available to the client. Likewise, the offender population should determine what programs are needed in the community and the matching of clients to programs must be based on client rather than on program needs.

Further, one can assume with a reasonable degree of confidence that client needs and the community-based programs will and should vary between and among affluent suburban areas, rural/small town areas, and the inner-city urban areas. This point is the crux of the question of universal applicability of the Advisory Commission's recommendations.

THE FUTURE

> *The ideal community . . .*
> *"When those who have not been injured*
> *become as indignant as those who have."*
>
> —Solon (638–559 B.C.)

The fact remains that a substantial number of people are sent to prison (penal institutions) when they do not need to be.[7] Do these people have to be "sent" anywhere? The future of community-based corrections rests on the degree of success we have in changing the traditional view of punishment, control, and isolation that is ingrained in much of American political, social, and correctional thought. If community-based corrections is going to work, several things must be done.

First, the corrections profession must recognize it is a dynamic and functional component contributing to the success or failure of a complex series of processes—the criminal justice system. The police, courts, legislative, and community (citizen) concerns with violent crime and drugs are realistic and legitimate. This official and public concern for crime can generate "hard line" public attitudes that will overshadow the professional and ideological commitment to community-based corrections. Until community-based correctional programs can show evidence of success in those areas of public concern (violent crime), it is likely that a direction away from the community-based concept will be forced upon the corrections community by the public and by the other components of the criminal justice system.

Secondly, evaluative research must be initiated when it is lacking and expanded where it is being done. Likewise, new and innovative programs must be developed, implemented, and evaluated.

Third, every effort must be made to prevent overreaction by the judiciary, the legislature, and the public when positive corrective results concerning violent offenders are not available. The truth remains that although public concern is focused primarily on the more visible, more aggressive offender, many other types of offenders are found in the correctional areas. Therefore, the success or failure of community-based programs to deal with the more visible, aggressive offender should not be allowed to determine the fate of the other programs that are designed for a different type of offender.

Fourth, community-based corrections must be a total planning effort. The concept of total correctional planning includes every aspect of corrections, the criminal justice system, and the community.

These four propositions have two common basic elements representing the fundamental dilemma confronting corrections. Reduced to simplest terms, corrections is lacking and in need of information and the capacity to adapt.

Information

Community-based corrections is the product of a decision-making process that modified the traditional correctional institution and values. Since information is the basic currency of all political and economic decision making, one can draw the inference that information modified the correctional scene. And future modification will depend upon the quality and quantity of information and the way it is collected, processed, presented, and amplified.

Corrections, in its entirety, is of social and political concern. As in all social and political conflicts, information is the weapon with which battles are fought. Henderson states that

> ... new or restructured information, when deployed and amplified can:
>
> • alter human perceptions of reality;

- create changes in personal values, preferences, and goals, which are later reflected in new collective and institutional goals;
- explode the boundaries of academic disciplines by creating cognitive dissonances and conflicts, often leading to gradual paradigm shifts;
- successfully challenge the rationality and legitimacy of resource allocations and decisions of governmental and private institutions;
- strengthen the power of consumers and citizens to perceive and protect their own interests and to understand how individual interests coincide more frequently when viewed within even larger system contexts until, when finally viewed in planetary and ecological contexts, they literally become identical;
- short-circuit hierarchical, pyramidal, and bureaucratic control;
- illuminate the intricate chains of causality and interdependence in complex societies and their reciprocal exchanges with equally complex host ecosystems.[8]

These assumptions provide the foundation for many citizen and interest groups of varying persuasions. Corrections has been the target of many such groups. Perhaps, the emphasis toward community-based correctional programs is not a product of the corrections professions's efforts, but of academicians and citizen interest group activities. (Private foundations have contributed considerable sums of money to various groups involved in penal reform.)

Information or input data necessary for correctional research is often difficult and even impossible to collect. Even the research that has been done has not provided empirical validated knowledge (information) to be utilized in developing a theory. Despite the lack of information, a major movement is taking place in penal reform. Penal reform is a response to the inadequacies of the past. These inadequacies occurred and continued to occur because knowledge of the social and psychological mechanisms of deterrence and rehabilitation have not been and are not available. Surprisingly, this knowledge is at best obscure. Yet, a new direction is being taken by corrections, based not on knowledge (information) but on human decency. It has been said that this decency originated outside the prison walls and is being taken inside a piece at a time. Perhaps penal reform must come from outside the walls; for, to leave correctional innovation to our jailers, wardens, and correctional staff is probably as ill-advised as it might have been to put the development of the automobile under the control of buggy-whip manufacturers.

Another aspect of information process must be considered, i.e., the absence of information as "corrections' defense mechanism." The lack of information precipitates ignorance. Moore and Lumin, say that ignorance serves the social purposes of: preserving privileged positions and social stereotypes, and re-enforcing traditional values.[9]

Such social purposes have little redeeming value in today's rapidly changing technological society. Nevertheless, one must wonder had the prison riots of the 60s and 70s not had the national coverage by the mass media that they had, would the corrections profession admit to the failure of its prisons? Does corrections assume that public ignorance (the lack of information) will place them in a privileged position, and reinforce the traditional values of punishment, isolation, and rehabilitation? Ralph Nader, the ACLU, and scores of educators, doctors, housewives, and a variety of others can and do conduct research and distribute their findings *to concerned* citizens. Is it naiveté?

The moral to the story is "if corrections does not do its homework someone else will." Whether the homework someone else does is done well is important, of course, but the critical question is why isn't corrections seeking its own answers—and better still, why isn't every effort being made to seek answers cooperatively, with others?

It is logical to assume that better information will yield better actions. And this information will determine which one position will be chosen when two are in conflict. In the case of community-based corrections and institutional corrections, who chooses? Are these two concepts, first of all, conflicting? Can they coexist and serve the client and the taxpayer better?

The role of information is crucial, not only for citizen groups in modifying correctional institutions and values, but also for correctional institutions in modifying themselves, other institutions, including citizen groups, and values. Information then plays a primary role in change, whether that change is within an organization or between organizations.

Adaptability

Adequate information availability is desirable prior to any decision-making process. Whether adequate information is available or not often does not lessen the need for a decision. Once the decision (good or bad) is made, it will have some subsequent effect. This effect is change, and organizational goals, purposes, and structures are subject to change. Furthermore the individuals within the organization establish the limitations of organizational change based upon their capability to adapt to change.

Corrections has demonstrated resistance to change. Correctional organizations, except for size, have remained virtually unchanged. The people who work in the various correctional occupations have for the most part done the same tasks the same way as their predecessors did years before. Correctional officers, the "key treatment agents" in institutions, have been and continue to be untrained and uneducated. Unfortunately, the situation has not been improved much with regards to correctional officers, wardens, and administrators. This lack of improvement or change indicates a deficiency in the ability of correctional personnel to adapt to social and technological requirements.

The dilemma is this: corrections has lacked information, perhaps by design, because information forces decisions which in turn effect change, and this change requires both individual and organizational adaptation. Most of the past correctional administrators and some even today lack the ability to adapt to change and, by virtue of this inability, they fail to seek new information. This has been a safe approach for management; for with no information they do not have to make any decisions, thus no change and no need for adaptation. Everyone can go on as before.

The concept of adaptability is crucial both in institutional and community corrections. First, the trend is away from the institution and toward community-based programs. Correctional administrators must adapt, both as individuals and as administrators (if such a distinction cannot be drawn). Nevertheless, if corrections administrators do not have the ability to adapt to this "new direction," and cannot demonstrate sufficiently the errors of this "new direction," they will experience increased antagonism from political, citizen, and inmate groups. The age-old measuring stick—correctional personnel opinions—is no longer a satisfactory index of how well we are "correcting" offenders. On the other hand, community workers' opinions are no more meaningful in determining success of community treatment programs. Corrections needs reliable and valid information upon which objective decisions for positive change can be made.

TRANSITION

Correctional institutions, for all practical purposes, are places to warehouse offenders. Admittedly, the sciences dealing with human behavior have not yet arrived at the level of sophistication to properly diagnose and treat all criminal behavior. Therefore, some offenders must be warehoused. On the other hand, those offenders who do not need warehousing should be returned to the community, not confined. Rehabilitation is not to institutionalize offenders as corrections has done in the past, but to prepare them for a noncriminal career upon return to their community. Successful reintegration into the community will not be achieved through manipulation schemes and artificial environments. Success will be derived from programs in an environment which meets the needs of the offender, and which provides the necessary qualities to stimulate and motivate the individual.

To achieve the idealistic, one must consider the pragmatic. Community-based programs in some instances are actually community-based confinement and, at best, community-based custody. Community-based treatment often is merely lip service. The move away from the institution and toward the community requires nothing less than total commitment. Certainly, it takes time, money, and most importantly, understanding, to re-orient an organization consisting of hundreds, even, thousands of employees. But a total commitment for finding alternatives to confinement is essential from the beginning. Anything less yields a poorly designed program necessitating more administration and management due to conflicting and vacillating priorities.

It is essential that corrections determine its priorities and direct all resources commensurately. That is, if community-based programs are to be developed and implemented, they must be developed within the current correctional organization. Since the current organization is primarily institutional, one could say that community-based programs for the confined offender must be developed "behind the walls" and implemented in the "free world." This statement touches upon a very serious and contemporary issue that must be considered.

We have said the institutions will develop community programs. To clarify this statement, we must recognize that community-based programs are concerned with offenders who are placed in a community program usually after they have been confined, and those offenders who are placed in a community program in lieu of confinement. Being aware of these considerations, one should be able to see a potential problem in setting priorities, i.e., should community programs be designed to reduce the current institutional population, or to divert others from entering the institutions?

The reality of developing community programs for the confined offender has many implications. The confined offender enters confinement and is diagnosed, evaluated, assigned, supervised, fed, watched, etc., etc., etc., by institutional employees. The offenders' records are compiled, evaluated, and maintained by institutional employees. Therefore, it is logical to assume that the institutional staff will influence the decision as to which offenders may participate in community programs. Can the institution, in fact, predetermine the success or failure of community-based programs as a result of their selection of participating offenders?

If the institution plays such an important role in the future of community-based correctional programs it would seem reasonable to make the institutional staff aware of their important, and although unrealized, changing roles. All those who work "behind the walls," the correctional officers and supervisors, administrators, academic and vocational teachers, farm and industry workers, food and health service personnel, case workers, and other professionals, must be trained and retrained, educated and re-educated if community-based corrections is to serve the offender rather than the offender serving the correctional bureaucracy. Police, judges, prosecutors, attorneys, probation and parole officers, and parole boards must likewise contribute to this effort because they are all equal partners in the criminal justice system and play important and necessary interacting roles.

Society has said penal reform must happen now. Community-based treatment has taken hold as a potential remedy for many of our prisons' ills. Corrections, however, must take the initiative in developing and implementing new and innovative programs because no one else will. Although corrections has many weaknesses, no one is better equipped to tackle the challenge of finding alternatives to institutionalization. On the other hand, perhaps no one has as much to lose as the correctional bureaucracy. Schrag states that ... "it costs only one-tenth as much to supervise an offender in the community as it does to confine him in an institution."[10] Others have reported on the cost advantage of community programs.[11] Corrections may view this improved efficiency as a reduction in budget—and even as a slow death to the old bureaucracy.

If the myth that the institution provides a means by which the inmate can earn his keep behind bars was dissolved and the facts made known that the community treatment was, in fact, a lesser burden on the taxpayers, would the correctional budget decrease? Simply, would the defensive, bureaucracy-protecting administrator realize a reduction in fiscal funding? Could the administrator justify continued appropriations when his "treatment" cost per offender is shrinking? How does the administrator justify funds for improving the quality of treatment programs? What measures would be used to determine the quality of treatment? These problems confront contemporary and future correctional efforts. They must be dealt with by men and women committed to improving the quality of life, not only for the confined, but also for all mankind.

CONCLUSION

Community-based corrections is an alternative to institutional confinement for many offenders. However, it is not a means by which maximum security facilities can be eliminated. Some authorities have suggested a total moratorium on the construction of all jails and prisons. Regional jails rather than prisons have been suggested as an alternative. The question underlying this argument is concerned with two basic factors—level of security and proximity to treatment resources.

The answer to this question has not been resolved and the probability of an absolute answer is remote. However, every state and local government involved in corrections will have to formulate a scheme of corrections. Correctional clients will have to be classified and matched to meaningful programs that will provide them with the best chance of returning to their communities and functioning successfully in noncriminal careers.

Total correctional planning must be utilized to arrive at a comprehensive correctional program. The nature of the correctional population, the correctional staff and services, the physical facility—construction and location—the level of security, and the treatment models are all factors that must be planned for.

> Many correctional systems currently are using community-based programs as part of their array of services in pursuit of reintegration. But few, if any, provide a full range of alternatives, and there is little evidence of systematic planning for development of the most appropriate and most needed programs at local and state levels. Rather, programs have sprung up as grant funds have been available or as a result of the specialized interest of a staff member or administrator. There is a clear need to systematize on a state level the orderly development of community corrections, with full consideration of specific local needs.
>
> The purpose of such effort is to insure that: (1) no individual who does not absolutely require institutionalization for the protection of others is confined; and (2) no individual should be subjected to more supervision or control than he requires. Over-restriction of offenders may have been practiced because alternative programs and understanding of offender needs have been lacking or inadequate. This situation should be changed by development of a systematic plan for creation of varied community-based programs that will best respond to the range of offender needs and community interests.[12]

The challenge facing corrections today is to determine this balance. The challenge for tomorrow will be maintaining the balance in a rapidly changing society. Determining and maintaining this balance will not be an easy task. The simplistic answers have been uttered and attempted with little positive results for years. The essayist, E. B. White, made an observation which is applicable to the difficult task standing before corrections, "what with the tendency of one thing to lead to another, I predict a bright future for complexity."

> *The first prison I ever saw had inscribed on it*
> *"cease to do evil: learn to do well";*

but as the inscription was on the outside,
the prisoners could not read it.

—George Bernard Shaw

NOTES

1. Vernon Fox, *Introduction to Corrections* (New Jersey: Prentice-Hall, Inc., 1972), p. 215.
2. American Correctional Association and Chamber of Commerce of the United States, "Community Corrections: A Cheaper and More Humane Approach," in *Penology: The Evolution of Corrections in America,* ed. by George G. Killenger and Paul F. Cromwell (St. Paul, Minnesota: West Publishing Company, 1973), p. 385.
3. The President's Commission on Law Enforcement and the Administration of Justice, *Task Force Report: Corrections,* Washington, D.C., Government Printing Office, 1967, p. 7.
4. Ibid., pp. 9–10.
5. Ibid., xiii.
6. National Advisory Commission on Criminal Justice Standards and Goals, *Corrections* (Washington, D.C., Government Printing Office, 1973), pp. 238–245.
7. Paul Togaki, "The Parole Violator: An Organizational Reject," *Journal of Research in Crime and Delinquency,* Vol. 1, No. 6 (1969), pp. 78–86.
8. Hazel Henderson, "Information and the New Movements for Citizen Participation," *The Annals,* Volume 412 (March 1974), p. 38.
9. Wilbert E. Moore and Melvin Tumis, "Some Social Functions of Ignorance," *American Sociological Review,* 14 (February 1949), pp. 787–795.
10. Clarence Schrag, *Crime and Justice: American Style,* National Institute of Mental Health, Rockville, Maryland, 1971, p. 188.
11. See *A Handbook on Community Corrections in Des Moines, LEAA,* Government Printing Office, 1973; Norval Morris and Gordan Hawkins. *The Honest Politicians' Guide to Crime Control* (Chicago: The University Press), 1970.
12. National Advisory Commission, p. 237.

TOPICS FOR DISCUSSION

1. Discuss the rehabilitative resources and services existing in the local community and the state.

2. Discuss a specific program in the local community that effectively re-integrates the offender into the community.

3. Discuss how realistic it is to make parole and probation supervision available for all offenders.

4. Discuss the future of community-based corrections.

5. Discuss the Martinson study and contrast its findings to community-based corrections. (Robert Martinson "What Works?—Questions and Answers About Prison Reform," *The Public Interest* (Spring 1974).

21

EUGENE H. CZAJKOSKI

Issues in probation
and parole

INTRODUCTION

Although different in terms of historical development, probation and
parole are typically glued together in much of the discussions that
appear in the general body of criminological literature. There are,
indeed, sufficient similarities between the two devices to warrant their
frequently being considered as a single entity. The issues affecting
one, more often than not, affect the other. Still, with all the congrui-
ties, it is worthwhile for the sake of a precise understanding of some
of the issues, to draw some fundamental distinctions between probation and parole.

Probation is essentially a judicial function traditionally managed
by the courts. The order for probation, the conditions of supervision,
and revocation are all court matters. It might be said that probation
arose out of humanitarian impulses. The roots of probation can be
found in the English Common Law. Several devices developed in
England in the 18th and 19th centuries for the purpose of ameliorat-
ing the harsh penalties that English judges regularly bestowed. At
one time, there were more than two hundred capital offenses in England. Crimes which today would be very lightly punished were in
those days attached to severe punishments, frequently death. Many
people of good will were dismayed by the array of harsh penalties
emanating from the English courts.

Combined with the factor of harsh penalties was the factor of
unrefined methods for determining guilt or innocence. There was not
the finely honed trial methodology that we enjoy today and judges
in those days were gnawed by the uncertainty that harsh punishments were being meted out to the appropriate individuals. Severe

penalties combined with rough methods for determining guilt made judges amenable to devices that might legitimately spare offenders from punishment.

Devices which emerged from the courts' humanitarian concerns were "benefit of clergy," "reprieve," and "filing." Such devices served to exempt defendants from punishment. The devices were essentially in the nature of a suspended sentence and until today some form of suspended sentence serves as a foundation for any probation order. (Today, probation is considered a sentence in itself but it still is built on the notion of some suspension of punishment, usually either fine or imprisonment.)

Despite its Common Law roots, probation probably experienced its greatest growth in the United States soon after John Augustus began "standing up" for the release of certain offenders and afterward undertaking a rudimentary form of supervision and record keeping. As it stands now, probation in the United States can be described as a judicial function carried out in lieu of imprisonment; usually having conditions of behavior and some form of official supervision of behavior incorporated in the function.

Although the history of parole also needs to be traced back to England, the conditions and the motivations that led to its development are different from those of probation. Parole grew out of a number of procedures that were determined more by a desire for efficient or practical handling of offenders than by any humanitarian motive. In the 18th century, England extensively engaged in "transporting" felons to her overseas colonies. Rogues were "banished beyond the seas" for two chief reasons. On the one hand, economic conditions were poor in England and there was a surfeit of labor. On the other hand, economic conditions were good in the North American colonies, but there was a shortage of labor there. In a very primitive kind of selection process, offenders who were physically able to work were spared imprisonment in England and instead were shipped to America to work off their sentence as forced labor. (After America gained her independence, British felons were transported in large numbers to Australia.) After a period of punitive labor, the transported criminals were granted "tickets of leave" permitting them to work for themselves within a restricted area under conditions of good behavior.

The "ticket of leave" concept, which essentially involved conditional freedom in the community, was incorporated by a British prison administrator, Captain Alexander Maconochie, into a scheme motivating prisoners during their confinement. Maconochie observed that when faced with rigid terms of confinement, prisoners could not be motivated to positively conform to the prison routine or to show themselves as being improved. He created a system of "marks" which prisoners could earn by work and good behavior while in prison. These earned "marks" could then be used toward early release accomplished in stages. One of the stages was the "ticket of leave." Walter Crofton developed a prison management scheme similar to Maconochie's and Crofton's so-called "Irish system" was adopted in the United States in 1870 in Elmira, New York. It would be fair to say that parole, unlike probation, did not receive its impetus from humanitarian reasons. However, in both probation and parole, rehabilitation and deterrence were not, at the outset, primary factors for implementation. Contemporary probation and parole, of course, set rehabilitation at the very top of any rationale for being.

By way of definition, parole can be described as an executive function which provides conditional release in the community, under official supervision, *after* some period of imprisonment has been served. The similarity between probation and parole is that they both involve supervising the offender in the community under specific conditions of behavior. The conditions are often identical and, given certain organizational structures, the supervising officers are also often identical. In the case of probation, granting and revocation are in the hands of a judge. In the case of parole, the granting or revocation are in the hands of an administrative board. Parole is almost always organized on a statewide basis while probation is frequently organized on county and municipal levels.

As has already been indicated, probation and parole are most often considered together in the literature. The important issues for probation apply equally to parole with few, if any, exceptions. The discussion which follows will review some key probation and parole issues under three categories: issues of fundamental mission; issues of organization and administration; and issues of due process and fairness.

FUNDAMENTAL MISSION

If one gazes backward at the historical development of probation and the historical development of parole, one might reasonably surmise that the basic mission of probation has something to do with bestowing leniency and that the basic mission of parole has something to do with incentive for the practical management of prisons. As we now see probation and parole, these suppositions would be incorrect, of course, but not entirely. Operationally, at least, leniency and incentive for conforming behavior is still very much a part of the motivational structure supporting probation and parole. The official ideological line is quite different however.

In a unique survey conducted by this writer a few years ago, probation and parole administrators overwhelmingly responded with the notion of "rehabilitation" when asked about the fundamental missions of their agencies. This response was wholly in accord with the dominant theme in probation and parole literature. Even the lay reader, bombarded as he has been by public relations statements emanating from the broad correctional field, can easily deduce that the catchword throughout all probation and parole is rehabilitation. As a slogan, rehabilitation has served probation and parole very well. The word has characteristics which ensure public support and admiration. First of all, it has a medical ring to it and therefore is able to borrow some of the prestige and good will that is generally accorded to that profession, one which has achieved a high degree of precise knowledge and effective results. Secondly, rehabilitation has a humanitarian connotation and is therefore in keeping with the liberal social forces tenuously prevailing over the activities of our contemporary society.

Rehabilitation has another advantage as a slogan. It is poorly defined, especially within the context of corrections. It is obvious that the general public doesn't understand what is meant by rehabilitation and, therefore, in typical paradoxical fashion, doesn't question it. The word rehabilitation is very loosely used by probation and parole and is ambiguous indeed when compared to medicine's use of the term. Some in probation and parole will say that rehabilitation means "treating the offender" instead of punishing him. Equating rehabilitation with treatment is plausible, but it actually substitutes one ambiguity for another. The suggestion that rehabilitation or treatment somehow means the absence of punishment may bring clearer meaning to the matter except that many argue that a lot of punishment is carried on under the rubric of rehabilitation.

Regardless of its vagueness, or perhaps because of it, the concept of rehabilitation is at the heart of any official statement of mission regarding probation and parole. Despite its conceptual thinness, it is alloyed with the concept of "protection of society" and forms the keystone of probation's and parole's manifest philosophy. In an official statement, the Federal Probation Officers Association indicated that the goal of probation and parole was the protection of society and the rehabilitation of the offender. To bring integrity to the philosophical position, the statement should be defined to read: "protection of society through the rehabilitation of the offender." The idea of protection of society retains a certain pre-eminence in the dogma of probation and parole, and rehabilitation is generally seen as the best means for achieving the protection of society. The concept is bent a little when the rationale for juvenile probation and parole is sought. In working with juveniles, the welfare of the child has priority attention, but it may mean only a small difference of philosophical thinking since it can be easily argued that the welfare of society depends on the welfare of its children.

If, without attempting to unravel the vagaries of rehabilitation in the context of probation and parole, we can accept it as the overt mission, we can proceed to examine its reality and latent characteristics.

As appealing as the notion of rehabilitation seems to be, even philosophically, there are still a number of arguments against it. Beccaria, of the classical school of criminology, who in his time was regarded as a reforming liberal, saw rehabilitation or reformation of the individual offender, as being outside the boundaries of state action. He felt that the state could not compel reformation but could, properly, only intercede in the life of the offender to the same extent that an offender's criminal act interfered with or harmed a victim. In his famous essay, "On Liberty," John Stuart Mill carries the message that the state can not interfere with an individual's life for the sake of the individual's own good. Only when the individual is acting in direct harm to others can the state take a compulsory hand in redirecting an individual's life, but still for the sake of society, not for the sake of the individual. Extending these arguments means that the state can take restraining action against an individual only for detrimental actions that the individual has actually taken against the state, and not for detrimental actions that the state augurs the individual will take. It is not difficult to see that probation and parole with its mission of rehabilitation, seeks to control an individual for what he is likely to do rather than for what he has actually done. Presentence investigation and other diagnostic processes help to determine the length of state control or release from state control by prognostications regarding what the offender's future behavior is likely to be. Thus it is acceptable, under the rehabilitation ideal for probation and parole, for one bank robber to be placed on probation because somehow it has been deduced that he is not likely to commit another crime, while another bank robber, committing an offense of equal characteristics, may be sentenced to many years in prison because it is somehow deduced that he is likely to repeat the crime.

The truth is that we dispose of our offenders on the basis of offense actually committed. This represents a profound philosophical decision even though it is seldom articulated. The issue is aggravated when estimated future behavior is not confined to actual criminal events. Using the example of two bank robbers committing equal offenses again, the bank robber who is sent to prison may earn that disposition by expectations that he might not keep a steady job, support his family, or otherwise be thought of as less than a useful citizen. The imprisoned bank robber may not be the victim of the guess that he would commit another crime, but he may very well be the victim of the guess that he would be nonconforming in ways not prescribed by the criminal law. The bank robber placed on probation or released on parole may have given indication that he would work regularly, go to church on Sundays, abstain from alcohol, and avoid keeping late hours, all of which behavior may be desirable but not clearly associated with a crime-free life.

As "critical criminology" comes to the fore, the latent motive of probation and parole is receiving scrutiny. The critical criminologist, the criminologist with the conflict-perspective, can easily see probation and parole as an instrument for maintaining the moral status quo. The behaviors which probation and parole seek to induce are, more often than not, behaviors to which the criminal law does not address itself. The effectors of probation and parole come from the middle-class stratum of society. They are allied with the dominant power structure and they seek a degree of conformity among probationers and parolees that is not even suggested within the criminal law. The conflict perspective challenges the idea that criminal law derives from a consensus to which even offenders ideally subscribe. The criminal law is seen rather to emerge from conflict between social groups. The criminal law, and ultimately probation and parole, is seen as an instrument whereby the politically powerful maintain control over the politically and socially disadvantaged. The rehabilitation light which guides probation and parole can be seen, from the conflict perspective, as bringing about a submissive conformity beyond the basic instrumentality of the criminal law. The techniques of rehabilitation used in probation and parole lead the offender to find fault within himself rather than within the system which controls him. He is asked to correct himself rather than the sociopolitical environment which holds him in a powerless condition.

In sum, the mission of probation and parole can be conceived of as erratically composed of four basic elements, none of which enjoy universal acceptance over a sustained period of time. There is first the humanitarian element which historically has been more appropriate to probation than to parole, but which nevertheless retains motivational drive for both services.

Second, there is the protection of society which seems to be too general a goal to have much operational poignancy. Grafted to the goal of the protection of society has been the goal of rehabilitation, the latter being seen as the best means for achieving the former. Still, rehabilitation deserves consideration, as a separate element, the third one, since in one of its variations (especially at the juvenile level), it benevolently holds the desirability of rehabilitation for the intrinsic good of the individual. Here, rehabilitation assumes a humanitarian shade.

The fourth element is a blend of the need to provide incentive structures for the practical management of persons in the custody of the state and the need, as the conflict theorists assert, for the sociopolitically powerful to maintain ascendancy over the sociopolitically powerless. Activation of this fourth element aims at maintaining the moral status quo and seeks a high degree of conformity to standards not directly addressed by the law.

In considering the consequences of the rehabilitation goal, the question arises, shall it be enough to simply reduce traditional crime or should the concept of criminal behavior be enlarged so as to justify concern with the optimal levels of happiness, security, and social conformity? Because of poor definitions surrounding rehabilitation and because of its general acceptability as a basic notion (something like public welfare), a lot of undesirable things can be carried out, consciously and unconsciously, under the guise of rehabilitation. Paradoxically, the undesirable extracts from rehabilitation effort run against the grain of humanitarian ideals and relate to deprivation of individual liberty and privacy.

ORGANIZATION AND ADMINISTRATION

In terms of macro-organizational aspects, probation and parole have been caught up in the current drive towards consolidation and centralization. It is axiomatic that centralization/decentralization is cyclical in nature. In other words, whenever organizational centralization is achieved, the seeds are sown for a decentralization movement, and vice versa. Corrections as a whole is in a long period of centralization movement. At the core of centralizing or consolidating correctional activity has been probation and parole.

Of the two, parole has experienced the most stable organizational structure. Rather uniformly, parole is organized on a statewide basis. There are state parole boards with field staffs centrally administered at the state level. Although this pattern remains firm, there have been in the past exceptions, especially in the area of juvenile parole (frequently called aftercare). For example, many states have had the juvenile parole functions carried out by the probation staffs of county level juvenile courts. As another example, New York City until a few years ago had a municipally organized parole system. Historically, parole originated in this country as a function of the individual prisons from which parolees were released. In recent years, many states have combined probation services and parole services under a single state agency (e.g., Florida Probation and Parole Commission).

In the case of probation, especially juvenile probation, the pattern has been for local control. Probation services are usually decentralized by attachment to individual county and municipal courts. Under such circumstances of organization, the state may only provide help in coordination and maintenance of standards.

As indicated earlier, probation is regarded as a judicial function while parole is regarded as an executive function. This tends to dictate separate management for each. At the federal level, for example, probation is managed generally by the Administrative Office of the United States courts and the actual hiring of federal probation officers is done by each U.S. District Court in the several states and territories. Federal parole is managed by the U.S. Board of Parole within the Department of Justice as part of the executive branch of government. The case at the federal level becomes convoluted by the situation wherein federal probation officers, of the judicial branch, undertake the supervision of federal parolees who are in custody of the executive branch.

Given the prevailing mood of consolidating correctional services, the problem has not been the administrative bringing together of probation and parole; this has easily been done in a number of states, but the problem is in the bringing together of probation and parole with prison agencies or departments of corrections. The ultimate goal of consolidating corrections would be a single agency housing probation services, parole services, and institutional services. There are the usual and obvious arguments supporting this arrangement such as: efficiency of management; economy; comprehensiveness of service; uniformity of professional standards; and facilitation of research. It is argued that rehabilitation of the offender represents a continuum of service that could best be maintained through a unified correctional body. The relative ease with which probation and parole have been administratively unified is probably due to a number of reasons, among them: similarities in the work function involving the conducting of field social investigations and supervising the offender in the community; nearly identical educational qualifications for professional probation and parole officers at the level of a college degree; and the quasijudicial atmosphere of both probation decisions and parole board decisions.

On the other hand, prison organizations or agencies of penal confinement involve markedly different work processes from those in probation and parole. Security is a major influence on prison programming and the educational qualification for a line worker in prisons is substantially less than a college degree. Moreover, prison agencies are large establishments which have more personnel and more funds than probation and parole. As a result, probation and parole tend to see consolidation as a case where the larger agency swallows up a smaller agency.

There are bureaucratic impediments to any process whereby one set of administrators is expected to give up a portion of autonomy to another set. That phenomenon has been extensively revealed at the juvenile court level in instances where efforts have been made to provide statewide probation services **or** statewide aftercare services by removing them from the control of the county level juvenile court and putting them in the hands of a state agency.

In resisting consolidation, probation and parole agencies seldom articulate latent reasons relating to bureaucratic survival and aggrandizement. Manifest, socially acceptable, arguments fall in the following lines:

1. Parole agencies argue that the parole board, in its quasijudicial functioning, must be independent in order to preserve the integrity of its quasijudicial character.
2. In the case where county probation faces consolidation with a state prison agency, or a state correctional agency, the argument is that consolidation would sacrifice grassroots involvement and responsiveness to local community interest. This argument has been made particularly by juvenile courts.
3. Probation agencies argue that since probation is an arm of the judiciary, it is imperative that judges maintain direct control over probation services in keeping with constitutional principles.
4. There is the general argument that within a super-agency structure, individual components, vital in themselves, lose attention and find program advancement difficult.
5. There is also a general argument that the increased administrative costs within a super-agency, because of coordination needs, counterbalance the usually perceived economies of consolidation.

DUE PROCESS AND FAIRNESS

A chronic and well-discussed fairness issue in probation and parole has to do with the confidentiality of the social investigation reports. The issue is particularly argued in regard to presentence reports conducted by probation officers. The confidentiality of parole investigations has somehow received little attention as an issue.

In referring to the issue of the confidentiality of the presentence reports, the question focuses on whether the offender or his counsel should have access to the report. Although some jurisdictions make presentence reports a matter of public record, there is fair consensus that presentence reports should not be generally open to the public. In terms of whether the offender should have access to the presentence reports, the pro and con arguments are as follows:

Pro:

1. The offender, by knowing what is said about him in a vital document such as the presentence report, can defend himself against error and prejudicial statements. Since the presentence report primarily determines the kind of sentence the offender will receive, the offender has a vital stake in the accuracy and fairness of the report.

2. By knowing the contents of the report, the offender becomes better involved in the judicial process and in whatever treatment process follows. For both judicial and treatment purposes, the cooperation of the offender is enhanced by his knowing why certain things are happening to him.

Con:

1. Probation officers argue that if the presentence report was known to be available to the offender, the sources of information used in preparing the report would "dry up." Informants would fear the offender's reaction to any information they provided.

2. Probation officers would be inhibited in making professional judgments and analyses, thereby leading to sterile reports confined to simple and verifiable facts.

3. Information in the presentence reports might be harmful to the offender if revealed to him.

The issue of confidentiality of the presentence reports remains largely unresolved, but in keeping with a general liberal trend there is strong movement for allowing offenders access to them. The Model Penal Code of the American Law Institute and the Model Sentencing Act of the National Council on Crime and Delinquency both lean, in their recommendations, to providing offenders and defense counsel with some knowledge of the contents of the presentence report. In some states, statutes require defendant access to the presentence reports. In general, however, the degree of defendant access to presentence reports is controlled by judicial discretion.

The question of fundamental fairness, as may be easily surmised, revolves about the quasijudicial functioning of probation and parole, especially probation. While there is a distinction to be made between judicial tasks and administrative tasks, the distinction often becomes blurred in the actual operation of probation and parole. Constitutionally, courts may delegate their administrative powers, but they may not delegate their judicial powers. Under the circumstances where judicial powers and administrative powers are becoming increasingly confused, probation and parole officers find themselves more and more in a quasijudicial position.

Unquestionably, there is a difference between administrative decision making and adjudication. Administrative decision making depends on free, extensive, and informal discussions with many interested and informed individuals or groups. Adjudication requires formalized procedures, the building of a record, and the presentation and cross-examination of evidence. In adjudication, the final judgment is based on the record alone. The aforementioned difference is well known and the ensuing discussion of the probation and parole officer's quasijudicial role does not rest on an analysis between judicial process and administrative process. It rests rather on an analysis of judicial effect. Questions are raised as to the propriety of probation and parole officer's achieving judicial effect without judicial process.

The case for the quasijudicial role of the probation and parole officer is made along five lines of functional analysis.*

(1) PLEA BARGAINING AND THE PROBATION OFFICER

It wasn't too long ago that plea bargaining was curtained off in the courtroom. To ensure a valid guilty plea, one which could not later be upset on appeal, judges engaged in a litany with the defendant wherein the question was asked, "Did anyone make you any promises?" Promises made to induce a guilty plea were, in effect, denied in open court. Everyone involved, including the judge, knew about the plea bargaining and the promises made, but all, especially the defendant (lest his deal be upset), denied the negotiated promises in open court. All seemed to have benefited from the charade except that it was unseemly for the court to participate in subterfuge and certainly the recipient of justice was often left with a quizzical notion of the basic honesty of the court. Now that plea bargaining is openly acknowledged and has the imprimatur of the United States Supreme Court, the air in the courtroom is a little clearer. Another result is that the pace of plea bargaining, with its newfound legal respectability, has been stepped up.

To even the most casual observer of the court, it is evident that the judge's role in sentencing has shrunk almost to that of a mere announcer. Not unwillingly it seems, the judge has abdicated a major portion of his sentencing role. It is the prosecutor, the chief plea bargainer, who in reality determines sentence.

*What follows from this point is adapted from the writer's article, "Exposing the Quasi-Judicial Role of the Probation Officer," which appeared in the September, 1973, issue of *Federal Probation.*

Completely ignoring the generally accepted correctional philosophy that sentencing should be in accord with the individual characteristics of the offender, the guidelines used by prosecutors are usually based on the crime committed. The prosecutor's influence in sentencing is drawing us further back toward classical concepts of penology (sentencing in accordance with the crime) even while lawyers in other contexts, such as through the Model Penal Code of the American Law Institute and the Model Sentencing Act of the National Council on Crime and Delinquency, espouse sentencing in accordance with the characteristics of the offender. It is doubtful that prosecutors are moved by one or the other of the two philosophical stands. It is more likely that they are motivated by production goals and by bureaucratic standards of efficiency and self-interest.

By permitting plea bargaining, judges have left themselves little to do other than to certify conditions previously agreed to by defendant, prosecutor, and police.

The abdication of sentencing responsibility to the plea bargaining system leaves the probation officer in an even more peculiar position than it leaves the judge. Theoretically, the probation officer is supposed to make sentencing recommendations to the judge on the basis of his professional estimate of the rehabilitation potential of the defendant. Whether or not a defendant is sentenced to probation probably depends more now on his success in plea bargaining than on his promise of reformation. How does the probation officer fit into this new scheme of extensive plea bargaining? What point is there in conducting an elaborate social investigation by evaluating rehabilitation potential? In answer to the first question, Professor Abraham Blumberg points out that the probation officer serves to "cool the mark" in the production-oriented and confidence game-like system of expeditiously moving defendants through the court by means of plea bargaining. The probation officer can assure the defendant of how wise it was for him to plead guilty and of how much benefit there is to be derived from the correctional efforts arising out of the sentence. In answer to the second question, social investigations of defendants (presentence reports) are becoming shorter, more factual, and less analytical.

Like the judge's role, the probation officer's role in sentencing is diminishing. If it has become the judicial role of the judge to simply certify the plea bargaining process, then the probation officer's role is quasijudicial in that he does the same thing. It is admittedly a peculiar argument, but where the probation officer does a perfunctory presentence report and aims his recommendation toward what he already knows will be the plea bargaining sentence, then he is indeed playing out a de facto judicial role.

It has long been argued that the probation officer's role in sentencing has been a quasijudicial one, especially where the judge more or less automatically imposes the sentence recommended by the probation officer. Various empirical studies have shown a very high correlation between probation officer recommendation and disposition made by the judge. Robert Carter and Leslie Wilkins have pointed out that judges have followed probation officer recommendations in better than 95 percent of the cases. Among the factors which might explain the high level of agreement between recommendations and dispositions, it was postulated that probation officers make their recommendations in anticipation of what the judge desires (second guessing the judge). Today, it is more likely that the prosecutor has found a way to communicate the plea bargaining agreement to the probation officer and the probation officer responds with an appropriate recommendation (or no recommendation) in his presentence report.

Insofar as it firmly determines sentence, the plea bargaining process clearly undermines the professional role of the probation officer. It is now probably more appropriate for the probation officer to counsel the prosecutor on rehabilitation potential than the judge. The prosecutor might want to use the probation officer's professional estimate in the plea bargaining. As a matter of fact, probation officers frequently conduct "prepleading investigations" which are used by both judge and prosecutor to decide plea matters.

(2) INTAKE PROCEDURE
AND PROBATION OFFICERS

Intake service by probation officers in adult courts is practically unknown. At the juvenile court level, however, it is considered good practice to have some form of intake apparatus.

When serving as a functionary in a juvenile court's intake unit, the probation officer is asked to decide which cases are appropriate for formal judicial processing. This kind of decision is obviously a judicial one somewhat akin to those made by judges or magistrates at preliminary hearings. Except for supervision within an administrative hierarchy, the probation officer in intake functions quite independently in his quasijudicial decision making. Despite the fact that the intake process does not meet the ordinary requirements for adjudication, there have been few complaints from defendants subjected to the process. Clearly, inasmuch as intake offers the defendant an opportunity for leniency and perhaps a chance for being saved from legal stigmatization, there is little inclination on the part of defendants to challenge the procedure. Indeed, very many of them consent to an informal probation supervision which is carried out in nearly the same way as adjudicated probation. Behavior required of the defendant is almost the same in both cases, and there is a "penalty" for failure under both formal and informal supervision. Under informal probation supervision, the penalty becomes referral to the court for formal judicial processing, the threat of conviction, and the likelihood of incarceration.

(3) SETTING THE CONDITIONS
OF PROBATION AND PAROLE

Oral or unrecorded conditions have been held generally to be invalid and in order for a defendant to be bound by conditions of probation or parole, they must be definite, clearly stated, and effectively communicated to the defendant. Unfortunately, conditions of probation and parole are notoriously vague and poorly communicated to the defendant. Typical conditions of probation and parole include such ambiguous requirements as: avoid undesirable associates, stay away from disreputable places, and do not keep late hours. Such conditions are obviously very difficult for the defendant to conscientiously manage. What is "undesirable"? What is "disreputable"? Standards for adhering to such conditions are seldom adequately set down and the enforcement of these conditions, where it is done at all, is left to the personal, and frequently capricious, judgment of the probation officer or parole officer. The indefinite conditions become a vehicle for maintaining the moral status quo as interpreted by the probation and parole officer. According to surveys made by Nat Arluke, conditions seem slow to change. While a few jurisdictions are turning to brief streamlined sets of conditions, for the most part, particularly in the juvenile courts, conditions of probation and parole remain moralistic, negativistic, and vague.

Apart from conditions of probation and parole serving as a means for controlling nonlegally proscribed behavior (behavior which is morally undesirable but not unlawful), conditions of probation and parole intrude upon or become substitutes for certain formal judicial processes. Many conditions involve monetary obligations. Some are the kind that any citizen may have (e.g., support of dependents), while others arise out of criminal conviction, such as fines or restitution. Because of the existence of such monetary conditions of probation and parole, the offender is deprived of the usual judicial safeguards and is placed in the administrative or quasijudicial hands of the probation and parole officer.

Consider, for instance, the matter of supporting dependents. Offenders who are placed on probation or parole as a result of a criminal conviction are seldom brought into civil or family court on the issue of supporting dependents. Dependents wishing support from the offender need only go to the probation and parole officer to obtain satisfaction. The probation and parole officer, using the conditions of probation and parole, can compel support payments in amounts determined by the probation and parole officer himself, through his own administrative investigation. Without a court hearing on the question of support payments, the order of the probation and parole officer in enforcing the conditions of probation and parole has significant judicial effect. Were he not on probation or parole for a criminal case, the offender might easily seek an adjudication process in the appropriate court on the question of support. Instead he is forced to submit to the judicial effect brought about by the probation and parole officer enforcing a standard condition of probation and parole. The offender makes his case before the probation and parole officer, and not before the court that is specially set up to adjudicate the question of family support.

A similar usurpation of civil court process occurs when a restitution condition is imposed on a criminal court probationer. It is usually left to the probation officer to determine the appropriate restitution payment. Too often, victims, particularly corporate victims, seek to gain through restitution conditions that which they would have great difficulty in gaining in civil court. Civil courts are comparatively careful in restoring exactly what has been lost. Relying on adversary proceedings, they analyze and evaluate the loss in fair detail. Civil courts may hold jury trials on matters of restitution. When the criminal court probation officer is given the responsibility of settling the matter of restitution, he does not have the same resources for hearing evidence on the loss as do the civil courts. He usually accepts the victim's flat statement as to what the loss was. The probationer, since he is not arguing the matter in a genuine court setting, can do little to rebut the victim's claim. Victims frequently do far better in gaining restitution through the criminal court probation officer than through a civil court. Because he is operating on the basis of a criminal conviction having occurred, the probation officer is bound to presume in favor of the victim in terms of both the quality and quantity of the restitution claim. Since the criminal court judge rarely conducts a full-dress hearing on the question of restitution, preferring to assign the resolution of the matter to the probation officer, the judicial effect of the probation officer's determination of restitution is significant indeed.

(4) PROBATION AND PAROLE VIOLATION PROCEDURES

The traditional view of both probation and parole has been that they are privileges rather than rights, and that as such they do not invoke ordinary due process. While this view has experienced considerable erosion in recent years, the revocation of probation or parole remains highly discretionary. In some jurisdictions, violation hearings closely approach the characteristics of a trial. Still, a hearing is not a trial and the courts and parole boards generally retain substantial discretion in revocation proceedings.

While it is the judge or the parole board who actually revokes probation or parole, it is the probation and parole officer who initiates the revocation action and largely controls it. In a very high proportion of cases, the judge's revocation action or the parole board's revocation action is in accord with the probation and parole officer's recommendation. The hegemony of the probation and parole officer in violation proceedings is well known and requires little unfolding here. It plainly casts the probation and parole officer in a quasijudicial role.

In the case of so-called technical violations, the judicial role of the probation and parole officer becomes amplified. Technical violations are those which are somehow covered by conditions of probation and parole but which are not specified in criminal statutes. Failure to report to the probation and parole officer or failure to avoid undesirable persons might be a type of technical violation. Oftentimes probation and parole officers proceed on the basis of technical violation when new criminal offenses are suspected but cannot be easily proved. Police and prosecutors regularly call upon the probation and parole officer to invoke some technical violation against a probationer or parolee whom they believe has committed a new crime. It is patently easier to put a defendant behind bars as a result of a probation or parole violation hearing than it is to send him to prison as a result of a full-fledged trial. In consenting to proceed on the basis of a technical violation when the real issue is a new criminal offense, the probation and parole officer is playing a judicial role. In effect, he is deciding that there is sufficient basis to conclude that the defendant is guilty of the new offense and thus deserves to have the technical violation placed against him. Given the vague and all encompassing nature of conditions of probation and parole, it is not difficult for the probation and parole officer to muster a technical violation as needed. Many probationers and parolees are in a steady state of violation as a result of conditions relating to keeping "decent hours," abstaining from alcohol, and various prohibitions relating to sexual activity. These violations usually go unenforced by the probation and parole officer until such time as he is given reason to believe that a new criminal offense has occurred. Invoking the technical violation thus becomes the result of the probation and parole officer's making the adjudication that a crime has been committed. The probationer or parolee has a hearing on the technical violation but is denied a trial on the suspected crime that triggered the technical violation.

(5) PUNISHMENT BY THE PROBATION AND PAROLE OFFICER

The legislator sets punishment, the judge imposes it, and the administrator executes it. Under our constitutional scheme, it is the judge who decides when a particular individual is to have legal punishment. While probation is a sentence, it is ideologically not a punishment. Neither is parole considered to be a punishment. Nevertheless, implicit in probation and parole supervision are numerous opportunities for punishment. With his awesome authority over the probationer or parolee, the probation and parole officer may in various ways restrict his liberty. It is easily argued that restriction of liberty amounts to punishment. The probation and parole officer, in the name of rehabilitation and under the banner of standard conditions of probation and parole, can demand that the probationer or parolee not live in or frequent certain areas, that he not engage in certain employment, and that he refrain from a number of interpersonal associations.

Sometimes probation and parole officer-decided punishments are more direct than denial of freedom. In some jurisdictions, a probationer or parolee may not receive a driver's license without the specific approval of the probation and parole officer. From place to place, various occupational licenses are subject to the approval of the probation and parole officer.

In sum, the probation and parole officer's role is multi-faceted. Many of the facets are not easily recognized and may be dysfunctional to our concepts of justice and due process. The issues which surround probation and parole are dynamic and not likely to be resolved with any overwhelming measure of consensus or permanence. Society itself is thrust upon change cycles which are exponential in rate. The changes in probation and parole reflect pervasive societal changes more than they do changes in esoteric knowledge or professional development.

TOPICS FOR DISCUSSION

1. Discuss the objectives of parole and probation.

2. Discuss the advantages and disadvantages of organizing parole and probation on a statewide basis.

3. Discuss the criterion validity of presentence investigations regarding the prediction of an offender's future behavior.

4. The author identifies the mission of probation and parole as being conceived of or emotionally composed of four basic elements. Discuss the conflict which exists between these elements.

5. Discuss the qualifications necessary to be a federal and a state parole/probation officer. Are the qualifications relevant and valid?

Index